Latinx Farmworkers in the Eastern United States

Thomas A. Arcury • Sara A. Quandt

Editors

Latinx Farmworkers in the Eastern United States

Health, Safety, and Justice

Second Edition

 Springer

Editors
Thomas A. Arcury
Department of Family and Community
Medicine
Wake Forest School of Medicine
Winston Salem, NC, USA

Sara A. Quandt
Department of Epidemiology
and Prevention
Division of Public Health Sciences
Wake Forest School of Medicine
Winston Salem, NC, USA

ISBN 978-3-030-36645-2   ISBN 978-3-030-36643-8   (eBook)
https://doi.org/10.1007/978-3-030-36643-8

This Springer imprint is published by the registered company Springer Nature Switzerland AG
The registered company address is: Gewerbestrasse 11, 6330 Cham, Switzerland

Contents

About the Authors

Thomas A. Arcury, PhD is a Professor in the Department of Family and Community Medicine and Director of the Center for Worker Health, Wake Forest School of Medicine, Winston-Salem, NC. He received his doctoral degree in anthropology from the University of Kentucky in 1983 and completed a postdoctoral fellowship in health services research at the Cecil G. Sheps Center for Health Services Research, University of North Carolina, Chapel Hill, in 1996. Dr. Arcury is a medical anthropologist and public health scientist with a research program focused on improving the health of rural and minority populations. Since 1996, he has collaborated in a program of community-based participatory research with immigrant farmworkers, poultry processing workers, construction workers, and their families focused on occupational and environmental health and justice. Although much of his research with farmworkers has focused on pesticide exposure, he has also directed projects examining green tobacco sickness, skin disease, migrant housing, and child labor. He has helped author over 250 refereed articles and chapters focused on the health of immigrant workers and the members of their families, and he has participated in the development of diverse educational materials intended to return research results to immigrant worker communities. He has also used research results to effect policy change. Dr. Arcury's contributions have been recognized by the 2004 Outstanding Researcher Award from the National Rural Health and the 2011 Distinguished Alumnus Award from the Department of Sociology, Duquesne University. He and Dr. Sara A. Quandt have jointly received the 2003 Praxis Award from the Washington Association of Professional Anthropologists, the 2006 National Occupational Research Agenda (NORA) Innovative Research Award for Worker Health and Safety from the National Institute for Occupational Safety and Health, the 2017 Defender of Justice Award for Policy Research and Advocacy from the North Carolina Justice Center, and the 2017 Alice Hamilton Award from the Occupational Health Section, American Public Health Association.

Taylor J. Arnold, MA is a Project Manager in the Department of Family and Community Medicine, Wake Forest School of Medicine, Winston-Salem, NC. He received his master's degree from the University of Memphis in 2015 with concentrations in medical anthropology and globalization, development, and culture. During his graduate studies, he completed the Occupational Health Internship Program (OHIP) with a placement at the National Farm Medicine Center in Marshfield, Wisconsin, where he contributed to a health and safety training program for immigrant dairy workers in Wisconsin. In Memphis, he worked on documenting the city's rich environmental justice (EJ) history through a community-based project with local activists and organizing an EJ conference. In his current role at Wake Forest School of Medicine, he manages a statewide community-based participatory research study examining the health and safety of hired Latinx child farmworkers.

Katherine F. Furgurson, MPH is a Research Associate in the Department of Social Sciences and Health Policy, Division of Public Health Sciences, Wake Forest School of Medicine, Winston-Salem, NC. She received her Master of Public Health from Emory University with a concentration in health policy and a certificate in socio-contextual determinants of health. Ms. Furgurson completed a fellowship with Student Action with Farmworkers and worked as the coordinator for the farmworker outreach program at the Surry County (NC) Health and Nutrition Center. During her graduate studies, she worked as a graduate assistant at the Mexican Consulate in Atlanta where she helped coordinate vision screening clinics for children of farmworker families in southern Georgia. At Wake Forest School of Medicine, she has assisted with several studies related to farmworker health. She currently serves as the vice-chair of the governing board for the North Carolina Farmworker Health Program.

Hannah T. Kinzer is a graduate student in Public Health with a concentration in Community Health Promotion at the University of Minnesota-Twin Cities. Her research interests include infectious disease, health communication, and community health. She earned her BA in Biology with minors in Creative Writing and Anthropology at Lawrence University in Appleton, WI. She completed post-baccalaureate research on *Chlamydia* vaccine development at Yale School of Medicine in New Haven, CT. Ms. Kinzer has contributed to the Surface-Enhanced Raman Spectroscopy (SERS) project examining pesticide exposure tools, the Farm Fresh Healthy Living community nutrition program, and research on migrant farmworker nutritional strategies at Wake Forest School of Medicine in Winston-Salem, NC.

John J. May, MD is a graduate of the University of Notre Dame and Case Western Reserve School of Medicine. He trained in internal medicine at the Mary Imogene Bassett Hospital in Cooperstown, New York, and the University of Colorado Medical Center, Denver, CO. Dr. May is a specialist in pulmonary medicine, having completed a fellowship at the University of Colorado. In addition to his pulmonary practice at Bassett Hospital in rural upstate New York, Dr. May began seeing patients with various agricultural occupational health problems over three decades ago. He is a cofounder and emeritus director of the New York Center for Agricultural Medicine and Health, which is one of the national centers designated by the National

Institute for Occupational Safety and Health. May has published widely in research areas that include respiratory, musculoskeletal, hearing, and other disorders affecting both family farmers and farmworkers in the northeastern United States. A particular interest is the application of community-based intervention methods in addressing occupational health challenges for migrant farmworkers. Dr. May now serves as a senior research scientist in the Bassett Research Institute in Cooperstown, New York.

Dana C. Mora, MPH is a Research Associate in the Department of Family and Community Medicine, Wake Forest University School of Medicine, Winston-Salem, NC. Ms. Mora received a BA in Sociology and a Master of Public Health with a concentration in epidemiology from the University of Florida. After graduate school Ms. Mora completed an internship with Hispanic-Serving Health Professions Schools (HSHPS) with a placement at the National Institute for Occupational Safety and Health (NIOSH) in Cincinnati, Ohio, where she contributed to research related to occupational health and women's reproductive cycle. She has managed several research projects related to occupational health among Latinx immigrant farmworkers and poultry processing workers in North Carolina. Currently, she is the project manager for two community-based participatory research projects. One project focuses on children of Latinx farmworkers; its main aim is to examine the effects of pesticides in the children's cognitive and brain development. The other project examines Surface-Enhanced Raman Spectroscopy (SERS) as a tool for the assessment of pesticide exposure.

Sara A. Quandt, PhD is a Professor in the Department of Epidemiology and Prevention, Division of Public Health Sciences, and in the Department of Family and Community Medicine, Wake Forest University School of Medicine, Winston-Salem, NC. She is an Adjunct Professor of Anthropology and an affiliate of the Maya Angelou Center for Health Equity at Wake Forest. Dr. Quandt was trained in medical anthropology and human nutrition at Michigan State University. Her research focuses on health disparities in rural and minority communities. Quandt and colleagues have conducted basic research on pesticide exposure among farmworker families; developed, tested, and implemented pesticide safety interventions; and initiated policy-relevant research at the request of the farmworker and medical communities in nutrition and growth of children in farmworker families, food insecurity, green tobacco sickness, mental health, housing, oral health, and skin disease. She serves on the Health and Safety Advisory Committee of East Coast Migrant Head Start Program and is on the Scientific Advisory Board of the Rutgers University Center for Environmental Exposures and Disease. She received the Outstanding Rural Health Researcher Award of the National Rural Health Association in 2007. She was co-recipient with Thomas A. Arcury of the 2006 National Occupational Research Agenda (NORA) Innovative Research Award for Worker Health and Safety for work on reducing the impact of green tobacco sickness among Latinx farmworkers; the 2017 Defender of Justice Award, for policy research and advocacy, of the North Carolina Justice Center; and the 2017 Alice Hamilton Award, for lifetime achievement in occupational safety and health, Occupational Safety and Health Section, American Public Health Association.

Joanne C. Sandberg, PhD is Associate Professor in the Department of Family and Community Medicine and is an affiliate faculty of the Maya Angelou Center for Health Equity at Wake Forest School of Medicine, Winston-Salem, NC. She received her doctoral degree in Sociology from Vanderbilt University. In addition to her focus on health disparities, minority health, and worker health, Dr. Sandberg's research interests include health and science communication and cancer survivorship.

Kathleen Sexsmith, PhD is Assistant Professor of Rural Sociology and Women's, Gender and Sexuality Studies at Penn State University. She holds a PhD in Development Sociology from Cornell University, an MPhil in Development Studies from the University of Oxford, and a BA in Economics from the University of Manitoba. Her research program focuses on occupational justice and social integration concerns for Latinx farmworkers and their families in the US rural Northeast. She has also conducted research for the International Institute for Sustainable Development (IISD) on the gendered impacts of voluntary sustainability standards among agricultural commodity producers in the Global South. Her research is driven by a participatory action agenda and she has worked with the Worker Justice Center of New York, the Workers' Center of Central New York, the Food Chain Workers' Alliance, and CARE.

Effie E. Palacios is a graduate student in Rural Sociology at Penn State University focusing on labor, migration, and social justice in the food system. Her research focuses on livelihood diversification among Haitian migrants and their descendants living in rural communities in the Dominican Republic. She completed her undergraduate degree at the University of Virginia in Spanish Language and Global Security and Justice. She has worked as a farmworker organizer for Legal Aid Justice Center in Charlottesville, Virginia, providing workers' rights training and legal advocacy for farmworkers. Ms. Smith has previously collaborated on a rural water system development project in El Corozo, Dominican Republic in conjunction with the US Agency for International Development, the Peace Corps, and the Dominican non-governmental organization REDDOM (Rural Economic Development-Dominica).

Grisel Trejo, MPH is a Research Associate in the Department of Family and Community Medicine, Wake Forest School of Medicine, Winston-Salem, NC. Ms. Trejo received a BA in Biology and a Master of Public Health in Community Health Education at the University of North Carolina at Greensboro. Ms. Trejo is the project manager for an educational intervention project that addresses informal STEM learning focused on genetic and genomic content for foreign born Latinx with limited literacy. She has taken part in a demonstration research study focused on providing pesticide safety training to farmworker families. She has also worked on a research study aimed at strengthening the empirical foundation upon which to build diet and physical activity intervention programs to address overweight and obesity among young Latinx farmworker children.

Melinda F. Wiggins, MTS is the Executive Director of Student Action with Farmworkers (SAF), a nonprofit organization that brings students and farmworkers together to learn about each other's lives, share resources and skills, improve conditions for farmworkers, and build diverse coalitions working for social change (www. saf-unite.org [saf-unite.org]). Ms. Wiggins is the daughter and granddaughter of sharecroppers who grew up in a rural farming community in the Mississippi Delta. She moved to North Carolina in 1992 to complete a Master of Theological Studies at Duke University. Before starting as the Director of SAF in 1996, she coordinated SAF's Into the Fields summer internship program for several years. She first joined the farmworker movement as a SAF intern with the Episcopal Farmworker Ministry during the summer of 1993. Wiggins is involved with many social and economic justice organizations and was instrumental in creating two statewide coalitions focused on immigrant and workers' rights—the Adelante Education Coalition and Farmworker Advocacy Network. She coedited *The Human Cost of Food: Farmworkers' Lives, Labor and Advocacy*, published by the University of Texas Press in 2002. In March 2012, Wiggins was honored by President Obama and the White House as a recipient of the "Cesar Chavez Champion of Change" award.

Chapter 1
The Health and Safety of Latinx Farmworkers in the Eastern United States: A Renewed Focus on Social Justice

Thomas A. Arcury and Sara A. Quandt

1.1 A Renewed Focus on Social Justice

The health and safety of farmworkers in the eastern United States (US) are a matter of social justice. Our definition of social justice is succinct. Social justice is the process that seeks fairness or equity in the distribution of social burdens and resources across all social groups and provides all people the opportunity to realize their full potential. For Latinx farmworkers, social justice includes working and living in environments that address health and safety hazards, receiving a living wage, living in communities free of discrimination, and having access to health, education, and social services.

Much about farmworker social justice in the eastern US has not changed since the first edition of this volume was published a little over 10 years ago (Arcury and Quandt 2009). Latinx farmworkers continue to experience discrimination due to their ethnicity, language, and immigration status. They perform strenuous labor that puts them at risk for occupational injuries and illnesses. They often work in isolated locales where they are exposed to heat and inclement weather. Many, due to a lack of documents, are separated from their families for years; others, with temporary work visas, are separated from their families for 3–9 months each year. The stress of discrimination, difficult work, and family separation places them at risk for mental illness.

Many farmworkers have the fortune of having their family live with them; these include many seasonally employed farmworkers, as well as some migrant farmworkers. Farmworker family members are exposed to many of the same occupational

T. A. Arcury (✉)
Department of Family and Community Medicine, Wake Forest School of Medicine, Winston-Salem, NC, USA

S. A. Quandt
Department of Epidemiology and Prevention, Division of Public Health Sciences, Wake Forest School of Medicine, Winston-Salem, NC, USA

1

and environmental hazards as are farmworkers, including living in substandard housing and being exposed to toxic agents such as pesticides (see Chaps. 6 and 7).

Although farmworkers and their families experience noteworthy physical and mental health hazards (see Chaps. 3, 6, and 7), they have poor access to health services (Arcury and Quandt 2007; Guild et al. 2016; Martinez-Donate et al. 2017). Many farmworkers have incomes that place them near or below poverty. Together with little income to pay for health care, few farmworkers have health insurance (see Chap. 3). Programs to address farmworker health disparities are limited. The number of community and migrant clinics supported with federal and states funds cannot meet the needs of the farmworker population in the eastern US.

All agricultural workers, but especially migrant and seasonal farmworkers, have fewer occupational health and safety protections than do other workers in the US (see Chap. 9). Investigators have consistently documented the limited regulatory protection for farm labor (Mitchell and Gurske 1956; President's Commission on Migratory Labor 1951; Schell 2002).

> [the US] depend[s] on misfortune to build up our force of migratory workers and when the supply is low because there is not enough misfortune at home, we rely on misfortune abroad to replenish the supply. (President's Commission on Migratory Labor 1951)

Most Latinx farmworkers lack knowledge of English and of the safety regulations that do exist. They seldom receive required safety training. Farmworkers often work in the face of unsafe conditions because they fear the loss of income to provide for their families. Many farmworkers do not have documentation; they will not report unsafe work or employers who do not follow regulations for fear of retaliation. Even farmworkers with documents often do not want to deal with government representatives because they fear harassment in an anti-immigrant environment.

Important characteristics of the Latinx farmworker population and the circumstances of agricultural work have also changed since 2010. Further, the level of scientific research and publication on the health and safety of Latinx farmworkers and their family members has increased, as have the topics addressed in this research. This volume documents how changes in the farmworker population, agricultural work, and the scientific literature reflect efforts to attain social justice for Latinx farmworkers in the eastern US.

Important changes in the Latinx farmworker population in the eastern US since 2010 include a significant decrease in migrant workers and a corresponding increase in seasonal workers. A substantial increase in the proportion of women Latinx farmworkers has accompanied this increase in seasonal workers. The number of Latinx farmworkers with H-2A temporary work visas has exploded in the last decade. Indications are that this growth in the number of Latinx farmworkers with temporary work visas will continue. More importantly, several legislative proposals for revised temporary work visa program would place greater restrictions on farmworkers and further erode justice.

Agriculture in the eastern US continues to experience consolidation, with the number of farms decreasing and the size of farms increasing. Consolidation is apparent in livestock and poultry production as well as crop production.

Consolidation in the dairy industry has led to an increase in the number of Latinx farmworkers on these farms. Agriculture in some parts of the eastern US has adopted a year-round production system, which, together with shortages of agricultural labor, is pushing farmers to adopt greater mechanization.

The changes in the farmworker population and agriculture occur within the greater US social and political environment. The 2010s have seen greater anti-immigrant political rhetoric and greater discrimination directed toward immigrants. The continuing debate about immigration reform and the drastic measures taken by Immigration and Customs Enforcement have increased fear among immigrants, including Latinx farmworkers.

Latinx farmworkers labor in extreme environmental conditions. Farmworkers face increasing temperatures resulting from climate change and therefore greater concern for heat-related illnesses.

Major policy changes in the past decade include the implementation of a revised US EPA Worker Protection Standard for pesticide safety. California and Washington have implemented heat standards for outdoor workers, including farmworkers, increasing pressure for similar standards in the eastern US (see Chap. 3). The Affordable Care Act has had limited effect on increasing access to health care among Latinx farmworkers, although this act requires farmworkers with H-2A temporary work visas to be insured (see Chap. 3). The work of grassroots organizations and programs to change the discussions around justice for Latinx farmworkers in the eastern US (see Chap. 9) may be more important than formal policy changes.

Latinx farmworker occupational health research expanded in the 2010s. More research has addressed women farmworkers and women in farmworker families (see Chap. 6), child farmworkers and children in farmworker families (see Chap. 7), the mental health of all farmworkers (see Chap. 4), and heat stress (see Chap. 3). Investigators have conducted some further research on pesticide exposure and health outcomes (see Chap. 3). Little further research has addressed infectious disease (STIs, HIV, TB) experienced by farmworkers. Little further research on farmworker housing is available, although the quality and availability of housing are major problems (see Chap. 2). Finally, investigators have made great use of community-engaged approaches, particularly community-based participatory research, to ensure that research addresses the concerns of farmworkers (see Chap. 8).

1.2 Organization of the Chapters

The chapters in this volume integrate knowledge of the health and safety of Latinx farmworkers in the eastern US, note continuing gaps in this knowledge, and recommend processes to improve social justice for farmworkers. The first chapters provide information on the risks for farmworkers and their families. These chapters define the context in which farmworkers in the eastern US labor and live (Chap. 2). They review specific aspects of health and safety for farmworkers, including occupational injuries (Chap. 3) and mental health (Chap. 4). The next chapters focus on three special populations for which research has expanded in the 2010s: livestock and poultry workers (Chap. 5), women farmworkers and women in farmworker families (Chap. 6), and children in farmworker families and child farmworkers (Chap. 7). The final chapters provide information about efforts to advocate for social justice for farmworkers through community-engaged research (Chap. 8) and advocacy (Chap. 9) and make recommendations for approaches to address social justice for farmworkers (Chap. 10).

1.3   Definitions and Conventions

We have presented our definition for the concept of social justice. We use the single word "farmworker" throughout this volume. This convention has no particular conceptual foundation; it reflects what the authors have always used.

The eastern US includes 23 states from Maine to Florida and from the Atlantic Coast to Ohio, Kentucky, Tennessee, and Mississippi. Since 1990, farmworkers in the eastern US have become overwhelmingly Latinx. The eastern US differs from the other major regions in which large numbers of farmworkers are employed, such as the West Coast and Southwest and Texas and the Midwest. The eastern US does not have the historically large rural Latinx population as do these other regions, and therefore, Latinx in the eastern US do not have the same levels of community organizations as do farmworkers with bases in California, Arizona, New Mexico, and Texas.

We call this region the eastern US, rather than the Eastern Migrant Stream. Many service agencies and publications refer to the Eastern Migrant Stream. However, a minority of the farmworkers in the eastern US migrate from place to place like a stream flowing to plant, cultivate and harvest crops. Some farmworkers in the eastern US do migrate to do farm work, but they generally move to one area and remain there for the season.

We use the term "Latinx" to describe the farmworker population on which we focus. We recognize that the people from nations in North and South America reflect diverse and rich cultures and histories. We further recognize that the term "Hispanic," often applied to these populations, has its roots in the colonial history and original Spanish conquest of these regions and was adopted in the 1980 US Census as a term imposed by the US government to count a subgroup for administrative purposes. The use of this category concealed rich diversity in language (Spanish, English, Portuguese, and dozens of indigenous languages), culture, and origin into a supposedly uniform group.

The term Hispanic was rarely adopted by the persons to whom it was applied. Rather terms such as Chicano/a and Latino/a were favored, as more specific (in the case of the former, applied in the southwestern US) and more general (in the case of the latter, applied to "New World" countries with a Latin-based language). In fact, Hispanic/Latino was adopted by the US Census in 2000. In recent years, the term

Latinx has been developed, as a term that removes the gendered terms Latino and Latina, and the use of Latino as a collective plural with its history of male dominance. Latinx has been particularly important to acknowledge gender and sexuality fluidity and to reject male domination in language and culture (Vidal-Ortiz and Martínez 2018). In using the term Latinx, authors in this book are not choosing to engage in a political debate about terminology. Rather, authors are acknowledging the diversity in the population from which farmworkers come and attempting to highlight the value of inclusivity in studying this population within a justice and, frequently, a CBPR framework.

1.4   The Chapters

In addition to this Introduction, this volume has nine chapters. Chapters 2 through 4 discuss the exposures that affect the health, safety, and justice experienced by Latinx farmworkers in the eastern US. Chapters 5 through 7 focus on health, safety, and justice for the specific farmworker populations. Chapters 8 and 9 examine efforts to promote farmworker social justice through community-engaged research and advocacy. The final chapter proposes an agenda to improve justice in health and safety for farmworkers.

The context for farmworkers in the eastern US affects the health, safety, and justice they experience. This context includes geographic, agricultural, demographic, housing, cultural, and political dimensions. In Chap. 2, Thomas A. Arcury and Dana C. Mora discuss each of these dimensions. Farmworkers are individuals involved in agricultural production, including planting, cultivating, harvesting, and processing crops for sale, and caring for animals. They include seasonal farmworkers, individuals whose principal employment is in agriculture on a seasonal basis, and migrant farmworkers, seasonal farmworkers who, for purposes of employment, establish a temporary home. Over the past decade, an increasing number of migrant farmworkers in the eastern US have had H-2A temporary work visas.

Agriculture involving farmworkers in the eastern US is concentrated in production that requires hand labor. This agriculture is changing, with consolidation, mechanization, and year-round production. Farmers and farmworkers have beliefs and behaviors that affect exposure to health and safety hazards and access to health care, often to the detriment of farmworkers. The political context within the US, with its biases toward protecting the "family farm" and against immigrants, as well as the impressive financial resources of the agricultural industry, circumscribes changes in policy and regulation that would protect farmworker health, safety, and justice.

Information needed to document each dimension of the context for farmworkers in the eastern US is often unavailable, making it difficult to understand who farmworkers are, their number, their personal characteristics, their exposures and health status, and how to best work toward justice for farmworkers and their families in the eastern US. Recommendations to improve health, safety, and justice include more complete and consistent reporting by state agencies of information they collect for farmworkers in their states and better documentation and reporting of study design by researchers.

John J. May and Thomas A. Arcury describe key occupational health challenges encountered by farmworkers in the eastern US in Chap. 3, They argue that agricultural work exposes farmworkers to risks for numerous occupational injuries, yet little has been done to document the injuries experienced by farmworkers or to provide sufficient health care when farmworkers experience occupational injuries and illness. The lack of appropriate support available to farmworkers and to health professionals providing their care is indicative of the lack of respect and justice our society affords these essential workers. These injustices are particularly provocative in light of recent changes to the health-care system, particularly the Affordable Care Act. They describe the causes and symptoms for occupational health problems common to farmworkers, including heat stress, pesticides, musculoskeletal injuries, skin disease, hearing loss, eye injury, and transportation-related injuries. They also discuss patterns of illness and injury for farmworkers that are common to orchard work, tobacco production, and vegetable and berry production, all important commodities in the eastern US. Importantly, they discuss community-based approaches for designing changes in tools used by farmworkers in agricultural production that can reduce their occupational injuries. They conclude with a list of recommended changes in the provision of health care for farmworkers, the organization of work, and procedures to redesign tools that will reduce injury and improve justice for farmworkers.

The mental health of Latinx farmworkers is the focus of expanding concern and research. In Chap. 4, Katherine F. Furgurson and Sara A. Quandt use the stress/distress model to delineate farmworker situational and structural stressors, and they summarize the meager mental health research literature among farmworkers in the eastern US. Situational stressors include family separation, social marginalization, housing conditions, work demands and conditions, and physical health, while structural stressors include discrimination, acculturation, documentation status, poverty, and limited access to health care. They report that mental health symptom levels for anxiety and depression are highly variable, with studies reporting 0–23% prevalence for anxiety and 7–52% for depression. Alcohol use disorder is common, particularly among men, with most studies reporting more than 30% prevalence. Although variable, the evidence suggests that Latinx farmworkers in the eastern US have a substantial burden of mental distress that is untreated by currently available resources.

The consolidation of livestock and poultry production has had a major effect on work in these enterprises. In Chap. 5, Effie E. Palacios and Kathleen Sexsmith comprehensively examine the health and safety issues faced by Latinx workers in the dairy, poultry, swine, and equine industries. They note that while environmental justice advocates have effectively called attention to the mistreatment of animals in livestock production, occupational justice for the farmworkers who care for them has been largely overlooked. As the size and scale of animal agriculture operations grow, farmers have become increasingly dependent on a Latinx workforce. As a result, Latinx livestock and poultry workers are exposed to new and different safety and health risks. Physical risks for livestock workers include direct traumatic injury from being kicked, bitten, or otherwise hurt by animals, musculoskeletal disorder from repetitive and awkward motions, respiratory illness or dysfunction from air pollutants, and mental health disorder related to stress, sleep disorders, and social and geographical isolation. The difficulty of accessing health care and social services compound the injuries and illnesses of Latinx livestock workers in the eastern US. Palacios and Sexsmith identify important gaps in the literature on occupational safety and health among livestock workers and conclude with recommendations to policymakers and to farm owners to improve occupational safety and health for Latinx livestock workers.

Women in the farmworker community include those who work themselves as hired farmworkers and those who are present as spouses, mothers, sisters, daughters, or other relatives of family or household members engaged in farm work. In Chap. 6, Sara A. Quandt, Hannah T. Kinzer, Grisel Trejo, Dana C. Mora, and Joanne C. Sandberg detail issues related to women in the farmworker community. The percentage of farmworkers who are women has increased nationally over the past several decades, and is higher in the eastern US than in other parts of the country where about one in three workers is female. While women face many of the same issues as men (e.g., social, economic, and ethnic discrimination), many of these issues are even more severe for women—they are paid even less than men and they endure discrimination and harassment based on gender. They also often have a double workload due to domestic responsibilities added onto paid employment. Health research on women in the farmworker community is spotty. When included in studies with male farmworkers, there are often too few women to be analyzed separately, and issues relevant particularly to women are not addressed. These include gender-related health outcomes (e.g., reproductive cancers) and failure to document variables such as body size and proportion that can affect rates of injuries such as musculoskeletal disorders. This chapter concludes with recommendations for further research, practice, and policy related to women in the farmworker community.

Children in Latinx farmworker communities are present as dependents of adult farmworkers or as hired farmworkers themselves. Both groups risk health effects from the hazards present in these communities. In Chap. 7, Sara A. Quandt and Taylor J. Arnold examine the current knowledge about the health and safety of both groups of children. Most children in farmworker families are US citizens. The farmworker child research based in the eastern US is fragmentary. Children in farmworker families face substantial health risks tied to poverty, rural residence, and documentation status (of the children as well as other members of their families). These children have limited access to both medical and dental care. Two of their primary health issues are risk for overweight and obesity and risk for exposure to pesticides. Hired child farmworkers face substantial occupational health risks due to their physical, behavioral, and emotional immaturity. Existing research notes dangers of pesticide and heat exposure in particular. Improving the health of children in farmworker communities may require providing greater access to government services and revision of existing labor laws that permit minor children to work in agriculture without the protections afforded for children in other industries.

Latinx migrant and seasonal farmworkers constitute a vulnerable and hidden population. Investigators use community-engaged approaches, community-based participatory research (CBPR) in particular, to engage the members of this population. In Chap. 8, Thomas A. Arcury and Sara A. Quandt argue that community-based participatory research (CBPR) and other forms of community-engaged research provide a framework for involving Latinx farmworkers in research that can result in their improved health, safety, and justice. Arcury and Quandt review the general characteristics of community-engaged research, particularly CBPR, and present a model for describing and evaluating this research. They review how community-engaged research addresses Latinx farmworker health, safety, and justice in the eastern US and summarize lessons learned from community-engaged research conducted with Latinx farmworker communities. Finally, they make recommendations to improve the conduct of community-engaged research with Latinx farmworker communities.

Achieving health, safety, and justice for farmworkers will require advocacy and intervention. Melinda F. Wiggins provides a list of specific changes for which advocates are working that will move farmworkers closer to social justice. In Chap. 9, Wiggins provides a historical context for farmworker advocacy. She notes that people of color have done most farm work. These people experience labor abuses and lack the power to make systemic change in the agricultural system. She documents that farmworkers suffer from "agricultural exceptionalism," the practice of excluding farmworkers from legal protections benefiting other workers. The agricultural industry has resisted changes to this system. Farmworkers, who are a primarily immigrant, undocumented, and disenfranchised population, have not been able to develop organizations to foster needed changes in this system. Wiggins also highlights major efforts of farmworkers to organize and provides a history of farmworker advocacy, giving examples of current national (Farmworker Justice) and state-specific (Justice for Farmworkers Campaign in New York, Farmworker Advocacy Network in North Carolina) farmworker advocacy organizations. Wiggins also considers the potential of community-academic alliances to further farmworker advocacy, focusing specifically on CBPR.

Improving health and safety and achieving social justice for Latinx farmworkers in the eastern US will require continued research and advocacy to change a variety of policies that regulate farm work and the lives of farmworkers. In the final chapter, Thomas A. Arcury and Sara A. Quandt summarize four themes common across the chapters of the book: (1) since 2009, changes have occurred in both the context for farm work and the composition of the Latinx workforce; (2) information to thoroughly document farmworker health and safety remains inadequate; (3) the changes of the past decade and the limited available information provoke grave concerns about farmworker health and justice; and (4) the deficits in farmworker health and failure to achieve farm labor justice result largely from agricultural labor policy. Arcury and Quandt present an updated agenda for farmworker social justice. They argue that social justice for farmworkers will require systemic changes in policy and regulation for labor, housing, pesticide safety, health care, wages, and immigration.

Acknowledgments The editors and authors received support from numerous people in producing this updated volume. The editors thank, in particular, Theresa L. Seering and Alice Arcury-Quandt, who carefully copyedited and formatted each chapter. Mark McKone, Coy C. Carpenter Library of Wake Forest School of Medicine, verified citations in all of the chapters. The editors thank him for his assistance, patience, and attention to detail.

Authors of several specific chapters enlisted the assistance of others and thank them for their work. For Chap. 3, Deborah Dalton, MLS, assisted in updating the literature review. For Chap. 4, Allison Lipscomb, MPH, North Carolina Farmworker Health Program, supplied information on current mental health programs for farmworkers. For Chap. 5, Alice E. Arcury-Quandt, MSPH, provided consultation and drafted text on zoonotic infectious disease. For Chap. 6, Haiying Chen, MD, PHD, provided analysis of data from women respondents in the 2016 National Agricultural Worker Survey data. For Chap. 9, Dave DeVito, Andreina Malki, and Bianca Olivares read and commented on the chapter. Joanna Welborn, Student Action with Farmworkers, helped locate suitable photographs for several chapters.

References

Arcury TA, Quandt SA (2007) Delivery of health services to migrant and seasonal farmworkers. Annu Rev Public Health 28:345–363

Arcury TA, Quandt SA (eds) (2009) Latino farmworkers in the eastern United States: health, safety, and justice. Springer, New York, NY

Guild A, Richards C, Ruiz V (2016) Out of sight, out of mind: the implementation and impact of the affordable care act in the U.S. farmworker communities. J Health Care Poor Underserved 27(4):73–82

Martinez-Donate AP, Ejcbc I, Zhang X et al (2017) Access to healthcare among Mexican migrants and immigrants: a comparison across migration phases. J Health Care Poor Underserved 28(4):1314–1326

Mitchell JP, Gurske PE (1956) Status of agricultural workers under state and federal labor laws. US Department of Labor, Bureau of Labor Standards, Washington, DC

President's Commission on Migratory Labor (1951) Migratory labor in American agriculture: report of the President's Commission on Migratory Labor. US Government Printing Office, Washington, DC

Schell G (2002) Farmworker exceptionalism under the law: how the legal system contributes to farmworker poverty and powerlessness. In: Thompson C, Wiggins M (eds) The human cost of food: farmworkers' lives, labor & advocacy. University of Texas Press, Austin, TX

Vidal-Ortiz S, Martínez J (2018) Latinx thoughts: Latinidad with an X. Lat Stud 16:384–395

Chapter 2
Latinx Farmworkers and Farm Work in the Eastern United States: The Context for Health, Safety, and Justice

Thomas A. Arcury and Dana C. Mora

2.1   Introduction

Understanding the health and safety of farmworkers in the eastern United States (US) and addressing justice for farmworkers require familiarity with the context in which farmworkers labor and live. This context has geographic, agricultural, demographic, housing, cultural, and political dimensions. Each of these dimensions has undergone considerable change in the past 50 years, and each continues to change.

The information needed to document the context for health, safety, and justice for farmworkers is often unavailable. The limited information makes it difficult to understand who farmworkers are, the number of farmworkers in the eastern US, their personal characteristics, their exposures and health status, and how best to work toward justice for these workers and their families. For this chapter, and for this volume, information from multiple sources was culled and integrated to document farmworker health, safety, and justice in the eastern US. Sometimes the information gathered about farmworkers appears contradictory. The reasons for apparent contradictions are several. Farmworkers in various sections of the eastern US are diverse, and those recording information about farmworkers use different methods. Regulations defining "farmworker" differ among agencies and among states, and the types and quality of information vary among states and among agencies. Clearly assessing what is known is an essential first step in promoting farmworker justice.

T. A. Arcury (✉) · D. C. Mora
Department of Family and Community Medicine, Wake Forest School of Medicine, Winston-Salem, NC, USA

© Springer Nature Switzerland AG 2020
T. A. Arcury, S. A. Quandt (eds.), *Latinx Farmworkers in the Eastern United States*, https://doi.org/10.1007/978-3-030-36643-8_2

2.2   Farmworkers Defined

We focus on seasonal and migrant farmworkers in this volume. The definition of who is a farmworker varies among analysts and for different programs and regulations. Factors included in defining farmworkers include the agricultural commodities (crops, dairy, poultry, livestock) and sectors (material processing, fisheries, forestry) in which an individual might work, migration statuses (e.g., family moved to seek farm work, change residence from one school district to another, establish temporary abode), their ages, and programmatic income requirements (e.g., none, income less than poverty while engaged in farm work) and eligibility periods (e.g., employed in farm work in the last 24 months, the last 36 months, 12 of the last 24 months).

In this volume, farmworkers include individuals who are involved in agricultural production, with agricultural production including planting, cultivating, harvesting, and processing crops for sale and caring for animals. Nonfood commodities, such as tobacco, Christmas trees, sod, flowers, and ornamental plants, are included as agricultural crops. Agricultural work excludes manufacturing activities, such as preserving fruits and vegetables, working in grain storage, slaughtering or butchering livestock and poultry, or making cheese and cooking food. *Seasonal farmworkers* are individuals whose principal employment is in agriculture on a seasonal basis. They do not change residence in order to work in agriculture. *Migrant farmworkers* are individuals whose principal employment is in agriculture on a seasonal basis and who, for purposes of employment, establish a temporary home. The migration may be within a state, interstate, or international.

The National Agricultural Workers Survey (NAWS) differentiates six types of farmworkers (Carroll et al. 2005; Hernandez et al. 2016a, b). The nonmigrant worker is equivalent to what we refer here to as a seasonal farmworker. The NAWS includes only crop workers and excludes livestock or poultry workers. It estimates nationally that the percentage of farmworkers who are nonmigrant has increased from 58% in 2002 to 84% for 2013–2014 and 81% in 2015–16. Migrants can be migrant newcomers (a foreign-born farmworker who has traveled to the US for the first time), international shuttle farmworkers (travel from permanent homes in a foreign country to the US for employment but work only within a 75 mile radius of that location), domestic shuttle farmworkers (have permanent residences in the US but travel 75 miles or more to do farm work in a single location and work only within a 75 mile radius of that location), international follow-the-crop farmworkers (travel to multiple US farm locations for work from permanent homes in a foreign country), and domestic follow-the-crop farmworkers (travel to multiple US farm locations for work from permanent homes in the US). The follow-the-crop farmworker most closely resembles the classic image of a migrant farmworker who moves in one of the "migrant streams" from south to north as crops ripen for harvest. In 2013–2014, national estimates based on the NAWS indicate that 11% of migrant farmworkers (1.8% of all farmworkers) were migrant newcomers, 37% were international shuttle migrants (5.9% of all farmworkers), 26% were domestic shuttle migrants (4.2% of all farmworkers), 3% were international follow-the-crop farmworkers (0.5% of all farmworkers), and 23% were domestic follow-the-crop migrants (3.7% of all farmworkers).

The decline in migrant versus seasonal farmworkers has several potential causes. Current political and legal pressure on undocumented farmworkers and on their employers has limited some movement. The larger number of Latinx farmworkers who have been born in the US (Hernandez et al. 2016a) are citizens and can obtain alternative local employment when agricultural work is not available. Anecdotal information indicates that changes to year-round agricultural production in Florida (and possibly other states) have made farm employment available year-round.

We include the spouses, children, and other family members of farmworkers in our discussions for this volume. Family members who live with farmworkers are often exposed to the same health risks as are the farmworkers. Often, they are employed in farm work (see Chaps. 6 and 7). They live in the same housing (Arcury et al. 2015e, 2017a), are exposed to agricultural and residential pesticides (see Chap. 3), encounter similar levels of health care (Arcury and Quandt 2007), and are confronted by similar stressors and hardships (see Chap. 4).

The NAWS does not include farmworkers with H-2A visas in its estimates. An H-2A visa allows an individual to enter the US to work in agriculture for a specified period for a particular employer. The employer is obligated to provide an average of 35 h of work per week, a specific hourly wage, and inspected housing and to meet all safety requirements, including Worker Protection Standard training (Fults 2017). Almost all farmworkers with H-2A visas are international shuttle migrants. A few are international follow-the-crop migrants; for example, some farmworkers with H-2A visas spend much of the agricultural season (May through September) in eastern North Carolina cultivating and harvesting tobacco but then travel several hundred miles to western North Carolina to harvest Christmas trees in October and November.

A large number of farmworkers with H-2A visas work in the eastern US (Table 2.1), and this number has greatly increased over the past decade. For example, while 8730 farmworkers with H-2A visas worked in North Carolina in 2007, the number of certified positions for farmworkers with H-2A visas increased to 19,786 in 2016 and 21,794 in 2018 (US Department of Labor (USDOL) 2019). Florida had 22,828 certified H-2A positions in 2016 and 30,462 in 2018, while Georgia had 17,392 in 2016 and 32,364 in 2018. Other eastern states with large numbers of workers with H-2A visas for 2018 include Louisiana (10,079), New York (7634), and Kentucky (7604).

Although farmworkers with H-2A visas have legal documents to work in the US and the program offers them some protections, they, like other Latinx farmworkers, face hardships. Research comparing the situations of those with H-2A visas in the eastern US with other migrant farmworkers indicates that those with H-2A visas have better living and working conditions (Arcury et al. 2012a, 2015d). In North Carolina, some farmworkers with H-2A visas have the additional protection of a union contract through the Farm Labor Organizing Committee. However, many farmers employing farmworkers with H-2A visas do not adhere to all the required

Table 2.1 H-2A positions certified in the eastern US 2016, by state

State	Total positions certified 2016
Alabama	972
Connecticut	2058
Delaware	392
Florida	22,828
Georgia	17,392
Kentucky	6779
Louisiana	8301
Maine	700
Maryland	804
Massachusetts	437
Mississippi	3580
New Hampshire	169
New Jersey	1016
New York	5522
North Carolina	19,786
Ohio	1297
Pennsylvania	892
Rhode Island	4
South Carolina	3896
Tennessee	3224
Vermont	520
Virginia	3432
West Virginia	116

https://foreignlaborcert.doleta.gov/

safety and housing standards. Further, advocates argue that the control and intimidation exerted over these workers by their employers limit workers' ability to voice concerns over safety and living conditions (Bauer 2013; Newman 2011).

2.3 Geographic Context

The eastern US for this volume includes 23 states (Fig. 2.1). They include the southeastern states bordering the Gulf of Mexico and Atlantic Ocean (Florida, Georgia, Alabama, Mississippi, Louisiana, South Carolina, North Carolina, and Virginia), the mid-Atlantic states (Maryland, Pennsylvania, Delaware, New Jersey, and New York), interior states (Tennessee, Kentucky, West Virginia, and Ohio), and New England (Massachusetts, Connecticut, Rhode Island, New Hampshire, Vermont, and Maine). This region is considered the "Eastern Migrant Stream." However, the 2002–2004 NAWS found that only 13% of farmworkers in the eastern US were follow-the-crop migrants (Carroll et al. 2005), and the proportion dropped to only 4% in the 2013–2014 NAWS national data (Hernandez et al. 2016a).

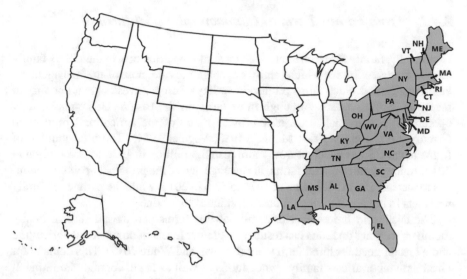

Fig. 2.1 Map of the USA, with shading indicating the 23 states considered part of the eastern US for this volume

Therefore, the idea of a stream of migrant farmworkers flowing from Florida and Texas, through the South, into the mid-Atlantic and on into New England as crops ripen is probably no longer accurate.

Little information actually documents the movement of farmworkers during an agricultural season. Quandt et al. (2002) used information from several studies in North Carolina to document the movement of farmworkers during an agricultural season. The farmworkers included in these studies were migrant farmworkers living in camps during the summer. Approximately one third of the workers moved during the course of the summer, with work availability and work-related illness being the major causes of their moving from a camp. Workers who migrated often returned to a camp that they left when more work became available.

2.4 Agricultural Context

Agriculture in the eastern US is diverse and changing. The agriculture that involves farmworkers is concentrated in those commodities that require hand labor: animal care or planting, cultivating, and harvesting crops. Some crops that historically required hand labor, such as cotton, are now mechanized. Mechanization remains limited for other crops, such as tobacco and most fruits and vegetables. However, efforts to increase mechanization in the production of all agricultural commodities are underway (Seabrook 2019; Charlton et al. 2019).

2.4.1   From Family Farm to Commercial Agriculture

Historically, family farms characterized most of the agriculture in the US. A family farm is an operation for which family members provide most of the management, labor, and capital. Such farms produce a variety of crops, livestock, and poultry to meet the family's needs. Although most farms in the eastern US remain family operations, commercial farms now provide much of the agricultural production (Arcury 2017; Kelsey 1994; Mooney 1988; Vogeler 1981). The total number of farms in the US has declined from more than 5.3 million in 1950 to two million in 2017. Among family-owned farms, the average age of the principal operator continues to increase, from 51.7 years in 1974 to 57.5 in 2017, while the number of family members living and working on farms continues to decline.

The decline in the number of family-owned farms and the number of family members working on farms has resulted in greater levels of commercial agriculture and a greater need for hired farm labor (Schewe and White 2017). This demand for hired farm labor affects family-owned farms as well as large, commercial farms. It affects all forms of agriculture: animal and dairy production as well as crop production. However, although agriculture is becoming more commercial and less family-based, the laws regulating agricultural labor still reflect the model of the family farm. Referred to as "agricultural exceptionalism" (Guild and Figueroa 2018; see Chap. 9), these labor regulations limit the requirements of safety regulations, workers' compensation, health insurance, and overtime pay for farmworkers, while allowing hired workers as young as 10 years of age to work in the fields (see Chap. 7).

2.4.2   The Risk and Safety Culture of US Farmers

US farmers have a distinct culture, a set of generally shared beliefs and values, that affects the health, safety, and justice for farmworkers. An analysis of in-depth interviews conducted with small crop and livestock farmers in the Northeast helps to describe the farm community's view of occupational hazards (Sorensen et al. 2008). Farmers do not view "risk" as undesirable. They have observed past generations accepting risk as inherent to their way of life. Many risk their entire fortune with each spring's planting. Thus, as a group they have a remarkably high tolerance for risk, believing that most things will work out in the end. While farmers readily acknowledge the dangers inherent in farming, they often adopt an optimistic bias with regard to hazard (Weinstein 1988). Their experience with risk leads them to believe that their own knowledge, experience, and skills exempt them from agriculture's dangers. Near misses only serve to reinforce this view. Most farmers place considerably greater priority on the efficient production of food and fiber than upon safety. As businesspersons, they see most safety measures as contributing little to their efficiency and productivity. This most certainly applies to their personal safety but, unfortunately, tends to carry over to safety in general. At the same time, these farmers express considerable concern regarding the safety of spouses, children, and employees. This attitude is reflected in decisions to personally undertake the riskiest tasks and results in elevated rates of injuries to farmers on small family farms when compared to employees (Pratt et al. 1992).

In studies among California farmworkers and farm owners, Grieshop et al. (1996) explored concepts related to the "locus of control" over safety and workplace injury. Farmworkers had a powerful and pervasive belief that the control of injury and illness for both the worker and farm owner was under external control. In contrast, farmers viewed injury prevention as under internal control rather than in the hands of luck or fate. These workers valued prevention efforts but believed equally in accepting the inherent dangers of the job and trusting in their ability to react or cope with hazards that arise.

The safety culture of farmers is reflected in their views toward risk for their own children. Current regulations (US Department of Labor, Wage and Hour Division 2016a) place no restriction on the ages at which a farmer's child can work on the farm or the hazardous tasks the child performs (see Chap. 7). Children working on parents' farms experience high rates of injury, illness, and death (Goldcamp et al. 2004; Hard and Myers 2006; Zaloshnja et al. 2012), and these children report engaging in hazardous work tasks and receiving very little safety training. Nevertheless, their parents are adamant that they know what is best for their children and oppose any policy that will limit their oversight of their children (Darragh et al. 1998; Neufeld et al. 2002; Summers et al. 2018; Westaby and Lee 2003).

The farmer's high tolerance of risk, denial of susceptibility, and skepticism regarding safety measures may contribute significantly to the problems encountered by some farmworkers. In some cases, exposure of farmworkers to heat, chemical, ergonomic, and other hazards may be deliberate and malicious (Salazar et al. 2005), while in others it may simply reflect an extension of the farmer's personal approach to risk and prevention. Unfortunately, the considerable power imbalance inherent in the farmer-farmworker relationship can amplify the risk encountered by these workers. This problem may be further exacerbated by farmworkers' priorities and beliefs. Farmworkers' perception of being in the hands of fate and their recognition of the extreme power imbalance both significantly reduce the likelihood of their objecting to observed hazards in the workplace. Many of these workers face an economic imperative to maximize work hours and weekly income. For many workers, physical work is inextricably linked to physical pain and musculoskeletal strain; Arcury et al. (2015b) provide an analysis of this perspective among Latinx poultry processing workers. The farmworkers' view that musculoskeletal injury is "just part of the job" contrasts notably with health professionals' view that "work shouldn't make you sick." The effects of these farmer values on health and safety for farmworkers are particularly seen in the discussion of farmworker injury and illness and exposure to pesticides (see Chap. 3).

2.4.3 Regional Crops in the Eastern US with Farmworker Involvement

Production of many agricultural commodities in the eastern US requires the hand labor of farmworkers for planting, cultivating, and harvesting. These commodities include fruits, such as apples, berries, citrus, melons, and peaches; vegetables, including cucumbers, mushrooms, onions, sweet potatoes, and tomatoes; and non-food commodities like Christmas trees, ferns, and tobacco. Table 2.2 provides information on some agricultural commodities that particularly involve farmworkers in the eastern US. Review of the farms and acreage devoted to these different commodities documents the variability in the work performed by farmworkers in the eastern US. For example, while cucumbers are produced in all the states, a large number of farms and acres are devoted to the production of cucumbers in the southeastern states. Within the states producing cucumbers, Florida stands out for the large proportion of acres (15,530 of 26,222 acres, 59%) harvested for processing (e.g., making pickles). Pennsylvania has by far the greatest need for workers to pick mushrooms. Maine leads the region in acres devoted to berries. North Carolina and Kentucky have the greatest acreage in tobacco.

The process of planting, cultivating, and harvesting different agricultural commodities places farmworkers at risk for different injuries and illnesses (see Chaps. 3 and 5). For example, pesticides, including fungicides, herbicides, and insecticides, are applied to all of these commodities; however, the toxicity of pesticides used for each commodity differs. Picking some fruits and vegetables, such as strawberries, cucumbers, and sweet potatoes, requires bending and lifting. Harvesting orchard fruits includes risks for falls and eye injuries. Tobacco harvesting exposes workers to nicotine and nicotine poisoning (green tobacco sickness) (Arcury et al. 2001, 2016a). Harvesting mushrooms requires work in humid environments with high levels of molds.

2.4.4 Livestock and Poultry

The number of Latinx immigrants working in livestock and poultry production, as well as in seafood processing, such as crab picking, is increasing. For example, in the Northeast, Latinx immigrants are being hired to work on dairy farms (Earle-Richardson and May 2002; Stack et al. 2006; Sexsmith 2016a, b; Schewe and White 2017), and in the mid-Atlantic, they are working on thoroughbred horse farms (Bush et al. 2018; Swanberg et al. 2013) (see Chap. 5). Individuals working in livestock and poultry production are often full-time, long-term employees and do not fit the definition of migrant and seasonal farmworker.

The number of concentrated animal feeding operations (CAFOs) for poultry and hogs has grown substantially since 1990, particularly in the Southeast (Table 2.3). The potential health effects of CAFOs for workers and on the surrounding commu-

Table 2.2 Number of farms and acres for selected crops produced in the eastern US, 2017

State	Cucumbers		Mushrooms		Peaches		Berries		Tobacco		Christmas trees	
	Farms	Acres	Farms	Sq. ft. under protection	Farms	Acres	Farms	Acres	Farms	Acres	Farms	Trees cut
Alabama	296	5376	10	7034	293	1818	725	1098	0	0	48	17,038
Connecticut	286	201	23	21,050	167	365	404	744	46	2204	358	98,500
Delaware	39	1016	2	–	11	269	52	94	0	0	21	5401
Florida	285	26,222	46	–	337	1025	1367	17,054	19	1135	55	13,968
Georgia	488	6140	31	293,876	289	11,877	1281	19,427	106	12,905	106	32,161
Kentucky	633	198	26	44,720	364	370	967	900	2618	80,544	61	5869
Louisiana	203	98	8	14,190	54	164	361	725	1	–	32	11,545
Maine	403	154	34	19,875	118	44	1054	39,930	0	0	244	128,601
Maryland	225	1495	27	–	134	831	328	593	40	315	113	52,677
Massachusetts	355	248	32	33,759	216	461	979	14,994	15	461	264	82,524
Mississippi	293	225	2	–	173	250	543	2131	0	0	51	12,889
New Hampshire	181	104	7	6900	114	83	371	754	0	0	181	106,703
New Jersey	385	2894	15	298,525	281	3362	607	13,649	0	0	639	85,781
New York	945	1359	117	101,919	431	1391	1659	4240	0	0	754	295,260
North Carolina	882	9568	178	143,959	323	930	1430	10,589	1294	167,781	653	4,031,864
Ohio	668	1950	44	32,915	547	1167	1309	1584	82	1046	449	155,572
Pennsylvania	791	619	113	17,314,135	849	4249	1802	2334	812	7476	962	1,050,159
Rhode Island	47	24	11	–	12	0	74	228	0	0	43	17,121
South Carolina	431	984	23	136,229	248	17,566	643	1589	117	12,176	81	27,578
Tennessee	547	253	48	–	406	638	1015	1164	598	20,751	74	54,005
Vermont	179	69	54	9960	40	13	478	662	0	0	163	110,459
Virginia	456	386	41	36,868	337	1032	903	1357	306	23,039	343	474,902
West Virginia	341	88	22	10,129	277	1088	1201	23,172	2	–	152	42,830
Total	9359	59,671	914	18,526,043	6021	48,993	19,547	159,012	6056	329,833	5847	6,913,407

USDA (2019) 2017 Census of Agriculture, Vol. 1, Chap. 2: US state level data https://www.nass.usda.gov/Publications/AgCensus/2017/Full_Report/Volume_1,_Chapter_2_US_State_Level/

Table 2.3 Number of farms producing selected livestock and poultry in the eastern US, 2017

State	Number of farms		
	Hogs and pigs	Milk cows	Any poultry
Alabama	1704	366	5954
Connecticut	214	198	1371
Delaware	55	50	782
Florida	1810	600	7029
Georgia	1091	572	7047
Kentucky	1805	1577	8965
Louisiana	874	132	3498
Maine	429	450	2059
Maryland	562	511	2724
Massachusetts	337	220	1845
Mississippi	784	108	4300
New Hampshire	281	216	1231
New Jersey	347	109	2156
New York	1739	4648	6172
North Carolina	2426	546	7875
Ohio	3484	3346	11,350
Pennsylvania	2777	6914	10,818
Rhode Island	60	16	257
South Carolina	1005	215	4332
Tennessee	1898	986	9662
Vermont	353	841	1596
Virginia	1461	1048	6789
West Virginia	892	458	4884

USDA (2019) 2017 Census of Agriculture, Vol. 1, Chap. 2: US state level data https://www.nass.usda.gov/Publications/AgCensus/2017/Full_Report/Volume_1,_Chapter_2_US_State_Level/

nities continue to be documented (Kirkhorn and Schenker 2002; Mirabelli et al. 2006; Tajik et al. 2008; Hofmann et al. 2018; Kilburn 2012). Little research has considered the ethnicity or immigration status of workers in these operations (see Chap 5). However, observations of workers in North Carolina indicate that many are Latinx immigrants. In the poultry industry, many of those who collect eggs are Latinx, and many of those "catching" chickens in poultry houses for shipment to processing plants are Latinx (Quandt et al. 2013a).

2.5 Demographic Context

Agricultural workers in the eastern US once included large numbers of local youth doing farm work as a summer job or working on family-owned operations. Migrant and seasonal agricultural workers, until recently, included substantial numbers of African Americans, Afro-Caribbeans, Native Americans, and Appalachian whites, as well as Latinx (Leone and Johnston 1954). Now, although each of these groups still remains involved in seasonal farm work, most farmworkers working in the eastern US are Latinx immigrants, with most of Mexican heritage (Hernandez et al. 2016a). The Latinx community is becoming the largest minority population in the US (Colby and Ortman 2015). In several eastern states, the growth of the Latinx population has been extraordinary. For example, the Latinx population of Georgia is estimated to have grown from 425,305 persons in 2000 to 950,471 persons in 2015, a 123% change; the estimated growth for North Carolina is from 367,390 persons in 2000 to 912,609 persons in 2015, a 148% change; and the estimated growth for South Carolina is from 90,263 persons in 2000 to 261,580 persons in 2017, a 188% change (Pew Research Center 2017). Although most farmworkers are Latinx, it is important to recognize that the proportion of farmworkers born in the US has increased; almost three-in-ten farmworkers interviewed for the 2013–2014 NAWS were US-born (Hernandez et al. 2016a).

2.5.1   Number of Farmworkers

Estimates of the number of farmworkers in the eastern US and nationally vary widely. A number frequently used to characterize the national farmworker population is 2.5–3 million; this number is probably an overestimate. The earliest national estimates were produced in 1990, but these estimates did not include all states (USDHHS 1990). Additional estimates for a few states were calculated in 2000 (Larson 2000). The 2002 Census of Agriculture provided three different indicators of the number of farmworkers in each state (USDA 2004). Data on "farms with hired migrant farm labor" and "farms reporting only contract migrant farm labor" were not reported in earlier censuses, and changes in the number of farms cannot be evaluated. The 2017 Census of Agriculture provided more detailed indicators of the size of the farmworker population (USDA 2019). Information provided included the number of farms with employees working fewer than 150 days as well as the number of workers employed fewer than 150 days. It also includes the number of farms with migrant workers and the number of migrant workers, and divides the number of farms with migrant labor into those with hired labor and those with only contract labor.

The number of farmworkers in each of the eastern states varies substantially. Comparing the 1990 migrant and seasonal farmworker estimates with the 2002 and 2017 Census of Agriculture data show some interesting patterns (Table 2.4). Some states with few farmworkers (e.g., Alabama, Tennessee) or for which the number of farmworkers was not estimated in 1990 (Kentucky, Louisiana, Mississippi) had large numbers of workers working less than 150 days and farms with migrant workers in 2002. These numbers then decrease precipitously by 2017. Other states with extremely large numbers of farmworkers in 1990 (e.g., Florida, North Carolina) experienced major declines in workers working less than 150 days and farms with migrant workers in 2002 and further declines through 2017. By 2017, only one

Table 2.4 Indicators of the number of farmworkers in the eastern US, by state

State	1990 Total number of MSFW[a]	2002 Census of Agriculture[b]			2017 Census of Agriculture[c]							
		Workers working less than 150 days	Farms with migrant workers	Farms with only contract workers	Workers working less than 150 days		Total migrant workers		Migrant farm labor on farms with hired labor		Migrant farm labor on farms reporting only contract labor	
					Farms	Workers	Farms	Workers	Farms	Workers	Farms	Workers
Alabama	6483	25,994	303	57	7653	16,402	175	1864	151	1573	24	291
Connecticut	9421	7559	135	7	1056	6079	95	688	91	679	4	9
Delaware	5397	2151	70	3	529	1900	45	648	45	648	–	–
Florida	435,373	68,971	1303	453	8076	45,849	913	34,177	707	30,932	206	3245
Georgia	93,604	42,307	858	141	8382	30,737	623	19,331	537	17,689	86	1642
Kentucky	–	99,003	3311	687	13,467	35,977	1418	10,605	1104	8452	314	2153
Louisiana	–	9683	363	46	5051	12,626	719	4528	681	4357	38	171
Maine	8660	13,551	137	14	1827	9314	108	2191	81	1786	27	405
Maryland	4267	10,551	212	11	2272	7472	138	1341	127	1318	11	23
Massachusetts	7813	8265	243	29	1817	7683	123	837	120	D	3	D
Mississippi	–	23,915	157	113	6803	16,331	229	3530	2056	2236	24	1294
New Hampshire	726	2789	41	113	761	3200	31	209	31	209	–	–
New Jersey	13,522	13,676	523	43	1815	15,298	303	10,675	294	10,621	9	54
New York	30,811	43,347	946	50	6457	29,742	929	11,821	880	11,512	49	309
North Carolina	344,944	97,138	3097	364	8850	39,618	1684	28,063	1467	25,333	217	2730
Ohio	11,621	54,180	518	108	12,649	37,086	259	3666	252	3626	7	40
Pennsylvania	24,711	41,606	745	59	9514	33,730	401	4731	375	4564	26	167

Rhode Island	459	677	26	5	24	981	7	14	6	D	1	D
South Carolina	18,560	18,650	469	57	3809	12,438	160	4693	136	4569	24	124
Tennessee	6571	43,366	1338	288	6597	14,954	113	493	111	D	2	D
Vermont	1785	4239	129	1	1494	4552	128	786	127	D	1	D
Virginia	15,079	34,367	1016	159	8261	23,977	492	5153	439	4766	53	387
West Virginia	2700	8441	99	17	2520	6441	40	475	38	D	2	D

D data withheld to avoid disclosing data for individual farms

[a]USDHHS (1990)

[b]USDA (2004) 2002 Census of agriculture, Vol. 1, Chap. 2: US state level data. http://usda.mannlib.cornell.edu/usda/AgCensusImages/2002/01/51/1709/Table-07.pdf (accessed April 16, 2019)

[c]United States Department of Agriculture (USDA), National Agricultural Statistics Service (2019) 2017 Census of agriculture, Vol. 1, Chap. 2: US state level data. https://www.nass.usda.gov/Publications/AgCensus/2017/Full_Report/Volume_1,_Chapter_2_US_State_Level/st99_2_007_007.pdf (accessed April 16, 2019)

state, Florida, had over 40,000 workers working fewer than 150 days, while several states had over 35,000 such workers (Kentucky, North Carolina, Ohio), and others had over 25,000 such workers (Georgia, New York, Pennsylvania). Florida also had the greatest number (34,177) of migrant farmworkers in 2017, with North Carolina having 28,063. Georgia, Kentucky, New Jersey, and New York had between 10,000 and 12,000 migrant workers.

Some states have other sources of information that estimate the number of farmworkers. For example, the North Carolina Division of Employment Security estimates the number of agricultural workers at "peak season" by county each year. Division of Employment Security staff have made public statements that their estimates are very conservative and probably underestimate the number of farmworkers. Their estimates for 2017 were 28,075 migrant farmworkers (down from 37,610 in 2007), 19,685 seasonal farmworkers (down from 25,407 in 2007), and 21,443 farmworkers with H-2A visas (up from 8730 in 2007). The number of migrant farmworkers they estimate is comparable to the number reported by the 2017 Census of Agriculture (28,075 versus 28,063). Assuming that those with H-2A visas are contract workers, the number reported by the Employment Security Commission is far greater than the number reported by the 2017 Census of Agriculture (21,443 versus 2730). Finally, the combined number of seasonal farmworkers, migrant farmworkers, and farmworkers with H-2A visas (69,203) is far greater than the number of workers working less than 150 days (39,618).

2.5.2   Farmworker Personal Characteristics

The 2014 and 2015–2016 NAWS (Hernandez et al. 2016a; Hernandez and Gabbard 2018) provide current information on the personal characteristics of farmworkers across the eastern US and the context for a comparison of farmworkers in the eastern US with national farmworker information (Table 2.5). Data from the 2002–2004 NAWS provides comparative data to estimate changes during the 2000s.

Eastern US farmworkers in 2014 had an average age of 36 years compared with an average of 34 years in 2002–2004. Although most farmworkers remained men (60%), the percent of farmworkers who were women increased from 19% to 40% in the eastern US. In 2014, Spanish remained the primary language of the majority (70%) of farmworkers in the eastern US, with the percent who stated that they could speak English well increasing from 37% to 43% since 2002–2004. Most remained foreign-born (58%), with 46% born in Mexico. The national farmworker population interviewed for the 2015–2016 NAWS was more Spanish speaking (77% versus 70%), foreign-born (76% versus 58%), and Mexico-born (69% versus 46%) than was the eastern US farmworker population in 2014. It is important to note that more than one third (39%) of the eastern US farmworkers interviewed by the 2014 NAWS indicated that they were not Hispanic or Latino.

Most (84%) farmworkers in the eastern US participating in the 2014 NAWS were not migrants; this is similar to the 2015–2016 national NAWS data (81%) and a

Table 2.5 Selected eastern US farmworker demographic characteristics in 2002–2004 and 2014, and national US farmworker demographic characteristics (2014–2015 and 2015–2016) from the National Agricultural Workers Survey

Demographic characteristic	Eastern US 2002–2004[a]	Eastern US 2014[b]	National US 2015–2016[c]
Mean age (years)	33.6	36	38
Female (%)	19	40	32
Language			
Spanish is primary language (%)	60	70	77
Able to speak English well (%)	37	43	29
Able to speak English at all or a little (%)	31	33	32
Ethnicity			
Foreign-born (%)	63	58	76
Born in Mexico of those foreign-born? (%)	55	46	69
Indigenous (2002) (%)		6	3
Stating not Hispanic or Latino (%)	31	39	16
Migration status			
Nonmigrant (%)	57	84	81
Migrant (%)	36	16	19
Newcomer (%)	13	2	18
Follow the crops (%)	13	4	27
Shuttle (%)	17	9	21
Weeks employed	32.8	33	35
Average range personal income ($)	14,168	15,000–17,499	17,500–19,999
Average range family income ($)	18,580	20,000–24,999	20,000–24,999
Percent with families below poverty (%)	26	35	33

[a]Carroll et al. 2005
[b]Calculated from the publically available NAWS data
[c]Hernandez and Gabbard 2018; Hernandez et al. 2016b

substantial increase from the 57% of eastern US nonmigrant farmworkers who participated in the 2002–2004 NAWS. The percent of newcomer migrants (2%), follow-the-crop migrants (4%), and shuttle migrants (9%) is smaller in the eastern US than nationally, and these percentages have decreased substantially in the eastern US since 2002–2004. Personal and family income for farmworkers in the eastern US in 2014 increased slightly from 2002 to 2004 and is about on par with national farmworker income ranges. The percent of farmworker families in the eastern US below poverty increased from 26% in 2002–2004 to 35% in 2014, about the same as the national farmworker rate of 33%.

Indigenous or native heritage is an important characteristic of many farmworkers recognized by service providers and researchers. Individuals of indigenous heritage often have a primary language such as Mixteco, Quiché, or Zapoteco, rather than Spanish. If these indigenous farmworkers speak Spanish at all, it is as a second language. Typically, 20–25% of North Carolina study participants are indigenous. A project conducted in Oregon has focused on the growing indigenous farmworker community (Farquhar et al. 2008). Being indigenous and speaking an indigenous language further limits farmworkers' access to health and other services, knowing their rights, and reporting situations in which occupational safety and health regulations are not followed.

2.6 Housing Context

An individual's house, the place in which they eat, sleep, and relax, is important to mental and physical health. This importance is reflected in Article 25 of the Universal Declaration of Human Rights (United Nations 1948), which proclaims adequate housing is a basic human right. However, the available research demonstrates that inadequate housing is the most egregious of all of the unjust and inequitable conditions endured by farmworkers in the eastern US (Arcury et al. 2012a, 2015e).

The provision of housing to farmworkers varies by whether they are migrant or seasonal workers and the region in which farmworkers live. Seasonal farmworkers are generally responsible for their own housing as are some migrant farmworkers. This housing is regulated by local and state housing codes. Many migrant farmworkers in the eastern US are provided housing by their employers. Employer-provided migrant farmworker housing is often referred to as a "farmworker camp." Employer-provided housing is regulated by the Migrant and Seasonal Agricultural Worker Protection Act (MSPA) (USDOL 2016b). A few states have adopted regulations that are stronger than the federal guidelines. Employers of farmworkers with H-2A visas are required to provide housing.

The quality and condition of housing available to farmworkers, whether employer-provided or obtained in the general housing market, are a continuing concern. Papers produced for a conference on farmworker housing quality and health (Arcury et al. 2015a; Arcury and Summers 2015) provide a review of current knowledge on the association of farmworker housing and health (Quandt et al. 2015), on the role of social factors in farmworker housing and health (Marsh et al. 2015), and on current federal farmworker regulations and their enforcement (Moss Joyner et al. 2015).

2.6.1 Employer-Provided Housing

Most employer-provided farmworker housing is in poor condition (Vallejos et al. 2011), none of it meets current regulations (Arcury et al. 2012a), and little of it provides farmworkers with a sense of safety or privacy (Arcury et al. 2012b). Employer-provided housing is associated with the risk of pesticide exposure (Arcury et al. 2014a; Levesque et al. 2012; Raymer et al. 2014) as well as the risk of heat stress (Quandt et al. 2013b). The water in one third of this housing does not meet basic public health standards (Bischoff et al. 2012), and those residing in this housing are at increased risk of infectious disease and parasites (Feldman et al. 1974; Russell et al. 2010) and skin diseases (Gustafson et al. 2014). This housing increases the risks for mental health problems and violence (Benson 2008; Kraemer Diaz et al. 2016; Mora et al. 2016; see Chap. 4).

Farmworker camps are often located so that they cannot be seen by the general public (Summers et al. 2015), with the newest camps (those that include barracks built especially for farmworkers) often being more hidden. When faced with the poor condition in which they are forced to live, migrant farmworkers adapt to it by developing an attitude of *aguantamos*, of putting up with the situation so that they can accomplish their responsibility to provide income for their families (Heine et al. 2017).

2.6.2 Non-Employer-Provided Farmworker Housing

The majority of Latinx farmworkers, including almost all seasonal farmworkers and many migrant farmworkers, do not reside in employer-provided housing. However, little research has addressed the housing quality or needs of these farmworkers. The residents of non-employer-provided farmworker housing acknowledge the poor housing conditions in which they live, describing their exposure to pesticides, safety concerns, pests, poor water and air quality, and lack of temperature control (Keim-Malpass et al. 2015). Much is rental housing (Arcury et al. 2017a). Many of the houses in which these farmworkers live (which include old trailers and farmhouses) are small, in disrepair, and crowded (Early et al. 2006; Gentry et al. 2007; Arcury et al. 2017b). These houses are often adjacent to agricultural fields. The poor housing conditions and crowding are associated with elevated stress and conflict (Arcury et al. 2015e). Few farmworker houses have enclosed play spaces for children, and traffic makes it difficult to walk on the street.

A single study focused on pesticide safety and behavior in farmworker houses found that workers try to follow recommended procedures for occupational pesticide safety (e.g., leaving pesticide containers at work, separate storage and laundry of work clothes), but following these behaviors is more difficult when a large number of persons reside in the house (Rao et al. 2006). At the same time, workers do not generally know and follow recommendations for general residential pesticide safety (Rao et al. 2006). As a result, most (95%) farmworker houses have residential or agricultural pesticides present, and these pesticides are present on children's hands and toys as well as floors (Quandt et al. 2004). Pesticide detection in farmworker houses is associated with the degree to which they were judged difficult to clean, an indicator of housing conditions (Quandt et al. 2004).

2.7 Cultural Context

Although the substantial majority of farmworkers in the eastern US are Latinx, the ethnic and cultural backgrounds of farmworkers in the eastern US vary. Over one third (39%) of farmworkers from the eastern US who participated in the 2014 NAWS reported that they were not Latinx (Table 1.5). Recent studies conducted in the Northeast include substantial numbers of Native Americans and Afro-Caribbeans (May et al. 2008; Rabinowitz et al. 2005); recent studies in the Southeast include substantial numbers of African Americans (Gadon et al. 2001).

Most Latinx farmworkers in the eastern US are of Mexican heritage. More than half (58%) of farmworkers from the eastern US who participated in the 2014 NAWS reported that they were foreign-born, with 46% of those foreign-born reporting being born in Mexico (Table 2.5). Most Latinx farmworkers who were born in the US are the children of immigrants from Mexico (Arcury et al. 2014b, 2015c, 2019a). Other Latinx farmworkers are natives of other Central American counties, such as Guatemala and Honduras, and others are from Caribbean locations, such as Puerto Rico and the Dominican Republic. Many of the Latinx farmworkers from Mexico and Central American nations are indigenous people (6% reported in the 2014 NAWS) who speak an indigenous language in addition to or instead of Spanish.

Although the ethnic and cultural variations among farmworkers are difficult to document, most attention to the culture, values, and beliefs of farmworkers has been focused on those who are Latinx and who are from Mexico. That all communities have culture, and that the shared beliefs that constitute culture affect behavior, should be remembered when discussing the culture of farmworkers and considering how the context of culture affects health, safety, and justice.

2.7.1 General Beliefs and Values of Latinx Farmworkers

Several aspects of the cultural context of Latinx farmworkers have important implications for health, safety, and justice. The most important of these are *familismo*, *personalismo*, and *respeto*. Latinx farmworkers have strong ties to their families, whether family members are with them in the US, remain in a home community elsewhere in the US, or are in a foreign country (e.g., Mexico). The persons and degrees of relation included as family among Latinx farmworkers often exceed those included by other North Americans. The sense of responsibility to family is also very strong among Latinx farmworkers. Many farmworkers laboring in the US are doing so to support families in their communities of origin. A key indicator of this sense of responsibility is the number of farmworkers—migrant and seasonal— who send remittances to family members in their home communities. The size and number of remittances are important for the survival of family members and have an important economic development effect in these communities (Grey and Woodrick 2002; Suro et al. 2002; Pew Research Center 2013). For example, Cortina and De la

Garza (2004) found that Mexican and El Salvadoran immigrants intended their remittances for food and basic consumption (67%), health care (9%), home building or improvement (5%), and education (3%). With the importance that Latinx farmworkers place on sending remittances to their families, they are inclined to continue working in difficult and dangerous situations and not engage in behaviors (e.g., refusing to work in unsafe conditions or reporting employers to regulatory agencies) that might result in job loss.

Latinx farmworkers expect to develop warm, friendly, and personal relationships and seek this *personalismo* with their employers as well as co-workers (Molina et al. 1994). They also expect to be treated with respect and dignity (*respeto y dignidad*) based on their age, gender, and social position and show this respect and dignity to others (Molina et al. 1994; Lecca et al. 1998). On the basis of these values, Latinx farmworkers expect their employer will protect them, but they are hesitant to disagree with their employer about occupational safety.

Machismo is an often-cited belief among Latinx men that refers to a strong sense of masculine pride. The degree to which *machismo* actually exists, as well as the degree to which it represents a set of risk behaviors and a chauvinistic attitude toward women, is a matter of debate. However, research with male farmworkers in the US and farmers in Mexico indicates that they are willing to forego occupational safety because they feel that, as strong men, they are immune to injury and that they should ignore risk (Hunt et al. 1999; Quandt et al. 1998). This attitude appears very similar to that described for US farmers (see Sect. 2.4.2).

2.7.2 Health Values, Beliefs, Behaviors

2.7.2.1 General Health Beliefs

Several general health beliefs have been identified among Latinx farmworkers that may affect their health and safety. One is that the locus of health or illness is outside the control of the individual, whether due to supernatural causes or due to God's will (Grieshop et al. 1996). Humoral medicine is a health belief system that is widely held among people native to Mexico and other Latin American countries (Rubel 1960; Weller 1983; Barker et al. 2017). Within this system of beliefs, substances and materials have different humors that make them "hot" or "cold." Depending on the beliefs of individuals, hot and cold may be concrete, referring to actual temperature, or metaphysical, referring to the nature of the substance regardless of its concrete temperature. For example, water is by nature cool (metaphysical), no matter what its temperature (concrete). Mixing substances or conditions that are hot with those that are cold will result in illness. Humoral medicine concepts are part of the health belief systems of many societies; for example, in the US, it is widely believed that an individual who goes outside into cold weather with wet hair will get sick.

These general health beliefs may reduce the occupational health and safety of Latinx farmworkers by limiting their use of appropriate conventional health services. They also limit workers' demands that employers adhere to occupational safety regulations (Grieshop et al. 1996). These beliefs also affect the adherence of Latinx farmworkers to occupational safety practices. For example, on the basis of humoral medicine beliefs, workers limit washing hands at work and showering immediately after work because they do not want to get ill from placing their hot body in water, which is considered metaphysically cold (Quandt et al. 1998; Flocks et al. 2007). This may lead to increased pesticide dose as pesticides remain on the skin for a longer time.

2.7.2.2 Lay-Defined Illness

Lay-defined illnesses not recognized by biomedicine have been documented in Latin American countries and among Latinx persons living in the US, including Latinx farmworkers (Baer and Bustillo 1993, 1998; Baer and Penzell 1993). These include the illnesses *susto*, *nervios*, *empacho*, and *mal de ojo* (O'Connor et al. 2015; Weller and Baer 2001; Weller et al. 1993, 2002, 2008). Latinx farmworkers also bring culturally based lay definitions to biomedically recognized illnesses, including green tobacco sickness (Rao et al. 2002), tuberculosis (Poss 1998), and diabetes (Heuer and Lauch 2006).

Latinx farmworkers are similar to all other people in applying lay definitions to illnesses. For Latinx farmworkers, applying lay definitions to illnesses that result from farm work may lead them to not seek needed health care and suffer more grave health effects of occupational injuries. For example, Baer and Penzell (1993) document that farmworkers exposed to pesticides in Florida interpreted the resulting symptoms within the framework of lay-defined *susto* and, therefore, did not seek needed medical care.

2.7.2.3 Self-Treatment Versus Medical Care

Although Latinx farmworkers acknowledge the efficacy of conventional medical care, they often limit their use of this care because of the costs (e.g., payment for care, lost time from work), the barriers to obtaining medical care in the US (e.g., hours of operation, transportation, language), and the desire to avoid interactions with authorities (Arcury and Quandt 2007). Latinx farmworkers utilize traditional healers and self-treatment when they lack access to conventional medical care (Arcury et al. 2016b, 2019b). Commonly utilized traditional healers include *curanderos*, *sobadores* (massage therapists), *hueseros* (bonesetters), and *yerberos* (herbalists).

Farmworkers will often ignore or self-treat injuries and illnesses rather than use medical care. In the case of green tobacco sickness, farmworkers report working sick for the entire season because they do not want to risk losing their jobs and do not know how to treat the illness effectively (Rao et al. 2002). Latinx farmworkers report using various traditional and home remedies to treat and prevent illnesses, including herbs, chlorine bleach, milk, and medicine purchased at *tiendas* (small local stores that serve Latinx communities in the US) (Poss et al. 2005; Arcury et al. 2006; Mainous III et al. 2005, 2008). Much of the self-treatment that farmworkers use is effective; however, it can have serious consequences (Cathcart et al. 2008).

The willingness of Latinx farmworkers to self-treat occupational injuries and illness rather than obtain formal medical care increases their risk for continued illness, complications, and long-term health effects. This approach also limits knowledge of the extent of occupational injuries and illnesses experienced by farmworkers (Feldman et al. 2009). Increasing health outreach to farmworkers that provides culturally appropriate treatment recommendations and health education is needed.

2.8 Political Context

The political context for farmworkers in the eastern US is shaped by major political processes, such as changes to immigration law and international trade agreements. In addition, political context is shaped by immigration laws, international trade agreements, occupational safety regulations, and wage and housing policies, which are affected by national and local political and advocacy organizations.

2.8.1 Political Processes

The loudest political process affecting farmworkers is the rhetoric surrounding immigration reform. Most farmworkers are immigrants, and many are undocumented workers. Many conservative political leaders and organizations describe the presence of the large number of Latinx immigrants in the US as destroying the character of the nation as well as a source of crime and infectious disease. Immigrant farmworkers are no exception to this characterization. Anti-immigrant sentiment has a long and virulent history in the US, and some anti-immigrant leaders today can only be described as xenophobic and vitriolic in their statements. Other leaders and organizations, including politicians, associations representing agricultural producers, and farmworker advocates, understand the need for Latinx immigrant farm labor. They recognize that the survival of an important industry and the economy of many rural communities are dependent on the labor of farmworkers, whether or not they have the needed documents to work in the US.

Several policies have been proposed to address the need for Latinx immigrant farmworkers. These include the new Agricultural Worker Program Act of 2019 and changes in the existing H-2A visa program. The Agricultural Worker Program Act of 2019 (S. 175/H.R. 641), also known as the "Blue Card Act," would allow certain farmworkers who meet agricultural work and national security clearance requirements to work legally in agriculture for 3–5 years and allow them the opportunity to earn immigration status with a path to citizenship (Farmworker Justice 2017). This program would not make any changes to the existing H-2A agricultural guest worker program. The H-2A program has expanded as indicated in Sect. 2.2. Recent efforts have included a proposed H-2C visa program to replace the H-2A program. This proposed H-2C visa program is more far-reaching than the H-2A program. For example, the proposed H-2C program would allow employers to keep workers for up to 3 years without their ability to return to their home communities; allow employment in year-round industries including aquaculture, dairy, meat and poultry processing, and forestry; tie wages to the federal minimum wage; require binding arbitration or mediation of grievances rather than litigation; require that 10% of workers' wages be placed into a trust fund that could only be accessed at a US embassy or consulate; not allow spouses and children to accompany workers; and make workers ineligible for any federal benefits, including Affordable Care Act subsidies, but require them to pay for health insurance.

The second major political process forming the political context for farmworkers is the globalization of agriculture. International treaties, in particular the North American Free Trade Agreement (NAFTA) and its replacement, the United States-Mexico-Canada Agreement (USMCA), have facilitated the movement of agricultural commodities across national borders. While such legislation continues to be criticized in the US for allowing low-skill manufacturing jobs to be exported to Mexico, its major effect has been to allow low-cost US agricultural products to be exported to Mexico. As a result, small Mexican farmers cannot compete, forcing many to look elsewhere for work. Many Mexicans are coming to do farm work in the US because they cannot make a living as farmers in Mexico.

2.8.2 Political Organizations

Political organizations representing the agricultural industry and labor work together to make changes in the political context of Latinx farmworkers. However, these organizations often work at cross-purposes. Both industry and labor argue that their goals are to improve the agricultural economy, while protecting the health and safety of agricultural workers.

Political organizations representing industry are numerous and well-funded. They include large, international agricultural processors such as ConAgra Foods and Archer Daniels Midland; trade associations for agricultural equipment and chemical industries, such as CropLife America, the major pesticide industry trade organization, and its state affiliates; national and state agricultural commodity groups, such as the International Tobacco Growers Association, North American Strawberry Growers Association, National Christmas Tree Association, and the National Dairy Council; and farmer advocacy groups, such as American Farm Bureau, state Farm Bureau Federations, and Cooperative Extension. State Farm Bureau Federations, as well as the American Farm Bureau, have their own lobbyists and political action committees for the purpose of effecting agricultural legislation. For example, the New York Farm Bureau Federation has a button for an "e-lobby center" at the top of its Web site. The Virginia Farm Bureau Federation founded the Virginia AgPAC in 1999.

Political organizations representing the agricultural industry generally argue that existing occupational safety regulations are sufficient to protect the health of farmworkers and that many regulations are unnecessary because threats to occupational exposures are overstated or because agricultural employers are conscious of the safety of their workers. They further argue that making policies and regulations more stringent, such as greater pesticide safety training, paying farmworkers overtime wages, or improving housing quality requirements, would be detrimental to the "family farm" (see Sect. 2.4.1). Organizations representing the agricultural industry often work to remove these policies and regulations unless they believe that policies and regulations that protect farmworkers and their families also have an economic benefit for their members. For example, in 2012, the Obama administration proposed new rules restricting the ages at which children could be hired to do farm labor and the hazardous tasks they could perform. These rules were withdrawn before the comment period had expired under a vicious attack from agribusiness interests that distorted the proposed regulations by claiming they would affect work performed by the children of farmers and thus destroy the "family farm" and rural way of life (CropLife News 2012; Leven 2012). Similarly, after a 10-year struggle, the US Environmental Protection Agency (US EPA) released the new Agricultural Worker Protection Standard (US EPA 2016) addressing pesticide safety in 2016. However, a US EPA official stated in a presentation to the 2016 North Carolina Farmworker Institute that the new regulations did not reflect what the science showed was needed; they reflected what the agency felt it could get through the approval process due to industry objections.

Political organizations representing farmworkers are neither numerous nor well-funded. Some of these organizations are discussed in Chap. 9. Nationally and regionally, they include unions, such as the United Farm Workers of America and the Farm Labor Organizing Committee, which are active in the eastern US; they also include advocacy groups, such as Farmworker Justice, Inc. and the Southern Poverty Law Center. Many political organizations representing labor are specific to states, such as El Comité de Apoyo a los Trabajadores Agrícolas (CATA)/The Farmworker Support Committee in New Jersey and Pennsylvania, Farmworker Advocacy Network in North Carolina, and Coalition of Immokalee Workers and The Farmworker Association of Florida, Inc. in Florida. These organizations actively support new state and national legislation that promotes health, safety, and justice for farmworkers and their families. For example, Coalition of Immokalee Workers is a major partner in the Fair Food Program; the North Carolina Farmworker Advocacy Network was a major force in the passage of farmworker housing legislation in 2007. These political organizations also work to amend existing "agricultural exceptionalism" laws that affect farmworker health, safety, and justice (e.g., Harris 2005).

2.9 Summary and Recommendations to Address Health, Safety, and Justice

The context for farmworker health, safety, and justice in the eastern US is complex and changing. This chapter has presented our definition of who we consider to be farmworkers and provided an overview of the geographic, agricultural, demographic, housing, cultural, and political dimensions of the context in which these farmworkers labor and live. Information on farmworkers and their context is inconsistent for the states in the eastern US. Little information is available for several of the dimensions, and different sources are, at times, contradictory in the information they provide. The lack of clarity in data describing farmworkers hampers our ability to address justice; health problems that are not defined or documented cannot be addressed. The descriptions of farmworkers and their contexts presented in this chapter may be different from the experience of some readers. This argues for a greater effort to document the work and health of all farmworkers. Knowing the actual variability and the actual needs of farmworkers in the eastern US will support an approach to justice for all farmworkers.

Farmworkers are involved in agricultural production, with agricultural production including planting, cultivating, harvesting, and processing crops for sale and caring for animals. The majority of farmworkers in the eastern US are Latinx, either immigrants from Mexico or Central America and their children. This population has beliefs, values, and behaviors that differ from many of those who provide services to this population, although this is changing with more Latinx people obtaining the education and training to provide these services. The ethnic composition of this population has resulted in growing anti-immigrant political and social rhetoric directed toward farmworkers. A continuing trend in farm work is the ongoing decline in the number of "family farms" and growth of large-scale commercialization in agriculture. This has created opportunities for farmworkers to obtain jobs in sectors of agriculture, such as dairy and poultry production, in which they had not worked previously. These changes also argue for changes in special regulatory protections that have been permitted for agriculture, such as no extra pay for overtime and lower ages for workers, to protect the "family farm." This agricultural exceptionalism limits the health, safety, and justice for farmworkers.

This review of the context for farmworkers in the eastern US supports two major recommendations. The first recommendation is that state agencies across the region work together to improve the consistency and quality of the information they collect and report about farmworkers. Further, more of the information that agencies have collected about farmworkers in their states needs to be made available. Making the collection of this regulatory information consistent and making existing data available will provide a more complete picture of the commonalities and variation among farmworkers. This information will provide a foundation for understanding the health and safety of farmworkers and help direct efforts needed to provide justice for farmworkers.

The second recommendation is that researchers investigating farmworkers in the eastern US better document the populations they study, their procedures for locating and recruiting participants, and their methods for collecting data. This documentation will provide a way to compare the different communities in which research is conducted. Therefore, rather than having results that are inconsistent across studies, a mechanism to appreciate the diversity of farmworkers and differences in their health and safety will be available.

References

Arcury TA (2017) Anthropology in agricultural health and safety research and intervention. J Agromedicine 22(1):3–8

Arcury TA, Quandt SA (2007) Delivery of health services to migrant and seasonal farmworkers. Annu Rev Public Health 28:345–363

Arcury TA, Summers P (2015) Farmworker housing: a photo essay. New Solut 25(3):353–361

Arcury TA, Quandt SA, Preisser JS (2001) Predictors of incidence and prevalence of green tobacco sickness among Latino farmworkers in North Carolina, U.S.A. J Epidemiol Community Health 55:818–824

Arcury TA, Vallejos QM, Feldman SR et al (2006) Treating skin disease: self-management behaviors of Latino farmworkers. J Agromedicine 11:27–35

Arcury TA, Weir M, Chen H et al (2012a) Migrant farmworker housing regulation violations in North Carolina. Am J Ind Med 55:191–204

Arcury TA, Weir MM, Summers P et al (2012b) Safety, security, hygiene and privacy in migrant farmworker housing. New Solut 22:153–173

Arcury TA, Lu C, Chen H et al (2014a) Pesticides present in migrant farmworker housing in North Carolina. Am J Ind Med 57:312–322

Arcury TA, Rodriguez G, Kearney GD et al (2014b) Safety and injury characteristics of youth farmworkers in North Carolina: a pilot study. J Agromedicine 19(4):354–363

Arcury TA, Jacobs IJ, Ruiz V (2015a) Farmworker housing quality and health. New Solut 25(3):256–262

Arcury TA, Mora DC, Quandt SA (2015b) "…you earn money by suffering pain": beliefs about carpal tunnel syndrome among Latino poultry processing workers. J Immigr Minor Health 17(3):791–801

Arcury TA, Kearney GD, Rodriguez G et al (2015c) Work safety culture of youth farmworkers in North Carolina: a pilot study. Am J Public Health 105(2):344–350

Arcury TA, Summers P, Talton JW et al (2015d) Job characteristics and work safety climate among North Carolina farmworkers with H-2A visas. J Agromedicine 20(1):64–76

Arcury TA, Trejo G, Suerken CK et al (2015e) Housing and neighbourhood characteristics and Latino farmworker family well-being. J Immigr Minor Health 17(5):1458–1467

Arcury TA, Laurienti PJ, Talton JW et al (2016a) Urinary cotinine levels among Latino tobacco farmworkers in North Carolina compared to Latinos not employed in agriculture. Nicotine Tob Res 18(6):1517–1525

Arcury TA, Sandberg JC, Mora DC et al (2016b) North Carolina Latino farmworkers' use of traditional healers: a pilot study. J Agromedicine 21(3):253–258

Arcury TA, Trejo G, Suerken CK et al (2017a) Stability of household and housing characteristics among farmworker families in North Carolina: implications for health. J Immigr Minor Health 19(2):398–406

Arcury TA, Suerken CK, Ip EH et al (2017b) Residential environment for outdoor play among children in Latino farmworker families. J Immigr Minor Health 19(2):267–274

Arcury TA, Arnold TJ, Sandberg JC et al (2019a) Latinx child farmworkers in North Carolina: study design and participant baseline characteristics. Am J Ind Med 62(2):156–167

Arcury TA, Furgurson KF, O'Hara HM et al (2019b) Conventional and complementary therapy use among Mexican farmworkers in North Carolina: applying the I-CAM-Q. J Agromedicine 24(3):257–267

Baer RD, Bustillo M (1993) Susto and mal de ojo among Florida farmworkers: EMIC and ETIC perspectives. Med Anthropol Q 7:90–100

Baer RD, Bustillo M (1998) Caida de mollera among children of Mexican migrant workers: implications for the study of folk illnesses. Med Anthropol Q 12:241–249

Baer RD, Penzell D (1993) Research report: Susto and pesticide poisoning among Florida farmworkers. Cult Med Psychiatry 17:321–327

Barker JC, Guerra C, Gonzalez-Vargas MJ et al (2017) An ethnographic study of salt use and humoral concepts in a Latino farm worker community in California's Central Valley. J Ethnobiol Ethnomed 13(1):11

Bauer M (2013) Close to slavery: guestworker programs in the United States. Southern Poverty Law Center, Montgomery, AL

Benson P (2008) El Campo: faciality and structural violence in farm labor camps. Cult Anthropol 23(4):589–629

Bischoff W, Weir M, Summers P et al (2012) The quality of drinking water in North Carolina farmworker camps. Am J Public Health 102:e49–e54

Bush AM, Westneat S, Browning SR et al (2018) Missed work due to occupational illness among Hispanic horse workers. J Agric Saf Health 24(2):89–107

Carroll D, Samardick RM, Bernard S et al (2005) Findings from the National Agricultural Workers Survey (NAWS) 2001–2002: a demographic and employment profile of United States farm workers (research report no 9). US Department of Labor, Washington, DC

Cathcart S, Feldman SR, Vallejos QM et al (2008) Self-treatment with bleach by a Latino farmworker. Dermatitis 19:102–104

Charlton D, Taylor JE, Vougioukas S et al (2019) Innovations for a shrinking agricultural workforce. Choices 34(2):1–8

Colby SL, Ortman JM (2015) Projects of the size and composition of the U.S. population: 2014 to 2060. Population estimates and projections. Current population reports. https://www.census.gov/content/dam/Census/library/publications/2015/demo/p25–1143.pdf. Accessed 13 May 2019

Cortina J, De la Garza R (2004) Immigrant remitting behavior and its developmental consequences for Mexico and El Salvador. Tomás Rivera Policy Institute, Los Angeles, CA

CropLife News (2012) ARA applauds department of labor's withdraw of the child labor proposal. https://www.croplife.com/management/legislation/ara-applauds-department-of-labors-withdraw-of-the-child-labor-proposal/. Accessed 11 Dec 2018

Darragh AR, Stallones L, Sample PL et al (1998) Perceptions of farm hazards and personal safety behavior among adolescent farmworkers. J Agric Saf Health 1:159–169

Earle-Richardson G, May JJ (2002) Tienes leche? The changing demographics of the dairy workforce. J Agric Saf Health 8:5–6

Early J, Davis SW, Quandt SA et al (2006) Housing characteristics of farmworker families in North Carolina. J Immigr Minor Health 8(2):173–184

Farmworker Justice (2017) Statement on the introduction of the agricultural worker program act of 2017. https://www.farmworkerjustice.org/press/2017/05/statement-introduction-agricultural-worker-program-act-2017. Accessed 13 May 2019

Farquhar S, Samples J, Ventura S et al (2008) Promoting the occupational health of indigenous farmworkers. J Immigr Minor Health 10:269–280

Feldman RE, Baine WB, Nitzkin JL et al (1974) Epidemiology of salmonella Typhi infection in a migrant labor camp in Dade County, Florida. J Infect Dis 130(4):334–342

Feldman SR, Vallejos QM, Quandt SA et al (2009) Healthcare utilization among migrant Latino farmworkers: the case of skin disease. J Rural Health 25:98–103

Flocks J, Monaghan P, Albrecht S (2007) Florida farmworkers' perceptions and lay knowledge of occupational pesticides. J Community Health 32:181–194

Fults J (2017) How to comply with the 2015 revised Worker Protection Standard for agricultural pesticides: what owners and employers need to know. Washington, DC: Pesticide Education Resources Collaborative, United States Environmental Protection Agency. http://www.pesticideresources.org/wps/htc/htcmanual.pdf. Accessed 13 May 2009

Gadon M, Chierici RM, Rios P (2001) Afro-American migrant farmworkers: a culture in isolation. AIDS Care 3:789–801

Gentry AL, Grzywacz JG, Quandt SA et al (2007) Housing quality among North Carolina farmworker families. J Agric Saf Health 13:323–337

Goldcamp M, Hendricks KJ, Myers JR (2004) Farm fatalities to youth 1995–2000: a comparison by age groups. J Saf Res 35:151–157

Grey MA, Woodrick AC (2002) Unofficial sister cities: meatpacking labor migration between Villachuato, Mexico, and Marshalltown, Iowa. Hum Organ 61:364–376

Grieshop JI, Stiles MC, Villanueva N (1996) Prevention and resiliency: a cross cultural view of farmworkers' and farmers' beliefs about work safety. Hum Organ 55:25–32

Guild A, Figueroa I (2018) The neighbors who feed us: farmworkers and government policy: challenges and solutions. Harvard Law Policy Rev 13:157–186

Gustafson CJ, Feldman SR, Quandt SA et al (2014) The association of skin conditions with housing conditions among North Carolina Latino migrant farmworkers. Int J Dermatol 53(9):1091–1097

Hard DL, Myers JR (2006) Fatal work-related injuries in the agriculture production sector among youth in the United States, 1992–2002. J Agromedicine 11:57–65

Harris C (2005) CATA policy manual: laws affecting the farmworker population and CATA's position. El Comité de Apoyo a los Trabajadores Agrícolas (CATA)/The Farmworker Support Committee, Glassboro, NJ

Heine B, Quandt SA, Arcury TA (2017) 'Aguantamos': limits to Latino migrant farmworker agency in North Carolina labor camps. Hum Organ 76(3):240–250

Hernandez T, Gabbard S (2018) Demographic and employment profile of United States farmworkers. Findings from the National Agricultural Workers Survey (NAWS) 2015–2016. Research report 13. US Department of Labor, Employment and Training Administration, Office of Policy Development and Research, Washington, DC

Hernandez T, Gabbard S, Carroll D (2016a) A demographic and employment profile of United States farmworkers. Findings from the National Agricultural Workers Survey (NAWS) 2013–2015. Research report 12. US Department of Labor, Employment and Training Administration, Office of Policy Development and Research, Washington, DC

Hernandez T, Georges A, Gabbard S et al (2016b) A demographic and employment profile of United States farmworkers. Findings from the National Agricultural Workers Survey (NAWS) 2011–2012. Research report 11. US Department of Labor, Employment and Training Administration, Office of Policy Development and Research, Washington, DC

Heuer L, Lauch C (2006) Living with diabetes: perceptions of Hispanic migrant farmworkers. J Community Health Nurs 23:49–64

Hofmann JN, Shiels MS, Friesen MC et al (2018) Industrial hog farming is associated with altered circulating immunological markers. Occup Environ Med 75(3):212–217

Hunt LM, Ojanguren RT, Schwartz N et al (1999) Balancing risks and resources: applying pesticides without using protective equipment in southern Mexico. In: Hahn RA (ed) Anthropology and public health: bridging differences in culture and society. Oxford University Press, Oxford

Keim-Malpass J, Spears Johnson CR, Quandt SA et al (2015) Perceptions of housing conditions among migrant farmworkers and their families: implications for health, safety and social policy. Rural Remote Health 15:3076

Kelsey TW (1994) The agrarian myth and policy responses to farm safety. Am J Public Health 84(7):1171–1177

Kilburn KH (2012) Human impairment from living near confined animal (hog) feeding operations. J Environ Public Health 2012:565690

Kirkhorn SR, Schenker MB (2002) Current health effects of agricultural work: respiratory disease, cancer, reproductive effects, musculoskeletal injuries, and pesticide-related illnesses. J Agric Saf Health 8:199–214

Kraemer Diaz AE, Weir MM, Isom S et al (2016) Aggression among male migrant farmworkers living in camps in eastern North Carolina. J Immigr Minor Health 18(3):542–551

Larson AC (2000) Migrant and seasonal farmworker enumeration profiles study. http://www.ncfh.org/00_ns_rc_enumeration.php. Accessed 17 Jul 2018

Lecca P, Nunes JV, Quervalu I (1998) Cultural competency in health, social, and human services: directions for the twenty-first century. Routledge, Garland, NY

Leone LP, Johnston HL (1954) Agricultural migrants and public health. Public Health Rep 69:1–8

Leven R (2012) Obama administration scraps child labor restrictions for farms. The Hill. https://thehill.com/business-a-lobbying/224169-obama-administration-scraps-child-labor-rules-for-farms. Accessed 23 Apr 2019

Levesque DL, Arif AA, Shen J (2012) Association between workplace and housing conditions and use of pesticide safety practices and personal protective equipment among North Carolina farmworkers in 2010. Int J Occup Environ Med 3(2):53–67

Mainous AG III, Cheng AY, Garr RC (2005) Non-prescribed antimicrobial drugs in Latino community, South Carolina. Emerg Infect Dis 11:883–888

Mainous AG III, Diaz VA, Carnemolla M (2008) Factors affecting Latino adults' use of antibiotics for self-medication. J Am Board Fam Med 21:128–134

Marsh B, Milofsky C, Kissam E et al (2015) Understanding the role of social factors in farmworker housing and health. New Solut 25(3):313–333

May J, Hawkes L, Jones A et al (2008) Evaluation of a community-based effort to reduce blueberry harvesting injury. Am J Ind Med 51:307–315

Mirabelli MC, Wing S, Marshall SW et al (2006) Asthma symptoms among adolescents who attend public schools that are located near confined swine feeding operations. Pediatrics 18:e66–e75

Molina C, Zambrana RE, Aguirre-Molina M (1994) The influence of culture, class, and environment on health care. In: Molina CW, Aguirre-Molina M (eds) Latino health in the US: a growing challenge. American Public Health Association, Washington, DC

Mooney PH (1988) My own boss? Class, rationality, and the family farm. Westview Press, Boulder, CO

Mora DC, Quandt SA, Chen H et al (2016) Associations of poor housing with mental health among North Carolina Latino migrant farmworkers. J Agromedicine 21(4):327–334

Moss Joyner A, George L, Hall ML et al (2015) Federal farmworker housing standards and regulations, their promise and limitations, and implications for farmworker health. New Solut 25(3):334–352

Neufeld S, Wright SM, Gaut J (2002) Not raising a "bubble kid": farm parents' attitudes and practices regarding the employment, training and supervision of their children. J Rural Health 18:57–66

Newman E (2011) No way to treat a guest: why the H-2A agricultural visa program fails U.S. and foreign workers. Washington, DC: Farmworker Justice. http://ncfan.org/research/2011/9/20/no-way-to-treat-a-guest-why-the-h2a-agricultural-visaprogra.html. Accessed 4 Dec 2018

O'Connor K, Stoecklin-Marois M, Schenker MB (2015) Examining nervios among immigrant male farmworkers in the MICASA study: sociodemographics, housing conditions and psychosocial factors. J Immigr Minor Health 17(1):198–207

Pew Research Center (2013) Remittances to Latin America recover—but not to Mexico. Pew Research Center, Washington, DC. http://www.pewhispanic.org/2013/11/15/remittances-to-latin-america-recover-but-not-to-mexico/. Accessed 5 Dec 2018

Pew Research Center (2017) Facts on U.S. Latinos, 2015: statistical portrait of Hispanics in the United States. Washington, DC: Pew Research Center. http://www.pewhispanic.org/2017/09/18/facts-on-u-s-latinos-current-data/. Accessed 13 May 2018

Poss JE (1998) The meanings of tuberculosis for Mexican migrant farmworkers in the United States. Soc Sci Med 47:195–202

Poss JE, Pierce R, Prieto V (2005) Herbal remedies used by selected migrant farmworkers in El Paso, Texas. J Rural Health 21:187–191

Pratt DS, Marvel LH, Darrow D et al (1992) The dangers of dairy farming: the injury experience of 600 workers followed for two years. Am J Ind Med 21:637–650

Quandt SA, Arcury TA, Austin CK et al (1998) Farmworker and farmer perceptions of farmworker agricultural chemical exposure in North Carolina. Hum Organ 57:359–368

Quandt SA, Preisser JS, Arcury TA (2002) Mobility patterns of migrant farmworkers in North Carolina: implications for occupational health research and policy. Hum Organ 61:21–29

Quandt SA, Arcury TA, Rao P et al (2004) Agricultural and residential pesticides in wipe samples from farmworker family residences in North Carolina. Environ Health Perspect 112:382–387

Quandt SA, Arcury-Quandt AE, Lawlor EJ et al (2013a) 3-D jobs and health disparities: the health implications of Latino chicken catchers' working conditions. Am J Ind Med 56(2):206–215

Quandt SA, Wiggins MF, Chen H et al (2013b) Heat index in migrant farmworker housing: implications for rest and recovery from work-related heat stress. Am J Public Health 103(8):e24–e26

Quandt SA, Brooke C, Fagan K et al (2015) Farmworker housing in the United States and its impact on health. New Solut 25(3):263–286

Rabinowitz PM, Sircar KD, Tarabar S et al (2005) Hearing loss in migrant agricultural workers. J Agromedicine 10:9–17

Rao P, Quandt SA, Arcury TA (2002) Hispanic farmworker interpretations of green tobacco sickness. J Rural Health 8:503–511

Rao P, Gentry AL, Quandt SA et al (2006) Pesticide safety behaviors in Latino farmworker family households. Am J Ind Med 49:271–280

Raymer JH, Studabaker WB, Gardner M et al (2014) Pesticide exposures to migrant farmworkers in eastern NC: detection of metabolites in farmworker urine associated with housing violations and camp characteristics. Am J Ind Med 57(3):323–337

Rubel AJ (1960) Concepts of disease in Mexican-American culture. Am Anthropol 62:795–814

Russell MD, Correa MT, Stauber CE et al (2010) North Carolina Hispanic farmworkers and intestinal parasitism: a pilot study of prevalence and health-related practices, and potential means of foodborne transmission. J Food Prot 73(5):985–988

Salazar M, Keifer M, Negrete M et al (2005) Occupational risk among orchard workers: a descriptive study. Fam Community Health 28:239–252

Schewe RL, White B (2017) Who works here? Contingent labor, nonfamily labor, and immigrant labor on U.S. dairy farms. Soc Curr 4:429–447

Seabrook J (2019) Machine hands: the future of farming is robots. The New Yorker 15:48–57

Sexsmith K (2016a) "But we can't call 9-1-1": undocumented migrant farmworkers and access to social protection in New York dairies. Oxf Dev Stud 45:96–111

Sexsmith K (2016b) Exit, voice, constrained loyalty, and entrapment: migrant farmworkers and the expression of discontent on New York dairy farms. Citizensh Stud 20(3–4):311–325

Sorensen JA, May JJ, Paap K et al (2008) Encouraging farmers to retrofit tractors: a qualitative analysis of risk perceptions among a group of high-risk farmers in New York. J Agric Saf Health 14:105–117

Stack SG, Jenkins PL, Earle-Richardson G et al (2006) Spanish-speaking dairy workers in New York, Pennsylvania and Vermont: results from a survey of farm owners. J Agromedicine 11:37–44

Summers P, Quandt SA, Talton JW et al (2015) Hidden farmworker labor camps in North Carolina: an indicator of structural vulnerability. Am J Public Health 105(12):2570–2575

Summers P, Quandt SA, Spears Johnson CR et al (2018) Child work safety on the farms of local agricultural market producers: parent and child perspectives. J Agromedicine 23:52–59

Suro R, Bendixen S, Lowell BL, et al (2002) Billions in motion: Latino immigrants, remittances and banking. A report produced in cooperation between the Pew Hispanic center and the multilateral investment fund. Washington, DC: Pew Hispanic Center. http://idbdocs.iadb.org/wsdocs/getdocument.aspx?docnum=548657. Accessed 17 Jul 2008

Swanberg JE, Clouser JM, Westneat SC et al (2013) Occupational injuries on thoroughbred horse farms: a description of Latino and non-Latino workers experiences. Int J Environ Res Public Health 10(12):6500–6516

Tajik M, Muhammad N, Lowman A et al (2008) Impact of odor from industrial hog operations on daily living activities. New Solut 18:193–205

United Nations (1948) Universal declaration of human rights. General Assembly resolution 217 A. Presented Paris, France, 10 December 1948. http://www.un.org/en/universal-declaration-human-rights/index.html. Accessed 4 Dec 2018

United States Department of Agriculture (USDA) (2004) State level data. In 2002 census of agriculture (Vol. 1). Washington, DC: USDA. http://usda.mannlib.cornell.edu/usda/AgCensusImages/2002/01/51/1709/Table-07.pdf. Accessed 16 Apr 2019

United States Department of Agriculture (USDA), National Agricultural Statistics Service (2019) 2017 Census of Agriculture. Washington, DC: USDA. https://www.nass.usda.gov/Publications/AgCensus/2017/Full_Report/Volume_1,_Chapter_1_US/usv1.pdf. Accessed 13 Aug 2019

United States Department of Health and Human Services (USDHHS) (1990) An atlas of state profiles which estimate number of migrant and seasonal farmworkers and members of their families. US Department of Health and Human Services Migrant Health Program. (ERIC document reproduction service no. ED332857), Rockville, MD

United States Department of Labor (USDOL) (2016a) Child labor bulletin 102. Child labor requirements in agricultural occupations under the Fair Labor Standards Act. WH1295. Washington, DC: Wage and Hour Division, US Department of Labor. https://www.dol.gov/whd/regs/compliance/childlabor102.pdf. Accessed 30 May 2018

United States Department of Labor (USDOL) (2016b) Migrant and Seasonal Agricultural Worker Protection Act (MSPA). Washington, DC: Wage and Hour Division, US Department of Labor. https://www.dol.gov/whd/mspa/. Accessed 3 Dec 2018

United States Department of Labor (USDOL) (2019) Office of Foreign Labor Certification performance data. US Department of Labor, Washington, DC. https://www.foreignlaborcert.doleta.gov/performancedata.cfm

United States Environmental Protection Agency (USEPA) (2016) Agricultural Worker Protection Standard. USEPA, Washington, DC. https://www.epa.gov/pesticide-worker-safety/agricultural-worker-protection-standard-wps

Vallejos QM, Quandt SA, Grzywacz JG et al (2011) Migrant farmworkers' housing conditions across an agricultural season in North Carolina. Am J Ind Med 54(7):533–544

Vogeler I (1981) The myth of the family farm: Agribusiness dominance of U.S. agriculture. Westview Press, Boulder, CO

Weinstein ND (1988) The precaution adoption process. Health Psychol 7(4):355–386

Weller SC (1983) New data on intracultural variability: the hot-cold concept of medicine and illness. Hum Organ 42:249–257

Weller SC, Baer RD (2001) Intra- and intercultural variation in the definition of five illnesses: AIDS, diabetes, the common cold, empacho, and mal de ojo. Cross-Cult Res 35:201–226

Weller SC, Pachter LM, Trotter RT II et al (1993) Empacho in four Latino groups: a study of intra- and inter-cultural variation in beliefs. Med Anthropol 15:109–136

Weller SC, Baer RD, Garcia de Alba J et al (2002) Regional variation in Latino descriptions of susto. Cult Med Psychiatry 26:449–472

Weller SC, Baer RD, Garcia de Alba J et al (2008) Susto and nervios: expressions for stress and depression. Cult Med Psychiatry 32:406–420

Westaby JD, Lee BC (2003) Antecedents of injury among youth in agricultural settings: a longitudinal examination of safety consciousness, dangerous risk taking, and safety knowledge. J Saf Res 34:227–240

Zaloshnja E, Miller TR, Lawrence B (2012) Incidence and cost of injury among youth in agricultural settings, United States, 2001–2006. Pediatrics 129:728–734

Chapter 3
Occupational Injury and Illness in Farmworkers in the Eastern United States

John J. May and Thomas A. Arcury

3.1 Introduction

Few populations of workers in the United States (US) are so readily acknowledged to be socially and economically disadvantaged as the nation's migrant and seasonal farmworkers. Agriculture as a whole is a dangerous industry, with rates of occupational fatality and injury that are seven times the national average (Bureau of Labor Statistics 2018). Migrant and seasonal farmworkers often face the worst working conditions within this dangerous industry.

Data on the degree to which the migrant and seasonal farmworker population experiences occupational injuries and illnesses are limited and generally inadequate. The traditional sources of such data simply do not provide reliable information for this population of workers. Injury logs used for reporting to the Occupational Safety and Health Administration (OSHA) and workers' compensation statistics are, at best, suspect with this group of workers. The problem of underreporting is substantial and leads to limited information being available to assess the issue of occupational illness and injury affecting workers in the eastern US (Azaroff et al. 2002).

Migrant and seasonal farmworkers are hired on a temporary basis, most without benefits or the protections other workers enjoy. Manual crop work often requires prolonged repetitive motion, lifting heavy weights, holding awkward postures for extended periods, exposure to toxic chemicals, and the use of sharp tools. These workers may be paid piece rate, which, under the pressure of the short harvest period, discourages adequate breaks and rest. Basic hydration and hygiene facilities are often not readily available at the work site. Workers' cultural and linguistic

J. J. May
Bassett Research Institute, Cooperstown, NY, USA

T. A. Arcury (✉)
Department of Family and Community Medicine, Wake Forest School of Medicine, Winston-Salem, NC, USA

© Springer Nature Switzerland AG 2020
T. A. Arcury, S. A. Quandt (eds.), *Latinx Farmworkers in the Eastern United States*, https://doi.org/10.1007/978-3-030-36643-8_3

isolation and their uncertain legal status create extreme dependency upon the employer. This marked imbalance of power serves to enhance their susceptibility to occupational safety risks (Wilk 1988; Mobed et al. 1992). Given the organizational structure of these jobs, it is unlikely that OSHA reporting mechanisms will ever accurately reflect illness and injury rates.

Agricultural work exposes the worker to myriad occupational health challenges. Some of these are issues familiar to the occupational health practitioner: people being forced to fit the job, rather than vice versa, employers focused entirely upon short-term issues of production and costs, unhealthy rates of work, and unhealthy work conditions. Other occupational problems for Latinx farmworkers in the eastern US may be less familiar to occupational health professionals: agrochemical intoxications, heat stress, unusual working conditions, limited access to care, and linguistic and cultural differences. These are complex issues that would challenge most occupational health experts. Currently, these issues are routinely presented to practitioners who have expertise in primary care but may feel ill equipped to address these occupational challenges (Institute of Medicine 1988; Liebman and Harper 2001).

This chapter provides an overview of some of the more significant occupational health problems experienced by migrant and seasonal farmworkers as they cultivate and harvest large proportions of eastern states' overall agricultural production. Examined first are some of the problems that may occur commonly in a number of locations and with many commodities. Subsequent discussion of selected specific commodities illustrates how each can present unique challenges that require the health professional to have some understanding of the specific work process. Throughout the chapter, limited comments on treatment and prevention are provided. Recommendations on steps to improve the understanding and prevention of occupational health problems in farmworkers in the eastern US are provided at the end of this chapter.

3.1.1 The Role of Culture in Farmworker Occupational Injury

Farmers have their own culture as do Latinx farmworkers (see Sect. 2.4.2). The farmer-farmworker interaction represents the intersection of these distinct cultures, readily understood by neither the health professional nor outside observer. Farmers combine a remarkably high tolerance for risk (Sorensen et al. 2008) with an optimistic bias (Weinstein 1988), leading them to believe that most things will work out in the end. They generally place greater priority on efficient production than on personal safety, and they see most safety measures as contributing little to their efficiency and productivity. At the same time, farmers express considerable concern regarding the safety of spouses, children, and employees. This attitude reflects decisions to undertake the riskiest tasks personally and in the resultant elevated rates of injuries to farmers compared to employees on small family farms (Pratt et al. 1992).

The farmer's high tolerance of risk, denial of susceptibility, and skepticism regarding safety measures may contribute significantly to the woes encountered by some farmworkers. The exposure of these workers to hazards, such as heat, chemicals, and falls, often reflects the farmers' personal approach to risk and prevention (Sorensen et al. 2008). Farmworkers' beliefs and values may exacerbate the potential for occupational injury. Their beliefs about the role of fate and supernatural factors in their health and safety, their recognition of their limited power relative to their employers, their expectation that work will be physically demanding, and their financial need to keep their jobs and maximize income may lead them to continue working in the face of imminent pain, injury, and illness (Faucett et al. 2001; Arcury et al. 2012).

3.1.2 Data on Farmworker Occupational Illness and Injury

Occupational injury and illness data are often incomplete for agriculture. In the case of farmworkers, this problem is compounded. Papers in the literature are limited, particularly when one focuses upon the experience of workers in the eastern US. Published rates are virtually nonexistent; for most of this work, there are significant questions regarding both numerators and denominators.

3.1.2.1 Numerator Problems

Many farmworkers are not particularly interested in being studied (Earle-Richardson et al. 1998). When they are injured, they have limited access to health care and, for financial, social, and legal reasons, may avoid interactions with the medical establishment. Many workers are just as likely to use home remedies or seek treatment from healers within their community (Arcury et al. 2016a, b). Certainly, those who are undocumented experience increasingly powerful disincentives to seek medical care or to participate in any research projects. This population can be hard to access, and much of the literature relies upon sampling that is little better than convenience sampling, with all of its attendant biases. Several methodologies have been developed that represent an improvement (Arcury et al. 2003a, b; Earle-Richardson et al. 2008; Scribani et al. 2013), but these continue to have limitations. The camp sampling methods used in North Carolina can suffer if some camps are not identified or are not sampled for reasons that might inject unrecognized biases (e.g., the camp owner does allow researchers access). The selection of those within the camp to sample can result in data that are not fully representative. The review of medical charts from migrant clinics and emergency rooms is labor intensive and presumes that those seeking care at these sites are representative of all farmworkers in the region. Problems can arise with accurate recognition, diagnosis, and sufficient documentation in the notes to enable identification of an occupationally related injury or illness in subsequent chart reviews. All of these issues lead to some uncertainty regarding the number of adverse health events actually being experienced by farmworkers in the eastern US.

Further complicating matters is the migratory nature of some of this work force. Does a musculoskeletal injury in a Pennsylvania orchard worker relate to orchard work? Might this injury actually relate to cucumber work done previously in North Carolina? In some cases, an injury may have occurred in one work setting but be further exacerbated by different work in a different location.

3.1.2.2 Denominator Problems

Although figures are quoted repeatedly throughout the literature and throughout this book, there is no clear understanding of how many farmworkers are employed in the eastern US or elsewhere in the country. Previous literature referred to estimates produced by the Health Resources and Services Administration (HRSA 1990), but the most recent substantial enumeration was done in 2000 and had a number of significant design flaws. Alternate estimates have been based upon the Larson's minimum labor demand methodology (Larson and Plascencia 1993; Larson 2000). Using figures relating the number of worker hours required to produce a given amount of a commodity product, Larson was able to estimate the total number of workers required in each state to account for its reported agricultural production of a series of different labor-intensive commodities.

Each state currently makes various estimates of the number of migrant farm-workers employed in the state. In New York, estimates are now made by both the Department of Agriculture and Markets and the Department of Labor. The traditional estimates made by the Department of Labor rely upon mandatory reporting by farms employing more than five workers or contractors employing any number of workers. Comparison of these figures with those derived using Larson's methodology shows considerable divergence, with Larson's minimum labor calculations estimating nearly twice as many workers (Earle-Richardson et al. 2005). Efforts based upon accumulating counts from various farmworker advocacy and support organizations have proven equally difficult (Borjan et al. 2008). These examples of the underlying uncertainty regarding the number of workers illustrate the challenges in any efforts aimed at establishing rates of injuries or illnesses in farmworkers.

The general absence of reliable numerator and denominator figures represents a substantial challenge to establishing priorities for intervention. Subsequently, this problem will also complicate the assessment of the effect of any interventions that are implemented. Assessment of long-term outcomes of either exposures or interventions is substantially challenged by the transient nature of this workforce.

3.2 Access to Optimal Health Care

Roughly 80% of America's 12 million undocumented residents are Latinx. An estimated 1–3 million of these undocumented residents work in agriculture. Like other immigrants, they have worse access to health care and worse health outcomes than other people in the US (Martinez-Donate et al. 2017). Among the contributing factors are low rates of health insurance coverage (Ortega et al. 2015). Employer-provided insurance is unlikely for those who work on smaller operations (<50 full-time equivalents) or who work for less than 120 days. For the roughly 1% of US farms obligated to provide insurance, the fines for failure to do so might be less than the cost of premiums, so insurance still might not be provided (Ahearn et al. 2015).

While the future of the 2010 Patient Protection and Affordable Care Act (ACA) remains politically uncertain, it is important to review ways in which this legislation affected health insurance coverage for farmworkers in the US. The act aimed to assure coverage for more than half of the 20% of America's uninsured population by (1) expanding Medicaid, (2) requiring coverage ("individual mandate") and awarding tax credits to make insurance purchased on the health insurance exchanges more affordable (Ahearn et al. 2015), and (3) increasing funding provided to the US Health Resources and Services Administration (HRSA) for its system of federally qualified health centers (Henry J. Kaiser and Family Foundation 2013). These approaches did succeed in substantially improving rates of insurance coverage but generally have had limited impact upon many farmworkers.

Medicaid expansion mainly assists US citizens and those legally residing in the US for greater than 5 years (Ahearn et al. 2015). Additionally, a number of the states opting out of the Medicaid expansion are those that employ substantial numbers of farmworkers.

Tax-incentivized insurance on the exchanges is available (and required) for US citizens and legal residents exceeding Medicaid poverty limits. H-2A farmworkers actually have the responsibility to be covered and may utilize tax incentives for this coverage (Guild et al. 2016). Unfortunately, workers are not well-informed and rely mainly upon traditionally trusted sources and media for information (Arcury et al. 2017) on this complex process. The challenges of applying are greatly increased for a population without access to computers, command of the English language, and established bank accounts and credit.

Increased funding for HRSA community health centers is the only ACA benefit for more than half of all farmworkers who are undocumented (HRSA 2015a, b). Unfortunately, this advantage may be offset by the considerable swelling of the ranks of immigration officers across the East (Graybill 2012), which has substantially diminished many workers' willingness to undertake off-farm activities, including medical care (Baker and Chappelle 2012; Sexsmith 2017; Graybill 2012).

Despite these hurdles, access to appropriate health care remains an important issue. As will be noted in this and subsequent chapters, farmworkers are at risk for a number of specific health problems related to their work and living situations. Data from farmworkers in New York and Maine indicate that nearly 60% of workers obtain care from either a local emergency department or, more commonly, from a nearby migrant health facility (Earle-Richardson et al. 2008; Brower et al. 2009). Reviews of migrant clinic charts in New York and Pennsylvania demonstrated that more than 10% of all visits are related to occupational problems (and in some clinics, considerably more) (Earle-Richardson et al. 2003).

3.3   Common Occupational Health Problems

In recent years, clinical chart review data, questionnaire data, and combined survey/review data have provided greater insight on the most common occupational issues affecting eastern farmworkers.

The most extensive of the chart review reports described only problems identified as work-related during the clinic visit. Charts were reviewed in migrant clinics extending from Maine to western New York to the eastern shore of Maryland (Scribani et al. 2013). Over a 2-year period, 2520 injuries were identified—30.27 injuries per 10,000 worker weeks or 12.7 per 100 full-time equivalent (FTE) workers. These were overwhelmingly strain/sprain injuries (56%), followed by contact with natural irritants (20%), contact with chemicals (5%), struck by object injuries (4.5%), and falls (3.9%). Orchard crops and bush crops figured more prominently than ground crops, and rates varied considerably from region to region.

Other chart studies also included nonoccupational diagnoses but still documented frequent problems likely related to agricultural work. A study of over 1100 clinical records from farm clinics serving Georgia onion workers from 2009 to 2011 showed leading diagnoses of back pain (11.8%), hypertension (11.4%), musculoskeletal problems (11.3%), gastrointestinal disorders (8.6%), eye problems (7.2%), dermatitis or rash (7.0%), and tinea or fungal skin infections (5.6%) (Luque et al. 2012). As in other occupational settings, there was a suspicion that some musculoskeletal problems might relate in part to stress and depressive symptoms (Arcury et al. 2012). Similar work with clinician-reported diagnoses on over 6000 workers per year from 2003 to 2005 was reported from the New York State Department of Health in 2010 (Emmi et al. 2010). The leading diagnostic groups were infections, often skin, musculoskeletal problems, respiratory disease, hypertension, and diabetes.

These clinical findings are supported by other questionnaire-based data. The most studied source is the National Agricultural Workers Study (NAWS), which relies upon a series of English or Spanish interviews of workers (though the NAWS does not include H-2A workers) on randomly selected, consenting farm operations within randomly selected farm areas across the US. Recent work compared responses from 1999 and 2002–2004 (Period I) with data from 2008 to 2010 (Period II) (Tonozzi and Layne 2016). Injury rates declined by 33% over this period, though not for older workers. The types of injuries reported depended, in part, on the structure of the NAWS question but included sprain/strain 38.8% (Period I) and 50.3% (Period II), cut/laceration 21.2% and 21.1%, fracture/dislocation 12.5% and 12.3%, and bruise/contusion 2.8% and 5.0%. Interviews in North Carolina of Latinx youths (age 10–17 years) working with tobacco, berries, sweet potatoes, and other commodities documented musculoskeletal injury in 54% (commonly shoulder and wrist), trauma (frequently a laceration) in 61%, and dermatologic problems including sun burn and skin rash in 72% (Arcury et al. 2014a, b). Although many of the occupational hazards encountered by migrant farmworkers are universal issues affecting workers across commodities and across the eastern US, others are quite specific issues encountered only in a specific commodity.

3.3.1 Heat Stress

Few would seriously contest that climate change is impacting work conditions in eastern agriculture. The effects of climate change are most apparent in the Southeast (Kunkel et al. 2013a), but changes are also affecting the Mid-Atlantic and Northeast regions (Kunkel et al. 2013b). Recent clinical reports on both heat illness and fatality appear to reflect these climatic trends. Combined data from 9 southeastern states show 8315 occupational heat-related illness (HRI) emergency visits (6.5/100,000 workers) and 1051 inpatient hospitalizations (0.61/100,000) in the Southeast over the 2007–2011 period (Harduar Morano et al. 2015). A detailed review of 359 deaths (2000–2010) from the Census of Fatal Occupational Injuries (Bureau of Labor Statistics 2018) showed that agriculture had 35 times the heat-related fatality risk of all other industries. Forty percent of the fatalities occurred in ten states, half of these being located in the eastern US. Latinx workers had about three times the risk of non-Latinx workers. Males had much higher fatality rates than females, and age was only of minor importance (Gubernot et al. 2015). It appears that the combination of high heat plus humidity may contribute to the high rates of heat fatality in the southeastern states and that some of these events can be anticipated. Investigators in North Carolina reported that the number of emergency visits increased modestly for each degree of ambient temperature between 90° and 98 °F and by tenfold for each degree beyond 98° (Rhea et al. 2012).

Questionnaire data have also shown high rates of HRI symptoms among farmworkers in several southeastern states. Of 405 predominantly Latinx workers harvesting corn, peppers, tomatoes, and other crops in Georgia in June 2011, 34% experienced three or more symptoms of heat illness (Flcischer et al. 2013). Two cross-sectional surveys in North Carolina found 40% and 72% of those working in extreme heat experienced at least some symptoms of illness (Mirabelli et al. 2010; Kearney et al. 2016a, b). A more recent survey of a convenience sample of Florida farmworkers found that during the preceding work week 84% of workers noted at least 1 symptom of HRI, with 40% reporting 3 or more symptoms (Mutic et al. 2017). Of these, 46% experienced combinations of symptoms suggesting moderate or severe illness. These were more commonly experienced by female workers.

3.3.1.1 Work-Related Hyperthermia

Farmworkers acquire heat from the environment and from solar radiation but mainly from heat generated by strenuous muscular activity. A recent study of mainly male workers in California assessed a number of variables and found that workers' core temperatures rising above 38 °C correlated most strongly with ambient temperature and intensity of work (Vega-Arroyo et al. 2019). Hyperthermia occurs with the failure of various regulatory mechanisms that normally compensate for this heat loading.

The farmworker's primary defense against overheating is evaporative heat losses through perspiration from the skin surface. Peak sweating rates may be as high as 2 L/h (Bouchama and Knochel 2002). Determinants affecting evaporative cooling include clothing, sufficient fluid volume for both redistribution of blood flow to the skin and maximal sweat production, and the ambient relative humidity (Armstrong and Maresh 1991). As humidity increases, evaporation slows and cooling is impaired.

Over several weeks of acclimatization, a worker's fluid intake increases, kidney mechanisms shift toward fluid preservation, blood volume increases, maximal sweat production goes up, and clothing and heat avoidance behaviors become refined. Before acclimatization, the worker is more susceptible to the risk of hyperthermia (Bouchama and Knochel 2002). An analysis of 2012–2013 nonagricultural illness/fatalities investigated by OSHA found that nine of the 13 heat-related deaths occurred within the first 3 days on the job (Arbury et al. 2014).

Early indicators of HRI include dehydration related to excessive fluid losses and inadequate intake. Declining urine output and rising urine concentration are signs of inadequate hydration. Headache, dizziness, and muscle cramps, particularly affecting the calves and abdomen, are other early symptoms. Heat exhaustion is present when body temperature exceeds 38 °C; headache, muscle pain, and lightheadedness are likely. The onset of confusion, nausea, and vomiting at this stage is particularly onerous because it removes the potential for oral rehydration. Heat stroke is associated with hot, dry skin and confusion, convulsions, or coma (Bouchama and Knochel 2002). This can lead to damage of multiple organs and even death.

Treatment of heat stroke focuses upon cessation of muscular activity, cooling (removal of clothing and application of cooling packs), and support of organ-system function. Aggressive rehydration with intravenous fluids is of great importance, though the total volume depletion may be less than would be expected in many of these patients (Seraj et al. 1991). The risk of serious complications in these workers is considerable, and urgent medical evaluation is needed.

3.3.1.2 Prevention of Heat Injury

Hats and lightweight, loose-fitting, light-colored, breathable clothes are important. Ready access to clean water is essential. One-half to one liter of water per hour may be needed as the temperature increases from 80 to 90 °F. Voiding should be frequent with light-colored, dilute urine. Use of coffee or sugary soft drinks is ill-advised. One potentially unanticipated problem is the belief among some groups that hot-cold imbalance leads to illness (Flores 2000), causing some workers to drink insufficient volumes of water.

Supervisors must be aware of the effects of temperature and humidity. Short work breaks and use of shade are encouraged. They must recognize the greater sensitivity of those who have not undergone the 2–3 weeks of acclimatization. Recognition of early warning signs such as cramping, muscle pain, weakness, and lightheadedness should prompt immediate cessation of physical exertion, aggressive oral hydration, and removal to a cooler environment.

Standards for prevention of heat injury have recently been published by the National Institute for Occupational Safety and Health (NIOSH 2016a). These include recommendations for workplace limits and surveillance, instituting a system of medical monitoring for employees, work modifications, and worker training.

3.3.1.3 Other Heat Considerations

Over the past two decades, an epidemic of unexplained chronic kidney disease, Mesoamerican nephropathy, has been recognized in the highly agricultural lowlands of Central America, with El Salvador, Honduras, and Nicaragua experiencing some of the highest rates of death from kidney disease in the world (Ramirez-Rubio et al. 2013; Johnson et al. 2019). The affected young male agricultural workers do not have obvious risk factors such as hypertension or diabetes, and the current view is that Mesoamerican nephropathy may be multifactorial. Among the leading suspects are repeated bouts of dehydration related to demanding physical work in hot conditions, possibly combined with use of nonsteroidal analgesics or other medications, and exposure to pesticides or arsenic and other heavy metals (Wesseling et al. 2014).

3.3.2 Health Effects of Pesticide Exposure

Pesticides are substances or mixtures of substances intended for (1) preventing, destroying, repelling, or mitigating any pest; (2) use as a plant regulator, defoliant, or desiccant; or (3) use as a nitrogen stabilizer (US Environmental Protection Agency 2019a). Numerous agricultural pesticides of different classes (e.g., organophosphates, pyrethroids, neonicotinoids) are used to address diverse agricultural pests (e.g., insects, weeds, rodents).

Farmworkers are exposed to pesticides where they work; they and the members of their families are also exposed to pesticides where they live. Pesticides are toxicants that can have immediate effects on health (Roberts and Reigart 2013). Pesticide exposure has also been linked to increased long-term risk for diseases, including cancer, reproductive health problems, neurodegenerative diseases, and respiratory diseases. Few regulations protect farmworkers or their family members from pesticide exposure, making this exposure an environmental and occupational injustice.

3.3.2.1 The Ubiquity of Farmworker Pesticide Exposure

Farmworkers in the eastern US are exposed to high levels of a wide variety of pesticides. Analysis of pesticide urinary metabolites from samples collected four times at 1-month intervals from farmworkers in 2007 showed that these farmworkers had high doses of a variety of different pesticides, including organophosphate insecticides, carbamate insecticides, pyrethroid insecticides, and herbicides (Arcury et al. 2009a, b). The detection and amount of each pesticide urinary metabolite varied across the agricultural season; for example, detection of the malathion pesticide urinary metabolite MDA increased from May to June and decreased in July and August, while detection for the chlorpyrifos pesticide urinary metabolite TCPy increased each month from May through June, July, and August (Arcury et al. 2009a, b). Finally, individual farmworkers were exposed to several different pesticides during the agricultural season, and they were often repeatedly exposed to the same pesticide. For example, the acephate pesticide urinary metabolite APE was detected at four different times for 15 of 196 farmworkers, while TCPy was detected four times for 20 of 196 farmworkers (Arcury et al. 2010). Data collected in North Carolina in 2010 (Raymer et al. 2014) and 2012 (Arcury et al. 2016a, b, 2018a, b) and in Florida in 2011 (Runkle et al. 2013) indicate that farmworker pesticide exposure continues. Research conducted in the western US indicates similar farmworker pesticide exposure (Coronado et al. 2006; Huen et al. 2012).

Farmworkers in the eastern US are exposed to pesticides in their homes. Quandt et al. (2004) documented the presence of an array of agricultural and residential pesticides in the homes of seasonal farmworkers in western North Carolina; for example, chlorpyrifos was found in 32 of the 41 houses, diazinon in 14, and oxyfluorfen in 10. Arcury et al. (2014a, b) reported that organophosphate insecticides were found in 166 of 176 migrant farmworker dwelling, and pyrethroid insecticides were found in 171 of these dwellings. As with pesticide urinary metabolites, research conducted in the western US also documented the presence of pesticides in farmworker dwellings (Bennett et al. 2019; Quirós-Alcalá et al. 2012).

3.3.2.2 The Health Effects of Farmworker Pesticide Exposure

Pesticides can have immediate acute and long-term chronic health effects. Pesticide health effects differ for adults and children (see Chap. 7 for effects on child health). The immediate health effects of pesticide exposure depend on the specific pesticide and the actual dose (Roberts and Reigart 2013). A very small dose of a pesticide may not result in any immediate sign or symptom. With increasing doses, pesticides can result in eye and skin irritation, dizziness, nausea, vomiting, and muscle ache. An extremely high pesticide dose can result in coma and death. All farmworkers and most other people in the US are regularly exposed to pesticides, but because the doses are small, they experience no immediate adverse effects (Centers for Disease Control and Prevention 2019).

Long-term effects can result from large doses of pesticides as well as from continuous small doses over extended periods. The Agricultural Health Study (2019a) has used a sample of 80,000 licensed pesticide applicators and their family members in Iowa and North Carolina to document the long-term adverse effects of pesticide exposure for those involved in agriculture. The size and longitudinal design (data collection began in 1994 and continues to the present) of the Agricultural Health Study has allowed the investigators to show that, in the long term, exposure to different pesticides increases the risk for specific types of cancer, respiratory problems, and neurocognitive decline (Agricultural Health Study 2019b). Other research has documented that pesticide exposure can affect the reproductive health of men and women (Rao 2008), increases the risk of depression and suicide (Freire and Koifman 2013), and results in DNA damage (McCauley et al. 2008).

Insecticides including the organophosphates, carbamates, pyrethroids, and neonicotinoids, are all neurotoxicants. Research has emphasized the potential long-term neurocognitive effects of insecticide exposure, including increased risk for general cognitive decline, Parkinsonism, dementia, and amyotrophic lateral sclerosis (ALS) (Alavanja et al. 2004; Kamel et al. 2012; Baldi et al. 2003). The longitudinal data needed to document neurocognitive disease outcomes among farmworkers are not available. However, research in the eastern US provides indicators of the neurocognitive effects of pesticide exposure among farmworkers. This research has documented relatively high cholinesterase inhibition among farmworkers (Quandt et al. 2010, 2015). It has shown that farmworkers had decreased olfactory function for odor threshold compared to non-farmworker Latinx participants (Quandt et al. 2016, 2017a, b, c, d) and that postural control differed in comparing farmworkers with non-farmworker Latinx (Sunwook et al. 2016; Kim et al. 2018)

3.3.2.3 Reducing Pesticide Exposure

Farmworkers are commonly exposed to pesticides, and this pesticide exposure affects their immediate and long-term health. Preventing all pesticide exposure may be impossible, given the widespread use of pesticides in agriculture and across contemporary society. Processes to reduce pesticide use in agriculture, including organic agriculture and integrated pest management, are important. However, strong regulations are needed that limit the types of pesticides that are used. Recent political processes that stopped the US Environmental Protection Agency from banning the use of the organophosphate pesticide chlorpyrifos document the difficulty of regulating pesticides (Lipton 2017, 2018). Regulations are also needed to control how pesticides are used (e.g., to reduce drift), for the improvement of field sanitation procedures and for mandating that farm work be organized to reduce the level of pesticide exposure.

Current policies and procedures to protect farmworkers from pesticide exposure remain limited. Two federal regulations address the reduction of farmworker pesticide exposure: (1) the US Environmental Protection Agency (US EPA) Worker Protection Standard (WPS; Environmental Protection Agency 2019b) and (2) OSHA field sanitation and housing regulations. Some states have instituted additional regulations to document pesticide use (Yanga et al. 2018) and reduce pesticide exposure for farmworkers who apply pesticides (Hofmann et al. 2008, 2010; Weyrauch et al. 2005), but these are located on the West Coast.

The Worker Protection Standard was first implemented in 1994. It was revised after a protracted political struggle, with the revision only being fully implemented in 2019. As one US EPA representative stated in a presentation to farmworker advocates and service providers in North Carolina, the revised Worker Protection Standard did not reflect the standards dictated by the current science, but what could be approved in the face of industry objections. The current Worker Protection Standard addresses three domains: information, protection, and mitigation. For information, the regulations require that farmworkers be trained annually and that they be provided access to information about pesticides applied where they work. The protection domain requires that workers be isolated from areas in which pesticides are being or have been recently applied and that necessary personal protective equipment be available. For example, a sign, such as Fig. 3.1, indicating that pesticides have been applied to an area should be posted until after the restricted entry interval has expired; the farmworker in Fig. 3.2 is wearing appropriate personal protective equipment for his work in applying herbicide from a backpack sprayer. The mitigation domain requires that decontamination supplies be available and that emergency assistance be provided in the case of pesticide exposure.

OSHA field sanitation and housing requirements are also very limited. The Occupational Safety and Health Act requires that all agricultural employers with 11 or more employees provide drinking water, toilet, and washing facilities for farmworkers while they are working in a field. A supply of cool, fresh water must be within 500 ft. of the working area. Toilet facilities must be located within 5 min travel time of the field. Hand-washing facilities should be provided and located near the toilets and within 5 min travel time of the field. Soap and individual towels should be supplied. Housing regulations, which apply only to housing for migrant

Fig. 3.1 Pesticide restricted entry interval sign (Photo by Thomas A. Arcury)

Fig. 3.2 Farmworker wearing appropriate personal protective equipment. Photo by Pesticide Safety Education Program of the Alabama Cooperative Extension System (Published with kind permission of © The Alabama Cooperative Extension System 2017. All Rights Reserved)

workers, are discussed in Chap. 2. These regulations address the number of bathing and laundry facilities provided for each worker.

Field sanitation and housing requirements are important to pesticide safety. Frequent hand-washing—particularly before eating and toileting—bathing immediately after finishing work, and wearing clean clothes each day all reduce the dose that results from pesticide exposure. Despite their importance, federal regulations requiring agricultural employers to provide toilets, drinking water, and handwashing facilities to workers in the fields have only been in effect since 1987.

Implementation of the Worker Protection Standard and OSHA field sanitation and housing requirements is hampered by limited resources for enforcement. These regulations are generally administered by state rather than federal agencies, with funding for enforcement reliant on state budgets. In North Carolina, for example, enforcement of the Worker Protection Standard is the responsibility of the Department of Agriculture and Consumer Services, and enforcement of OSHA field sanitation and housing requirements is the responsibility of the Department of Labor. Each agency has 10 staff members for enforcement across the state's 100 counties and thousands of farms.

Neither set of regulations has been evaluated to address whether they reduce farmworker pesticide exposure. The Worker Protection Standard is limited to training and reacting to pesticide exposure events; it does little to change how pesticides are used or how farm work is organized. The Worker Protection Standard training may increase the knowledge farmworkers have about pesticides, but it is not clear if it actually reduces exposure. Although the field sanitation requirements should make personal hygiene facilities available, the only evaluations of whether these requirements are actually enforced have not been positive (e.g., Arcury et al. 2001a, b). If the goal of these regulations is to reduce pesticide exposure, then an evaluation that tests whether they decrease farmworker pesticide exposure and dose is needed. Such an evaluation could test for individual exposure (e.g., monitoring cholinesterase inhibition or pesticide urinary metabolites) or environmental contamination (e.g., the presence of pesticides in the work environment and in housing).

3.3.3 Musculoskeletal Injuries and Illness

3.3.3.1 Musculoskeletal Injuries Affecting Farmworkers

The National Institute for Occupational Safety and Health defines musculoskeletal disorders (MSDs) as "injuries or disorders of the muscles, nerves, tendons, joints, cartilage, and spinal discs." Among these are "sprains, strains, tears; back pain; … carpal tunnel syndrome" and other problems occurring in response to "bending, climbing, crawling, reaching, twisting, overexertion, or repetitive motion" (NIOSH 2004). These disorders include a broad spectrum of problems that can be placed into three groups: (1) peripheral neuropathies arising from carpal and cubital tunnel syndromes, (2) tendonitis and epicondylitis, and (3) other musculoskeletal disorders, including strains and muscle pain, rotator cuff injuries, bursitis, and others (Morse et al. 2005). Major factors are excessive load, rapidly repeating motions, and sustained awkward postures—all common experiences for the farmworker. In most cases, these MSDs represent an accumulation of microtrauma for a worker who has insufficient opportunity to recover. Any activity requiring moderate or greater force, work cycles of 30 s or less, or consistently less recovery time than work time in a cycle places the worker at considerable risk of MSD (Latko et al. 1999; Stock 1991).

Work-related MSDs are among the most common problems affecting farmworkers. These MSDs account for half of all agricultural occupational injuries reported in the 2008–2010 NAWS (Tonozzi and Layne 2016). Data from North Carolina and several northeastern states describe musculoskeletal complaints affecting 39–56% of farmworkers (Arcury et al. 2012; Scribani et al. 2013). These problems are often chronic and of sufficient severity that in one report half of those affected had to modify their normal activities and a third had changed their jobs. Back, shoulders, neck, and upper extremities are most affected by the repetitive, work-related overloading of selected muscle groups. The median age for workers reporting MSD in the NAWS survey was 39 years. Migrant workers, those hired directly by farmers, working women, and possibly those with an underlying health condition had higher risk (Tonozzi and Layne 2016; Xiao et al. 2013).

In the Northeast, Scribani et al. (2013) conducted a systematic review of medical visits to migrant health facilities and emergency rooms across seven states to identify over 2500 occupational injury/illness cases occurring in 2001 and 2002. Strain/sprain injuries accounted for 56% of the total. Sixty percent of these affected the back, trunk, and shoulders, with the remainder involving the extremities. The rates were significantly higher for bush crops and orchards than for ground crops.

Cross-sectional surveys have also found high rates of MSD. Arcury et al. (2012) collected information on musculoskeletal discomfort, working while injured, and depressive symptoms from a sample of randomly selected workers within randomly selected farmworker camps in North Carolina. Of the 300 tobacco workers studied, 39% reported musculoskeletal discomfort. Risk appeared to be higher for older workers, those performing loading and barning of tobacco, and those with depressive symptoms. In a convenience sample of 120 sweet potato workers in North Carolina, nearly 80% of respondents described "any pain," with back and shoulder being the regions of highest reported pain. Sixty percent of respondents described pain at level three or greater on a scale of six. Older workers reported more back and knee pain, while younger workers noted more shoulder pain (Kearney et al. 2016a, b).

Other commodities have been associated with different types of musculoskeletal risks. Data from wild blueberry rakers in Maine suggest that the tendonitis and epicondylitis pain is common. Harvesting some vegetables involves the combined motions of spinal flexion and extension, partial rotation of the trunk, and throwing the produce back over the shoulder. All of this is repeated several times a minute for long days with limited recovery time. Mushroom work often requires sustained difficult postures. Harvesting mushrooms exposes workers to highly repetitive movements at high rates of speed. Work with onions combines heavy loads and near-continuous stooping with intermittent heavy overhead loads.

3.3.3.2 Diagnosis and Treatment of Musculoskeletal Disorders

Diagnosis of musculoskeletal disorders is seldom challenging for the health professional who has even limited insight into the nature of the work being performed. Usually a few extra moments learning from the patient about the motions and forces associated with any repetitive tasks can readily explain the etiology of most musculoskeletal complaints. The intensity of the worker's symptoms generally correlates well with the intensity of the work. For some of these disorders, the role of underlying medical conditions such as diabetes, hypothyroidism, obesity, arthritis, and depression (Arcury et al. 2012) must be considered.

Musculoskeletal disorders are caused by overuse and are ideally treated with rest, anti-inflammatory agents, and, when appropriate, splinting, physical therapy, and gradual rehabilitation. Unfortunately, farmworkers are subject to considerable pressure, both internal and external, to continue to work at highly productive rates. Advice that they rest more and slow down is not helpful. Ready access to joint injections, splinting, physical therapy modalities, and rehabilitation is possible for some workers in America but not the farmworker population. Many farmworkers currently rely upon home remedies and over-the-counter anti-inflammatory agents while they continue injurious repetitive work activities. Reliance upon manipulative treatments offered by traditional healers (e.g., *sobadores*) appears to be common in some communities (Quandt et al. 2017a, b, c, d).

3.3.3.3 Musculoskeletal Disorder Solutions

One solution to physically demanding, highly repetitive agricultural work is increased mechanization. In commodities in which this approach has been taken, the small number of remaining workers may be exposed to a new set of mechanical hazards, while the majority of workers no longer have a job. Mechanization is feasible for major crops like apples, citrus, strawberries, leafy greens, and grapes (Seabrook 2019). Other commodities continue to rely upon manual labor based upon considerations of capital expenditures, terrain, availability of reliable workers, and various social and economic considerations. The challenge is to address those aspects of the work that are most demanding and most likely to induce musculoskeletal disorders.

Interventions, ranging from administrative changes to altered work procedures to redesign of commonly used tools, can reduce the hazard from physically demanding repetitive tasks (Fathallah 2010). Job redesign efforts in California reduced awkward postures, forceful thumb-finger pinches, and repetitive bending and twisting (Janowitz et al. 1998). Introduction of hourly 5-min rest breaks significantly decreased musculoskeletal disorder symptoms in California farmworkers (Faucett et al. 2007). Adoption of different tools and processes led to fewer MSD hazards among midwestern vegetable producers with production equal to or improved compared to baseline levels (Chapman et al. 2004). Community-based approaches can effectively combine the expertise of ergonomists and researchers with the expertise of the workers, farm owners, and cooperative extension personnel (Scharf et al. 1998; Hawkes et al. 2007). Process and tool redesign approaches can be considered and interventions can be systematically tested. With key contributions from northeastern farmworkers and their employers, this approach has led to successful redesign of the rake used for harvesting blueberries with attendant improved ergonomics, less pain, and higher productivity (May et al. 2008).

3.3.4　Skin Disease

3.3.4.1　Skin Disorders Affecting Farmworkers

Occupational dermatitis occurs much more commonly in production agriculture than in the general population of American workers (Bureau of Labor Statistics 2007). Rates are particularly high for the "crop production" category, especially greenhouse, nursery, floriculture, and fruit farming. Among farmworkers in the eastern US, this has been best studied in North Carolina, where more than half of the farmworkers described skin problems. Sunburn and fungal infection led the list, followed by acne, "skin rash," and "itching" reported by more than 40% (Vallejos et al. 2008). It appears that these problems may evolve over the course of the growing season, rising from nearly 25% early to 37% late in the season (Arcury et al. 2003a, b). Dermatological examination of residents of two camps in North Carolina documented the presence of skin disease in 47 of 59 (80%) workers examined (Krejci-Manwaring et al. 2006).

Fungal infection of the skin, scalp, and nails is commonly reported. In the 47 cases noted above, fungal infections of the feet and nails accounted for 28 (nearly 60%) of the cases. These infections can be readily transmitted person-to-person, from animals, or from contaminated surfaces. The housing conditions and shared shower facilities in many migrant farmworker camps (Early et al. 2006) likely play a significant role in the persistence and spread of these problems.

Six to twelve percent of skin disease noted in surveys of North Carolina farmworkers was related to contact dermatitis (Krejci-Manwaring et al. 2006; Arcury et al. 2008). In 2018, the federally funded migrant health programs reported roughly 18,000 contact dermatitis cases (HRSA 2015b), which could be in response to a primary irritant or to an allergic sensitizing agent. Irritant contact dermatitis (80% of all contact dermatitis) is a nonallergic reaction appearing within minutes of contact with a wide variety of irritating substances. The itchy eruptions affecting the upper extremity flexor surfaces of North Carolina tobacco workers, noted by Abraham et al. (2007), may well be examples of irritant-induced contact dermatitis. These reactions may occur to endogenous plant components or to chemicals that have been applied to the plants (Schuman and Dobson 1985).

Allergic contact dermatitis requires a period of 1–3 weeks for the initial sensitization. With subsequent contacts, dermatitis appears within hours or days. As most people do not react to the majority of sensitizers, allergic contact dermatitis is relatively uncommon. An exception to this is urushiol, the allergen found in poison ivy, oak, and sumac, to which a majority of the population reacts. This most certainly includes farmworkers who are likely to be exposed, while working in orchards and other sites. A systematic review of agricultural contact dermatitis cited pesticides, rubber products, disinfectants, and plant materials (notably tobacco) as leading causes but acknowledged that meaningful data from patch testing was only available for the first two of these (Irby et al. 2009).

The ultraviolet waves of the sun are a significant skin hazard. Phototoxic or photoallergic reactions to a sensitizing agent (topical or systemic) can cause itching, local redness, and blistering in sun-exposed workers. Antibiotics and other drugs, as well as a number of plant-derived compounds, can be responsible for these reactions. Typically, these occur on the sun-exposed surfaces of individuals with relatively limited pigment in their skin.

Solar radiation of ultraviolet light (UV) is clearly associated with skin cancers (Schmitt et al. 2011). The more common UVA rays penetrate more deeply and also prematurely age the skin. UVB rays are more superficial but have also been associated with skin cancer. The occurrence of premalignant and malignant skin lesions is fairly common in farmers. At public screening events in New York and Pennsylvania, roughly 25% of farmers are typically referred to a dermatologist for evaluation of a lesion (Evans and May, unpublished data). The vast majority of these prove to be premalignant changes such as actinic keratoses, generally appearing upon sun-exposed surfaces of the face, ears, or upper extremities. While there is clearly a selection bias in these public screening events, the more systematic selection involved in the New York Farm Family Health and Hazard Survey yielded quite similar findings (May, unpublished data). Of the malignancies detected, two-thirds were basal cell cancers, and nearly all others were squamous cell cancers. It should be noted that these findings apply to a population composed largely of farmers of northern European ancestry. There are remarkably few data regarding the rates of these problems in eastern farmworkers, and this should be an area of future study.

3.3.4.2 Skin Disease Solutions

Clothing worn in the field can prevent some contact dermatitis problems. However, such clothing is also potentially contaminated, so it should be removed promptly at the end of the work day and laundered separately from other non-contaminated clothing. Using gloves when feasible for the job may be helpful in reducing some of the mechanical and chemical trauma to the skin. Daily showering and routine use of nonirritating cleansing agents are recommended.

Ideally, solar radiation should be avoided. The use of light, loose-fitting clothing and hats that shade the face and neck can do much to reduce skin damage from UVA and UVB light. Topical sun-blocking agents can substantially reduce exposure, but it is unlikely that most farmworkers will routinely apply sufficient amounts to make this an effective strategy.

3.3.5 Hearing Loss

3.3.5.1 Hearing Loss Occurring in Eastern Agriculture

Hearing loss, typically noise-induced, is very common among farm populations (Marvel et al. 1991; Gomez et al. 2001). Substantial noise has been documented around agricultural equipment in New York (Dennis and May 1995). Information on hearing loss for farmworkers in the eastern US is limited to one report focusing upon a self-selected group of 150 predominantly Mexican men (mean age 34 years) in Connecticut River Valley migrant camps (Rabinowitz et al. 2005). The majority were tobacco workers; smaller proportions worked in nurseries and fruit orchards. They were thoroughly evaluated with a survey questionnaire, tympanometry, and pure tone audiometry. Twelve percent of these workers met criteria for hearing impairment, and more than half showed evidence of deficits ($\geq$25 dB) at one or more frequencies. Subjectively, 35% complained of difficulty hearing or under-standing speech. When compared with the findings of the 1982–1984 Hispanic Health and Nutrition Examination Survey, the farmworkers demonstrated consistently worse high-frequency perception in all age groups.

3.3.5.2 Causes of Hearing Loss in Farmworkers

The obvious cause of these findings (Rabinowitz et al. 2005) is exposure to hazardous noise (>80 dB) in the work environment, particularly as only 14% of workers, mainly nursery workers, reported using appropriate hearing protection. However, currently no data regarding the level of noise encountered by these workers are available, and it might be expected that, because of less exposure to farm machinery, their total noise exposures would be less than other agricultural workers. Baseline information on rates of hearing loss among workers in their native populations would be of interest. The effects of recreational noise, agrichemicals, and other toxin exposures need further investigation. A better understanding of other nonagricultural occupational exposures encountered by these workers might provide important insight into their increased levels of hearing loss. Further audiometric assessment of other migrant populations would be of considerable interest as would systematic area or personal noise sampling of the various work environments commonly encountered.

3.3.5.3 Hearing Loss Solutions

As in other prevention situations, engineering approaches to hearing loss are preferred. In agriculture, minor adjustments such as tightening a few screws to reduce metal vibration on machinery and replacing defective mufflers can do much to reduce ambient noise. However, the most apparent solution to this problem is provision of inexpensive hearing protection for workers and instruction on its proper use. Earmuffs can be put on and off easily, but they are bulky and can be misplaced. Therefore, earplugs are preferred by many workers. These should be available in any setting where background noise requires workers to raise their voices to be heard. Attention must be given to proper insertion techniques and to the cleanliness of the earplugs after repeated use. Care must be taken to avoid contamination with agrichemicals prior to insertion in the ear.

3.3.6 Eye Injury

3.3.6.1 Eye Injuries Affecting Eastern Farmworkers

The National Electronic Injury Surveillance System recorded 131,000 emergency room visits for occupational eye injuries in 2016 (NIOSH 2016b). Eye injuries have been reported in agriculture for many decades (Smith 1940). These certainly can affect farmworkers. Penetrating ocular injuries or other acute trauma can result from contact with plants, particularly in orchard work, or tasks such as the sharpening of a hoe. However, accurate recording of eye injury in agriculture is suspect. It is estimated that the Bureau of Labor Statistics captures less than a quarter of the actual number of events (Lacey et al. 2007). Recent questionnaire data on eye injuries affecting a population of predominantly H-2A workers in North Carolina confirmed that a substantial number of these injuries go unreported. The self-reported lost work injury rate was three times that previously described, with the majority of these being penetrating injuries mostly from vegetation (Quandt et al. 2017a, b, c, d).

Exposure to agrichemicals poses some specific risks for workers. In one older study, nearly 20% of workers with a mean of 8 years of exposure to fenthion (organophosphate) were found to have macular changes (Misra et al. 1985). Data from pesticide applicators in North Carolina and Iowa suggest that several types of fungicide are related to retinal degeneration in both applicators and their wives (Kirrane et al. 2005). The most common specific agents were three dithiocarbamate compounds: maneb, mancozeb, and ziram. The Japanese literature describes a series of disorders ("Saku disease") related to organophosphate agents, which can be readily absorbed into the chambers of the eye following topical application, eventually reaching the cells of the retina (Boyes et al. 1994). Manifestations of these exposures range from problems at the level of the lens to pathologic changes in the retina (Dementi 1994).

3.3.6.2   Chronic Irritation of the Eyes

Most commonly, farmworkers experience problems with chronic conjunctivitis affecting the tissue covering the eye, or blepharitis, an inflammation affecting the margin of the lid. When North Carolina farmworkers from randomly selected housing sites were interviewed over the course of a growing season, they noted the presence of a number of eye symptoms. This predominantly Mexican group of 197 tobacco and cucumber workers experienced eye pain (40%), redness (43%), itching (25%), and blurred vision (13%). More than 98% of these workers wore no sunglasses while in the fields. Half stated that sunglasses interfered with their work and their ability to differentiate ripe from green leaves (Quandt et al. 2001a, b). Vegetable workers (and farm owners) in New York complain that the fine black soil of the region produces eye irritation. In a cohort of 120 of these workers, 67% described one or more of the of eye symptoms described in North Carolina: eye pain (29%), redness (49%), itching (43%), and blurred vision (43%) (Earle-Richardson et al. 2014).

3.3.6.3   Cataract and Pterygium

Although there are no reports on cataract rates in eastern farmworkers, their extensive exposure to solar UV radiation would be expected to result in elevated risk for the opacities of the lens. Another effect of solar radiation, combined with other sources of chronic irritation (wind, dust), is the development of pterygium. This wedge-shaped fleshy growth of conjunctival tissue extends across the surface of the eye, typically extending from the inner corner of the eye toward the pupil. These may grow to be large enough to actually obscure vision, though this is rare. More commonly pterygia cause ongoing irritation and redness by interfering with the normal lubricating mechanism of the eye. In the only relevant study of this problem, digital photographs of 304 North Carolina farmworkers documented a 23% prevalence (10% bilateral) of this problem (Taylor et al. 2006). Treatment of these lesions may require surgery if it becomes so extensive as to obscure vision, though more often lubricating eye drops, possibly topical steroid drops, and sunglasses or protective UV-blocking glasses are recommended.

3.3.6.4 Eyesight and Eye Care

Good vision is important for safety in hazardous occupations such as farm work. Only a few studies have explored the visual acuity of farmworkers in the eastern US and the eye care they have received. Using interviews and Snellen charts with 289 farmworkers in North Carolina, Quandt et al. (2017a, b, c, d) assessed the previously reported high frequency of vision complaints (Quandt et al. 2008). Three-quarters had not had previous vision screening. Two-thirds described visual acuity that was only moderate or worse. Vision testing revealed normal distance vision in 98% and normal near vision in 93% of workers. It appears that farmworkers in the eastern US have generally excellent vision despite concerns to the contrary. It is also clear that routine eye care occurs infrequently if at all.

3.3.6.5 Eye Injury Solutions

Relying entirely upon protective equipment is not viewed as desirable in occupational health, but in this case, use of carefully selected protective glasses is the most realistic solution. Such eyewear should provide protection from both UVA and UVB rays, thus reducing risk of problems such as cataract and pterygium. These high-impact glasses should have side shields to limit the risk of foreign bodies and trauma from plants and also to reduce exposure of the conjunctiva and cornea to the effects of dust and wind. Unfortunately, the experience in the Midwest has been that workers resist use of protective glasses because of appearance, discomfort, perspiration and fogging, slowing work processes, and interference with vision (Forst et al. 2006). Less than 10% of North Carolina workers use protective glasses for many of the same concerns. Other major factors were lack of education—roughly three-quarters had not been trained and did not believe they had much risk—and failure of most employers (92%) to provide eye protection (Verma et al. 2011).

The experience with workers in New York who adopted use of safety glasses after distribution of eyewear and training by community health workers (Earle-Richardson et al. 2014) parallels that of Midwest farmworkers (Forst et al. 2004). Initially, New York vegetable workers experienced fogging and discomfort with some designs and problems seeing spoilage on lettuce leaves with dark lenses. But after some trial and error, they settled upon designs that were comfortable, socially

Fig. 3.3 Camp health aide demonstrates emergency use of eye wash in the fields (Photo by Jason Lind. Published with kind permission of © Jason Lind 2007. All Rights Reserved)

acceptable, and functional for their specific tasks. They were able to identify lens colors (yellow) that did not interfere with their work efficiency. As the wearing of protective glasses became a social norm, general acceptance increased substantially. Following early season trainings, the use of sunglasses or protective eyewear ("sometimes" or "always") was in the range of 90% (Earle-Richardson et al. 2014). In a study comparing workers on control and intervention farms, the use of small plastic vials of sterile saline solution for immediate eye irrigation/moisturizing combined with protective eyewear significantly reduced eye pain and redness (Earle-Richardson et al. 2014) (Fig. 3.3).

The training of respected workers to model behavior, distribute glasses, administer first aid, and provide peer-to-peer education increased utilization at 15 weeks of protective eyewear among intervention (11–27%) compared to control (2.4–2.6%) groups of Florida citrus workers (Monaghan et al. 2011).

A review from the Midwest encouraged redesign of tasks or selection of alternate tools in order to reduce the risk of eye injury (Lacey et al. 2007).

3.3.7 Transportation

3.3.7.1 Transportation Injuries Affecting Farmworkers

There is remarkably little in the scientific literature regarding transportation deaths in migrant farmworkers, particularly in the eastern US. This is surprising as motor vehicle incidents are the leading contributor to overall occupational fatality and appear to be a significant source of fatality among migrant farmworkers (NIOSH 2003). A study of proportionate mortality in California among United Farm Workers members found a ratio of observed to expected deaths of 1.78 (95% confidence limits 1.61, 1.98) for transportation injuries, higher for passengers and pedestrians (Mills et al. 2006). In a 2001 report of farmworker deaths across 24 states, farmworkers from the Northeast and Southeast accounted for nearly 60% of the total. Of the injury-related deaths in the group, 53% were due to motor vehicles (Colt et al. 2001). The agriculture, forestry, and fishing sectors consistently have rates of highway fatalities that are second only to the transportation industry itself (MMWR 2004). Considerable confusion surrounds the interpretation of "transportation fatalities" and the distinction of "vehicle" vs. "machinery" in some of the published literature. Unfortunately, the Bureau of Labor Statistics has further confounded the situation by distributing tractor-related fatalities among the vehicle, machinery, and several other categories in the Census of Fatal Occupational Injuries (CFOI) statistics (Murphy and Yoder 1998). To compound the problems, the determination of when a highway collision is "occupational" is also arbitrary. The CFOI database excludes incidents involving the commute to or from work, unless traveling from a camp.

Farmworkers, particularly those born outside the US and whose English language skills are limited, are at risk on rural highways when they are going to and from work or traveling between fields. A study on farmworkers in California's Central Valley assessed driving behaviors by using both questionnaires and unobtrusive systematic observations of 126 vehicles being driven in Central Valley labor camps. This work documented an increased incidence of adverse outcomes (including revoked licenses, citations, and crashes) and unsafe driving behaviors among those licensed in Mexico and those driving without licenses. Among all drivers, 79% were licensed. Only 58% learned to drive in the US, and those who learned to drive in Mexico learned at an early age (20% between ages 8 and 14 years). Observed use of seat belts was 37%, and compliance with belting of passengers, children, and use of child seats was low (Stiles and Grieshop 1999), though this situation may have changed since 1999. In Steinhorst's study of Latinx farmworkers admitted to a North Carolina trauma center, 51% of injuries were related to motor vehicle crashes, though the vast majority of these were not work-related. Significant factors in the incidence and severity of these injuries included the low rates of seat belt and airbag usage (40%) and the high rates of positive blood alcohol levels (66%) (Steinhorst et al. 2006).

More information is available from the insurance industry, which identified "a dozen accidents that left 38 dead and nearly 200 injured" in 2015–2016 (Breed 2016). Key considerations in some Florida incidents were unsafe vehicles not registered with the Labor Department, lack of a commercial operator's license, worn tires, and inadequate insurance. The dependence of workers upon predatory *raiteros* (paid drivers who transport low-wage workers to their jobs) for necessary transportation places them at considerable risk. Enforcement of transportation regulations in the Migrant and Seasonal Agricultural Worker Protection Act has been limited at best (Breed 2016).

It is likely that the factors traditionally associated with fatal crashes (e.g., running off the road or failing to stay in the proper lane, driving over the speed limit or too fast for conditions, driver inattention, and driver drowsiness [MMWR 2004]) are involved in these farmworker crashes as well. These workers often have little recourse other than the use of old, poorly maintained vehicles that are often overcrowded. Poor understanding of traffic laws, unavailability of seatbelts or lack of seatbelt use, and, in some cases, the use of alcohol certainly contribute to the hazard. When incidents do occur, payment of medical costs, lost work, and even repatriation of remains often fall upon the farmworker and family.

3.3.7.2 Transportation Solutions

In situations where farmworkers are being transported by an employer or contractor, strict enforcement of licensing requirements for drivers, inspection and safety requirements for vehicles, and occupancy and seatbelt laws for passengers by local and state police is needed. Substantial fines from local traffic enforcement and from OSHA are entirely appropriate. Similar enforcement is appropriate for farmworkers driving personal vehicles, but educational interventions might also be used in an effort to reduce both crashes and problems with law enforcement. Undocumented farmworkers' inability to obtain drivers licenses may not restrict their driving but certainly restricts opportunities to train and regulate their driving. Licensing efforts in a number of states now aim to educate and enhance the driving skills of undocumented workers (Arnold 2019).

3.4 Commodity-Specific Occupational Illness and Injury

With the obvious exception of pesticide exposures (Sect. 3.3.2), the occupational health challenges described above are those that might generally be expected to affect farmworkers in nearly any agricultural setting. In addition to these universal problems, there are a number of exposures and health problems that are specific for a given commodity.

3.4.1 Orchard Work

Orchard fruits are major production commodities in much of the eastern US. Citrus production, which is largely limited to Florida, accounts for nearly 70% of the nation's total acreage of citrus orchards. Other significant orchard fruits include peaches (Georgia, South Carolina, Pennsylvania, New York), pears (Pennsylvania, New York), and apples (Pennsylvania, New York).

3.4.1.1 The Nature of Orchard Work

The vast majority of the manual labor associated with orchard production relates to the harvesting of the fruit. Some ergonomic exposures are associated with off-season pruning, and some potential exposures are related to application of pesticides and plant hormones prior to harvest. However, the number of workers exposed is far less than the number associated with harvest.

Orchard work is quite similar across commodities, with the main variation in the work relating to the size of the trees and the nature of the fruit. Some fruits are increasingly grown on dwarf trees, which reduce ladder work but may increase the amount of stoop work. The durability of the fruit also dictates some of the specific practices. Because apples bruise after any impact, they are harvested in buckets smaller than those for citrus. At about 45 lb., a full apple bucket weighs considerably less than a full citrus bag. The citrus worker can stand upright while dumping the bag of fruit, while the apple harvester must fully flex forward with a loaded bucket to release the apples from the bottom of the bucket into the apple bin.

Detailed ergonomic data are available on the harvesting process. A standardized time sampling technique demonstrated that New York apple harvesters spend 63% of their time with one or both arms extended above the head reaching for apples. Often this is with a nearly filled bucket on the shoulder. Buckets are at least partially loaded nearly 80% of the time. Nearly 10% of the time is spent with the spine acutely forward flexed over the edge of a bin as the buckets are emptied (Earle-Richardson et al. 2004).

Unless dwarf trees are being harvested, the ladder is a major component of the job. Motivated in part by the piecework pay strategy, workers try to minimize the number of times the ladder is repositioned. Harvesters will place one foot off to the side of the ladder upon a convenient branch to extend their picking range without having to move the ladder. Often this involves repeated shifts of the bag or bucket from one hip to the other. Conditions in the orchard for the first half of each day tend to be wet from dew in the grass and trees, so footing on ladders and branches can be insecure. The demand for reaching highly placed fruit and for extending reach means that workers routinely use the top two steps of the ladder, thus reducing its stability and increasing their chances of falling (Salazar et al. 2005).

3.4.1.2 Occupational Health Problems Associated with Orchard Work

On the basis of review of charts from migrant health programs and from nearby emergency departments, a cohort of 303 work-related injuries affecting apple workers has been analyzed. Sixty percent of these related to musculoskeletal strain, 11% to contact with an irritant material, and 8% to falls. The most common medical diagnoses are shown in Fig. 3.4. These include musculoskeletal disorders from the repetitive motions, load bearing, acute flexion, and overhead work noted above. Eight percent of injuries relate to falls, probably a common occurrence that often does not result in a medical visit but can result in sprains, contusions, and broken

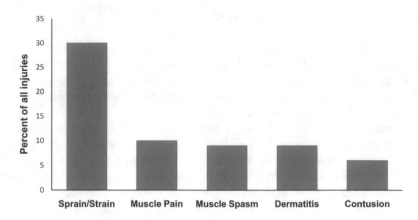

Fig. 3.4 Distribution of 303 injuries to orchard workers noted at New York and Pennsylvania migrant health program chart audits (Data from The New York Center for Agricultural Medicine and Health)

bones. These falls may relate to inadequate maintenance of ladders, wet and slippery footwear, overreaching, and inadequate attention to the proper placement of the ladder. A smaller number of eye injuries may follow trauma from vegetation in the trees and rebounding branches. This risk is present early in the season when a small number of workers are pruning and at harvest when a large number of workers are on the trees.

3.4.1.3 Orchard Work Injury Solutions

In the orchard, greater awareness of the safety challenges of the work might substantially reduce the risk of injury (Salazar et al. 2005). Some of the solutions here could relate to reengineering the job or the equipment. Other challenges might be addressed by administrative changes in the pay structure of the job.

For eye injuries, reliance upon protective equipment is perhaps the most direct approach to the issue. The use of polycarbonate lenses with side guards will greatly reduce the risk of eye trauma related to tree branches.

Falls from ladders are complex and related to the condition of both the ladder and the worker's footwear. Behaviors such as the setting of the ladder, the height ascended, the extent of reach beyond the ladder, and behaviors such as stepping onto adjacent branches and shifting a loaded bucket also are key determinants of risk. To reduce falls, each of these issues must be addressed. Unsafe ladders need to be retired. The positioning and use of ladders cannot be hurried. The use of piece-rate pay strategies encourages inappropriate haste and shortcuts, which may well heighten injury risk. More data on the unrecognized costs of piece-rate strategies could be effective in discussing this practice with farmers.

Mechanization efforts may address a number of the challenges of orchard picking. Mobile picking platforms afford a stable work surface for pickers as the platform maneuvers around trees (Elkins et al. 2011). Mechanical means to elevate bins are also available. The major limitation of this approach relates to the layout of existing orchards and the size and shape of trees relative to optimum for the platform. Considerable progress has been made with robotic picking devices that may eventually obviate these barriers, while also displacing most of the hired workers (Silwal et al. 2017)

3.4.2 Tobacco Production

The termination of the USDA tobacco allotment program has caused substantial changes in tobacco production. Despite a 27% decline in US production, approximately 700 million pounds of tobacco are still produced annually. Although some states in the Northeast are involved in production, the majority of the nation's production occurs in the Southeast (Statista 2019).

3.4.2.1 The Nature of Tobacco Production Work

The process of tobacco production extends from setting the plants and early cultivation to curing and baling the harvested leaves toward the end of the season (Arcury and Quandt 2006). Over the middle third of the season, workers remove flowers ("topping" the plants) to direct the growth to the leaves, and they cultivate and harvest the earlier maturing leaves. Harvesting varies with the type of tobacco. Burley is harvested by the entire stalk, while flue-cured tobacco is harvested by the leaf ("primed"). This begins with the larger lower leaves that contain less nicotine. Typically, about three leaves are taken from the plant with each cycle of picking. As each is picked, it is placed with others in a stack held under the worker's arm. Toward the end of the season, the smaller "tip" leaves containing the highest concentrations of nicotine are taken. "Curing" the leaf begins as it is picked. For burley tobacco, several tobacco plants are attached to long wooden poles and lifted up four to five levels into the rafters of the barn for air curing. For flue-cured tobacco, curing involves packing the tobacco into "bulk barns" in which the heat and humidity are automatically controlled. Cured leaves are then retrieved from the different barns. For burley tobacco, the leaves are manually stripped from the stalks and baled; for flue-cured tobacco, the leaves are removed from the barns and baled.

3.4.2.2 Occupational Health Problems Associated with Tobacco Production

For a review of occupational health problems associated with tobacco production, see Arcury and Quandt (2006). Areas of potential hazard in this process include repetitive motion and sustained awkward postures, as ergonomic challenges are associated with planting in the initial weeks of the season and with the harvest season for burley and for flue-cured in the early harvest when the lower leaves are being primed. A variety of potentially toxic chemicals are applied to tobacco over the course of the growing season, including insecticides and growth regulators. Heat and humidity are significant problems for workers throughout the most active portions of the season. For burley tobacco, potential hazards include lacerations from the "knives" used to cut the tobacco stalks and "spear points" put on sticks that allow impaling the stalks. Harvest is also associated with considerable dermal contact with the tobacco leaves. Using digital photography of the face, hands, arms, and feet to look specifically for skin rash, 304 systematically selected workers were followed at 3-week intervals through the season. More than 40% of participants reported symptoms of itch or skin rash, and the two were highly correlated. A dermatologist reviewed the photographs and noted traumatic skin lesions in 16.8% of workers and contact dermatitis in 12.2% (Arcury et al. 2008). For burley tobacco, the curing process requires considerable climbing on barn rafters, while holding poles with the attached leaves. Although there are no data available on fall rates associated with the suspending of leaves from barn rafters, there is clearly risk there.

Green tobacco sickness is a common occupational illness that results from tobacco work. It results from nicotine absorbed through the skin from plant leaves and nicotine-containing dew or rain saturating the workers' clothes (Gehlbach et al. 1975). Over the course of the season, roughly one-quarter of tobacco workers are likely to experience at least some of the symptoms of green tobacco sickness. These include nausea, vomiting, abdominal pain, diarrhea, dizziness, palpitations, and headache. Most commonly noted are headache, dizziness, vomiting, and nausea occurring in the evening or night following a day of working with tobacco (Arcury et al. 2001a, b). The illness is self-limited once continuous dermal absorption of nicotine is interrupted. Levels of the nicotine breakdown product, cotinine, in workers' saliva and incidence of green tobacco sickness symptoms increase across the course of the season, likely related to the progressively more intense dermal contact associated with the common methods of harvest (Quandt et al. 2001a, b). Work conditions associated with increased occurrence of symptoms and levels of salivary cotinine include harvesting, late season, and wet leaves (Arcury et al. 2003a, b). Other worker characteristics that have been associated with increased risk of green tobacco sickness include age, experience, nonoccupational exposure to nicotine, and type of tobacco work (Quandt et al. 2001a, b). Older, more experienced workers have fewer symptoms, likely reflecting both learned avoidance behaviors and some "healthy worker" effect. The 40% of Latinx farmworkers who smoke (Spangler et al. 2003) or use chewing tobacco have notably lower rates of green tobacco sickness symptoms (Arcury et al. 2001a, b). The presence of self-reported skin rash significantly increased the odds of green tobacco sickness (odds ratio, 3.30; 95% confidence interval 2.17, 5.02) (Arcury et al. 2008).

Shade tobacco, which is grown to produce wrapper leaves for cigars and is largely confined to New England, is not associated with symptoms of green tobacco sickness or measurable increases in salivary cotinine levels, perhaps because this tobacco is generally not harvested wet and, once picked, leaves are minimally handled by workers (Trapé-Cardoso et al. 2005).

Although tobacco workers do not seem to experience elevated rates of most respiratory symptoms, there is a relative increase in the rate of wheeze in workers engaged in topping, barning, and baling of tobacco (Mirabelli et al. 2011).

3.4.2.3 Occupational Health Solutions in Tobacco Production

The use of water-repellent clothing can reduce the incidence of symptoms (Arcury et al. 2002), but this presents a potential hyperthermia problem. The use of gloves and changes in how the leaves are held after picking (i.e., not under the arm) can reduce skin injury and nicotine absorption. Changing out of wet clothing during the day or at the end of the day and showering immediately after work should reduce nicotine exposure as well.

3.4.3 Vegetables

Tomatoes, melons, beans, cucumbers, peppers, and cabbages are among the leading vegetable commodities in the eastern US. Each of these requires substantial input of farmworker labor. There can be no single description for vegetable work, but many commodities do share some similar tasks that can be associated with occupational health problems. Planting vegetables may involve seeding but often involves planting seedlings, while riding on the back of a slowly moving tractor. This work involves the ergonomic challenges of rapid, continually repeated movements, often in an awkward sustained posture. Depending upon the use of plastic mulch, more or less cultivating and thinning of seedlings may be required. In some situations this can be done mechanically, but, more often, it is done either manually or chemically, both of which can present potential occupational health problems for farmworkers. Harvest work usually involves the use of blades with associated risk of lacerations. Issues of posture and repetitive motions are likely to be prominent in harvest work as well. Farmworkers are at risk of skin and eye injuries related to sun and heat problems throughout most vegetable work.

The Northeast, Mid-Atlantic, and Southeast have substantial production of onions, potatoes, and sweet potatoes. The harvesting of these root crops may be ergonomically challenging with prolonged bending, stooping, and kneeling. Transfer of the produce from field to truck requires repeated lifting and heaving of substantial loads. Ergonomic assessments of packing house workers in New York identified the transferring and stacking 80 pound bags of onions as major risk factors for musculoskeletal injury. Sweet potato workers in North Carolina report frequent lifting and carrying of loaded baskets, typically lifting and dumping one every 2 min. Seventy-nine percent of these workers reported pain, most commonly in the back (especially lumbar region), shoulder, and knee. Of these, 60% ranked their pain level at three or higher on a scale of six (Kearney et al. 2016a, b).

3.4.4   Wild Blueberries

3.4.4.1   The Work of Harvesting Wild Blueberries

Blueberry production in many states centers upon bush fruit, while Maine blueberries are "wild," growing on scrubby plants no higher than 6–8 in. off the ground. The terrain is sometimes rocky and quite irregular. The wild berries are harvested in midsummer by "raking" with comblike metal rakes with an attached collecting box. These rakes come in varying widths and usually weigh 3.5–10 pounds. The traditional rake has a single, short, horizontally oriented central handle (Fig. 3.5) that requires repeated forceful motions of the wrist to engage the foliage with the rake and then pull directly up. Bending at the waist and working at a rate often exceeding 30 cycles per minute, the worker might pause only intermittently to empty the rake's collecting box. Considerable force is required to pull the rake up through the foliage.

3.4.4.2   Occupational Injury Associated with Wild Blueberry Work

Evidence from a variety of sources shows that the traditional approach to blueberry raking is associated with ergonomic challenges and related worker injuries (Tanaka et al. 1994; Estill and Tanaka 1998). Ergonomic problems affecting the elbows, shoulders, and particularly the back and wrist have been noted in association with blueberry raking (Millard et al. 1996). Chart review data from the Maine Migrant Health Program showed 86 clinic visits for complaints identified as related to blueberry raking. Sixty-five of these (76%) were musculoskeletal problems. Of these,

Fig. 3.5 The traditional center-handled rake used in harvesting of wild blueberries (Photo by New York Center for Agricultural Medicine and Health. Published with kind permission of © The New York Center for Agricultural Medicine and Health 2006. All Rights Reserved)

Fig. 3.6 A blueberry rake with 12 in. handle extensions (Photo by New York Center for Agricultural Medicine and Health. Published with kind permission of © The New York Center for Agricultural Medicine and Health 2006. All Rights Reserved)

38% related to back problems; 32% related to shoulder, wrist, and hand problems; and 18% related to knee problems (Hawkes et al. 2007). Twelve percent related to skin problems.

3.4.4.3   Solutions for Injuries in Wild Blueberry Work

Previously, a work team composed of farmworkers and farm owners worked to examine various alternative rake designs. A long-handled design (Fig. 3.6) was found to enhance productivity and was preferred by the workers, who noted less force required and less pain associated with harvest work (May et al. 2008). Video analyses of postures showed that the long-handle rake was associated with less squatting and less moderate to severe flexion of the torso (May et al. 2012). Currently, rake manufacturers are offering long-handle models and are selling inexpensive handle conversion kits for traditional rakes.

3.5   Personal Protection

For many of the occupational hazards described above, the most suitable solutions are redesign of the job, tools, or work organization. Institution of short rest periods, rotation of tasks, and changes in piece-rate pay strategies can do much to alleviate many of the problems experienced by farmworkers in the eastern US. Personal protective equipment is the least desirable "solution" to a hazard exposure because it depends on human behavior and so is likely to provide less than complete protection. However, the realities of the workplace make use of personal protective equipment a necessary option.

There are limited data regarding farmworkers' use of hearing protection. In a convenience sample of 150 Connecticut farmworkers, 10% of apple workers, 36% of nursery workers, and 7% of tobacco workers—14% of all workers tested—reported use of hearing protection (Rabinowitz et al. 2005). The challenges of eye protection are outlined above, with fewer than 10% of North Carolina workers using protective glasses and fewer than 10% of employers providing such protection (Verma et al. 2011). However, work from both New York and Florida suggests that making eyewear readily available, offering choices well suited for the work and the workers, training workers, and modeling the behavior can substantially enhance the use of protective glasses (Monaghan et al. 2011; Earle-Richardson et al. 2014).

There are limited data on respiratory protection despite common hazards of inhaled dust and chemicals. A cohort of 56 New York vegetable workers was assessed for respirator fit testing. Eleven of these workers (20%) described actual use of respirators on the job. Only one of the cohorts had previously undergone fit testing. These Latinx workers proved to be harder to fit with the commonly approved respirators, with only 41% achieving protection with a respirator that typically fits the vast majority of Anglo workers (Earle-Richardson et al. 2014). This combination of rarely undergoing fit testing and frequent misfits with usual respirators suggests that the majority of those farmworkers who are using an approved respirator is not protected by it. Recent changes in EPA regulations may increase the frequency and suitability of respirator use by farmworkers.

3.6   Conclusions

As agriculture evolves, shifts in commodities and modification of production methods will change some of the hazards experienced by Latinx farmworkers. Work in tobacco may decline, while work in other commodities is likely to increase. Severe acute injury and fatality may become more significant threats as farmworkers experience increased exposure to large animals and machinery. The more traditional, highly repetitive manual labor will remain in many commodities. Occupational health threats relating to heat, musculoskeletal injury, and injury to eyes, ears, and skin will continue to be challenges for this population of workers and for those providing support for them.

That people who perform difficult work and provide such a vital service to our society remain at the very bottom of America's economic and social order is a curious and unfortunate phenomenon. The social and economic inequities imposed on these workers certainly compound the occupational hazards inherent in their work. To some degree the problems experienced by farmworkers relate directly to the behaviors of some of their employers. However, on a larger scale, farmworkers and farmers alike are victims of both economic policies and evolving market forces. The phenomenon of vertical integration (e.g., a firm marketing chicken meat owns the chicks, provides the feed and bedding, and controls the entire process, simply renting the farmer's space and labor) and the impact of competition from subsidized foreign producers are just two recent and powerful factors that threaten the existence of many farms. While some operations thrive, many chronically operate on very thin margins. It is easy and sometimes appropriate to view the farm owner as the cause of the farmworkers' problems, but this approach can be both incorrect and counterproductive. In many ways the producer shares the same concerns as the farmworker. They both want the farm to stay in business and provide employment. They want the workers to be productive and to avoid injuries. Most farm owners want their workers to stay through the season and return for the next. Many employers can be effective partners in seeking ways to keep their employees safe. The combined wisdom and experience of farmworkers and farm owners can be invaluable in devising solutions to the daunting problems described above. The challenge for the farmworker advocate is to seek just treatment for workers without squandering the possibilities for effective collaboration with farm owners.

3.7 Recommendations

A variety of initiatives would likely enhance our understanding of the causes and remedies for some of the occupational health challenges discussed above. These include the following:

- Rest periods have been recommended for both musculoskeletal and heat-related problems. Study the effects of regular short rest periods upon overall productivity for employers and personal income for workers.
- Conduct a true cost-benefit analysis of various pay strategies (e.g., piece-rate pay strategies), in terms of injuries, medical expenses, retention of work force, and overall productivity.
- Examine the impact on workers (social, economic, and health) of mechanization in orchard, berry, and vegetable work.
- Develop algorithms predicting a worker's heat injury risk and specifying supervisor interventions. These might include temperature, humidity, weeks on the job, age, and chronic health conditions.
- Collaboration with insurers, police, and departments of motor vehicles to develop reliable surveillance of transport incidents involving farmworkers.
- Study the impact of driver licenses for undocumented workers in states where such legislation has been effected.
- Improve surveillance of occupational illness and injury in farmworkers.
- Increase access to occupational health support and expertise for migrant clinicians.

- Examine social marketing and other approaches aimed at enhancing employers' provision of personal protection and workers' adoption of protection.
- Develop labor-management safety committee approaches to enhancing worker safety in agriculture.
- Assure adequate resources to federal and state agencies for development of interventions demonstrated to effectively reduce occupational injury and illness in farmworkers.

References

Abraham NF, Feldman SR, Vallejos Q et al (2007) Contact dermatitis in tobacco farmworkers. Contact Dermatitis 57:40–43

Agricultural Health Study (2019a) About the study. https://aghealth.nih.gov/about/. Accessed 11 Jul 2019

Agricultural Health Study (2019b) Publications. https://aghealth.nih.gov/news/publications.html. Accessed 11 Jul 2019

Ahearn MC, Williamson JM, Black N (2015) Implications of health care reform for farm businesses and families. Appl Econ Perspect Policy 37(2):260–286

Alavanja MC, Hoppin JA, Kamel F (2004) Health effects of chronic pesticide exposure: cancer and neurotoxicity. Annu Rev Public Health 25:155–197

Arbury S, Jacklitsch B, Farquah O et al (2014) Heat illness and death among workers—United States, 2012–2013. MMWR Morb Mortal Wkly Rep 63(31):661–665

Arcury TA, Quandt SA (2006) Health and social impacts of tobacco production. J Agromedicine 11(3–4):71–81

Arcury TA, Quandt SA, Cravey AJ et al (2001a) Farmworker reports of pesticide safety and sanitation in the work environment. Am J Ind Med 39(5):487–498

Arcury TA, Quandt SA, Preisser JS et al (2001b) The incidence of green tobacco sickness among Latino farmworkers. J Occup Environ Med 43(7):601–609

Arcury TA, Quandt SA, Garcia DI et al (2002) A clinic-based, case–control comparison of green tobacco sickness among minority farmworkers: clues for prevention. South Med J 95(9):1008–1011

Arcury TA, Quandt SA, Mellen BG (2003a) An exploratory analysis of occupational skin disease among Latino migrant and seasonal farmworkers in North Carolina. J Agric Saf Health 9(3):221–232

Arcury TA, Quandt SA, Preisser JS et al (2003b) High levels of transdermal nicotine exposure produce green tobacco sickness in Latino farmworkers. Nicotine Tob Res 5(3):315–321

Arcury TA, Vallejos QM, Schulz MR et al (2008) Green tobacco sickness and skin integrity among migrant Latino farmworkers. Am J Ind Med 51(3):195–203

Arcury TA, Grzywacz JG, Chen H et al (2009a) Variation across the agricultural season in organophosphorus pesticide urinary metabolite levels for Latino farmworkers in eastern North Carolina: project design and descriptive results. Am J Ind Med 52(7):539–550

Arcury TA, Grzywacz JG, Isom S et al (2009b) Seasonal variation in the measurement of urinary pesticide metabolites among Latino farmworkers in eastern North Carolina. Int J Occup Environ Health 15(4):339–350

Arcury TA, Grzywacz JG, Talton JW et al (2010) Repeated pesticide exposure among North Carolina migrant and seasonal farmworkers. Am J Ind Med 53(8):802–813

Arcury TA, O'Hara H, Grzywacz JG et al (2012) Work safety climate, musculoskeletal discomfort, working while injured, and depression among migrant farmworkers in North Carolina. Am J Public Health 102(S2):S272–S278

Arcury TA, Lu C, Chen H et al (2014a) Pesticides present in migrant farmworker housing in North Carolina. Am J Ind Med 57(3):312–322

Arcury TA, Rodriguez G, Kearney GD et al (2014b) Safety and injury characteristics of youth farmworkers in North Carolina: a pilot study. J Agromedicine 19(4):354–363

Arcury TA, Laurienti PJ, Chen H et al (2016a) Organophosphate pesticide urinary metabolites among Latino immigrants: North Carolina farmworkers and non-farmworkers compared. J Occup Environ Med 58(11):1079–1086

Arcury TA, Sandberg JC, Mora DC et al (2016b) North Carolina Latino farmworkers' use of traditional healers: a pilot study. J Agromedicine 21(3):253–258

Arcury TA, Jenson A, Mann M et al (2017) Providing health information to Latino farmworkers: the case of the affordable care act. J Agromedicine 22(3):275–281

Arcury TA, Chen H, Laurienti PJ et al (2018a) Farmworker and nonfarmworker Latino immigrant men in North Carolina have high levels of specific pesticide urinary metabolites. Arch Environ Occup Health 73(4):219–227

Arcury TA, Laurienti PJ, Talton JW et al (2018b) Pesticide urinary metabolites among Latina farmworkers and nonfarmworkers in North Carolina. J Occup Environ Med 60(1):e63–e71

Armstrong LE, Maresh CM (1991) The induction and decay of heat acclimatisation in trained athletes. Sports Med 12(5):302–312

Arnold A (2019) New York approves driver's licenses for undocumented immigrants. Huff Post. https://www.huffpost.com/entry/drivers-liscense-undocumented-immigrants_n_5d02934ce4b0dc17ef06422f?guccounter=1. Accessed 17 Jun 2019

Azaroff LS, Levenstein C, Wegman DH (2002) Occupational injury and illness surveillance: conceptual filters explain underreporting. Am J Public Health 92(9):1421–1429

Baker D, Chappelle D (2012) Health status and needs of Latino dairy farmworkers in Vermont. J Agromedicine 17(3):277–287

Baldi I, Lebailly P, Mohammed-Brahim B et al (2003) Neurodegenerative diseases and exposure to pesticides in the elderly. Am J Epidemiol 157(5):409–414

Bennett B, Workman T, Smith MN et al (2019) Longitudinal, seasonal, and occupational trends of multiple pesticides in house dust. Environ Health Perspect 127(1):17003

Borjan M, Constantino P, Robson MG (2008) New Jersey migrant and seasonal farm workers: enumeration and access to healthcare study. New Solut 18(1):77–86

Bouchama A, Knochel JP (2002) Heat stroke. N Engl J Med 346(25):1978–1988

Boyes WK, Tandon P, Barone S Jr et al (1994) Effects of organophosphates on the visual system of rats. J Appl Toxicol 14(2):135–143

Breed A (2016) Dangerous transportation option faces migrant farm workers. Claims J. https://www.claimsjournal.com/news/national/2016/12/21/275722.htm. Accessed 14 Sept 2018

Brower MA, Earle-Richardson GB, May JJ et al (2009) Occupational injury and treatment patterns of migrant and seasonal farmworkers. J Agromedicine 14(2):172–178

Bureau of Labor Statistics (2007) Illness rates by type of illness—detailed industry, 2006. http://www.bls.gov/iif/oshwc/osh/os/ostb1760.txt. Accessed 30 Mar 2008

Bureau of Labor Statistics (2018) National census of fatal occupational injuries in 2017. https://www.bls.gov/news.release/pdf/cfoi.pdf. Accessed 27 Jan 2019

Centers for Disease Control and Prevention (2019) Fourth national report on human exposure to environmental chemicals with updated tables, February 2015–2019 update. https://www.cdc.gov/exposurereport/index.html. Accessed 30 Apr 2019

Chapman LJ, Newenhouse AC, Meyer RH et al (2004) Evaluation of an intervention to reduce musculoskeletal hazards among fresh market vegetable growers. Appl Ergon 35(1):57–66

Colt J, Stallones L, Cameron LL et al (2001) Proportionate mortality among US migrant and seasonal farmworkers in twenty-four states. Am J Ind Med 40(5):604–611

Coronado GD, Vigoren EM, Thompson B et al (2006) Organophosphate pesticide exposure and work in pome fruit: evidence for the take-home pesticide pathway. Environ Health Perspect 114(7):999–1006

Dementi B (1994) Ocular effects of organophosphates: a historical perspective of Saku disease. J Appl Toxicol 14(2):119–129

Dennis JW, May JJ (1995) Occupational noise exposure in dairy farming. In: McDuffie HH, Dosman JA, Semchuk KM, Olenchock SA, Senthilselvan A (eds) Agricultural health and safety: workplace, environment, sustainability. Lewis, Boca Raton, pp 363–367

Earle-Richardson G, May JJ, Ivory JF (1998) Planning study of migrant and seasonal farmworkers in New York State: understanding the occupational safety environment using focus groups. J Agric Saf Health 1:111–119

Earle-Richardson G, Jenkins PL, Slingerland DT et al (2003) Occupational injury and illness among migrant and seasonal farmworkers in New York State and Pennsylvania, 1997–1999: pilot study of a new surveillance method. Am J Ind Med 44(1):37–45

Earle-Richardson G, Fulmer S, Jenkins P et al (2004) Ergonomic analysis of New York apple harvest work using a posture-activities-tools-handling (PATH) work sampling approach. J Agric Saf Health 10(3):163–176

Earle-Richardson G, Jenkins PL, Stack S et al (2005) Estimating farmworker population size in New York State using a minimum labor demand method. J Agric Saf Health 11(3):335–345

Earle-Richardson GB, Brower MA, Jones AM et al (2008) Estimating the occupational morbidity for migrant and seasonal farmworkers in New York State: a comparison of two methods. Ann Epidemiol 18(1):1–7

Earle-Richardson GB, Wyckoff L, Carrasquillo M et al (2014) Evaluation of a community-based participatory farmworker eye health intervention in the "black dirt" region of New York State. Am J Ind Med 57(9):1053–1063

Early J, Davis SW, Quandt SA et al (2006) Housing characteristics of farmworker families in North Carolina. J Immigr Minor Health 8(2):173–184

Elkins RB, Meyers JM, Duraj V et al (2011) Comparison of platform versus ladders for harvest in northern California pear orchard. Acta Hortic 909:241–249

Emmi K, Jurkowski JM, Codru N et al (2010) Assessing the health of migrant and seasonal farmworkers in New York State: statewide data 2003–2005. J Health Care Poor Underserved 21(2):448–463

Estill CF, Tanaka S (1998) Ergonomic considerations of manually harvesting Maine wild blueberries. J Agric Saf Health 4(1):43–57

Fathallah FA (2010) Musculoskeletal disorders in labor-intensive agriculture. Appl Ergon 41(6):738–743

Faucett J, Meyers J, Tejeda D et al (2001) An instrument to measure musculoskeletal symptoms among immigrant Hispanic workers: validation in the nursery industry. J Agric Saf Health 7(3):185–198

Faucett J, Meyers J, Miles J et al (2007) Rest break interventions in stoop labor tasks. Appl Ergon 38(2):219–226

Fleischer NL, Tiesman HM, Sumitani J et al (2013) Public health impact of heat-related illness among migrant farmworkers. Am J Prev Med 44(3):199–206

Flores G (2000) Culture and the patient–physician relationship: achieving cultural competency in health care. J Pediatr 136(1):14–23

Forst L, Lacey S, Chen HY et al (2004) Effectiveness of community health workers for promoting use of safety eyewear by Latino farm workers. Am J Ind Med 46(6):607–613

Forst L, Noth IM, Lacey S et al (2006) Barriers and benefits of protective eyewear use by Latino farm workers. J Agromedicine 11(2):11–17

Freire C, Koifman S (2013) Pesticides, depression and suicide: a systematic review of the epidemiological evidence. Int J Hyg Environ Health 216(4):445–460

Gehlbach S, Williams W, Perry L et al (1975) Nicotine absorption by workers harvesting green tobacco. Lancet 305(7905):478–480

Gomez MI, Hwang SA, Sobotova L et al (2001) A comparison of self-reported hearing loss and audiometry in a cohort of New York farmers. J Speech Lang Hear Res 44(6):1201–1208

Graybill L (2012) Border patrol agents as interpreters along the northern border: unwise policy, illegal practice. American Immigration Council, Washington, DC

Gubernot DM, Anderson GB, Hunting KL (2015) Characterizing occupational heat-related mortality in the United States, 2000–2010: an analysis using the census of fatal occupational injuries database. Am J Ind Med 58(2):203–211

Guild A, Richards C, Ruiz V (2016) Out of sight, out of mind: the implementation and impact of the Affordable Care Act in the U.S. farmworker communities. J Health Care Poor Underserved 27(4A):73–82

Harduar Morano L, Bunn TL, Lackovic M et al (2015) Occupational heat-related illness emergency department visits and inpatient hospitalizations in the southeast region, 2007–2011. Am J Ind Med 58(10):1114–1125

Hawkes L, May J, Earle-Richardson G et al (2007) Identifying the occupational health needs of migrant workers. J Community Pract 15(3):57–76

Health Resources and Services Administration (HRSA) (1990) An atlas of state profiles which estimate the number of migrant and seasonal workers and members of their families. Health Resources Services Administration, Washington, DC

Health Resources and Services Administration (HRSA) (2015a) Bureau of primary health care. Health center program fact sheet. http://bphc.hrsa.gov/about/healthcenterfactsheet.pdf. Accessed 17 Oct 2018

Health Resources and Services Administration (HRSA) (2015b) Uniform data system. Table 6: selected diagnoses and services rendered. https://bphc.hrsa.gov/uds/datacenter.aspx?q=t6a&year=2018&state=&fd=mh. Accessed 13 Aug 2019

Hofmann JN, Carden A, Fenske RA et al (2008) Evaluation of a clinic-based cholinesterase test kit for the Washington State cholinesterase monitoring program. Am J Ind Med 51(7):532–538

Hofmann JN, Keifer MC, De Roos AJ et al (2010) Occupational determinants of serum cholinesterase inhibition among organophosphate-exposed agricultural pesticide handlers in Washington State. Occup Environ Med 67:375–386

Huen K, Bradman A, Harley K et al (2012) Organophosphate pesticide levels in blood and urine of women and newborns living in an agricultural community. Environ Res 117:8–16

Institute of Medicine (1988) Role of the primary care physician in occupational and environmental medicine (IOM Publication No 88–05). National Academies Press, Washington, DC

Irby CE, Yentzer BA, Vallejos QM et al (2009) The prevalence and possible causes of contact dermatitis in farmworkers. Int J Dermatol 48(11):1166–1170

Janowitz I, Meyers JM, Tejeda DG et al (1998) Reducing risk factors for the development of work-related musculoskeletal problems in nursery work. Appl Occup Environ Hyg 13(1):9–14

Johnson RJ, Wesseling A, Newman LS (2019) Chronic kidney disease of unknown cause in agricultural communities. N Engl J Med 380:1843–1852

Kaiser HJ, Kaiser Family Foundation (2013) Summary of the affordable care act. https://www.kff.org/health-reform/fact-sheet/summary-of-the-affordable-care-act/. Accessed 11 Jul 2019

Kamel F, Umbach DM, Bedlack RS et al (2012) Pesticide exposure and amyotrophic lateral sclerosis. Neurotoxicology 33(3):457–462

Kearney GD, Allen DL, Balanay JA et al (2016a) A descriptive study of body pain and work-related musculoskeletal disorders among Latino farmworkers working on sweet potato farms in eastern North Carolina. J Agromedicine 21(3):234–243

Kearney GD, Hu H, Xu X et al (2016b) Estimating the prevalence of heat-related symptoms and sun safety-related behavior among Latino farmworkers in eastern North Carolina. J Agromedicine 21(1):15–23

Kim S, Nussbaum MA, Laurienti PJ et al (2018) Exploring associations between postural balance and levels of urinary organophosphorus pesticide metabolites. J Occup Environ Med 60(2):174–179

Kirrane EF, Hoppin JA, Kamel F (2005) Retinal degeneration and other eye disorders in wives of farmer pesticide applicators enrolled in the Agricultural Health Study. Am J Epidemiol 161(11):1020–1029

Krejci-Manwaring J, Schulz MR, Feldman SR et al (2006) Skin disease among Latino farmworkers in North Carolina. J Agric Saf Health 12(2):155–163

Kunkel KE, Stevens LE, Stevens SE et al (2013a) Regional climate trends and scenarios for the U.S. National climate assessment: part 2. Climate of the southeast U.S. NOAA Technical Report 142–2. https://data.globalchange.gov/report/noaa-techreport-nesdis-142-2. Accessed 2 Nov 2018

Kunkel KE, Stevens LE, Stevens SE et al (2013b) Regional climate trends and scenarios for the U.S. national climate assessment: part 1. Climate of the northeast U.S. NOAA technical report 142–1. https://data.globalchange.gov/report/noaa-techreport-nesdis-142-1. Accessed 2 Nov 2018

Lacey S, Forst L, Petrea R et al (2007) Eye injury in migrant farmworkers and suggested hazard controls. J Agric Saf Health 13(3):259–274

Larson AC (2000) Migrant and seasonal farmworkers enumeration profiles study. Migrant Health Program, Bureau of Primary Health Care, Health Resources and Services Administration. http://www.ncfh.org/00_ns_rc_enumeration.php. Accessed 30 Mar 2008

Larson AC, Plascencia L (1993) Migrant enumeration project. Office of Migrant Health, Bureau of Primary Health Care, Health Resources and Services Administration. Migrant Legal Services, Washington, DC

Latko WA, Armstrong TJ, Franzblau A et al (1999) Cross-sectional study of the relationship between repetitive work and the prevalence of upper limb musculoskeletal disorders. Am J Ind Med 36(2):248–259

Liebman A, Harper S (2001) Environmental health perceptions among clinicians and administrators caring for migrants. MCN Streamline 7(2):1–4

Lipton E (2017) E.P.A. chief, rejecting agency's science, chooses not to ban insecticide. The New York Times. https://www.nytimes.com/2017/03/29/us/politics/epa-insecticide-chlorpyrifos.html?action=click&module=RelatedCoverage&pgtype=Article&region=Footer. Accessed 1 May 2019

Lipton E (2018) Court Orders E.P.A. to ban chlorpyrifos, pesticide tied to children's health problems. The New York Times. https://www.nytimes.com/2018/08/09/us/politics/chlorpyrifospesticide-ban-epa-court.html. Accessed 1 May 2019

Luque JS, Reyes-Ortiz C, Marella P et al (2012) Mobile farm clinic outreach to address health conditions among Latino migrant farmworkers in Georgia. J Agromedicine 17(4):386–397

Martinez-Donate AP, Ejebe I, Zhang X et al (2017) Access to healthcare among Mexican migrants and immigrants: a comparison across migration phases. J Health Care Poor Underserved 28(4):1314–1326

Marvel ME, Pratt DS, Marvel LH et al (1991) Occupational hearing loss in New York dairy farmers. Am J Ind Med 20(4):517–531

May J, Hawkes L, Jones A et al (2008) Evaluation of a community-based effort to reduce blueberry harvesting injury. Am J Ind Med 51(4):307–315

May E, Scribani M, Wyckoff S et al (2012) Ergonomic assessment of the long handle blueberry harvesting rake. Am J Ind Med 55(11):1051–1059

McCauley LA, Lasarev M, Muniz J et al (2008) Analysis of pesticide exposure and DNA damage in immigrant farmworkers. J Agromedicine 13(4):237–246

Millard PS, Shannon SC, Carvette B et al (1996) Maine students' musculoskeletal injuries attributed to harvesting blueberries. Am J Public Health 86(12):1821–1822

Mills PK, Beaumont JJ, Nasseri K (2006) Proportionate mortality among current and former member so the United Farm Workers of America, AFL-CIO, in California 1973–2000. J Agromedicine 11(1):39–48

Mirabelli MC, Quandt SA, Crain R et al (2010) Symptoms of heat illness among Latino farm workers in North Carolina. Am J Prev Med 39(5):468–471

Mirabelli MC, Hoppin JA, Chatterjee AB et al (2011) Job activities and respiratory symptoms among farmworkers in North Carolina. Arch Environ Occup Health 66(3):178–182

Misra UK, Nag D, Misra NK et al (1985) Some observations on the macula of pesticide workers. Hum Exp Toxicol 4(2):135–145

MMWR (2004) Work-related roadway crashes—United States, 1992–2002. MMWR Morb Mortal Wkly Rep 53(12):260–264

Mobed K, Gold EB, Schenker MB (1992) Occupational health problems among migrant and seasonal farm workers. West J Med 157(3):367–373

Monaghan PF, Forst LS, Tovar-Aguilar JA et al (2011) Preventing eye injuries among citrus harvesters: the community health worker model. Am J Public Health 101(12):2269–2274

Morse T, Dillon C, Kenta-Bibi E et al (2005) Trends in work-related musculoskeletal disorder reports by year, type and industrial sector: a capture–recapture analysis. Am J Ind Med 48(1):40–49

Murphy DJ, Yoder AM (1998) Census of fatal occupational injury in the agriculture, forestry and fishing industry. J Agric Saf Health 1:55–66

Mutic AD, Mix JM, Elon L et al (2017) Classification of heat-related illness symptoms among Florida farmworkers. J Nurs Scholarsh 50(1):74–82

National Institute for Occupational Safety and Health (2003) Work-related roadway crashes—challenges and opportunities for prevention. NIOSH publication no. 2003–119. National Institute for Occupational Safety and Health, Cincinnati, OH

National Institute for Occupational Safety and Health (2004) Worker health chartbook. NIOSH publication no. 2004–146. National Institute for Occupational Safety and Health, Cincinnati, OH

National Institute for Occupational Safety and Health (2016a) NIOSH criteria for a recommended standard: occupational exposure to heat and hot environments. DHHS (NIOSH) publication no. 2016–106. National Institute for Occupational Safety and Health, Cincinnati, OH. https://www.cdc.gov/niosh/docs/2016-106/pdfs/2016-106.pdf. Accessed 21 Oct 2019

National Institute for Occupational Safety and Health (2016b) Injury@Work: statistics—annual eye injuries 2016. National Institute for Occupational Safety and Health, Cincinnati, OH. https://wwwn.cdc.gov/wisards/workrisqs/workrisqs_estimates_results.aspx. Accessed 25 Jan 2019

Ortega AN, Rodriguez HP, Vargas-Bustamante A (2015) Policy dilemmas in Latino healthcare and implementation of the Affordable Care Act. Annu Rev Public Health 36:525–544

Pratt DS, Marvel LH, Darrow D et al (1992) The dangers of dairy farming: the injury experience of 600 workers followed for two years. Am J Ind Med 21(5):637–650

Quandt SA, Arcury TA, Preisser JS et al (2001a) Environmental and behavioral predictors of salivary cotinine in Latino tobacco workers. J Occup Environ Med 43(10):844–852

Quandt SA, Elmore RC, Arcury TA et al (2001b) Eye symptoms and use of eye protection among seasonal and migrant farmworkers. South Med J 94(6):603–607

Quandt SA, Arcury TA, Rao P et al (2004) Agricultural and residential pesticides in wipe samples from farmworker family residences in North Carolina and Virginia. Environ Health Perspect 112(3):382–387

Quandt SA, Feldman SR, Vallejos QM et al (2008) Vision problems, eye care history, and ocular protective behaviors of migrant farmworkers. Arch Environ Occup Health 63(1):13–16

Quandt SA, Chen H, Grzywacz JG et al (2010) Cholinesterase depression and its association with pesticide exposure across the agricultural season among Latino farmworkers in North Carolina. Environ Health Perspect 118(5):635–639

Quandt SA, Pope CN, Chen H et al (2015) Longitudinal assessment of blood cholinesterase activities over 2 consecutive years among Latino nonfarmworkers and pesticide-exposed farmworkers in North Carolina. J Occup Environ Med 57(8):851–857

Quandt SA, Walker FO, Talton JW et al (2016) Olfactory function in Latino farmworkers: subclinical neurological effects of pesticide exposure in a vulnerable population. J Occup Environ Med 58(3):248–253

Quandt SA, Sandberg JC, Graham A et al (2017a) Mexican sobadores in North Carolina: manual therapy in a new settlement context. J Immigr Minor Health 19(5):1186–1195

Quandt SA, Schulz MR, Chen H et al (2017b) Visual acuity and self-reported visual function among migrant farmworkers. Optom Vis Sci 93(10):1189–1195

Quandt SA, Schulz MR, Talton JW et al (2017c) Occupational eye injuries experienced by migrant farmworkers. J Agromedicine 17(1):63–69

Quandt SA, Walker FO, Talton JW et al (2017d) Olfactory function in Latino farmworkers over 2 years: longitudinal exploration of subclinical neurological effects of pesticide exposure. J Occup Environ Med 59(12):1148–1152

Quirós-Alcalá L, Bradman A, Smith K et al (2012) Organophosphorous pesticide breakdown products in house dust and children's urine. J Expo Sci Environ Epidemiol 22(6):559–568

Rabinowitz PM, Sircar KD, Tarabar S et al (2005) Hearing loss in migrant agricultural workers. J Agromedicine 10(4):9–17

Ramirez-Rubio O, McClean MD, Amador JJ et al (2013) An epidemic of chronic kidney disease in Central America: an overview. J Epidemiol Community Health 67(1):1–3

Rao P (2008) Reproductive health effects of pesticide exposure. Farmworker Justice, Washington, DC.   https://www.farmworkerjustice.org/sites/default/files/documents/Reproductive%20 Health%20Effects%20of%20Pesticide%20Exposure.pdf. Accessed 1 May 2019

Raymer JH, Studabaker WB, Gardner M et al (2014) Pesticide exposures to migrant farmworkers in eastern NC: detection of metabolites in farmworker urine associated with housing violations and camp characteristics. Am J Ind Med 57(3):323–337

Rhea S, Ising A, Fleischauer AT et al (2012) Using near-time morbidity data to identify heat-related illness prevention strategies in North Carolina. J Community Health 37(2):495–500

Roberts JR, Reigart JR (2013) Recognition and management of pesticide poisonings, 6th edn. Office of Pesticide Programs, US Environmental Protection Agency, Washington, DC. https:// www.epa.gov/pesticide-worker-safety/recognition-and-management-pesticide-poisonings. Accessed 22 Apr 2019

Runkle JD, Tovar-Aguilar JA, Economos E et al (2013) Pesticide risk perception and biomarkers of exposure in Florida female farmworkers. J Occup Environ Med 55(11):1286–1292

Salazar MK, Keifer M, Negrete M et al (2005) Occupational risk among orchard workers: a descriptive study. Fam Community Health 28(3):239–252

Scharf T, Kidd P, Cole H et al (1998) Intervention tools for farmers—safe and productive work practices in a safer work environment. J Agric Saf Health 1:193–203

Schmitt J, Seidler A, Diepgen TL et al (2011) Occupational ultraviolet light exposure increases the risk for the development of cutaneous squamous cell carcinoma: a systematic review and meta-analysis. Br J Dermatol 164(2):291–307

Schuman SH, Dobson RL (1985) An outbreak of contact dermatitis in farm workers. J Am Acad Dermatol 13(2 Pt 1):220–223

Scribani M, Wyckoff S, Jenkins P et al (2013) Migrant and seasonal crop worker injury and illness across the Northeast. Am J Ind Med 56(8):845–855

Seabrook J (2019) Machine hands. The age of robot farmers: picking strawberries takes speed, stamina and skill. Can a robot do it? (pp. 48–57). The New Yorker

Seraj MA, Channa AB, al Harthi SS et al (1991) Are heat stroke patients fluid depleted? Importance of monitoring central venous pressure as a simple guideline for fluid therapy. Resuscitation 21(1):33–39

Sexsmith K (2017) "But we can't call 911": undocumented immigrant farmworkers and access to social protection in New York. Oxf Dev Stud 45(1):96–111

Silwal A, Davidson J, Karkee M et al (2017) Design, integration, and field evaluation of a robotic apple harvester. J Field Robotics 34:1140–1159

Smith FPE (1940) Eye injuries in agriculture. Trans Ophthalmol Soc UK 60:252–257

Sorensen JA, May JJ, Paap K et al (2008) Encouraging farmers to retrofit tractors: a qualitative analysis of risk perceptions among a group of high-risk farmers in New York. J Agric Saf Health 14(1):105–117

Spangler JG, Arcury TA, Quandt SA et al (2003) Tobacco use among Mexican farmworkers working in tobacco: implications for agromedicine. J Agromedicine 9(1):83–91

Statista (2019) Leading tobacco producing U.S. states. https://www.statista.com/statistics/192022/ top-10-tobacco-producing-us-states/. Accessed 27 Jan 2019

Steinhorst B, Dolezal JM, Jenkins NL et al (2006) Trauma in Hispanic farm workers in eastern North Carolina: 10-year experience at a level I trauma center. J Agromedicine 11:5–14

Stiles M, Grieshop J (1999) Impacts of culture on driver knowledge and safety device usage among Hispanic farm workers. Accid Anal Prev 31(3):235–241

Stock SR (1991) Workplace ergonomic factors and the development of musculoskeletal disorders of the neck and upper limbs: a meta-analysis. Am J Ind Med 19(1):87–107

Sunwook K, Nussbaum MA, Quandt SA et al (2016) Effects of lifetime occupational pesticide exposure on postural control among farmworkers and non-farmworkers. J Occup Environ Med 58(2):133–139

Tanaka S, Estill CF, Shannon SC (1994) Blueberry rakers' tendinitis. N Engl J Med 331(8):552

Taylor SL, Coates ML, Vallejos Q et al (2006) Pterygium among Latino migrant farmworkers in North Carolina. Arch Environ Occup Health 61(1):27–32

Tonozzi TR, Layne LA (2016) Hired worker injuries on farms in the United States: a comparison of two survey periods from the National Agriculture Workers Survey. Am J Ind Med 59(5):408–423

Trapé-Cardoso M, Bracker A, Dauser D et al (2005) Cotinine levels and green tobacco sickness among shade tobacco workers. J Agromedicine 10(2):27–37

United States Environmental Protection Agency (2019a) Basic information about pesticide ingredients. United States Environmental Protection Agency, Washington, DC. https://www.epa.gov/ingredients-used-pesticide-products/basic-information-about-pesticide-ingredients. Accessed 23 Apr 2019

United States Environmental Protection Agency (2019b) Agricultural Worker Protection Standard. In: Pesticide worker safety. United States Environmental Protection Agency, Washington, DC. https://www.epa.gov/pesticide-worker-safety/agricultural-worker-protection-standard-wps#main-content. Accessed 22 Apr 2019

Vallejos QM, Schulz MR, Quandt SA et al (2008) Self report of skin problems among farmworkers in North Carolina. Am J Ind Med 51(3):204–212

Vega-Arroyo AJ, Mitchell DC, Castro JR et al (2019) Impacts of weather, work rate, hydration, and clothing in heat-related illness in California farmworkers. Am J Ind Med 62:1038–1046

Verma A, Schulz MR, Quandt SA et al (2011) Eye health and safety among Latino farmworkers. J Agromed 16(2):143–152

Weinstein ND (1988) The precaution adoption process. Health Psychol 7(4):355–386

Wesseling C, Crowe J, Hogstedt C et al (2014) Resolving the enigma of the Mesoamerican nephropathy: a research workshop summary. Am J Kidney Dis 63(3):396–404

Weyrauch KF, Boiko PE, Keifer M (2005) Building informed consent for cholinesterase monitoring among pesticide handlers in Washington State. Am J Ind Med 48(3):175–181

Wilk VA (1988) Occupational health of migrant seasonal farmworkers in the U.S.: progress report. Farmworker Justice Fund, Washington, DC

Xiao H, McCurdy SA, Stoecklin-Marois MT et al (2013) Agriculture work and chronic musculoskeletal pain among Latino farm workers: the MICASA study. Am J Ind Med 56(2):216–225

Yanga N, Wofford P, DeMars C et al (2018) Pesticide use reporting data in pesticide regulation and policy: the California experience. In: Zhang M, Jackson S, Robertson MA, Zeiss MD (eds) Managing and analyzing pesticide use data for pest management, environmental monitoring, public health, and public policy. American Chemical Society, Washington, DC, pp 97–114

Chapter 4
Stress and Distress: Mental Health Among Latinx Farmworkers in the Eastern United States

Katherine F. Furgurson and Sara A. Quandt

4.1 Introduction

The hazards of farm labor in the United States (US) have significant implications for mental health, as well as injury and illness. Working in physically demanding conditions with inadequate pay and other pressures is stressful. Migrant farmworkers spend extended periods of time away from home, family, and social support. Both migrant and seasonal farmworkers, who live year-round in the community in which they work, find themselves in isolated, rural areas with limited mental health services available. Language barriers and lack of health insurance further complicate mental health-care access for many farmworkers. Like other Latinx immigrants, many farmworkers face racial and ethnic discrimination in the US. The mental health challenges confronted by farmworkers and the lack of mental health services available to them are particularly noteworthy in the eastern US where historically there were few Latinx residents. Resources for this population are underdeveloped today (see Chap. 2).

One of the first reports to document US farmworkers' mental health found that nearly 20% of California farmworkers experienced levels of depressive symptoms suggesting clinically significant mental health problems (Vega et al. 1985). In the eastern US, one of the earliest studies related to mental health was conducted among farmworkers in Florida (Baer and Penzell 1993). Investigating responses to a pesticide exposure emergency, this study found that an estimated 20% of farmworkers reported experiencing *susto*, a culture-bound syndrome that attributes physical dis-

K. F. Furgurson
Department of Social Sciences and Health Policy, Division of Public Health Sciences,
Wake Forest School of Medicine, Winston-Salem, NC, USA

S. A. Quandt (✉)
Department of Epidemiology and Prevention, Division of Public Health Sciences,
Wake Forest School of Medicine, Winston-Salem, NC, USA

© Springer Nature Switzerland AG 2020
T. A. Arcury, S. A. Quandt (eds.), *Latinx Farmworkers in the Eastern United States*, https://doi.org/10.1007/978-3-030-36643-8_4

tress to a frightening experience (Rubel 1964). The first known epidemiologic study of farmworker mental health, using a modified version of the World Health Organization's Composite International Diagnostic Interview (Kessler and Üstün 2004), was published in 2000 (Alderete et al. 2000). This study found that 20.6% of farmworkers in California met clinical criterion for lifetime incidence of one or more psychiatric disorders. The most common classes of psychiatric disorder among farmworkers were anxiety disorder (12.5%), substance use disorder (8.7%) and mood disorder (5.7%) (Alderete et al. 2000).

Hovey and Magaña identified a set of stressors commonly experienced by migrant farmworkers in Michigan and Ohio (Hovey and Magaña 2000; Magaña and Hovey 2003). Using their research as a foundation, an adapted stress process model (after Pearlin et al. 1981) is proposed for understanding farmworker mental health (Fig. 4.1). In this model, an individual's stress level is a continuum. All individuals experience some level of stress. Various circumstances and experiences, or stressors, can contribute to an individual's stress level. The individual may attempt to mitigate this stress level with coping behaviors, which can be positive or negative. Positive coping behaviors, which can reduce stress and promote healthy outcomes, can include exercise or spending time with family. Negative coping behaviors, such as drug or alcohol misuse, may result in increased stress and poor health outcomes. As an individual's stress level increases, so does the risk for distress, which includes mental health diagnoses such as anxiety and depression. In this chapter, two types of stressors are examined: situational and structural. Situational stressors are individual circumstances or environmental conditions that can change over time and particularly across the agricultural season (Grzywacz et al. 2010). Structural stress-

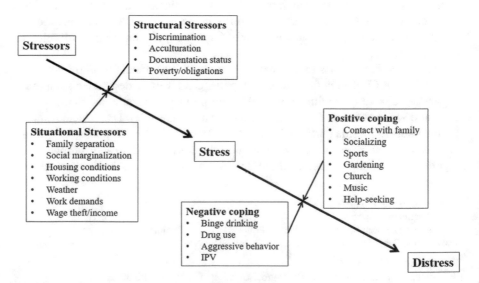

Fig. 4.1 Conceptual model of the stress process for migrant and seasonal farmworkers

ors are broader social and economic forces that affect farmworkers, such as discrimination and poverty. They remain relatively stable over time and across the growing season (Grzywacz et al. 2010).

This chapter summarizes results of recent research on the prevalence of depression, anxiety, and alcohol use disorder symptoms among the Latinx farmworker population in the eastern US. After describing research on these three disorders, this chapter uses the stress model as a framework to identify the unique factors that contribute to farmworker mental health problems and to describe the coping mechanisms farmworkers use to manage stress. Severe mental illnesses and culture-bound syndromes are beyond the scope of this chapter. This chapter focuses on the eastern US but includes relevant studies conducted elsewhere because of the limited research base.

4.2   Evidence of Distress Among Farmworkers

Stress is the body's physical, mental, and emotional response to change. Chronic stress can lead to distress or disruption in the body's equilibrium. Distress can result in both physical symptoms, such as headaches, an upset stomach, and elevated blood pressure, emotional problems, such as depression and anxiety, and potentially harmful behaviors such as alcohol use (Cleveland Clinic 2015).

4.2.1   Anxiety

Nearly one in five (19.1%) adults in the US has an anxiety disorder (NIMH 2017). Anxiety disorders include panic disorder, generalized anxiety disorder, agoraphobia, specific phobia, social anxiety disorder, post-traumatic stress disorder, obsessive-compulsive disorder, and separation anxiety disorder. People of Latinx ethnicity are less likely to be diagnosed with anxiety disorders compared to non-Latinx white individuals (Asnaani et al. 2010): 15.7% of Latinx individuals will be diagnosed with an anxiety disorder during their lifetime (Alegría et al. 2007).

Five studies examined anxiety symptoms among farmworkers in the eastern US (Table 4.1). The Personality Assessment Inventory (PAI) has been the most commonly used instrument to measure anxiety among farmworkers. Additional measures include the Beck Anxiety Inventory (BAI) and the Generalized Anxiety Disorder Scale (GAD-7). All three measures are self-report instruments with versions in Spanish that are valid and reliable for use with Latinx immigrant populations (Mills et al. 2014; Fantoni-Salvador and Rogers 1997; Magan et al. 2008). The five studies reviewed focus primarily on men and on migrant farmworkers.

Less than 3% of farmworkers have a clinically diagnosed anxiety disorder (Boggess and Bogue 2016). However, evidence suggests that anxiety disorders are underdiagnosed among farmworkers. In the five studies reviewed, the prevalence of

Table 4.1 Prevalence of anxiety symptoms among farmworkers in the eastern US

Study	Data collection	Location	Migrant/ seasonal	Gender	Measure	Sample size	Prevalence (%)
Hiott et al. (2008)	2003	NC	Migrant	Male	PAI	125	18.4
Cherry and Rost (2009)	2008	FL	Both	Both	GAD-7	276	23.2
Crain et al. (2012)	2009	NC	Migrant	Male	BAI	69	16.4
Mora et al. (2016)	2010	NC	Migrant	Male	PAI	371	8.8
Sandberg et al. (2016)	2012	NC	Migrant	Male	PAI	147	0
Boggess and Bogue (2016)	2012	National	Both	Both	ICD-9	793,188	2.5

PAI Personality Assessment Inventory, *GAD-7* Generalized Anxiety Disorder scale, *BAI* Beck Anxiety Inventory

anxiety symptoms at the level of possible loss of functioning among farmworkers in the eastern US ranged from 0% (Sandberg et al. 2016) to 23% (Cherry and Rost 2009) (Table 4.1). Differences in timing of survey administration during the growing season could explain some of this variability. The use of different measurement instruments and scoring thresholds also likely contributes to the inconsistency in these results.

4.2.2 Depression

Approximately 8% of US adults meet criteria for depression (Brody et al. 2018). Prevalence is higher for women (10.4%) than for men (5.5%). The difference in prevalence of depression among people who are Latinx, non-Latinx white, and non-Latinx black is not significant (Brody et al. 2018). The prevalence of depression is almost twice as high (15.8%) for US adults living below the federal poverty level, compared to those with higher incomes (Brody et al. 2018).

Fourteen studies measured the prevalence of depressive symptoms among farmworkers in the eastern US (Table 4.2). The most common instrument used was some variant of the Center for Epidemiologic Studies Depression (CES-D) scale (Radloff 1977). Other instruments included the Patient Health Questionnaire (PHQ-9 or PHQ-2) depression scale and the Beck Depression Inventory II (BDI) (Beck 1972; Kroenke et al. 2001, 2003).

Similar to anxiety disorders, depression is likely to be underdiagnosed among farmworkers. Three percent of farmworkers and their dependents treated in Migrant Health Centers are diagnosed with depression each year (Boggess and Bogue 2016), though the prevalence of elevated depressive symptoms among farmworkers in the

Table 4.2 Prevalence of depressive symptoms among farmworkers in the eastern US

Study	Data collection	Location	Migrant/ seasonal	Gender	Measure	Sample size	Prevalence (%)
Hovey and Magaña (2000)	1998	OH/MI	Migrant	Both	CES-D 20	45	37.8
Grzywacz et al. (2006)[a]	2003	NC	Migrant	Male	CES-D 20	60	40
Hiott et al. (2008)[a]	2003	NC	Migrant	Male	CES-D 20	125	41.6
Grzywacz et al. (2010)	2007	NC	Both	Both	CES-D 10 (3 items removed)	288	24
Kim-Godwin et al. (2014)	2007	NC	Both	Both	CES-D 20	291	32.2
Cherry and Rost (2009)	2008	FL	Both	Both	PHQ-9	276	24.3
Grzywacz et al. (2011)[b]	2008	NC	Both	Both	CES-D 10	122	45
Nguyen et al. (2012)[b]	2008	NC	Both	Both	CES-D 10	123	22
Georges et al. (2013)	2008–2010	National	Both	Both	CES-D 10	2905	10.5
Sánchez (2015)	2008–2010	FL	Migrant	Both	BDI	278	Minimal 42.1 Moderate to severe 24.5
Crain et al. (2012)	2009	NC	Migrant	Male	CES-D 20	69	52.2
Sandberg et al. (2012)	2009	NC	Migrant	Both	CES-D 10	300	28
Grzywacz et al. (2014)	2009–2010	National	Both	Both	CES-D 10	3691	8.7
Luque et al. (2012)	2010	GA	Both	Both	PHQ-2	100	7
Mora et al. (2016)	2010	NC	Migrant	Male	CES-D-10	371	16.7
Pulgar et al. (2016), Roblyer et al. (2016), Arcury et al. (2015)[c]	2011–2012	NC	Both	Female	CES-D 10	248	31.3
Arcury et al. (2018) and Marshall et al. (2018)[d]	2012	NC	Seasonal	Female	CES D-10 (Boston 4)	35	28.6

(continued)

Table 4.2 (continued)

Study	Data collection	Location	Migrant/ seasonal	Gender	Measure	Sample size	Prevalence (%)
Arcury et al. (2016)[e]	2012	NC	Migrant	Male	CES D-10 (Boston 4)	235	8.9
Boggess and Bogue (2016)	2012	National	Both	Both	ICD-9 diagnosis	793,188	3.1[f]
Sandberg et al. (2016)[e]	2012	NC	Migrant	Male	CES-D 10	147	6.12
Ramos et al. (2015)	2013	NE	Migrant	Both	CES-D 20	200	45.8
Tribble et al. (2016)	2013	NC	Migrant	Male	CES-D 10	189	9.2
Chaney and Torres (2017)	2014	NC	Seasonal	Both	10-item shortened version of Chaney scale (2010)	150	11.3

[a]Both papers use data from the Casa y Campo study
Both papers use data from the MICASA study
[b]Both papers use data from the same study
[c]All three papers use data from the Niños Sanos study
[d]Both papers use data from the same study
[e]Both papers use data from the same study
[f]This is the prevalence of both depression and mood disorders

National Agricultural Worker Survey (NAWS) is between 8.7% and 10.5% (Grzywacz et al. 2014; Georges et al. 2013), similar to the prevalence among the general US population. Elevated depressive symptoms among farmworkers in the eastern US are more common, ranging from 6% to 45% (Table 4.2). The studies that used the full CES-D scale had some of the highest levels of depressive symptoms; all estimated a prevalence above 30% (Crain et al. 2012; Grzywacz et al. 2011; Hiott et al. 2008; Kim-Godwin et al. 2014). Depressive symptoms for migrant farmworkers appear to fluctuate throughout the growing season. In one longitudinal study, migrant farmworkers in North Carolina reported the highest depression symptoms at the beginning of the agricultural season. Their symptoms then declined until the end of the season, when they began to increase once again (Grzywacz et al. 2010).

The Niños Sanos study followed 248 women in farmworker families and measured depression nine times over 2 years using the 10-item CES-D (Marshall et al. 2018). This prospective design allowed the investigators to characterize four distinct patterns of depression: those who experienced few or no depressive symptoms (32.2%); those who experienced moderate symptoms, but episodically (41.0%); those who experienced severe symptoms, but episodically (15.4%); and those who experience chronic depressive symptoms (11.5%). This study demonstrates that depressive symptoms are highly prevalent among women in farmworker families (two-thirds of the women met criteria for depression at least once), but relatively few women are persistently symptomatic.

4.2.3 Alcohol Use Disorders

Half of US adults who experience a substance use disorder have a co-occurring mental illness (National Alliance on Mental Illness 2019). Most studies of substance use among farmworkers have focused on alcohol. Alcohol use disorders include dependence, abuse, harmful drinking, hazardous drinking, and heavy drinking (Reid et al. 1999). Alcohol use disorders are risk factors for fetal alcohol spectrum disorders, hypertension, cardiovascular disease, stroke, liver cirrhosis, cancer, pancreatitis, type 2 diabetes, and injury (Grant et al. 2017).

The prevalence of alcohol use disorders among the general US population is between 6.2% (Center for Behavioral Health Statistics and Quality [CBHSQ] 2016) and 12.7% (Grant et al. 2017). Among Latinx adults, the prevalence of alcohol use disorders is close to the US average, between 7% (CBHSQ 2016) and 12% (Grant et al. 2017).

Ten studies measure alcohol use disorders among farmworkers in the eastern US (Table 4.3). The CAGE (a screening test that asks about four aspects of alcohol use) was the most frequently used instrument. One study used the Alcohol Use Disorders Identification Test (AUDIT), and one study used the Rapid Alcohol Problems Screen (RAPS4-QF). All instruments have been validated for use in Spanish (Saitz et al. 1999; Babor et al. 2001). These three instruments measure slightly different aspects of alcohol use disorders. The CAGE measures only alcohol abuse and dependence, while the AUDIT also measures risky drinking (Reid et al. 1999). The RAPS4-QF measures alcohol dependence and harmful drinking (Cherpitel 2002).

Less than 1% of farmworkers are diagnosed with alcohol use disorders annually (Boggess and Bogue 2016). However, 5.7–52.7% of farmworkers in the eastern US reported symptoms of alcohol use disorders (Table 4.3). Most studies estimated prevalence to be above 30%. Of the studies reviewed, the lowest prevalence (5.7%) was found among a sample of female seasonal farmworkers in North Carolina (Arcury et al. 2018). Few other studies have measured alcohol use among female farmworkers in the eastern US. A couple of studies found that female farmworkers consume less alcohol and are less likely than male farmworkers to be at risk for alcohol use disorders (Cherry and Rost 2009; Sánchez 2015).

4.3 Stress

Most studies reviewed used the Migrant Farm Worker Stress Inventory (MFWSI) to measure stress among farmworkers. The MFWSI is a 39-item self-report instrument developed by Hovey (2001) including potential stressors identified through interviews with farmworkers in Michigan and Ohio. The instrument uses a 5-point Likert scale (0, have not experienced; 1, not at all stressful; 2, somewhat stressful; 3, moderately stressful; and 4, extremely stressful) to measure exposure to common stressors and the perceived severity of these stressors. Scores on the MFWSI range from

Table 4.3 Prevalence of alcohol use disorder symptoms/risk among farmworkers in the eastern US

Study	Data collection	Location	Migrant/ seasonal	Gender	Measure	Sample size	Prevalence (%)
Hiott et al. (2008)	2003	NC	Migrant	Male	CAGE	125	37.6
Grzywacz et al. (2007)	2005	NC	Both	Male	CAGE	151	52.7
Kim-Godwin et al. (2014)	2007	NC	Both	Both	CAGE[a]	289	38.7
Cherry and Rost (2009)	2008	FL	Both	Both	RAPS4-QF	276	43.8
Rhodes et al. (2010)	2008	NC	Migrant	Male	Binge drinking during past year	100	58
Mora et al. (2016)	2010	NC	Migrant	Male	AUDIT-C	371	50.1
Arcury et al. (2018)	2012	NC	Seasonal	Female	CAGE	35	5.7
Arcury et al. (2016)[b]	2012	NC	Migrant	Male	CAGE	235	37.9
Sandberg et al. (2016)[b]	2012	NC	Migrant	Male	CAGE	147	38.1
Sánchez (2015)	2008–2010	FL	Migrant	Both	CAGE	278	8.5
Arcury et al. (2015)	2012–2013	NC	Migrant	Male	CAGE	101	34.7

[a]Used a lower scoring threshold (>1)
[b]Both papers use data from the same study

0 to 156 with higher scores indicating more stress and scores above 80 indicating a risk for negative mental health outcomes (Hovey and Magaña 2002). The MFWSI demonstrates high reliability and was validated with the Center for Epidemiologic Studies Depression (CES-D) scale and the Beck Hopelessness Scale (Hovey 2001). Two studies have used principal component analysis to identify factors within the instrument. Hiott et al. (2008) identified five factors among farmworkers in North Carolina: legality and logistics, social isolation, work conditions, family, and substance abuse by others. Ramos et al. (2015) identified eight factors among farmworkers in Nebraska: economics and logistics, acculturation and social isolation, relationship with partner, health, immigration issues, entertainment, concerns with children, and substance abuse by others.

Other methods of measuring farmworker stress include an instrument developed by Chaney et al. (2011) to assess stress, depression, and coping behaviors. The instrument demonstrated adequate reliability, but researchers did not evaluate it for construct validity in the initial study. Some studies have used the Perceived Stress

Table 4.4 Stress prevalence among farmworkers in the eastern US

Study	Data collection	Location	Migration status	Gender	Measure	Sample size	Prevalence (%)
Hiott et al. (2008)	2003	NC	Migrant	Men	MFWSI 39	125	38
Kim-Godwin et al. (2014)	2007	NC	Both	both	MFWSI 39	291	25.6
Tribble et al. (2016)	2013	NC	97% H-2A	Men	MFWSI 17	111	2.9
Chaney and Torres (2017)	2014	NC	Seasonal	both	Chaney—8	150	12.7
Pulgar et al. (2016)	2011–2012	NC	Both	Women	MFWSI 25	248	25.4

Scale (PSS) instead of, or in addition to, scales specific to farmworkers. Higher scores indicate higher levels of perceived stress. There is no standard cutoff. Crain et al. (2012) and Smith et al. (2015) used the 10-item version of the PSS. The 10-item version has been validated for use with Hispanic Americans (in a predominantly Mexican American sample) (Baik et al. 2019).

Results vary significantly on the prevalence of high levels of stress among farmworkers. Studies have found prevalence as low as 3% (Tribble et al. 2016) and as high as 38% (Hiott et al. 2008) (Table 4.4). To account for the different instruments to measure stress, Table 4.5 presents the percent of total score for the averages reported. None of the studies found average stress scores greater than 50% of the total possible score. The two studies with the highest percent of total possible score were all-women samples (Arcury et al. 2018; Pulgar et al. 2016). Evidence suggests that farm work-related stressors, those specific to migrant lifestyle measured using the MFWSI, are more closely associated with depression while general stressors, measured using the PSS, are more associated with anxiety (Crain et al. 2012).

4.4   Coping

The way individuals cope with stress can influence health outcomes. Coping behaviors can be positive, producing more favorable health outcomes, or negative, having deleterious effects on health. Farmworkers practice both negative and positive coping behaviors. Negative coping behaviors practiced by farmworkers include drinking beer, overeating, playing the lottery, or refraining from talking about or acknowledging stress (Winkelman et al. 2013; Arcury et al. 2019). Positive coping behaviors noted by researchers include spending time with friends, playing with

Table 4.5 Average stress scores among farmworkers in the eastern US

Study	Data collection	Location	Migrant/ seasonal	Gender	Measure	Sample size	Average score	% of possible total score
Arcury et al. (2016)	2012	NC	Migrant	Male	MFWSI 17	235	17.3	25
Nguyen et al. (2012)	2008	NC	Both	Both	MFWSI 17	123	24.8	36
Arcury et al. (2018)	2012	NC	Seasonal	Female	MFWSI 17	35	27.7	41
Arcury et al. (2015)	2012– 2013	NC	Both	Female	MFWSI 25	220	25.8	26
Pulgar et al. (2016)	2011– 2012	NC	Both	Female	MFWSI 25	248	38.5	39
Crain et al. (2012)	2009	NC	Migrant	Male	MFWSI 39	69	57.7	37
Kim-Godwin et al. (2014)	2007	NC	Both	Both	MFWSI 39	291	67.7	43
Crain et al. (2012)	2009	NC	Migrant	Male	PSS—10	69	14.2	36

their children, dancing, listening to music, getting extra sleep, taking a hot shower, drinking cinnamon tea, joking, setting goals, praying, talking to a counselor, and consulting with a physician (Winkelman et al. 2013; Arcury et al. 2019). Additional protective factors specifically for female farmworkers may include having a future goal in mind and having pride in their work (Dueweke et al. 2015). The ability to utilize positive coping behaviors is often limited by farmworkers' living situations. For example, people living in very remote areas may not have access to cell service and Internet to communicate with loved ones. Getting enough sleep may be difficult in shared, crowded housing and during peak growing season when working hours are long. Although these coping behaviors are labeled here as "positive" and "negative," due to their health implications, farmworkers may not perceive them this way. For example, binge drinking is labeled as negative coping for its health and behavioral implications, but farmworkers may value the social aspect of drinking to relax and bond with their coworkers (García 2008). It is important for clinicians, researchers, and public health practitioners to consider these factors when developing interventions.

4.5 Situational Stressors

Pearlin et al. (1981) describe two broad circumstances that can be sources of stress: discrete events and continuous problems. Here these discrete events are discussed using the term "situational stressors" from Grzywacz et al. (2010). Situational stressors can change quickly depending on environmental conditions and individual circumstances. Some of the most common situational stressors for farmworkers include family separation and responsibilities, social marginalization, poor housing conditions, strenuous work conditions, high-level work demands, and poor physical health. Existing studies examining the relationship between various stressors and mental health outcomes are listed in Table 4.6. Results of these studies are discussed in detail below.

4.5.1 Family Separation and Responsibilities

Family separation is a common stressor among migrant farmworkers (Hovey and Magaña 2000). Migrant workers may travel alone during the growing season or leave behind both nuclear and extended family members in their home countries (Winkelman et al. 2013). Compared to farmworkers travelling with family, unaccompanied farmworkers experience lower levels of family support (O'Connor et al. 2015). Being away from family was identified as the greatest stressor among farmworkers in North Carolina (Kim-Godwin and Bechtel 2004). Family separation is also associated with depressive symptoms (Grzywacz et al. 2010). Seasonal farmworkers may also experience stress from family separation. Many leave parts of their extended family, as well as some of their children, in their countries of origin.

Family responsibilities are also a source of stress for farmworkers (Winkelman et al. 2013). Family responsibilities include taking care of their spouses and children as well as cooking and housework. Having to fulfill these responsibilities after a long day of working and commuting further compounds stress. Stress related to family separation and familial responsibilities is strongly associated with anxiety symptoms (Grzywacz et al. 2006). Migration can also "generate conflict within families" (Rumbaut 1997). Greater family conflict is associated with higher percentages of elevated depressive symptoms (Roblyer et al. 2016). While family separation and conflict may be associated with distress, relationships can also positively contribute to mental health. For example, being married may be a protective factor for alcohol dependence (Grzywacz et al. 2007; Arcury et al. 2016).

Table 4.6 Studies examining the association between various stressors and farmworker mental health

Stressors	Outcomes			
	Stress	Anxiety	Depression	Alcohol use disorders
Situational				
Family separation and responsibility	Kim-Godwin and Bechtel (2004); Winkelman et al. (2013)	Grzywacz et al. (2006)	Grzywacz et al. (2010); Roblyer et al. (2016)	Grzywacz et al. (2007); Arcury et al. (2016)
Social marginalization	Kim-Godwin and Bechtel (2004)	Hiott et al. (2008); Crain et al. (2012)	Grzywacz et al. (2010); Hiott et al. (2008); Crain et al. (2012)	
Housing conditions		Mora et al. (2016); Grzywacz et al. (2010)	Mora et al. (2016); Grzywacz et al. (2010, 2011)	
Working conditions and work demands	Winkelman et al. (2013); Arcury et al. (2015)		Hiott et al. (2008); Grzywacz et al. (2014); Arcury et al. (2015)	
Poor physical health	Tribble et al. (2016)		Shipp et al. (2009); Tribble et al. (2016); Ramos et al. (2015, 2016); Xiao et al. (2014); Marshall et al. (2018)	
Structural				
Discrimination	McClure et al. (2015)		Roblyer et al. (2016); Grzywacz et al. (2010)	
Acculturation		Hovey and Magaña (2000)	Hovey and Magaña (2000); Grzywacz et al. (2010)	
Documentation status	Chaney and Torres (2017); Grzywacz et al. (2014); Winkelman et al. (2013)		Chaney and Torres (2017); Grzywacz et al. (2014); Winkelman et al. (2013); Grzywacz et al. (2010)	
Poverty	Winkelman et al. (2013)		Roblyer et al. (2016); Xiao et al. (2014); Ramos et al. (2015); Pulgar et al. (2016); Weigel et al. (2007)	
Limited access to health care	Chaney and Torres (2017); Clingerman and Brown (2012)			

4.5.2   Social Marginalization

Most farmworkers live in rural communities, many of which have not historically had large Latinx immigrant populations. Many migrant farmworkers may not have access to transportation to leave the labor camps during their free time. Seasonal farmworkers often limit their driving due to lack of valid licenses or threats of immigration-related arrests. Language is also a barrier to establishing social support in a new community. These factors can lead to a sense of social marginalization. Evidence of the association between social marginalization and mental health is somewhat mixed. Grzywacz et al. (2010) found that greater social marginalization was associated with increased depressive symptoms. Hiott et al. (2008) found that, compared to other types of stressors associated with farm work, social isolation had the strongest potential effect on anxiety. Hiott et al. (2008) also found that social isolation was associated with depression. Kim-Godwin and Bechtel (2004) found that a stronger social support system (which farmworkers identified as family and church) was associated with lower levels of stress. However, Crain et al. (2012) found no evidence that social isolation was associated with depressive or anxiety symptoms.

4.5.3   Housing Conditions

Farmworkers often live in substandard housing (see Chap. 2). Migrant housing is often crowded, in poor repair, lacking in security and privacy, and, at least in the southeastern US, excessively hot (Arcury and Summers 2015; Arcury et al. 2012a, b; Quandt et al. 2013). Seasonal farmworker housing is similarly deficient (Early et al. 2006; Gentry et al. 2007). Home disrepair (the presence of water leaks, mold, and cockroaches) is associated with higher odds of *nervios*, a culture-bound syndrome that is related to stress (O'Connor et al. 2015). Farmworkers who feel crowded in their homes have higher rates of depressive and anxiety symptoms (Mora et al. 2016; Grzywacz et al. 2010). Lack of home security (feeling that belongings were secure and having a key to the outside door) is also associated with depression and anxiety among farmworkers (Mora et al. 2016). Type of housing may also affect depressive symptoms. Farmworkers who lived in barracks had higher prevalence of depressive symptoms than farmworkers who lived in trailers or houses (Grzywacz et al. 2011).

4.5.4   Working Conditions and Work Demands

Farmworkers endure physically strenuous labor and frequently are denied common workplace rights. Results of interviews conducted with migrant and seasonal farmworkers in North Carolina show that demanding supervisors, unreasonable production standards, and language barriers contribute to stress in the workplace

(Winkelman et al. 2013). Stressful working conditions are associated with depressive symptoms, according to a study conducted with migrant farmworkers in North Carolina (Hiott et al. 2008). Low job control (inability to make decisions about the way work is performed) and elevated psychological demand (psychological stressors arising from the timing and pace of work) are associated with elevated depressive symptoms (Grzywacz et al. 2014). Arcury et al. (2015) found that psychological demand was associated with stress, but not with depressive symptoms.

4.5.5   Poor Physical Health

Several studies across the US have examined the relationship between poor physical health and mental health. These studies mostly focus on physical health as it pertains to occupational injuries as opposed to chronic or communicable diseases. A study conducted with farmworkers in Texas found that chronic back pain was associated with depressive symptoms during migration (Shipp et al. 2009). Neck/shoulder and wrist/hand pain were positively associated with depressive symptoms, but not stress, in a sample of Latinx manual laborers, including farmworkers, in North Carolina (Tribble et al. 2016). Health problems due to the physical nature of farm work were significantly correlated with depression scores among migrant farmworkers in Nebraska (Ramos et al. 2015). Another study conducted with migrant farmworkers in Nebraska found that those who had been injured on the job were seven times more likely to report being depressed (Ramos et al. 2016). A population-based study conducted in California found that occupational injury was significantly associated with depression and *nervios* among farmworkers (Xiao et al. 2014).

Most of these studies of mental health and its association with physical health are cross-sectional, so establishing causation is difficult. One exception is the longitudinal study by Marshall et al. (2018) of maternal depression. This implicates maternal depression in the physical health (specifically, obesity and overweight) of their children. Those mothers with severe episodic depressive symptoms over 2 years were more likely to have children who were overweight and obese than mothers who displayed other patterns of depressive symptoms. Mothers with different depression phenotypes over time had child feeding styles and dietary quality that varied, probably underlying the differences in child weight status.

4.6   Structural Stressors

The second type of circumstance that can be a source of stress, according to Pearlin et al. (1981), includes conditions that are generally stable over time. In this chapter, these fixed circumstances that are generally beyond the control of farmworkers are referred to as "structural stressors" (Grzywacz et al. 2010). These include, but are not limited to, discrimination, acculturation, documentation status, poverty, and limited access to health care.

4.6.1 Discrimination

Many farmworkers experience discrimination while living and working in the US (Hovey and Magaña 2000). In the general population, perceived discrimination negatively affects mental health outcomes (Pascoe and Smart Richman 2009). Few studies have examined the effects of discrimination on the mental health of farmworkers in the eastern US. McClure et al. (2015) did not find a correlation between perceived discrimination and stress. However, Roblyer et al. (2016) found a positive correlation between perceived racial or ethnic discrimination and depressive symptoms among women in farmworker families. Grzywacz et al. (2010) also found that greater perceived discrimination and marginalization were associated with higher depressive symptoms.

4.6.2 Acculturation

Acculturative stress, the stress related to the social, cultural, and psychological changes that occur when adapting to the dominant culture of a new community, is common among immigrants (Hovey and Magaña 2000). In a study of migrant farmworkers in Nebraska, Ramos et al. (2015) found that stress over acculturation and social isolation was positively associated with poor self-rated health. Hovey and Magaña (2000) found that migrant farmworkers in Ohio and Michigan experienced elevated levels of acculturative stress and reported high levels of anxiety and depression. In contrast, Grzywacz et al. (2010) found no association between acculturation (measured by English fluency) and depressive symptoms among migrant and seasonal farmworkers in North Carolina.

4.6.3 Documentation Status

Almost half of farmworkers do not have legal authorization to live or work in the US (see Chap. 2). Lack of work authorization or legal residency status is associated with increased stress and depressive symptoms among farmworkers (Chaney and Torres 2017; Grzywacz et al. 2014; Winkelman et al. 2013). Concerns about documentation are also associated with higher depressive symptoms among North Carolina farmworkers (Grzywacz et al. 2010). Concerns about immigration issues are also associated with poor self-rated health among farmworkers in Nebraska (Ramos et al. 2015).

4.6.4   Poverty

Among the general US population, people living in poverty are more likely to be depressed (Brody et al. 2018). Farm labor is paid low wages, and workers on farms with less than ten workers are generally exempt from overtime and minimum wage provisions of the Fair Labor Standards Act; they are often subject to wage theft (Robinson et al. 2011). Many states in the eastern US, particularly in the Southeast, have fewer state-based stringent laws than those in New England and the West Coast (Gamer 2015; US Department of Labor 2019). The temporary, seasonal nature of farm work (and, therefore, income) is also a source of stress among farmworkers (Winkelman et al. 2013). Economic insecurity is positively associated with depressive symptoms among farmworkers (Roblyer et al. 2016). In a study of California farmworkers, lower-income participants had higher prevalence of depression and *nervios* (Xiao et al. 2014). Ramos et al. (2015) found that stressors related to economics and logistics (e.g., not having reliable transportation, not getting credit from family for work, difficulty completing paperwork for services) were associated with depressive symptoms.

Food insecurity, or being without reliable access to quality, affordable food, is another stressor related to poverty that affects many farmworkers in the eastern US (Hill et al. 2011; Ip et al. 2015; Quandt et al. 2006). Women from farmworker families with low food security were more than twice as likely to report significant depressive symptoms as were women with high food security (Pulgar et al. 2016). Depression and *nervios* are more common in food insecure compared to food secure farmworker households in Texas and New Mexico (Weigel et al. 2007).

4.6.5   Limited Access to Health Care

Farmworkers face many barriers to accessing health care. They often live in isolated rural locations, particularly in the eastern US, and may not have personal transportation. Most farmworkers do not receive benefits such as paid sick leave or health insurance. Those who do, e.g., guest workers on H-2A visas, may not know how to use the health insurance or may be under pressure to work rather than take time for medical appointments (Arcury and Quandt 2007; Hoerster et al. 2011).

Few studies have examined the relationship between access to health care and mental health. Lack of health insurance is associated with higher stress among farmworkers (Chaney and Torres 2017). Farmworkers in Texas identified lack of access to medical care as the most significant stressor they worried about before migration (Clingerman and Brown 2012). Limited access to health care also makes it more difficult for farmworkers to seek treatment for mental health problems. Less than 2% of farmworkers who accessed services at Federally Qualified Health Centers (FQHCs) in North Carolina received mental health services (Lambar and Thomas 2019).

4.7   Discussion

Many factors specific to their occupation cause stress among farmworkers. Between 3% and 38% of farmworkers report elevated stress levels. Situational stressors, such as family separation, social marginalization, housing conditions, working conditions, and poor physical health, and structural stressors, such as discrimination, acculturation, documentation status, poverty, and limited access to health care, contribute to mental health problems among farmworkers. However, the exact pathways by which these stressors influence mental health and which specific mental health outcomes they affect are unclear. The effects of some potential stressors, such as wage theft, weather, and immigration and labor policies, have not yet been systematically measured. No studies were found examining the association between these factors and farmworkers' mental health in the eastern US.

Although numerous studies have measured mental health among farmworkers in the eastern US, actionable knowledge is limited. There is significant variability in the reported prevalence of mental health problems among these farmworkers. The prevalence of anxiety symptoms ranges from 0% to 23%. The prevalence of depressive symptoms ranges from 6% to 45%. The prevalence of alcohol use disorder symptoms ranges from 5.7% to 52.7%. Most evidence suggests that these problems are underdiagnosed.

The wide range of results is likely due to the variety of instruments and different definitions of identifying cases used to estimate prevalence of mental health symptoms. Differences in sample demographics and exposure to situational and structural stressors may also explain some of the variance across studies. The cross-sectional design of most studies limits our ability to determine causality and estimate prevalence, given evidence that symptoms of distress may fluctuate throughout the agricultural season. The small geographic scope of the existing studies on farmworker mental health also contributes to limited understanding of the problem. Most studies have been conducted in eastern North Carolina. Furthermore, research has been disproportionately focused on male farmworkers, although more recent studies have included a large sample of women in farmworker families (Arcury et al. 2018; Marshall et al. 2018; Pulgar et al. 2016; Roblyer et al. 2016).

One component of mental health not included in the stress model is biological pathways. In addition to the psychosocial factors influencing mental health, genetics also play a role in stress mitigation and mental illness (Herbert 1997). Biological pathways could explain some of the significant variability in the prevalence of mental health symptoms in the studies reviewed. For example, the PON1 gene plays a role in detoxifying organophosphorus pesticides and has been linked to cognitive illnesses and mood symptoms in Parkinson's and Alzheimer's diseases (Paul et al. 2017). More research is needed on the interactions between biological and psychosocial pathways. Research on the prevalence of somatic symptoms of stress among farmworkers in the eastern US is also lacking. It is possible that Latinx farmworkers express reactions to stress through physical (somatic) as well as mental symptoms.

4.8 Conclusions and Recommendations

Farmworkers in the eastern US are subject to significant stressors and have insufficient coping resources. As a result, the stress experience is manifest in significant rates of distress, as is evident in the rates of anxiety, depression, and alcohol use disorders.

Most of the research on the mental health of farmworkers in the US has been done with relatively small, regional samples. Additional large-scale epidemiological studies are needed. Mental health measures could be incorporated into forthcoming versions of the National Agricultural Worker Survey to get a more complete understanding of the prevalence of mental health problems among farmworkers nationwide. Future studies should include more women participants and farmworkers across the eastern US. There is also a need for more longitudinal studies. Future research should further examine additional stressors, such as wage theft, weather, and immigration and labor policies. In summary, recommendations for future research are:

- Incorporate mental health measures into national surveys of farmworker health.
- Include more women participants in studies.
- Include participants from less studied areas of the eastern US.
- Conduct more longitudinal studies.
- Examine additional stressors, such as wage theft, weather, and immigration and labor policies.
- Use consistent, validated measures to assess mental health.

There is a need for clinical screening for mental illness among this population. Lack of adequate mental health resources in rural areas where farmworkers live may be a barrier to screening for some organizations. Implementing telehealth services could be an effective strategy to increase access to culturally appropriate mental health care for farmworkers. Such services are currently being implemented and evaluated in North Carolina by the NC Farmworker Health Program (A. Lipscomb, pers. comm., 5 August 2019). They include an assessment completed over a tablet computer with a farmworker in a local clinic or camp and a mental health professional in an urban clinic, and, if a diagnosis is made that warrants treatment, up to three follow-up visits with the mental health professional, facilitated by a clinic outreach worker with the farmworker over the tablet computer. To address farmworker mental health problems, interventions beyond clinical treatment for mental illness are also needed. These interventions can build on the coping mechanisms identified in previous research and increase farmworkers' capacity to utilize positive coping behaviors rather than negative or unhealthy behaviors. Researchers, advocates, and service providers should work together to develop culturally appropriate stress management interventions for farmworkers. In summary, recommendations to public health practitioners are:

- Screen farmworkers for mental illness.
- Invest in training and recruitment for bilingual mental health providers.

- Explore telehealth services as a way to expand access to care in remote areas.
- Develop interventions to build stress management and coping capacity.

Ultimately, policy change is required to alleviate many of the situational and structural stressors associated with farm work. Several changes in labor and immigration policy have the potential to contribute to improved mental health among farmworkers. Specifically, recommendations to policymakers are:

- Amend the Fair Labor Standards Act to include farm labor in wage and hour protections.
- Implement a national heat standard for occupational safety.
- Elevate standards for employer-provided housing.
- Dedicate additional resources to enforcing labor policies in the agricultural sector.
- Reform the immigration system to allow farmworkers to travel and live with their families.

References

Alderete E, Vega WA, Kolody B et al (2000) Lifetime prevalence of and risk factors for psychiatric disorders among Mexican migrant farmworkers in California. Am J Public Health 90:608–614

Alegría M, Mulvaney-Day N, Torres M et al (2007) Prevalence of psychiatric disorders across Latino subgroups in the United States. Am J Public Health 97:68–75

Arcury TA, Quandt SA (2007) Delivery of health services to migrant and seasonal farmworkers. Annu Rev Public Health 28:345–363

Arcury TA, Summers P (2015) Farmworker housing: a photo essay. New Solut 25:353–361

Arcury TA, Weir MM, Summers P et al (2012a) Safety, security, hygiene and privacy in migrant farmworker housing. New Solut 22:153–173

Arcury TA, Weir M, Chen H et al (2012b) Migrant farmworker housing regulation violations in North Carolina. Am J Ind Med 55:191–204

Arcury TA, Trejo G, Suerken CK et al (2015) Work and health among Latina mothers in farmworker families. J Occup Environ Med 57:292–299

Arcury TA, Talton JW, Summers P et al (2016) Alcohol consumption and risk for dependence among male Latino migrant farmworkers compared to Latino nonfarmworkers in North Carolina. Alcohol Clin Exp Res 40:377–384

Arcury TA, Sandberg JC, Talton JW et al (2018) Mental health among Latina farmworkers and other employed Latinas in North Carolina. Rural Ment Health 42:89–101

Arcury TA, Furgurson KF, O'Hara HM et al (2019) Conventional and complementary therapy use among Mexican farmworkers in North Carolina: applying the I-CAM-Q. J Agromedicine 24:257–267

Asnaani A, Richey JA, Dimaite R et al (2010) A cross-ethnic comparison of lifetime prevalence rates of anxiety disorders. J Nerv Ment Dis 198:551–555

Babor TF, Higgins-Biddle JC, Saunders JB et al (2001) The alcohol use disorders identification test: guidelines for use in primary care, 2nd edn. World Health Organization, Geneva

Baer RD, Penzell D (1993) Research report: susto and pesticide poisoning among Florida farmworkers. Cult Med Psychiatry 17:321–327

Baik SH, Fox RS, Mills SD et al (2019) Reliability and validity of the Perceived Stress Scale-10 in Hispanic Americans with English or Spanish language preference. J Health Psychol 24:628–639

Beck AT (1972) Measuring depression: the depression inventory. In: Katz MM, Williams TA, Shield JA (eds) Recent advances in the psychobiology of the depressive illnesses. US Government Printing Office, Washington, DC, pp 299–302

Boggess B, Bogue HO (2016) The health of U.S. agricultural worker families: a descriptive study of over 790,000 migratory and seasonal agricultural workers and dependents. J Health Care Poor Underserved 27:778–792

Brody DJ, Pratt LA, Hughes JP (2018) Prevalence of depression among adults aged 20 and over: United States, 2013–2016. NCHS Data Brief, no 303. https://www.cdc.gov/nchs/products/databriefs/db303.htm. Accessed 6 Aug 2019

Center for Behavioral Health Statistics and Quality (2016) Results from the 2015 National Survey on Drug Use and Health: detailed tables. Rockville, MD: Center for Behavioral Health Statistics and Quality, Substance Abuse and Mental Health Services Administration. https://www.samhsa.gov/data/sites/default/files/NSDUH-DetTabs-2015/NSDUH-DetTabs-2015/NSDUH-DetTabs-2015.pdf. Accessed 6 Aug 2019

Chaney BH, Torres E (2017) Covariates of identified stress and depression among seasonal farmworkers. Int J Environ Res Public Health 14:E711

Chaney EH, Burke SC, Rager RC et al (2011) Development of an instrument to assess stress, depression, and coping among Latino migrant and seasonal farmworkers. Am J Health Stud 26:236–248

Cherpitel CJ (2002) Screening for alcohol problems in the US general population: comparison of the CAGE, RAPS4, and RAPS4-QF by gender, ethnicity, and service utilization. Alcohol Clin Exp Res 26:1686–1691

Cherry DJ, Rost K (2009) Alcohol use, comorbidities, and receptivity to treatment in Hispanic farmworkers in primary care. J Health Care Poor Underserved 20:1095–1110

Cleveland Clinic (2015) What is stress? Cleveland, OH: Cleveland Clinic. https://my.clevelandclinic.org/health/articles/11874-stress. Accessed 6 Aug 2019

Clingerman EM, Brown A (2012) Stress in migrant farmworkers during premigration. Biol Res Nurs 14:27–37

Crain R, Grzywacz JG, Schwantes M et al (2012) Correlates of mental health among Latino farmworkers in North Carolina. J Rural Health 28:277–285

Dueweke AR, Hurtado G, Hovey JD (2015) Protective psychosocial resources in the lives of Latina migrant farmworkers. Rural Ment Health 39:162–177

Early J, Davis SW, Quandt SA et al (2006) Housing characteristics of farmworker families in North Carolina. J Immigr Minor Health 8:173–184

Fantoni-Salvador P, Rogers R (1997) Spanish versions of the MMPI-2 and PAI: an investigation of concurrent validity with Hispanic patients. Assessment 4:29–39

Gamer S (2015) Farmworker overtime across the states. The Issue Spotter, Cornell Journal of Law and Public Policy. http://jlpp.org/blogzine/farmworker-overtime-across-the-states/. Accessed 25 Jul 2019

García V (2008) Problem drinking among transnational Mexican migrants: exploring migrant status and situational factors. Hum Organ 67:12–24

Gentry AL, Grzywacz JG, Quandt SA et al (2007) Housing quality among North Carolina farmworker families. J Agric Saf Health 13:323–337

Georges A, Alterman T, Gabbard S et al (2013) Depression, social factors, and farmworker health care utilization. J Rural Health 29:s7–s16

Grant BF, Chou SP, Saha TD et al (2017) Prevalence of 12-month alcohol use, high-risk drinking, and DSM-IV alcohol use disorder in the United States, 2001–2002 to 2012–2013: results from the National Epidemiologic Survey on Alcohol and Related Conditions. JAMA Psychiat 74:911–923

Grzywacz JG, Quandt SA, Early J et al (2006) Leaving family for work: ambivalence and mental health among Mexican migrant farmworker men. J Immigr Minor Health 8:85–97

Grzywacz JG, Arcury TA, Márin A et al (2007) Work-family conflict: experiences and health implications among immigrant Latinos. J Appl Psychol 92:1119–1130

Grzywacz JG, Quandt SA, Chen H et al (2010) Depressive symptoms among Latino farmworkers across the agricultural season: structural and situational influences. Cultur Divers Ethnic Minor Psychol 16:335–343

Grzywacz JG, Chatterjee AB, Quandt SA et al (2011) Depressive symptoms and sleepiness among Latino farmworkers in eastern North Carolina. J Agromedicine 16:251–260

Grzywacz JG, Alterman T, Gabbard S et al (2014) Job control, psychological demand, and farmworker health: evidence from the National Agricultural Workers Survey. J Occup Environ Med 56:66–71

Herbert J (1997) Fortnightly review: stress, the brain, and mental illness. BMJ 315:530–535

Hill BG, Moloney AG, Mize T et al (2011) Prevalence and predictors of food insecurity in migrant farmworkers in Georgia. Am J Public Health 101:831–833

Hiott AE, Grzywacz JG, Davis SW et al (2008) Migrant farmworker stress: mental health implications. J Rural Health 24:32–39

Hoerster KD, Mayer JA, Gabbard S et al (2011) Impact of individual-, environmental-, and policy-level factors on health care utilization among US farmworkers. Am J Public Health 101:685–692

Hovey JD (2001) Depression in migrant farmworkers. Farmworker News 7:1–4

Hovey JD, Magaña CG (2000) Acculturative stress, anxiety, and depression among Mexican immigrant farmworkers in the Midwest United States. J Immigr Health 2:119–131

Hovey JD, Magaña CG (2002) Mental health assessment: breaking new ground in Colorado. In: Paper presented at the 12th Migrant Farmworker Midwestern Stream Forum, Austin, TX

Ip EH, Saldana S, Arcury TA et al (2015) Profiles of food security for US farmworker households and factors related to dynamic of change. Am J Public Health 105:e42–e47

Kessler RC, Ustün TB (2004) The World Mental Health (WMH) Survey Initiative Version of the World Health Organization (WHO) Composite International Diagnostic Interview (CIDI). Int J Methods Psychiatr Res 13:93–121

Kim-Godwin YS, Bechtel GA (2004) Stress among migrant and seasonal farmworkers in rural southeast North Carolina. J Rural Health 20:271–278

Kim-Godwin YS, Maume MO, Fox JA (2014) Depression, stress, and intimate partner violence among Latino migrant and seasonal farmworkers in rural southeastern North Carolina. J Immigr Minor Health 16:1217–1224

Kroenke K, Spitzer RL, Williams JB (2001) The PHQ-9: validity of a brief depression severity measure. J Gen Intern Med 16:606–613

Kroenke K, Spitzer RL, Williams JB (2003) The Patient Health Questionnaire-2: validity of a two-item depression screener. Med Care 41:1284–1292

Lambar EF, Thomas G (2019) The health and well-being of North Carolina's farmworkers: the importance of inclusion, accessible services and personal connection. N C Med J 80:107–112

Luque JS, Reyes-Ortiz C, Marella P et al (2012) Mobile farm clinic outreach to address health conditions among Latino migrant farmworkers in Georgia. J Agromedicine 17:386–397

Magan I, Sanz J, Garcia-Vera MP (2008) Psychometric properties of a Spanish version of the Beck Anxiety Inventory (BAI) in general population. Span J Psychol 11:626–640

Magaña CG, Hovey JD (2003) Psychosocial stressors associated with Mexican migrant farmworkers in the midwest United States. J Immigr Health 5:75–86

Marshall SA, Ip EH, Suerken CK et al (2018) Relationship between maternal depression and child weight outcomes in Latino farmworker families. Matern Child Nutr 14:e12614

McClure HH, Josh Snodgrass J, Martinez CR Jr et al (2015) Stress, place, and allostatic load among Mexican immigrant farmworkers in Oregon. J Immigr Minor Health 17:1518–1525

Mills SD, Fox RS, Malcarne VL et al (2014) The psychometric properties of the Generalized Anxiety Disorder-7 Scale in Hispanic Americans with English or Spanish language preference. Cultur Divers Ethnic Minor Psychol 20:463–468

Mora DC, Quandt SA, Chen H et al (2016) Associations of poor housing with mental health among North Carolina Latino migrant farmworkers. J Agromedicine 21:327–334

National Alliance on Mental Illness (2019) Mental health by the numbers. Arlington, VA: National Alliance on Mental Illness. https://www.nami.org/learn-more/mental-health-by-the-numbers. Accessed 6 Aug 2019

National Institute of Mental Health (NIMH) (2017) Any anxiety disorder. https://www.nimh.nih.gov/health/statistics/any-anxiety-disorder.shtml. Accessed 6 Aug 2019

Nguyen HT, Quandt SA, Grzywacz JG et al (2012) Stress and cognitive function in Latino farmworkers. Am J Ind Med 55:707–713

O'Connor K, Stoecklin-Marois M, Schenker MB (2015) Examining nervios among immigrant male farmworkers in the MICASA study: sociodemographics, housing conditions and psychosocial factors. J Immigr Minor Health 17:198–207

Pascoe EA, Smart Richman L (2009) Perceived discrimination and health: a meta-analytic review. Psychol Bull 135:531–554

Paul KC, Sinsheimer JS, Cockburn M et al (2017) Organophosphate pesticides and PON1 L55M in Parkinson's disease progression. Environ Int 107:75–81

Pearlin LI, Lieberman MA, Menaghan EG et al (1981) The stress process. J Health Soc Behav 22:337–356

Pulgar CA, Trejo G, Suerken C et al (2016) Economic hardship and depression among women in Latino farmworker families. J Immigr Minor Health 18:497–504

Quandt SA, Shoaf JI, Tapia J et al (2006) Experiences of Latino immigrant families in North Carolina help explain elevated levels of food insecurity and hunger. J Nutr 136:2638–2644

Quandt SA, Wiggins MF, Chen H et al (2013) Heat index in migrant farmworker housing: implications for rest and recovery from work-related heat stress. Am J Public Health 103:e24–e26

Radloff LS (1977) The CES-D Scale: a self-report depression scale for research in the general population. Appl Psychol Meas 1:385–401

Ramos AK, Su D, Lander L et al (2015) Stress factors contributing to depression among Latino migrant farmworkers in Nebraska. J Immigr Minor Health 17:1627–1634

Ramos AK, Carlo G, Grant K et al (2016) Stress, depression, and occupational injury among migrant farmworkers in Nebraska. Safety (Basel) 2:23

Reid MC, Fiellin DA, O'Connor PG (1999) Hazardous and harmful alcohol consumption in primary care. Arch Intern Med 159:1681–1689

Rhodes SD, Bischoff WE, Burnell JM et al (2010) HIV and sexually transmitted disease risk among male Hispanic/Latino migrant farmworkers in the Southeast: findings from a pilot CBPR study. Am J Ind Med 53(10):976–983

Robinson E, Nguyen HT, Isom S et al (2011) Wages, wage violations, and pesticide safety experienced by migrant farmworkers in North Carolina. New Solut 21:251–268

Roblyer MI, Grzywacz JG, Suerken CK et al (2016) Interpersonal and social correlates of depressive symptoms among Latinas in farmworker families living in North Carolina. Women Health 56:177–193

Rubel AJ (1964) The epidemiology of a folk illness: Susto in Hispanic America. Ethnology 3:268–283

Rumbaut RG (1997) Introduction: Immigration and incorporation. Sociol Perspect 40:333–338

Saitz R, Lepore MF, Sullivan LM et al (1999) Alcohol abuse and dependence in Latinos living in the United States: validation of the CAGE (4M) questions. Arch Intern Med 159:718–724

Sánchez J (2015) Alcohol use among Latino migrant workers in South Florida. Drug Alcohol Depend 151:241–249

Sandberg JC, Grzywacz JG, Talton JW et al (2012) A cross-sectional exploration of excessive daytime sleepiness, depression, and musculoskeletal pain among migrant farmworkers. J Agromedicine 17:70–80

Sandberg JC, Nguyen HT, Quandt SA et al (2016) Sleep quality among Latino farmworkers in North Carolina: examination of the job control-demand-support model. J Immigr Minor Health 18:532–541

Shipp EM, Cooper SP, del Junco DJ et al (2009) Chronic back pain and associated work and nonwork variables among farmworkers from Starr County, Texas. J Agromedicine 14:22–32

Smith MN, Wilder CS, Griffith WC et al (2015) Seasonal variation in cortisol biomarkers in Hispanic mothers living in an agricultural region. Biomarkers 20:299–305

Tribble AG, Summers P, Chen H et al (2016) Musculoskeletal pain, depression, and stress among Latino manual laborers in North Carolina. Arch Environ Occup Health 71:309–316

US Department of Labor (2019) Minimum wage laws in the states. https://www.dol.gov/whd/minwage/america.htm. Accessed 25 Jul 2019

Vega W, Warheit G, Palacio R (1985) Psychiatric symptomatology among Mexican American farmworkers. Soc Sci Med 20:39–45

Weigel MM, Armijos RX, Hall YP et al (2007) The household food insecurity and health outcomes of U.S.–Mexico border migrant and seasonal farmworkers. J Immigr Minor Health 9:157–169

Winkelman SB, Chaney EH, Bethel JW (2013) Stress, depression and coping among Latino migrant and seasonal farmworkers. Int J Environ Res Public Health 10:1815–1830

Xiao H, Stoecklin-Marois M, Li CS et al (2014) Depression, perceived stress and nervios associated with injury in the MICASA study, a California farm worker population. Field Actions Sci Rep 2014:10

Chapter 5
Occupational Justice for Latinx Livestock Workers in the Eastern United States

Effie E. Palacios and Kathleen Sexsmith

5.1 Introduction

While animal welfare scholars and advocates have effectively called attention to the mistreatment of animals under the rapid consolidation and industrialization of animal agriculture (Fraser 2008; PETA 2019), occupational justice for the mostly Latinx farmworkers who care for them has been largely overlooked. Moreover, the literature on worker health and safety in US animal agriculture industries is thin, leaving policymakers and worker advocates with limited evidence to make claims for the need for improved farm-level practices and regulations. Although there is a growing literature on occupational safety and health concerns faced by Latinx dairy farmworkers, very little information exists on Latinx workers in poultry, swine, and equine production even though those industries are increasingly dependent on this workforce. The purposes of this chapter are to summarize and assess the available evidence regarding occupational safety and health concerns faced by Latinx farmworkers in animal agriculture industries and to identify parallels and trends that emerge from the workplace conditions of animal agriculture and the inherent characteristics of working with live animals. The chapter highlights how, as the size and scale of animal agriculture operations continue to grow, farmers have come to depend more on Latinx workers, who are exposed to safety and health risks specific to animal agriculture. Moreover, the chapter argues that the health concerns of Latinx livestock workers in the eastern United States (US) are compounded by language barriers and by their social and geographic isolation, which impede preventive measures such as training and use of personal protective equipment, as well as access to medical care.

E. E. Palacios · K. Sexsmith (✉)
Department of Agricultural Economics, Sociology, and Education, Pennsylvania State University, University Park, PA, USA

© Springer Nature Switzerland AG 2020
T. A. Arcury, S. A. Quandt (eds.), *Latinx Farmworkers in the Eastern United States*, https://doi.org/10.1007/978-3-030-36643-8_5

This chapter focuses on workers in four types of animal agricultural operations: dairy, poultry, swine, and equine (horse). The term *livestock workers* is used throughout the chapter when referring to this group of workers as a whole. Livestock workers are defined by the US Department of Agriculture (USDA) and the National Agricultural Statistics Service as "employees tending livestock, milking cows, or caring for poultry, including operation of farm machinery on livestock or poultry operations" (USDA 2012). While this chapter focuses on the safety and health conditions of livestock workers only, it should be noted that Latinx workers are also widely employed in animal processing, where their safety and health concerns are also at risk (Marín et al. 2009; Oxfam America 2015; Quandt et al. 2006; Ribas 2015). In fact, growing attention to slaughterhouses and poultry processing plants and the significant occupational safety concerns they present may have overshadowed persistent dangers in animal production. Animal agriculture is among the most dangerous industries in the US. The growth and concentration of animal production facilities, and attendant switch to a primarily Latinx labor force, have had significant implications for the labor process and, thus, worker safety and health on large farms. At the same time, farms with smaller workforces receive exemptions from Occupational Safety and Health Administration (OSHA) inspection and enforcement mechanisms, weakening safety protections in these workplaces.

The chapter proceeds as follows. First, a statistical profile of structural transformation in animal agriculture operations is presented. The profile includes an explanation of how labor processes have changed in these operations due to industrial consolidation and how these changes have coincided with increasing dependence on the Latinx workforce. It also presents injury rates in animal agriculture and describes OSHA coverage and exemptions for the dairy, poultry, swine, and equine industries. Second, the chapter synthesizes findings from a literature review of occupational safety and health risks faced by Latinx livestock workers, focusing on traumatic injury, musculoskeletal disorder, respiratory illness and dysfunction, infectious disease, and mental health disorders. Third, it explains how access to preventive and remedial measures is limited in the contexts in which Latinx livestock workers live and work. In the final section, significant research gaps in the extant literature are identified, and recommendations are presented for farmers and policymakers for improved occupational safety and health among Latinx livestock workers.

5.2 Structural Change, Latinx Workforces, and Risk of Injury in Animal Agriculture Industries

Animal agriculture has become heavily consolidated and industrialized across the US. Historical data from the US Census of Agriculture demonstrate rapid rates of consolidation in the dairy and swine industries, with the elimination of hundreds of thousands of farms from 1978 to 2017 (Fig. 5.1). The number of equine farms has stayed relatively stable with a slight rise in numbers over the same period (Fig. 5.1). This may be due to a change in data collection methods in 2002, in which the

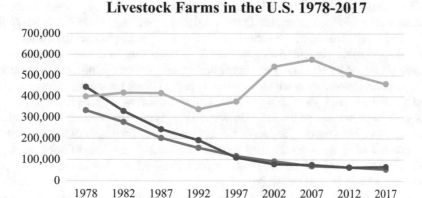

Fig. 5.1 Livestock farms in the US 1978–2017, from Census of Agriculture (USDA 1999, 2004, 2009, 2014, 2019; USDC 1981, 1984, 1989, 1994)

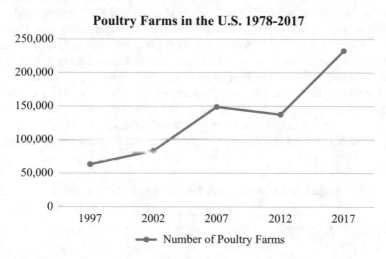

Fig. 5.2 Poultry farms in the US 1997–2017, from Census of Agriculture (USDA 1999, 2004, 2009, 2014, 2019)

National Agricultural Statistics Service tried to survey a larger number of small and minority-owned farms (USDA 2004). Poultry production grew from 1997 to 2007, with a decline from 2007 to 2012, followed by a rapid increase between 2012 and 2017 (Fig. 5.2). As of the most recently available Census of Agriculture (USDA 2019), there were an estimated 54,499 dairy farms, 66,439 swine farms, 459,526 equine farms, and 232,500 poultry farms in the US (Figs. 5.1 and 5.2).

The consolidation of animal farms has coincided with rising dependence on Latinx workers in the eastern US (Mares 2019; Schewe and White 2017; Sexsmith 2016, 2017). However, information on the geographic distribution and sociodemographic characteristics of Latinx farmworkers in animal agriculture is extremely limited, particularly for swine and equine workers. Similar to other kinds of agricultural work, many livestock workers in the US are immigrants from Mexico and Central America. According to 2016 USDA estimates, 31% of livestock workers were born outside of the US (USDA 2018a). While the number of total hired workers, whether contract laborers or direct hires, in animal agriculture has fallen, the number of those workers born outside the US has increased (Boesson et al. 2018; USDA 2018a). The average salary for a livestock worker in the US in April 2018 was $12.78/h (USDA 2018b).

Animal agriculture work is dangerous. According to the Bureau of Labor Statistics (BLS), in 2017, there were 33 reported fatalities in dairy and milk production, 12 in poultry and egg production, and 10 in equine production (Fig. 5.3). Fatal injury data for the swine industry were not reported. Nonfatal injuries are reported as an incidence rate of number of injuries and illnesses per 100 full-time worker equivalent (FTE) employees. There were 5.5 nonfatal injuries per 100 FTE reported in dairy and milk production, 7.7 per 100 FTE in pig and hog farming, and 6.1 per 100 FTE in poultry and egg production (Fig. 5.4). Nonfatal injury data for equine production were not reported. In comparison, the incidence rate of nonfatal occupational injuries and illnesses for all private industry was only 2.8 per 100 FTE (BLS 2017b). It is important to note that there is a well-documented undercount in BLS data on nonfatal injuries and illnesses, which, in agriculture, has been attributed to exemptions for certain farms from government data sets, the fact that agricultural work is often part-time, and failure by employers to record injuries in OSHA logs (Leigh et al. 2014). One study that attempted to adjust for these factors using 2011

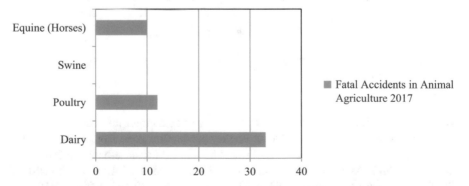

Fig. 5.3 Number of fatal accidents in animal agriculture 2017, excluding data from farms with fewer than 11 hired workers; fatality data were not reported for the swine industry (Bureau of Labor Statistics 2017a)

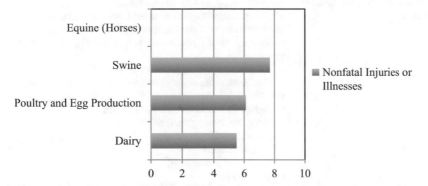

Fig. 5.4 Nonfatal injury or illness rates per 100 FTE in animal agriculture 2017, excluding data from farms with fewer than 11 hired workers; nonfatal injuries were not reported for the equine industry (Bureau of Labor Statistics 2017b)

BLS data suggested that the undercount of nonfatal injuries and illnesses in animal agriculture is severe. The authors estimated that the BLS missed 81.9% of all injuries or illnesses on animal agriculture operations that year; that is, over 68,000 injuries and illnesses occurred, rather than the BLS estimate of 12,400 (Leigh et al. 2014).

OSHA oversight in agricultural operations, including animal agriculture farms, is limited. Since 1976, OSHA has operated under the "small farm exemption," precluding OSHA from inspecting a farm "with ten or fewer non-family employees that has not maintained a temporary labor camp within the preceding twelve months" (OSHA 2014). While all farms in the US with employees are technically required to maintain the safety standards laid out in the OSH Act of 1970, no inspection or oversight program for farms fits the small farm criteria above, even if a violation of OSHA rules has been reported or if someone dies on the farm from an occupational injury (Fox et al. 2017; Wolfe 2018). Due to the lack of systematic data on numbers of Latinx workers on animal agriculture farms, it is not possible to specify how many work on farms outside of OSHA jurisdiction, but there is reason to believe the numbers are substantial. For example, it has been estimated that only 18% of New York dairy farmworkers are on farms eligible for OSHA inspections (Keller et al. 2017). Furthermore, according to statements by telephone on March 29, 2019, by representatives from both the OSHA Maryland and OSHA Harrisburg offices, OSHA coverage for swine, poultry, and equine production is limited by the lack of inspection lists specific to these operations in order to ensure worker health and safety. The incompleteness of OSHA oversight in animal agriculture has serious negative implications for the protection of farmworkers in such workplaces and presents a serious occupational injustice.

Table 5.1 Standards from the Occupational Safety and Health Act of 1970 applicable to agriculture

Parts of Sect. 1910 applicable to agriculture	
1910.142—Temporary labor camps	Proper housing for laborers includes: • Adequate drainage around the labor camp to prevent collection of water and the spread of disease by mosquito • Grounds shall be maintained clean and free of debris and trash • All laborers will be provided beds • Adequate water supply for drinking, cooking, bathing, and laundry • Adequate toilet and bathing facilities • Adequate laundry facilities • Proper sewage disposal systems • Proper lighting • Insect and pest control • First aid kit
1910.111—Storage and handling of anhydrous ammonia	• All ammonia must be contained, stored, and handled according to OSHA regulation and procedure
1910.266—Logging operations	• Mandates safety practices, means, methods, and operations for all types of logging, regardless of the end use of the wood
1910.145—Specifications for accident prevention signs and tags	• All facilities must have adequate signage detailing health and safety procedures and measures in the workplace and must be displayed according to OSHA regulation and procedure
1910.1200—Hazard communication	• All facilities must properly label all chemicals on site and make employees aware of their existence and use
1910.1027—Cadmium	• If using cadmium on site, all employees handling cadmium must be adequately trained and equipped with personal protective equipment. Cadmium must be stored according to OSHA regulation and procedure
1910.1201—Retention of DOT markings, placards, and labels	• All facilities must have adequate signage for any and all hazardous materials on site and the vehicles in which the hazardous materials are transported, and these labels must be displayed according to OSHA regulation and procedure
OSHA regulations specific to agriculture—Sect. 1928 of OSHA regulations	
1928.51–53—Rollover protection measures	• All agricultural tractors must be up to standard with the proper safety equipment according to OSHA regulation
1928.57—Guarding of farm field equipment, farmstead equipment, and cotton gins	• All farm equipment with moving parts must have safety guards to protect employees from injury or death
1928.110—Field sanitation	All facilities or fields where agricultural employees engaged in hand labor must have access to: • Potable water (suitably cool and sufficient amounts) • Toilets • Handwashing facilities

Clear information and guidelines for OSHA standards for animal agriculture are difficult to find. However, Table 5.1 demonstrates the general standards applicable to all agricultural industries, found in Sections 1910 and 1928 of the OSHA regulations. All employers must also adhere to the General Duty Clause from the OSH Act of 1970, which states that employers must "furnish to each of his employees employment and a place of employment which are free from recognized hazards that are causing or are likely to cause death or serious physical harm to his employees" (29 USC § 645.5(a)). The General Duty Clause stands in lieu of industry-specific standards. Individual inspectors use their discretion in deciding how to enforce it on US farms.

5.3 Dairy

The number of dairy farms in the US has declined dramatically from 312,095 farms in 1978 to just 54,499 farms in 2017 (Fig. 5.1). Consolidation has particularly far-reaching effects in the dairy industries of the eastern and midwestern US, with their small dairying tradition (Sexsmith 2019; Keller 2019). This consolidation has led to dramatic changes in the nature of dairy farm work in the last few decades, with significant safety ramifications for the new Latinx workforce.

While there are no systematic data available on the number of Latinx immigrants working in the dairy industry, a 2015 survey of dairy farmers estimated there are 76,968 foreign-born workers on US dairies, slightly more than half of employees (Adcock et al. 2015). A New York study found that dairy farmers claim that local laborers are no longer interested or sufficiently reliable for milking work and so they turn to Latinx immigrant labor to fill the labor gap (Sexsmith 2019). Latinx dairy farmworkers in the eastern US tend to be male Latinos who immigrated to the US from Mexico and Central America (Baker and Chappelle 2012; Fox et al. 2017; Jenkins et al. 2009; Liebman et al. 2016; Mares 2019; Schewe and White 2017; Sexsmith 2016). Existing guest worker visa programs (e.g., H2-A, see Chap. 1) cover only seasonal employment. Therefore, the absence of a guest worker visa program for dairy workers, who work year-round, suggests that the vast majority of these workers are undocumented.

5.3.1 Dairy Worker Tasks

In dairy production, Latinx workers are most often hired to milk and "push" cows, but they also often care for calves and receive promotions to herdsmen (Fox et al. 2017). A study of Latinx dairy workers in Vermont found that 91.6% were employed as milkers but also conducted other farm tasks, such as barn cleaning, feeding cattle, and care of young stock (Baker and Chappelle 2012). Latinx workers also commonly "push cows" from stables to milking parlors, either rotating shifts between milking and pushing throughout the work week or, on some large farms, exclusively working as a pusher. Caring for calves is a feminized job, often assigned to the small numbers of Latina women employed on dairy farms (Fox et al. 2017). Calf care is almost exclusively outdoor work and entails providing water, milk, and feed and monitoring health (Fox et al. 2017). Latinx workers with experience and who have learned sufficient English to communicate with the farm employer sometimes obtain promotions to herdsmen, which involves overseeing herd health and well-being (Fox et al. 2017).

Despite the turn to automated milking machines, most Latinx dairy farmworkers milk cows, a task that still requires significant round-the-clock labor inputs. Smaller farms still often milk cows manually, though most farms today have automated parlors (Douphrate et al. 2013). A dairy parlor can be arranged in several ways. The three most common parlor arrangements in the US are the herringbone (cows face away from milkers at a slight diagonal so that milking occurs from the side), parallel (cows face away from milkers and are directly adjacent to one another so that milking occurs from behind), and the rotary system (cows enter a carousel and rotate around a single milker) (Douphrate et al. 2013). The rotary system is found on the largest farms and is the most labor-efficient approach. The specific tasks entailed in milking a cow are (1) "pre-dipping" or sanitizing the teats, (2) wiping them dry with a clean cloth, (3) "stripping" or stimulating milk let-down through a gentle tugging motion and checking the pre-milk for any sign of mastitis, (4) attaching the automated milker or "cluster," (5) waiting several minutes (depending on the cow) during the milking procedure, (6) detaching the cluster, and (7) "post-dipping" or sanitizing the teats (Douphrate et al. 2013).

Several aspects of industrialized milking pose health and safety risks for Latinx farmworkers. On large farms, the milking procedures described above are managed by farm owners down to a matter of seconds in order to maximize labor efficiency and milk output (Sexsmith 2017). This emphasis on speed and efficiency poses a risk for workers because increased milking speeds call for faster repetitions of tasks and reduced rest times (Douphrate et al. 2009a, 2013). Moreover, since many farmers have increased milkings from two times per day to three to maximize production, milking parlors must be operated 24 h/day, often creating the need for a new all-night work shift that disrupts sleep routines (Sexsmith 2016, 2017). Latinx farmworkers often work these shifts because they typically live in employer-provided housing on the farm premises and are available constantly for work (Sexsmith 2019). Language barriers with their employers and the fear of speaking up when occupational safety risks are detected, often due to their undocumented legal status, exacerbates the risk of injury and death on dairy farms for Latinx workers.

OSHA has taken several measures to promote worker safety in recognition of the risks and dangers posed by dairy farming work, taking specific notice of the special risks faced by Latinx dairy workers. OSHA maintains a detailed inspection checklist specific to dairy farms referred to as the "Dairy Dozen." This list includes items from general OSHA regulations, as well as hazards more specific to work on dairy farms (Skjolaas 2015). The Dairy Dozen includes consideration of proper manure storage facilities, proper animal handling and worker positioning to avoid injury to both animals and employees, electric shock hazards, proper machinery maintenance and use (OSHA 29 CFR 1928.51 and 1928.57), hazards communication (OSHA 29 CFR 1928.21(a)(5) refers to 1910.1200), confined spaces, horizontal bunker silos, and noise protection (Skjolaas 2015). In response to high rates of occupational injuries and fatalities as well as rising dependence on Latinx workers in Wisconsin and New York, OSHA announced Local Emphasis Programs (LEPs) in these states in 2011 and 2014, respectively (Liebman et al. 2018). The LEPs entail unannounced inspections of compliance with the Dairy Dozen on a random sample of farms not meeting the OSHA small farm exemption criteria. Thus far, the LEPs have had some success in motivating farmers to make changes that improve safety for the Latinx workforces on their farms (Liebman et al. 2018).

5.4   Poultry

Poultry production involves the production of eggs and broilers (chickens raised specifically for meat). An estimated 83% of US poultry farms are located in the northeastern, Appalachian, southeastern, Delta, and Corn Belt regions (Perry, Banker and Green 1999) and are therefore part of or adjacent to the eastern US. Like most agricultural industries in the US, in recent decades, poultry production has been consolidated into fewer and larger farms (Perry et al. 1999). While it is known that the industry is dependent on foreign-born workers, information on poultry farmworkers is limited.

The work involved in egg and broiler production differs. There is almost no published literature on egg production workers. Broiler production facilities require only one operator, who is in charge of the feeding and care of eggs and poultry, as well as the maintenance of the facility (Perry et al. 1999). The operator is generally American-born and may or may not own the poultry facility (Perry et al. 1999). While larger broiler facilities are likely to employ more individuals to help distribute the work, there is limited information on their immigration statuses (Perry et al. 1999). In general, chicken production sites do not have employees and instead contract a professional chicken catching service to come collect broilers when they are ready for processing, according to a statement by telephone from a representative from the OSHA Maryland office on March 29, 2019. A small academic literature on Latinx chicken catchers details their labor process, occupational illness and injury hazards, and risk-taking behaviors on North Carolina poultry operations (Quandt et al. 2013a). The chicken catchers' tasks included forklift operation, catching chickens, latching all cages, and transporting chickens between chicken farms and processing plants (Quandt et al. 2013a). All were male, Latino, immigrant workers.

Poultry production poses particular risks to workers in the industry. The literature on the industry, not restricted to the Latinx workforce, generally lists pulmonary and respiratory illness from dust, illness from ammonia, animal handling, and hazards from equipment as risks for workers laboring in confined spaces in poultry production (Center for Rural Design 2013; Williams Ischer et al. 2017; Mora et al. 2016; Morris et al. 1991; Quandt et al. 2013b; Senthilselvan et al. 2011).

OSHA focuses most of its inspections on poultry processing facilities. There are no poultry production-specific inspection lists like the "Dairy Dozen," despite recognized risks for workers in this sector, a finding confirmed via telephone conversations with representatives from the OSHA Maryland and OSHA Harrisburg offices on March 29, 2019.

5.5   Swine

The greatest volume of swine production facilities in the US is in the Midwest and South. In 2012, Iowa, North Carolina, and Oklahoma alone produced 55% of pork in the US (USDA 2014). There has been a reduction in the number of pork production facilities, but a general increase in herd size, requiring a larger labor force in each facility (Boessen et al. 2018). Large-scale swine production occurs almost exclusively in concentrated animal feeding operations (CAFOs). Latinx workers perform tasks that include tracking and recording stages of production of each animal (e.g., farrowing); breeding; feeding; heat checking; setting up and breaking down feeders, crates, and floor mats to be moved for power washing; sow/gilt handling; treating and processing pigs; walking aisles to check on the animals; and weaning (O'Shaughnessy et al. 2009).

Little information on swine farmworkers is available. From a review of the literature, one can infer that, similar to other animal farmworkers, many employees in swine production are Latinx immigrants (Boessen et al. 2018; García-Pabón 2014; Ramos et al. 2018). Although no specific numbers are available, the Ramos et al. (2018) study of Latinx farmworkers in confined swine facilities in Missouri gives reason to believe that the employment of Latinx immigrants is increasingly the norm among swine workers in the US.

Swine production poses risks akin to those in dairy farm work. There are three principal hazard areas: animal handling, manure handling, and management of ventilation systems (Center for Rural Design 2013). Work-related symptoms reported by Latinx farmworkers in swine production facilities include "burning eyes, muscular pain, headaches, coughing, nausea, nasal congestion, and sneezing" (Ramos et al. 2018). Other health risks for individuals working in swine production include long-term respiratory ailments (O'Shaughnessy et al. 2009) and musculoskeletal disorders (Stål and Englund 2005). Many swine farms fall under OSHA's "small farm exemption" because they have so few employees and therefore do not receive OSHA inspections. Additionally, swine production facilities do not have industry-specific guidelines for operation like the Dairy Dozen.

5.6 Horses

The production and use of horses occur in all 50 states in the US. Kentucky has the largest number, with 19,000 farms and 141,800 horses and ponies (USDA 2017). The majority (67.3% in 2015) of equine operations in the US have between five and nine horses, and on 38.1% of those operations, horses are for personal or recreational use (USDA 2017). The second most common use of horses on US farms—25%—is for ranch work (USDA 2017). Because this chapter is focused on agricultural production, analysis is limited to Latinx workers in ranch work, but their significant presence on recreational stables is acknowledged, too.

The limited published information on equine workers shows that, like other farmworkers in the US, many equine workers are Latinx immigrants (Flunker et al. 2017; Swanberg et al. 2013, 2016, 2017). One study estimates that "a large proportion of the thoroughbred [horse] industry's 460,000 full-time workers are Latino or foreign-born, and over 50% of the year-round, frontline workforce on Southeast thoroughbred farms is Latino" (Swanberg et al. 2017). The majority of horse farmworkers are male; however, according to a joint survey of 225 workers by Swanberg et al. (2016) and Clouser et al. (2018), 14.2% of those workers were female. Because the labor force works year-round and no specific visa is available to the industry, one can assume that many of these workers, as in the dairy industry, are undocumented. Most activities performed by Latinx horse workers on ranches occur unmounted, not while the worker is sitting on the horse's back (Swanberg et al. 2016). The routine tasks include walking and leading horses to and from pastures and stables, mucking stalls, bringing food and water, and grooming and bathing (Swanberg et al. 2016, 2017).

Similar to dairy and swine production, working with horses poses physical risks to workers. The most common injuries reported across the literature are bruises, sprains, and cuts from horse kicks, while performing routine tasks (Bush et al. 2018; Swanberg et al. 2016, 2017). There are no studies on respiratory illnesses for horse farmworkers. However, similar to work across the agricultural industry, work-related stress and other mental health issues may pose problems for workers (Clouser et al. 2018).

5.7 Occupational Safety and Health Risks Faced by Latinx Workers in Livestock Industries

Farm work with animals is similar to crop work in that it is intensely physically demanding. However, farmworkers in animal agriculture face unique occupational health and safety hazards stemming from interaction with live animals, operating heavy machinery, working in confined spaces, and exposure to animal feed, animal waste, chemicals, and airborne endotoxins. These aspects of their jobs, coupled with the year-round nature of animal farm work, pose unique occupational safety and health risks for livestock workers.

5.7.1   Traumatic Injury

Latinx workers interacting with animals risk traumatic physical injury. The most dangerous injuries occur from being kicked or bitten by large animals like cows and horses, slipping on wet barn floors, and being injured by machinery (Mitloehner and Calvo 2008; Quandt et al. 2013a, b).

Dairy farmworkers face many risks from working with large animals and equipment in confined spaces like barns, stables, and milking parlors. In their review of workers' compensation claims among livestock workers in Colorado, Douphrate et al. (2009b: 410–411) found that "31% of all dairy injuries were associated with livestock-handling activities, and nearly 50% of these claims were associated with the worker performing a milking task in a dairy parlor." In a qualitative study of Wisconsin dairy farmworkers by Liebman et al. (2016), one worker recounts two instances of traumatic injuries on his time at the farm, revealing the recurring instances of such injuries:

> …because the first time it was the cow that landed on me. There was snow and the snow served as a cushion, so it didn't do anything to me. But this time, it was inside the pen and my ribs were pressed against a tube…. I fell down. It was painful; I had to go to the hospital….

Little information about traumatic injury among poultry workers and swine workers is available. Quandt et al. (2013b) highlight the potential for several kinds of injuries for chicken catchers, such as forklifts hitting workers; falling fan blades, water fountains, and chicken feeders to cut or otherwise injure workers; electric shock from electrical cables on the floor; and an increased risk of injury due to the fast pace of work. Additionally, Quandt et al. (2013a, b) found that workers face risk of infection due to scratches from chickens on their hands. Studies on traumatic injuries among swine production workers are still emerging. In a study of 40 swine production workers in Missouri, Ramos et al. (2018) found that 13 workers had experienced an injury on the job, ranging from broken bones, sprains and strains, and inhalation injuries, to injections/needle stabs. Of the 13 workers that responded, ten stated that an animal was the cause of their injuries, two stated that a machine was the cause, and one worker cited "other" as the main cause (Ramos et al. 2018).

Equine farmworkers also face many risks from working with large animals. In a survey of 225 Latinx farmworkers, Swanberg et al. (2016; 513) found that nearly half of all horse farmworkers experienced an injury in the previous year, "often involving a horse". Injuries often include bruises and sprains or strains in the facial and abdominal regions from being kicked or crushed by a horse while unmounted and performing routine activities (Swanberg et al. 2016). Farmworkers also reported more extreme injuries such as contusions, fractures, and abrasions or lacerations (Swanberg et al. 2016).

5.7.2 Musculoskeletal Disorders

The literature on musculoskeletal disorders or discomfort (MSD) among livestock workers is the most well-developed of the occupational safety and health concerns reviewed for this chapter. This is perhaps because the solutions to MSD, technological improvements or alterations to the work process, are easier to achieve than the more fundamental changes to the structure of work that are required to prevent traumatic injury, respiratory health, and mental health concerns. MSD is a function of the specific technology and work process and generally refers to "pain in muscles, joints, and skeletal regions" and can have both short-term and long-term effects on worker performance (Swanberg et al. 2017). Mitloehner and Calvo (2008) found that laboring in CAFOs creates an increased risk for the development of MSD issues for animal agricultural workers.

Due to repetitive motions during milking and other tasks, dairy farm laborers experience high levels of MSD, particularly in the upper back, low back, hip, knee, wrist, and hand (Douphrate et al. 2009a). Musculoskeletal symptoms (MSS) in the knees have been associated with tasks associated with working in a stanchion milking system (see Sect. 5.3) (Douphrate et al. 2009a). Douphrate et al. (2009a) argue that the stanchion milking system poses increased musculoskeletal health risks for workers in comparison with other milking systems. Additionally, Kolstrup (2012) and Stål et al. (1996) have shown that milking tasks have a greater impact on women's musculoskeletal systems than that of men. Although no literature from the US has reported on female milkers, this is an important consideration for future research. Associations between upper back, lower back, hip, knee, and wrist/hand MSS were also found with manually cleaning animal stalls; and upper back, hip, and knee symptoms were associated with greater time working on the dairy farm (Douphrate et al. 2009a).

Among poultry workers, the potential for repetitive motions, such as bending down and catching chickens, may pose long-term musculoskeletal problems (Mora et al. 2016; Quandt et al. 2006, 2013a). There is limited information about MSD among swine workers. However, Kolstrup et al. (2006) interviewed swine workers in Sweden, and 78% reported at least 1 MSD issue in the previous 12 months. The most common symptom was pain in the upper extremities, especially the shoulders and lower back, because of short stature, repetitive work, and working in awkward positions (Kolstrup et al. 2006). Equine ranch workers also experience MSD, but less frequently, as their tasks do not require much awkward, repetitive movement (Swanberg et al. 2017). However, in circumstances in which laborers are working longer hours or have a longer tenure in the equine industry, they might be more likely to develop MSD issues over time (Swanberg et al. 2017).

5.7.3   Respiratory Illness or Dysfunction

The causes for respiratory symptoms and illnesses among animal agriculture workers are similar across types of operations. Dust from animal feed, animal waste, and chemicals used in the workplace can cause both short- and long-term respiratory problems (Linaker and Smedley 2002; Mitloehner and Calvo 2008; Olson and Bark 1996). Symptoms may include inflammation, shortness of breath, wheezing, coughing, bronchial reactivity or hyperresponsiveness, and decrease in pulmonary function (Mitloehner and Calvo 2008). The air contaminants found in CAFOs are more concentrated than on smaller farms, likely with effects on worker health. According to several studies on dairy workers, engineering solutions have reduced risks to respiratory health (Nonnenmann et al. 2017). These respiratory issues appear to be prevalent among farmworkers across the US and globally, regardless of farm size (Eastman et al. 2010; Liebman et al. 2016; Linaker and Smedley 2002; Mitchell et al. 2015; Terho et al. 1985).

Although little empirical evidence exists for respiratory illness among workers in the poultry industry, several studies have outlined the potential risks of working in confined spaces with chickens. Morris et al. (1991) reported high rates of chronic respiratory symptoms among chicken catchers in confinement facilities; these symptoms included cough, phlegm, wheezing, and shortness of breath. Respiratory issues may arise due to dust and ammonia inhalation, while working in confined spaces (Williams Ischer et al. 2017; Mora et al. 2016; Senthilselvan et al. 2011). Williams Ischer et al. (2017) argue for the adoption of sprinkler cooling systems to combat dust and ammonia inhalation in these facilities.

In the swine industry, workers laboring in confined animal facilities, particularly during winter months and when working with moving animals, face increased risks for acquiring respiratory illnesses and chronic ailments (Mitloehner and Calvo 2008). O'Shaughnessy et al. (2009) found that, while toxic hydrogen sulfide poisoning may happen, workers most often experience "acute and chronic airway conditions" from exposure to dust, gases, and high levels of endotoxins, which lead to lung function decline. Ramos et al. (2018) found that respiratory issues were more prevalent and of concern to swine production workers than traumatic injuries on the job. Of the 40 employees interviewed, several cited chronic symptoms that indicate respiratory issues or illness, such as coughing (17.5%), eyes burning (25.0%), and sneezing (15.0%) (Ramos et al. 2018).

Laborers in the equine industry also experience high instances of respiratory issues. Dust samples from horse barns show a host of endotoxins (components of bacteria cell walls that are associated with inflammation), horse hair, dander, ammonia, saw dust, and hydrogen sulfide that can cause respiratory issues and illness (Bush et al. 2018; Flunker et al. 2017). In a study of 225 horse workers, Swanberg et al. (2015) found that 62% of workers presented with respiratory symptoms and 44% had a cough within the past 12 months. In a survey of 80 horse farmworkers, 79% reported experiencing any upper or lower respiratory symptoms in the past

12 months (Flunker et al. 2017). The most common symptoms were cough (56%), wheezing (24%), chest tightness (24%), shortness of breath (30%), difficulty breathing (19%), nasal irritation (30%), and throat trouble (30%) (Flunker et al. 2017). Both studies found that few workers wore dust masks while at work, and Swanberg et al. (2015) found a significant connection between not wearing a face mask and increased risk for respiratory issues.

5.7.4 Zoonotic Infections

Zoonotic infections, or zoonoses, are a potential, but understudied, hazard for livestock workers because these infections can be transmitted between animals and humans (LeJeune and Kersting 2010). Zoonotic food- and water-borne pathogens, such as *Salmonella* spp. and *Giardia*, are well-known causes of human illness and frequently have a fecal-oral transmission route.

Many emerging and reemerging infectious diseases are also zoonotic. Emerging infectious diseases are caused by pathogens that have recently been recognized as human pathogens, like Q fever. "Reemerging" infectious diseases are well known as human illnesses, like rabies or brucellosis, but are uncommon in high-income countries. They are considered reemerging because, due to climate change, globalization, or other factors, their incidence in humans in high-income countries is increasing or has the potential to increase.

Influenza causes respiratory illness in humans, birds, swine, and several other animals. Influenza A viruses are commonly known by antigenic subtype (e.g., H3N2), but different strains within each subtype usually only infect one type of animal. However, mutations and antigenic shifts can result in, for example, animal influenza strains infecting humans (CDC 2017). The result of this can be sporadic cases of human influenza caused by infection with animal strains. While this sometimes results in limited infection, as in single infections by avian H7N9 and H5N1 influenza viruses that do not spread, it sometimes results in widely spread strains, as in the 2009 H1N1 pandemic strain.

Livestock workers are more likely to have had zoonotic infections than non-livestock workers in their communities (Brennan et al. 2016; Kayali et al. 2010; Osadebe et al. 2013; Withers et al. 2002), which is in line with research conducted with abattoir workers and veterinarians (Bosch et al. 2015; Brennan et al. 2016; Dal Pozzo et al. 2017; Dreyfus et al. 2014; Lord et al. 2016). Prolonged, close contact with animals and animal waste increases the likelihood of zoonotic infection and the risk for infection by animal-only strains and pathogens that mutate and gain the ability to infect humans (Klous et al. 2016; Kreuder Johnson et al. 2015; Plowright et al. 2017). Individuals who already have poor health or are immunocompromised due to age, stress, or underlying health conditions are at the greatest risk (Kreuder Johnson et al. 2015).

5.7.5 Mental Health Disorders

Research on mental health among animal agriculture workers is limited. There is mixed evidence of depression and anxiety among Latinx workers. While these mental health problems have been found at elevated levels by some research (Baker and Chappelle 2012; Fox et al. 2017), other assessment of depression has found low levels (Griffin et al. 2019), which the authors attributed to self-selection for resilience in these workers. Animal agriculture workers in the eastern US may experience an elevated prevalence of depression and anxiety, as they tend to be geographically and socially isolated and separated for extended periods from families.

Work-related stress may also increase workers' risks of occupational injury (Griffin et al. 2019; Clouser et al. 2018; Grzywacz et al. 2009, 2014, as cited in Bush et al. 2018). This stress may be caused by productivity demands from employers, employers' inability to speak Spanish, and supervisor unfairness toward workers (Clouser et al. 2018; Griffin et al. 2019). Two dairy farmworker participants corroborated this relationship in a study on occupational hazards in dairy production by Liebman et al. (2016). One stated that: "They [owner/supervisor] pressure you. That is when accidents happen" (Liebman et al. 2016, p. 232). The other worker expanded on the issue, saying: "…because they [the owner/supervisor] only give you so many hours [in a shift] you aren't getting the work done, they are yelling at you, you have to run more when you are milking" (Liebman et al. 2016, p. 232). These quotations suggest that demands on farmworkers in the workplace can increase risk of injury, as workers are more preoccupied with achieving tasks than on their own safety. An additional stressor cited by Griffin et al. (2019) is local attitudes toward immigration. One worker in a focus group stated, "We felt better before the [2016] elections. Now things are changing, and we don't want to leave the farm as much because we worry that they will catch us any time." Information on mental health issues among swine, poultry, and horse workers is quite limited. More studies are needed to fill this gap.

5.8 Preventive and Remedial Measures for Occupational Injuries among Latinx Livestock Workers

The described occupational safety and health concerns are socially and legally constructed and, thus, often largely preventable. Workplace conditions, regulatory compliance failures, and social dynamics between workers and farmers often underlie injuries. Moreover, medical care once an injury occurs is rendered difficult to access by workers' immigration status, geographic isolation, laws and practices surrounding access to healthcare, and language barriers.

5.8.1 Safety and Health Training and Use of Personal Protective Equipment

The published literature on training activities and personal protective equipment (PPE) uptake among Latinx livestock workers is limited. Quandt et al. (2013a, b) found that very few chicken catchers receive health and safety training upon starting their jobs, yet many are forced to sign a statement saying that they have received it. Older research by Tripp et al. (1998) found that about half of swine industry employers did not plan health and safety trainings for their workers. These low training rates are comparable to other agricultural industries where training is inadequate and training mandates are under-enforced. Federal agencies often delegate enforcement to state agencies, either of convenience or because they are mandated to do so. Doing this helps ensure compliance with health and safety regulations and improves the effectiveness of regulations in reducing injury. Studies show work organization needs to be restructured to allot more time for workers to don and doff PPE, check on tools, and make any adjustments needed for efficiency and safety (Autenrieth et al. 2016; Menger et al. 2016; Rosecrance et al. 2013).

Several other factors compound the challenges of effective safety and health training for Latinx livestock workers. Language barriers can make it difficult for Latinx farmworkers to understand employers' instructions and safely carry out their tasks (Arcury et al. 2010; Fox et al. 2017; Bush et al. 2018; Hagevoort et al. 2013; Liebman et al. 2016; Clouser et al. 2018). Additionally, cultural barriers, such as differences in customary workplace environment and management, may cause confusion and dissatisfaction for farmworkers (Baker and Chappelle 2012; García-Pabón 2014).

5.8.2 Limited Access to Healthcare

Geographical isolation creates a significant healthcare access barrier for livestock workers in the eastern US farms. Worker housing often is in rural areas and sometimes far away from even small local health clinics. Additionally, language barriers, the cost of medical care, cultural ideas about medicine and illness, fear of law enforcement, and fear of termination from their jobs further solidify barriers to healthcare access for Latinx workers (Arcury and Quandt 2007; Sexsmith 2016). In this context, dairy farmworkers self-treat using simple first aid procedures for most injuries and may only go to the doctor's office as a last resort (Baker and Chappelle 2012). Workers are more likely to visit emergency rooms than to schedule appointments (Baker and Chappelle 2012). Sexsmith (2016) finds that immigrant dairy farmworkers in New York rely on their employers to drive them to the hospital and so may face language barriers in communicating the need for hospital treatment. Sometimes workers have informal networks of friends and family members nearby that they can call on for help. Farm owners and employers often want to protect their labor force but lack the resources and human resource management training to do so (Hagevoort et al. 2013; Tripp et al. 1998).

The limited literature on horse workers suggests that the healthcare situation on horse farms is similar to that in dairy. Workers fear similar perceived barriers and often opt to go to the emergency room only once an injury or illness has become severe (Swanberg et al. 2016). In the swine and poultry industries, studies of or referring to access to healthcare for Latinx workers are not available.

5.9 Justice for Latinx Livestock Workers: Research and Policy Recommendations

This chapter has conducted a review of the literature on occupational safety and health concerns faced by Latinx livestock workers, including discussions of the challenges to effective uptake of preventive measures such as training and use of PPE and of the barriers they face in accessing healthcare when needed. Latinx livestock workers in the eastern US do face, or are likely to face, occupational safety and health challenges stemming from the nature of work with animals, often large animals, in confined spaces and using heavy machinery, their social and geographic isolation, and language barriers. This concluding section outlines the research gaps in this area and provides recommendations to enhance occupational justice for Latinx livestock workers.

5.9.1 Research

There is a significant gap with regard to virtually all aspects of occupational safety and health for horse, poultry, and swine production workers, with somewhat more research on dairy workers. The most salient research gaps include the following:

- For all four industries, there is a gap in knowledge on the mental health of farmworkers. This is a critical area for research, given that working with animals may introduce forms of emotional stress not experienced in crop agriculture.
- The literature is almost completely silent on gender disparities in occupational safety and health. This does not just mean uncovering the specific occupational safety and health risks faced by women livestock workers (such as Latina women caring for calves on dairy farms). It also means that a rigorous analysis of men and masculinity norms that shape exposure to occupational safety and health concerns is needed. Literature from the construction and other industries shows that Latino masculinity norms can undermine worker safety if workers are encouraged to undertake risky behaviors or limit their use of PPE around animals, heavy machinery, and chemicals (Arcury et al. 2014; Hunt et al. 1999; Quandt et al. 1998).

- While it is known that animal agriculture workers in the eastern US are geographically and socially isolated, more research is needed to understand the impacts of this isolation on their general health. Mares (2019) has found that Latinx dairy workers in Vermont face a unique set of structural vulnerabilities that puts their food security at risk. More work in this area is needed.
- There appear to be no published studies of Latinx worker safety and health under organic animal farming in the US. Organic standards introduce changes to the labor process that could expose workers to different health and safety risks than in conventional agriculture. For example, organic dairy farmers may not dock the tails of milking cows, introducing a new risk to workers of being hit by a heavy, dirty tail.

5.9.2 Policy Recommendations

The remainder of this section provides recommendations for achieving occupational justice among farmworkers. Better technology is necessary but not sufficient to create occupational justice for Latinx animal agriculture issues. Rather, institutional changes are necessary at multiple levels, from the farm to OSHA and immigration policy.

- *Farmer investment in research and development for new, safer technologies*: There have been many improvements to technology in the last couple of decades that make farm work with animals safer for immigrant laborers. In the dairy industry, the adoption of retractable milking arms and adjustable floors reduces instances of MSD and traumatic injuries among farmworkers as they do not need to reach as far to milk the cow and risk being kicked or stepped on by the animal (Cockburn et al. 2015; Douphrate et al. 2013). Manure treatments and manure storage systems could reduce the amount of endotoxins in the air on dairy farms (Mitlochner and Calvo 2008; Manbeck et al. 2016). Engineering controls such as rail feed dispensers and surface manure scrapers have also been shown to reduce the amount of endotoxins and dust in enclosed dairy operations and subsequently reduce respiratory issues among dairy farmworkers (Nonnenmann et al. 2017). A similar technological advancement in the poultry industry of sprinkler cooling systems has also been proven to reduce dust, endotoxin, and ammonia levels in chicken production facilities and may reduce instances of respiratory illness in poultry workers (Williams Ischer et al. 2017). Flunker et al.'s (2017) research on horse farmworkers in the US indicates that the adoption of face mask usage is a simple solution to reducing respiratory illness among workers. Finally, newer construction of animal production facilities could use designs and materials that are less noise reflective and could reduce hearing problems (Mitloehner and Calvo 2008).

  Adoption of new technology by employers is difficult for a variety of reasons, including cost and cultural repudiation by older generations of farmers. Paradoxically, many of the cost-saving technologies that have led to increased concentration in the animal agricultural sectors, such as milking machinery, cause work to be more dangerous for workers (Douphrate et al. 2009a; Tripp et al. 1998). Often the championing of worker health and safety on animal agricultural farms is seen as being in direct conflict with farm efficiency and employer well-being. One study addressed this issue by undertaking a 4-year investigation in social marketing in which they sent out information to dairy farmers in Wisconsin and Maryland about cost-saving technologies that could also improve safety for workers on the farms. Researchers found that the most effective methods to encourage technological adoption was through peer-to-peer marketing via other farmers, public events, and equipment dealers (Chapman et al. 2011). Education and research and development investments that reduce the cost of new technologies are necessary in order to encourage adoption by farm employers.

- *More rigorous on-farm enforcement of work safety practices*: On the farms themselves, employers must be more involved in the enforcement of safe work practices and a healthy work environment. They must be regularly educated on current health and safety guidelines, new risk-reducing farm technologies, and human resource management. They must make sure that rigorous safety training is provided in the workers' native language by a professional or by a senior member of the farm staff. Finally, this education must be applied to the organization of work on farms to ensure efficient and safe working conditions for farm laborers. As part of this, employers must create a workplace safety culture that encourages workers to report health and safety concerns and injuries on the job.
- *Greater presence of OSHA on animal agriculture farms*: OSHA must have a greater presence on animal farms to ensure compliance with health and safety regulations. The OSHA rider that prevents the agency from conducting any of its work on small farms must be eliminated to ensure protection for all farmworkers.
- *On-farm healthcare programs for workers*: On-farm healthcare delivery by county health departments, private clinics, and community organizations are increasingly common in rural areas with high concentrations of Latinx workers. Such programs should be made more available in the rural, eastern US where workers live and work in locations that are particularly remote. Such programs often involve traveling nurses who visit farms to give vaccinations, perform basic blood tests, and do checkups. Ideally, programs offer transportation from the farm to the clinic for appointments with a doctor or specialist.
- *Improved delivery of legal aid:* Justice for farmworkers necessitates better access to legal aid. Isolation on farms and the fear of deportation limit workers' ability to receive legal assistance if they have been hurt on the job or otherwise had their legal rights violated. One measure to improve access to legal aid is to enforce farmworkers' rights to receive visitors when living in farm-provided housing.
- *Worker-led corporate responsibility programs*: Programs like the Coalition for Immokalee Workers' Fair Food Campaign or the Milk with Dignity campaign developed by Migrant Justice in Vermont are promising ways to ensure workers' perspectives and needs are incorporated into responsible supply chain governance; to promote consumer awareness about safety, health, and other employment issues in animal agriculture; and to place a rightful focus on occupational justice for workers alongside the attention to animal welfare in US livestock industries.

References

Adcock F, Anderson D, Rosson P (2015) The economic impacts of immigrant labor on U.S. dairy farms. Center for North American Studies. Available via Texas A&M University. https://www. nmpf.org/wp-content/uploads//immigration-survey-090915.pdf. Accessed 11 Jul 2019

Arcury TA, Quandt SA (2007) Delivery of health services to migrant and seasonal farmworkers. Annu Rev Public Health 28:345–363

Arcury TA, Estrada JM, Quandt SA (2010) Overcoming language and literacy barriers in safety and health training of agricultural workers. J Agromedicine 15:236–348

Arcury TA, Summers P, Carrillo L et al (2014) Occupational safety beliefs among Latino residential roofing workers. Am J Ind Med 57:718–725

Autenrieth DA, Brazile WJ, Douphrate DI et al (2016) Comparing occupational health and safety management system programming with injury rates in poultry production. J Agromedicine 21:364–372

Baker D, Chappelle D (2012) Health status and needs of Latino dairy farmworkers in Vermont. J Agromedicine 17:277–287

Boessen C, Artz G, Schulz L (2018) A baseline study of labor issues and trends in U.S. Pork Production. Des Moines, IA: National Pork Producers Council. http://nppc.org/wp-content/uploads/2018/04/Boessen-Artz-Schulz-NPPC-Labor-Study-Submitted-2018-03-07.pdf. Accessed 11 Jul 2019

Bosch T, Verkade E, van Luit M et al (2015) Transmission and persistence of livestock-associated methicillin-resistant *Staphylococcus aureus* among veterinarians and their household members. Appl Environ Microbiol 81:124–129

Brennan GI, Abbott Y, Burns A et al (2016) The emergence and spread of multiple livestock-associated clonal complex 398 methicillin-resistant and methicillin-susceptible *Staphylococcus aureus* strains among animals and humans in the Republic of Ireland, 2010–2014. PLoS One 11:e0149396

Bureau of Labor Statistics (BLS) (2017a) Fatal occupational injuries by industry and event or exposure, all United States, 2017. https://www.bls.gov/iif/oshwc/cfoi/cftb0313.htm. Accessed 11 Jul 2019

Bureau of Labor Statistics (BLS) (2017b) Incidence rates of nonfatal occupational injuries and illnesses by industry and case types, 2017. https://www.bls.gov/web/osh/summ1_00.htm. Accessed 11 Jul 2019

Bush AM, Westneat S, Browning SR et al (2018) Missed work due to occupational illness among Hispanic horse workers. J Agric Saf Health 24:89–107

Center for Rural Design (2013) Design guidelines for health and safety in animal agriculture production systems. http://umash.umn.edu/wp-content/uploads/2015/12/crd-report-final.pdf. Accessed 11 Jul 2019

Centers for Disease Control and Prevention (CDC) (2017) How the flu virus can change. https://www.cdc.gov/flu/about/viruses/change.htm. Accessed 2 Aug 2019

Chapman LJ, Brunette CM, Karsh BT et al (2011) A 4-year intervention to increase adoption of safer dairy farm working practices. Am J Ind Med 54:232–243

Clouser JM, Bush A, Gan W et al (2018) Associations of work stress, supervisor unfairness, and supervisor inability to speak Spanish with occupational injury among Latino farmworkers. J Immigr Minor Health 20:894–901

Cockburn M, Savary P, Kauke M et al (2015) Improving ergonomics in milking parlors: empirical findings for optimal working heights in five milking parlor types. J Dairy Sci 98:966–974

Dal Pozzo F, Martinelle L, Léonard P et al (2017) Q fever serological survey and associated risk factors in veterinarians, southern Belgium, 2013. Transbound Emerg Dis 64:959–966

Douphrate DI, Nonnenmann MW, Rosecrance JC (2009a) Ergonomics in industrialized dairy operations. J Agromedicine 14:406–412

Douphrate DI, Rosecrance JC, Stallones L et al (2009b) Livestock-handling injuries in agriculture: an analysis of Colorado workers' compensation data. Am J Ind Med 52:391–407

Douphrate DI, Lunner Kolstrup C, Nonnenmann MW et al (2013) Ergonomics in modern dairy practice: a review of current issues and research needs. J Agromedicine 18:198–209

Dreyfus A, Benschop J, Collins-Emerson J et al (2014) Sero-prevalence and risk factors for leptospirosis in abattoir workers in New Zealand. Int J Environ Res Public Health 11:1756–1775

Eastman C, Mitchell DC, Bennett DH et al (2010) Respiratory symptoms of California's dairy workers. Field Actions Sci Rep 2010:2

Flunker JC, Clouser JM, Mannino D et al (2017) Pulmonary function among Latino thoroughbred horse farmworkers. Am J Ind Med 60:35–44

Fox C, Fuentes R, Valdez FO et al. (2017) Milked: Immigrant farmworkers in New York State. Workers' Center of Central New York and the Worker Justice Center of New York. https://milkedny.files.wordpress.com/2017/05/milked_053017.pdf. Accessed 11 July 2019

Fraser D (2008) Animal welfare and the intensification of animal production. In: Thompson PB (ed) The ethics of intensification. Springer, Heidelberg, Germany, pp 167–189

García-Pabón J (2014) Managing Latino labor in the pork industry. Available via pork information gateway. http://porkgateway.org/resource/managing-latino-labor-in-the-pork-industry/. Accessed 11 Jul 2019

Griffin GM, Floyd EG, Dali SS et al (2019) Assessing mental health concerns of Spanish-speaking dairy farm workers. J Agromedicine 25:115–121. https://doi.org/10.1080/1059924X.2019.1656130

Hagevoort GR, Douphrate DI, Reynolds SJ (2013) A review of health and safety leadership and managerial practices on modern dairy farms. J Agromedicine 18:265–273

Hunt LM, Ojanguren RT, Schwartz N et al (1999) Balancing risks and resources: applying pesticides without using protective equipment in southern Mexico. In: Hahn RA (ed) Anthropology and public health: bridging differences in culture and society, 1st edn. Oxford University Press, Oxford, NY, pp 235–256

Jenkins PL, Stack SG, May JJ et al (2009) Growth of the Spanish-speaking workforce in the Northeast dairy industry. J Agromedicine 14:58–65

Kayali G, Ortiz EJ, Chorazy ML et al (2010) Evidence of previous avian influenza infection among US turkey workers. Zoonoses Public Health 57:265–272

Keller J (2019) Milking in the shadows: migrants and mobility in America's dairyland. Rutgers University Press, New Brunswick, NJ

Keller JC, Gray M, Harrison JL (2017) Milking workers, breaking bodies: health inequality in the dairy industry. New Labor Forum 26:36–44

Klous G, Huss A, Heederik DJJ et al (2016) Human-livestock contacts and their relationship to transmission of zoonotic pathogens, a systematic review of literature. One Health 2:65–76

Kolstrup CL (2012) Work-related musculoskeletal discomfort of dairy farmers and employed workers. J Occup Med Toxicol 7:23

Kolstrup C, Stål M, Pinzke S et al (2006) Ache, pain, and discomfort: the reward for working with many cows and sows? J Agromedicine 11:45–55

Kreuder Johnson C, Hitchens PL, Smiley Evans T et al (2015) Spillover and pandemic properties of zoonotic viruses with high host plasticity. Sci Rep 5:14830

Leigh JP, Du J, McCurdy SA (2014) An estimate of the U.S. government's undercount of nonfatal occupational injuries and illnesses in agriculture. Ann Epidemiol 24:254–259

LeJeune J, Kersting A (2010) Zoonoses: an occupational hazard for livestock workers and a public health concern for rural communities. J Agric Saf Health 16:161–179

Liebman AK, Juarez-Carrillo PM, Reyes IA et al (2016) Immigrant dairy workers' perceptions of health and safety on the farm in America's heartland. Am J Ind Med 59:227–235

Liebman A, Franko E, Reyes I et al (2018) An overview and impact assessment of OSHA large dairy local emphasis programs in New York and Wisconsin. Am J Ind Med 61:658–666

Linaker C, Smedley J (2002) Respiratory illness in agricultural workers. Occup Med (Lond) 52:451–459

Lord H, Fletcher-Lartey S, Weerasinghe G et al (2016) A Q fever cluster among workers at an abattoir in South-Western Sydney, Australia, 2015. Western Pac Surveill Response J 7:21–27

Manbeck HB, Hofstetter DW, Murphy DJ et al (2016) Online design aid for evaluating manure pit ventilation systems to reduce entry risk. Front Public Health 4:108

Mares TM (2019) Life on the other border: farmworkers and food justice in Vermont. University of California Press, Oakland, CA

Marín AJ, Grzywacz JG, Arcury TA et al (2009) Evidence of organizational injustice in poultry processing plants: possible effects on occupational health and safety among Latino workers in North Carolina. Am J Ind Med 52:37–48

Menger LM, Pezzutti F, Tellechea T et al (2016) Perceptions of health and safety among immigrant Latino/a dairy workers in the U.S. Front Public Health 4:106

Mitchell DC, Armitage TL, Schenker MB et al (2015) Particulate matter, endotoxin, and worker respiratory health on large Californian dairies. J Occup Environ Med 57:79–87

Mitloehner FM, Calvo MS (2008) Worker health and safety in concentrated animal feeding operations. J Agric Saf Health 14:163–187

Mora DC, Arcury TA, Quandt SA (2016) Good job, bad job: occupational perceptions among Latino poultry workers. Am J Ind Med 59:877–886

Morris PD, Lenhart SW, Service WS (1991) Respiratory symptoms and pulmonary function in chicken catchers in poultry confinement units. Am J Ind Med 19:195–204

Nonnenmann MW, Gimeno Ruiz de Porras D, Levin J et al (2017) Pulmonary function and airway inflammation among dairy parlor workers after exposure to inhalable aerosols. Am J Ind Med 60:255–263

O'Shaughnessy PT, Donham KJ, Peters TM et al (2009) A task-specific assessment of swine worker exposure to airborne dust. J Occup Environ Hyg 7:7–13

Occupational Safety and Health Administration (OSHA) (2014) Policy clarification on OSHA's enforcement authority at small farms. https://www.osha.gov/dep/enforcement/policy_clarification_small_farms.html. Accessed 15 Jul 2019

Olson DK, Bark SM (1996) Health hazards affecting the animal confinement farm worker. AAOHN J 44:198–204

Osadebe LU, Hanson B, Smith TC et al (2013) Prevalence and characteristics of Staphylococcus aureus in Connecticut swine and swine farmers. Zoonoses Public Health 60:234–243

Oxfam America (2015) Lives on the line: the high human cost of chicken. Washington, DC: Oxfam America. https://www.oxfamamerica.org/livesontheline/. Accessed 15 Jul 2019

People for the Ethical Treatment of Animals (PETA) (2019) Animals used for food. https://www.peta.org/issues/animals-used-for-food/. Accessed 15 Jul 2019

Perry JE, Banker DE, Green RC (1999) Broiler farms' organization, management, and performance. Resource Economics Division, Economic Research Service, U.S. Department of Agriculture, Washington, DC

Plowright RK, Parrish CR, McCallum H et al (2017) Pathways to zoonotic spillover. Nat Rev Microbiol 15:502–510

Quandt SA, Arcury TA, Austin CK et al (1998) Farmworker and farmer perceptions of farmworker agricultural chemical exposure in North Carolina. Hum Organ 57:359–368

Quandt SA, Grzywacz JG, Marin A et al (2006) Illnesses and injuries reported by Latino poultry workers in western North Carolina. Am J Ind Med 49:343–351

Quandt SA, Arcury-Quandt AE, Lawlor EJ et al (2013a) 3-D jobs and health disparities: the health implications of Latino chicken catchers' working conditions. Am J Ind Med 56:206–215

Quandt SA, Kucera KL, Haynes C et al (2013b) Occupational health outcomes for workers in the agriculture, forestry and fishing sector: implications for immigrant workers in the southeastern US. Am J Ind Med 56:940–959

Ramos AK, Fuentes A, Carvajal-Suarez M (2018) Self-reported occupational injuries and perceived occupational health problems among Latino immigrant swine confinement workers in Missouri. J Environ Public Health 2018:8710901

Ribas V (2015) On the line: slaughterhouse lives and the making of the New South. University of California Press, Oakland, CA

Rosecrance J, Tellechea T, Menger L et al (2013) Health and safety challenges associated with immigrant dairy workers. J Agric Eng 44:645–648

Schewe RL, White B (2017) Who works here? Contingent labor, nonfamily labor, and immigrant labor on U.S. dairy farms. Curr Sociol 4:429–447

Senthilselvan A, Beach J, Feddes J et al (2011) A prospective evaluation of air quality and workers' health in broiler and layer operations. Occup Environ Med 68:102–107

Sexsmith K (2016) 'But we can't call 911': undocumented immigrant farmworkers and access to social protection in New York. Oxf Dev Stud 45:96–111

Sexsmith K (2017) Milking networks for all they're worth: precarious migrant life and the process of consent on New York dairies. In: Garcia M, DuPuis EM, Mitchell D (eds) Food across borders. Rutgers University Press, New Brunswick, NJ, pp 201–218

Sexsmith K (2019) Decoding worker "reliability": modern agrarian values and immigrant labor on New York dairy farms. Rural Sociol 84:706–735. https://doi.org/10.1111/ruso.12267

Skjolaas C (2015) OSHA LEP "dairy dozen" continues for 2015–16. Available via University of Wisconsin-Madison Division of Extension. https://fyi.extension.wisc.edu/agsafety/2015/12/01/osha-lep-dairy-dozen-continues-for-2015-16/. Accessed 15 Jul 2019

Stål M, Englund JE (2005) Gender difference in prevalence of upper extremity musculoskeletal symptoms among Swedish pig farmers. J Agric Saf Health 11:7–17

Stål M, Moritz U, Gustafsson B et al (1996) Milking is a high-risk job for young females. Scand J Rehabil Med 28:95–104

Swanberg JE, Clouser JM, Browning SR et al (2013) Occupational health among Latino horse and crop workers in Kentucky: the role of work organization factors. J Agromedicine 18:312–325

Swanberg JE, Clouser JM, Gan W et al (2015) Individual and occupational characteristics associated with respiratory symptoms among Latino horse farm workers. Am J Ind Med 58:679–687

Swanberg JE, Clouser JM, Bush A et al (2016) From the horse worker's mouth: a detailed account of injuries experienced by Latino horse workers. J Immigr Minor Health 18:513–521

Swanberg J, Clouser JM, Gan W et al (2017) Poor safety climate, long work hours, and musculoskeletal discomfort among Latino horse farm workers. Arch Environ Occup Health 72:264–271

Terho EO, Husman K, Vohlonen I et al (1985) Allergy to storage mites or cow dander as a cause of rhinitis among Finnish dairy farmers. Allergy 40:23–26

Tripp RS, Shutske JM, Olson DK et al (1998) Needs assessment of employers in swine production facilities regarding employee health and safety. J Agric Saf Health 4:231–243

United States Department of Agriculture (USDA), Animal and Plant Health Inspection Service (2017) Equine 2015: changes in the U.S. equine industry, 1998–2015. Accessed July 15, 2019, from https://www.aphis.usda.gov/animal_health/nahms/equine/downloads/equine15/Eq2015_Rept2.pdf

United States Department of Agriculture (USDA), Economic Research Service (2018a) Farm labor. https://www.ers.usda.gov/topics/farm-economy/farm-labor/. Accessed 15 Jul 2019

United States Department of Agriculture (USDA), National Agricultural Statistics Service (1999) 1997 census of agriculture. http://usda.mannlib.cornell.edu/usda/AgCensusImages/1997/01/51/1997-01-51-intro.pdf. Accessed 15 Jul 2019

United States Department of Agriculture (USDA), National Agricultural Statistics Service (2004) 2002 census of agriculture. http://usda.mannlib.cornell.edu/usda/AgCensusImages/2002/01/51/2002-01-51-intro.pdf. Accessed 15 Jul 2019

United States Department of Agriculture (USDA), National Agricultural Statistics Service (2009) 2007 census of agriculture. https://www.nass.usda.gov/Publications/AgCensus/2007/Full_Report/Volume_1,_Chapter_1_US/usv1.pdf. Accessed 15 Jul 2019

United States Department of Agriculture (USDA), National Agricultural Statistics Service (2014) 2012 census of agriculture. https://www.nass.usda.gov/Publications/AgCensus/2012/Full_Report/Volume_1,_Chapter_1_US/usv1.pdf. Accessed 15 Jul 2019

United States Department of Agriculture (USDA), National Agricultural Statistics Service (2019) 2017 census of agriculture. https://www.nass.usda.gov/Publications/AgCensus/2017/Full_Report/Volume_1,_Chapter_1_US/usv1.pdf. Accessed 15 Jul 2019

United States Department of Agriculture (USDA), National Agricultural Statistics Service, Agricultural Statistics Board (2012) Farm labor. https://www.nass.usda.gov/Publications/Todays_Reports/reports/fmla1112.txt. Accessed 15 Jul 2019

United States Department of Agriculture (USDA), National Agricultural Statistics Service, Agricultural Statistics Board (2018b) Farm labor. https://downloads.usda.library.cornell.edu/usda-esmis/files/x920fw89s/hd76s1508/4j03d115j/FarmLabo-05-17-2018.pdf. Accessed 15 Jul 2019

United States Department of Commerce (USDC), Bureau of the Census (1981) 1978 census of agriculture. http://usda.mannlib.cornell.edu/usda/AgCensusImages/1978/01/51/1978-01-51-intro.pdf. Accessed 15 Jul 2019

United States Department of Commerce (USDC), Bureau of the Census (1984) 1982 census of agriculture. http://usda.mannlib.cornell.edu/usda/AgCensusImages/1982/01/51/1982-01-51.pdf. Accessed 15 Jul 2019

United States Department of Commerce (USDC), Bureau of the Census (1989) 1987 census of agriculture. http://usda.mannlib.cornell.edu/usda/AgCensusImages/1987/01/51/1987-01-51-intro.pdf. Accessed 15 Jul 2019

United States Department of Commerce (USDC), Bureau of the Census (1994) 1992 census of agriculture. http://usda.mannlib.cornell.edu/usda/AgCensusImages/1992/01/51/1992-01-51-intro.pdf. Accessed 15 Jul 2019

Williams Ischer S, Farnell MB, Tabler GT et al (2017) Evaluation of a sprinkler cooling system on inhalable dust and ammonia concentrations in broiler chicken production. J Occup Environ Hyg 14:40–48

Withers MR, Correa MT, Morrow M et al (2002) Antibody levels to hepatitis E virus in North Carolina swine workers, non-swine workers, swine, and murids. Am J Trop Med Hyg 66:384–388

Wolfe E (2018) When workers are killed on small farms, OSHA's hands are tied. Available via salon. https://www.salon.com/2018/12/08/when-workers-are-killed-on-small-farms-oshas-hands-are-tied_partner/. Accessed 15 Jul 2019

Chapter 6
The Health of Women Farmworkers and Women in Farmworker Families in the Eastern United States

Sara A. Quandt, Hannah T. Kinzer, Grisel Trejo, Dana C. Mora, and Joanne C. Sandberg

6.1 Introduction

Women are integral members of the farmworker community, both as farmworkers themselves and as members of households that contain one or more farmworkers. Nationwide, the percentage of women in farm work has steadily increased from 21% in 2001 to 32% in 2016 (USDOL 2005, 2016). The increase is attributed to both increased opportunity for young men in other sectors of the economy and the increased adoption of mechanical aids that allow women to perform jobs previously done by young men (USDA 2019). Women in the farmworker community are exposed to dangerous chemicals and pesticides and, for those who do crop work, physical demands and grueling workday hours. Women farmworkers also experience sexual harassment and abuse in the workplace. In addition to any paid employment, women in this community who are employed as farmworkers or in other occupations have primary responsibility for domestic work and family care. At home, they may be subject to intimate partner violence.

Women who are undocumented themselves or who have family members with them in the United States (US) who are undocumented may be particularly vulnerable. At the same time, they and their family often have very limited financial resources, and most lack access to healthcare. Farmworker women experience substantial rates of mental illness. Few studies have sought to examine the experiences

S. A. Quandt (✉)
Department of Epidemiology and Prevention, Division of Public Health Sciences, Wake Forest School of Medicine, Winston-Salem, NC, USA

H. T. Kinzer
School of Public Health, University of Minnesota, Minneapolis, MN, USA

G. Trejo · D. C. Mora · J. C. Sandberg
Department of Family and Community Medicine, Wake Forest School of Medicine, Winston-Salem, NC, USA

© Springer Nature Switzerland AG 2020
T. A. Arcury, S. A. Quandt (eds.), *Latinx Farmworkers in the Eastern United States*, https://doi.org/10.1007/978-3-030-36643-8_6

of women in the farmworker community, in the workplace, and in US society and how those experiences impact their health and well-being. Even less research has been conducted on farmworker women and women in farmworker families in the eastern US. Little of the existing research takes a social justice approach.

This chapter summarizes current research on the physical and mental health of women in the farmworking community, including those who do farm work. It will also consider policy and public health interventions to improve these unjust conditions. Finally, it will consider how much is known about women in farmworker communities in the eastern US and make recommendations in the areas of research, policy, and practice.

6.2 Characteristics of Women Farmworkers and Women in Farmworker Families

Women comprise a minority of Latinx farmworkers nationwide. Data from the 2015–2016 National Agricultural Workers Survey (NAWS), which used an employer-based sampling strategy, indicate that 32% and 40%, respectively, of US and Eastern Region farmworkers are women (USDOL 2016). The numbers for the Eastern Region may be slightly inflated, as the NAWS excludes farmworkers with H-2A visas, most of whom are men and many of whom work in the eastern US (see Chap. 2). The average age of Eastern Region women farm laborers is 35 years old; their mean educational attainment is 9.5 years. Most were born in Mexico (47%), the US (39%), or Central America (9%). A minority of Eastern Region farmworker women (16%) are migrant workers, i.e., they travel more than 75 miles to find work. As reported in a study of farmworker households with young children in North Carolina, most women (60.9%) in farmworker households are in the labor force, with farm work being the most common occupation (Arcury et al. 2015b).

6.2.1 Social, Socioeconomic, and Domestic Context

The eastern US, particularly the Southeast, has long been home to agriculture that is dependent on large amounts of low-cost labor. While early agriculture depended on slaves of African origin, subsequent production relied on African American and white tenant farmers. Today, agricultural production relies on the labor of seasonal and migrant workers who are predominantly Latinx. Throughout this history, the social context of agriculture has been characterized by white domination over workers who have largely been people of color. These systems of production have fostered, maintained, and exacerbated strong racist and nativist sentiments, reinforced by laws and by social institutions that promote discrimination.

Within this backdrop of racism and discrimination, the socioeconomic status of the Latinx farmworker community exerts effects that have health ramifications.

Poverty and concerns about documentation status, either their own or that of family members, create stress for farmworkers (see Chap. 4). One-third of farmworker families nationwide and one-third of Eastern Region Latina farmworkers reported living below the poverty threshold in 2016 (USDOL 2016). The threat of deportation for undocumented farmworkers can increase stress from poverty. Even if they are eligible, farmworker families are significantly less likely to access social safety net programs like SNAP (Supplemental Nutrition Assistance Program) due to poverty status and concerns about legal documentation (Padilla et al. 2014). Less than 1% of all farmworkers use general assistance welfare, 2% use social security, and less than 15% use Medicaid (USDOL 2016). The impact of financial distress and documentation status may therefore be extreme. Additionally, farmworker women face discrimination and harassment in the workplace including wage theft, sexual harassment, and a lack of a reliable reporting system. Furthermore, many farmworker women and women in farmworker households have substantial domestic demands, and they experience social and linguistic isolation (TePoel et al. 2017).

Despite contextual factors that affect health, women in farmworker communities face restricted access to health services. They often lack health insurance and money to pay for care, have limited transportation in rural areas without adequate public transportation, experience language barriers, and lack knowledge about health resources available. Lack of documentation of selves or a family member may also serve as a barrier to seeking or receiving health services. Few employers provide health insurance.

6.2.1.1   Documentation Status

Accurate data regarding the percentage of undocumented women in the farmworker community are difficult to obtain. Data from an employer-based sample indicate that slightly fewer than half (47%) of Eastern Region Latina farmworkers lack documentation (USDOL 2016). However, these data may underrepresent the presence of a number of undocumented workers. For example, a recent North Carolina study reports that 89% of women in the farmworker community, i.e., farmworkers or women in a farmworker household, are undocumented (Arcury et al. 2015b). Undocumented farmworker women experience substantial stress due to lack of work permits and concerns about potential deportation (Fox and Kim-Godwin 2011). Furthermore, Latinas who share households with undocumented immigrants may also experience elevated stress.

Undocumented farmworkers have less secure work, have more onerous work tasks, earn less money, have less access to healthcare, have less health insurance coverage, and are more likely to live in poverty than documented Latinx farmworkers (Reid and Schenker 2016). The position of an undocumented female farmworker is even more tenuous. When compared to their male counterparts, they tend to have less secure employment, are more likely to be a seasonal vs. year-round worker, and are more likely to have a family income below the poverty level (Fox and Kim-Godwin 2011).

6.2.1.2   Workplace Harassment and Discrimination

Unfair Labor Practices and Discrimination

Latina farmworkers experience workplace harassment, discrimination, and unfair labor practices. The National Labor Relations Act and the Fair Labor Standards Act exempt farmworkers from many protections, making farmworkers vulnerable to some types of abuse, including discrimination and wage theft (Robinson et al. 2011; see Chaps. 2 and 9). The degree of authority crew leaders and other supervisors hold over workers, especially undocumented workers who have limited employment options, bolsters an environment of abuse (Human Rights Watch 2012). While undocumented female farmworkers are entitled to minimum wage under the Fair Labor Standards Act, many are fearful of being reported to immigration authorities or losing their livelihood if they complain about their employer (Bauer and Ramírez 2010). Thus, wage theft, including less or no pay for hours worked, is widespread.

Latina farmworkers also face unfair labor practices due to gender discrimination. Employment rates indicate that employers have historically preferred men for most farm work, and most current field teams and supervisory roles are male dominated (Dominguez 1997; Waugh 2010). Employers often give fewer opportunities for advancement, fewer hours, and less favorable assignments to women. Some Latina farmworkers are paid on a male relative's paycheck, limiting their financial independence (Bauer and Ramírez 2010). Often, female farmworkers are the first to be laid off. Foreign-born farmworker women, both documented and undocumented, are more likely to perform preharvest and harvest tasks, be contracted by a farm labor contractor, earn less, and be paid piece rate than US-born farmworker women (Reid and Schenker 2016). Payment by piece rate rather than hourly pay puts women at a disadvantage if they are smaller or slower than men. When Latina farmworkers do question the discrepancies, they are ignored, fired, or threatened with being reported to immigration authorities (Bauer and Ramírez 2010).

Harassment

Latina farmworkers are vulnerable to sexual harassment and assault at their worksite. The limited amount of research on sexual harassment among Latina farmworkers suggests that it is widespread, with one report indicating that 80% of this population has been sexually harassed at work (Bauer and Ramírez 2010; Human Rights Watch 2012; Kim et al. 2016; Murphy et al. 2015; Waugh 2010,).

Harassment and Workplace Environment. Working conditions that conceal harassers' behaviors from others nearby, such as laboring alone in remote fields or in between rows of tall crops, can enable male co-workers and supervisors to sexually harass these women without detection (Waugh 2010). Furthermore, farmworkers are often required to bend over, climb, and crawl for their work. For farmworker women, assuming the positions necessary to do their job increases their risk of being sexually harassed by their male co-workers. Indigenous status, poverty, age, and marital status may influence farmworker women's susceptibility to sexual harassment and assault. Young, single, and indigenous women living in poverty may be targeted more often due to their lower social status, discrimination against indigenous groups, and heightened need to keep their jobs (Murphy et al. 2015).

Types of Harassment. Female farmworkers face sexual harassment in the forms of gender harassment, unwanted sexual attention, and sexual coercion (Waugh 2010). Gender harassment, including sexist, degrading, and insulting comments or behaviors, is common. In a sample of Mexican female farmworkers working in California, 97% of respondents who experienced sexual harassment reported gender harassment from co-workers and superiors (Waugh 2010). Unwanted sexual attention ranges from inappropriate verbal or physical advances to grabbing and rape. Waugh (2010) found that more than half (53%) of respondents who were sexually harassed experienced unwanted sexual attention. Sexual coercion includes blackmail and demands of sexual favors in exchange for advancement in the workplace. Waugh (2010) found that almost a quarter (24%) of respondents experienced sexual coercion. Sexual coercion is so common that fellow farmworkers often assume women who receive preferential treatment by supervisors have provided sexual favors (Human Rights Watch 2012). Those assigned to more strenuous or lower-paying tasks are assumed to have rejected sexual advances.

Barriers to Reporting. Sexual harassment is underreported. Stigma, fear of retaliation, and dismissal are well-known barriers to reporting. Latina farmworkers face even more barriers to reporting including living in rural isolated areas, little access to legal help, limited knowledge of US laws, fear of deportation, and loss of vital family income. Many do not know whom to trust or to whom they can report the incident (Murphy et al. 2015). Often, women work at the same sites as their relatives and the perpetrator's relatives; therefore, they risk social ostracism, losing their reputation, and criticism from family members if they report an incident. Waugh (2010) found that almost a quarter (22%) of Mexican female farmworkers in the study told no one about their incidents of sexual harassment. Furthermore, many farmworker women are reluctant to report harassment due to fear of retaliation against other family members employed by the same contractor. Women who do report their incidents of harassment have been dismissed, lost their reputation, been evicted from employer-provided housing, and been fired along with their family members (Human Rights Watch 2012).

Reduction and Coping Strategies. Many farmworker women tolerate harassment to keep their jobs. These women may use a variety of strategies to reduce harassment such as confronting the perpetrator, avoiding or ignoring perpetrators, wearing shapeless clothing, and calling on social contacts for support or protection. Waugh (2010) found that almost half (46%) of the women they interviewed confronted the perpetrator, asking them to stop the behavior or threatening to tell a superior. Almost a quarter (21%) reported ignoring the perpetrator. Additionally, female farmworkers often mask their bodies with baggy pants and shirts tied around their waists to cover their buttocks. In addition, they often cover their face with kerchiefs, wear bulky shirts, and do not wear makeup while working (Fig. 6.1). The layers of clothing cover the body from unwanted gazes and signal to fellow female co-workers that an

Fig. 6.1 South Carolina
farmworker in onion fields
(Photo by Lucero Galvan
and Guillermo Alvarado.
Published with kind
permission of © Student
Action with Farmworkers
2012. All Rights Reserved)

individual is virtuous (Castañeda and Zavella 2003). Family and friends who do
support a woman during incidents of harassment may accompany her to work, quit
their job along with her, confront the perpetrator, or encourage her to confront the
perpetrator. Others may console the individual but have little ability to change her
work conditions.

The Fair Food Program, in recognition of the problems with sexual harassment
and assault, has made the protection of women one of the key elements of its Fair
Food Agreements (CIW 2012). Under the Fair Food Code of Conduct, employers
are required to create a complaint resolution system for farmworkers and conduct
trainings to educate workers on their rights against sexual harassment. Furthermore,
market pressure holds growers directly accountable as growers lose business from
large grocery stores if incidents of sexual harassment occur. While improvements
have been made through this agreement, only a small portion of the total number of
growers participate in this agreement. More work still needs to be done to ensure
that the rights of women farmworkers are not violated.

6.2.1.3 Domestic Obligations

Many Latina farmworkers and women in farmworker households have substantial
domestic obligations associated with being a wife or mother. More than two-thirds
(66%) of Eastern Region Latina farmworkers are married (USDOL 2016). Women
who labor as farmworkers or are part of farmworker households bear primary
responsibility for housework such as cleaning, laundry, and meal preparation, even
after long work hours of paid labor (Quandt et al. 2014). The competition between

work and domestic obligations may be particularly acute for these women and may result in elevated levels of work-family conflict compared to their male counterparts (TePoel et al. 2017). Latina farmworkers with children bear most of the child-rearing responsibilities (TePoel et al. 2017). Most (66%) Eastern Region farmworker women have at least one child in their household; almost one-quarter of Eastern Region farmworker women have a child younger than 6 years of age in their household and therefore have substantial child-rearing responsibilities compared to those with older children (USDOL 2016).

Finding and securing affordable childcare for young children can be a great source of stress and a limiting factor for seeking employment in farm work or other occupations. Many farmworker families live in rural areas with limited childcare options. They rely primarily on informal and unlicensed childcare providers such as babysitters, family members, and neighbors (Liebman et al. 2017). Even if they are licensed, mothers may be skeptical of caregivers outside of their network (Reschke 2012). Requirements regarding migration status or income, lack of available slots at childcare centers, and difficulty completing applications for services due to language barriers and unfamiliarity with the system limit access to some programs. As demonstrated in a survey of Florida farmworker mothers, transportation and inconsistent or long work hours pose challenges to those who have arranged for childcare (Liebman et al. 2017). Furthermore, maintaining childcare organizations and retaining staff members available for this population is challenging given the seasonality of their work (Liebman et al. 2014). Migrant and Seasonal Head Start is a program to accommodate the migrant lifestyle and limited resources of farmworker families, but it is unable to meet the needs of all migrant and seasonal families who are eligible due to the limited number of sites (O'Brien et al. 2011; Liebman et al. 2017). Farmworker women who cannot find or afford childcare often stay home to take care of children, and they may resort to taking the children to the fields with them. This may distract the woman from her work and places children in danger (see Chap. 5).

6.2.1.4 Physical, Social, and Linguistic Barriers in Community of Residence

Many Latina farmworkers and Latinas in farmworker households experience considerable physical and social isolation while in the US. They usually live in rural communities, sometimes at considerable distance from other persons and from other Latinas, thereby fostering social isolation. Even if they have access to cars, they are often reluctant to drive for fear of being stopped to have documents checked (Quandt et al. 2014). Limited English fluency impedes communication and development of friendships with proximal non-Spanish-speaking neighbors and interactions with the community at large, adding to the isolation. Low English fluency and literacy also makes it very difficult for women in the farmworker community to identify, access, and successfully navigate services in their communities to address housing, insurance, healthcare, and schooling; lack of English and literacy skills

Fig. 6.2 North Carolina
farmworker (Photo by
Koehler Briceño.
Published with kind
permission of © Student
Action with Farmworkers
2009. All Rights Reserved)

contributes to elevated levels of stress (Fox and Kim-Godwin 2011). Linguistic barriers may be even greater for indigenous Latina women from southern Mexico and Central America, for whom Spanish is their second language, if spoken at all. The percentage of Latina farmworkers from Mexico and Central America who report speaking and reading English not at all or a little is 58% and 42%, respectively (USDOL 2016). English fluency is even lower among indigenous Latina farmworkers (Fox and Kim-Godwin 2011; Reid and Schenker 2016). The lack of English or Spanish proficiency and available interpreters often adds a layer of isolation for these women, even within the Latinx community (Reid and Schenker 2016) (Fig. 6.2).

6.3 Health

Although women make up a third of farmworkers and an unknown number are present in farmworker communities as family members who do not participate in farm work, the literature on their health is sparse. For women in the eastern US, there is even less documentation.

Occupational hazards that Latina farmworkers are subject to include heat-related illness (HRI), musculoskeletal injuries, and pesticide poisoning. Especially during periods of high temperatures and humidity, few breaks and inadequate workplace amenities put farmworkers in the southeastern US at particularly high risk of HRI. While research on musculoskeletal injuries among Latina farmworkers is limited, assignment to fast-paced and repetitive tasks, use of tools designed for men, and workplace harassment may contribute to risk of musculoskeletal injuries.

Many Latina farmworkers work during their childbearing years. Pesticide exposure is known to affect the health of women farmworkers and their children during pregnancy. Additional challenges to the reproductive health of these women include breast cancer, cervical cancer, human immunodeficiency virus (HIV), and other sexually transmitted infections (STIs). Barriers to cancer screening and limited health knowledge contribute to reproductive health issues in this population.

Stress from family conflict, domestic abuse, workplace conditions, job insecurity, and immigration status contribute to depression among Latina farmworker women (see Chap. 4). Many of these women experience considerable isolation while in the US (Fox and Kim-Godwin 2011; Reid and Schenker 2016).

6.3.1   Occupational Injuries and Exposures

HRI, musculoskeletal injuries, and pesticide exposure are known occupational health problems among farmworkers. However, knowledge about incidence of occupational injuries among Latina farmworkers is limited. Women are less likely to have secure employment than men (Reid and Schenker 2016). Quinlan et al. (2001) found that part-time, temporary, and other contingent work arrangements are associated with greater hazard exposure and injury rates and with lower worker knowledge of occupational safety and health. The findings suggest that women may experience more injuries and receive less safety training than men. Latina farmworkers have higher rates of HRI and acute pesticide-related illnesses than do male farmworkers.

6.3.1.1   Heat Stress

HRI is an occupational hazard for women laboring in the fields, greenhouses, or ferneries. During the summer months, the mid- and southeastern US can see temperatures in the high 90s and that even exceed 100° F. Especially when combined with high humidity, periods of extreme heat in this region can cause HRI in workers. Climate change is expected to increase temperatures, thereby increasing risk of HRI. Physical exertion and being in direct sunlight increase heat exposure; lack of adequate access to water, shade, and rest breaks also contributes to the development of HRI (Arcury et al. 2015a). Unlike California and Washington, none of the states in the eastern US have a heat standard requiring employers to provide shade or extra breaks in periods of high temperatures.

HRI symptoms include heavy sweating, headaches, dizziness, muscle cramps, nausea and vomiting, fainting, and confusion. A survey of predominantly Latinx farmworkers in Florida, 61% of whom were female, indicated that 40% of participants had reported at least three symptoms during the prior week (Mutic et al. 2018). Women farmworkers had three times the odds of experiencing three or more heat-related symptoms than men, controlling for health and work characteristics. This greater odds of HRI symptoms can be due to lower water intake, a strategy some women employ if toilets are not available, or the heavy clothing some women wear as protection from sexual harassment. Women's higher percentage of body fat may result in greater heat retention than men. Hyperthermia, heat exhaustion, stroke, and even death can result if the core body temperature exceeds the body's ability to dissipate heat.

Attention has recently focused on chronic kidney disease (CKD) and the associated condition of acute kidney injury (AKI). Both heat stress and dehydration are associated with development of kidney stones and chronic kidney disease. They can ultimately result in kidney failure (Nerbass et al. 2017). It has been hypothesized that repeated dehydration and resulting volume depletion leads to CKD. Among a predominantly Latinx sample of agricultural workers in Florida, a majority of whom were female, almost one-third of participants experienced decreased kidney function across the workday on at least 1 of the 3 days for which measurements were obtained (Mix et al. 2018). Women were less likely to be dehydrated than men; fernery and field crop workers were more likely than nursery workers to be dehydrated. Among women farmworkers in California, neither heat strain nor being overweight was associated with AKI (Moyce et al. 2017). Being paid piece rate and years in agricultural work were associated with an increased risk of having AKI.

6.3.1.2 Musculoskeletal Injuries

Musculoskeletal disorders (MSDs) are injuries to the bones, nerves, ligaments, joints, cartilage, and spinal discs. MSDs often occur when the body reacts to sudden or strenuous movements such as bending, climbing, crawling, reaching, or twisting or to overexertion of repetitive motion (Mora et al. 2016). High rates of MSDs have a significant impact on work productivity and work absenteeism (Summers et al. 2015). Agriculture had the highest incidence of nonfatal occupational injuries and illnesses (including MSDs) in the US in 2017 (U.S. Bureau of Labor Statistics 2017). Gender is a risk factor associated with the development of MSDs (Treaster and Burr 2004; Hamilton et al. 2019). In women, pregnancy is a major risk factor for carpal tunnel syndrome (Ganjoo et al. 2018). In a study of vineyard workers in Oregon, 75% of women reported a musculoskeletal symptom compared to only 45% of the male farmworkers (Brumitt et al. 2011). In a study on agricultural work and chronic musculoskeletal pain among Latinx farmworkers in California, Xiao et al. (2013) reported that women have a higher prevalence of chronic pain in the hips, hands, neck, and fingers and it increased with age. For women, stooping or bending for more than 30 h/week was significantly associated with chronic pain, and kneeling and crawling for more than 35 h/week were associated with back pain and knee pain, respectively. In a study among male farmworkers in southern Georgia, 81.9% of the participants reported pain most often localized in the back (Brock et al. 2012). Fatigue and tiredness were stated as the cause of pain by the workers, and the workers further agreed that they had little freedom in deciding how to do their work.

However, data on the types and incidence of MSDs among women farmworkers are scant. Research on Latina manual workers (including poultry, construction, and manufacturing workers) in North Carolina found that the most commonly reported MSDs were epicondylitis, rotator cuff syndrome, back pain, and carpal tunnel syndrome (Arcury et al. 2014a). Awkward posture, psychological demand, decreased skill variety, and decreased job control were related to carpal tunnel syndrome. There was no strong difference in the proportion of MSD diagnoses between the all-female study sample and a previously studied larger sample of men and women manual laborers.

While little is known about Latina farmworker MSD incident rates, women engaging in farm work, especially those who are undocumented or indigenous, tend to work in preharvest and harvest tasks. These tasks are typically more physically taxing and therefore place women at increased risk of developing MSDs (Reid and Schenker 2016). Although tasks that women workers perform can sometimes be perceived as less physically demanding, they tend to be fast-paced. Such tasks require precision and involve repetitive use of small muscles (Treaster and Burr 2004). Additionally, women farmworkers must often work with tools that are designed for men, making women more likely to develop MSDs (Habib et al. 2014; Treaster and Burr 2004). In addition to physical factors, women are exposed to psychological stressors. Women face verbal and physical harassment as well as sexual assault, particularly from farm labor contractors and those who provide transportation to work (Reid and Schenker 2016). Stress can result in release of epinephrine which increases individuals' risk of injury. In a study by Arcury et al. (2012), workers who perceived a less safe work climate had a higher risk of experiencing musculoskeletal discomfort. Additionally, women are often responsible for performing household chores that could further exacerbate the MSDs. Work safety climate is important to the occupational health of Latina farmworkers.

6.3.1.3   Pesticide Exposure

Most workplace pesticide exposure among women farmworkers is due to pesticide drift away from the treatment site or contact with pesticide residue on a treated surface (Kasner et al. 2012). In addition to occupational pesticide exposure, both farmworker women and women in farmworker households may be exposed to pesticides through pesticide drift from agricultural fields near their homes to the residence. They may also be exposed to pesticides that enter their home on the skin, clothing, shoes, and tools of family members. Residential pesticide use can also be an exposure route.

Acute effects of pesticide exposure include headaches, dizziness, nausea, rash, and eye irritation. Except among pesticide handlers, women farmworkers have a higher acute pesticide-related illness and injury rate than men (Kasner et al. 2012). This may be explained by women, in general, having smaller body sizes than men. Smaller individuals often have greater pesticide doses due to a greater surface area to volume ratio. Long-term health effects of pesticide exposure include an increased risk of developing cancers, neurological diseases—such as Alzheimer's disease, Parkinson's disease, and amyotrophic lateral sclerosis—and respiratory diseases including asthma and chronic bronchitis (Mostafalou and Abdollahi 2017). Exposure to pesticides widely used in agriculture has also been linked to reduced female (and male) fertility (Snijder et al. 2012).

Although little is known about the outcome of exposure to pesticide residues on plants, it may contribute to the development of skin rashes on farmworkers. Handwashing, personal protective equipment, and good hygiene are methods by which workers protect themselves from pesticide residue. Campbell et al. (2017) found that greater access to handwashing facilities for fernery and nursery workers lowered the risk of skin rashes. Pregnant farmworkers may have an increased risk of developing skin rashes associated with their work. Among nursery and fernery workers, pregnant women were more likely than non-pregnant women to report skin rashes (Campbell et al. 2017). Pregnancy results in physiological changes, including changes to growth factor levels and blood flow, and can worsen skin conditions.

Researchers tested for the presence of 11 organophosphorous (OP) and 14 pyrethroid pesticides in 176 North Carolina migrant farmworker houses; one or more females lived in approximately a quarter of the houses tested (Arcury et al. 2014c). OPs and pyrethroids were found in all but ten and five houses, respectively, with a mean of 2.4 and 4.3 pesticides, respectively. Having a female resident was not significantly associated with the presence of any of the OPs or pyrethroids, suggesting that the contamination of housing is not dependent on or prevented by specific female behaviors.

6.3.2   Reproductive Health

Farmworker women often face reproductive oppression. This is the regulation of their reproduction and exploitation of their bodies and labor as a result of long-standing systems of oppression based on race, class, gender, sexuality, ability, age, and immigration status. This oppression is manifest through their exposure to factors such as work, family, community, and national and international policies that have direct or indirect consequences on their physical and mental health, their economic conditions, and the wellbeing of them and their families (Galarneau 2013).

Although many female farmworkers work during their childbearing years, there is limited information on factors affecting pregnancy and childbirth in this population. Pesticide exposure and the physical demands of work may affect pregnancy outcomes. Additionally, breast and cervical cancer are challenges to female farmworker reproductive health. However, research on cancer incidence among Latina farmworkers is limited. Breast cancer survival rates are lower among Latinas than non-Latina white women, and cervical cancer incidence in Latinas is higher than in other minorities (Cronin et al. 2018). Obstacles to cancer screening, including schedule conflicts, transportation, limited health knowledge, and language barriers, likely contribute to cancer outcomes among Latina farmworkers.

6.3.2.1   Pregnancy

Substantial numbers of women in prime childbearing years work as farmworkers or live with farmworkers. The mean age of farmworkers is 38, and slightly fewer than half (44%) are 35 years old and under (USDOL 2016). Limited research has been conducted on pregnancy among farmworker women or women in the farmworking community in the eastern US. Female farmworkers are exposed to the same elevated occupational risks and dangerous hazards as their male counterparts. Occupational risk factors that may harm the health of the pregnant mother or fetus include heavy lifting, elevated temperatures, and pesticide exposure. Although not focused on agricultural work, research by Runge et al. (2013) shows that heavy lifting is associated with preterm birth. Additional research on non-farmworkers indicates a relationship between exposure to elevated temperatures and increased risk of premature birth, premature rupture of membranes, birth weight, neonatal stress, and congenital heart defects (Auger et al. 2014; Kuehn and McCormick 2017; Lin et al. 2018). These findings suggest that farm work poses risks to developing fetuses.

Pesticide exposure during pregnancy can be hazardous to developing embryos and fetuses. Although the findings are not uniform, in utero pesticide exposure has been associated with behavioral and cognitive challenges in both non-farmworker and farmworker populations in an agricultural region in California (Eskenazi et al. 2007; Gunier et al. 2017; Marks et al. 2010; Sagiv et al. 2018; see Chap. 3). There is some evidence in the North Carolina general population that maternal residential exposure during preconception and pregnancy is associated with a number of different types of birth defects (Rappazzo et al. 2016), but it is likely that the small size and mobility of the farmworker population will prevent assessment of such findings among farmworker women.

6.3.2.2   Reproductive Cancers

Breast Cancer

Research regarding the association between pesticide exposure and the development of breast cancer is mixed (Lerro et al. 2012; Fenga 2016). A recent analysis based on Agricultural Health Study data reported that personal use (e.g., mixing or applying) of two specific pesticides, chlorpyrifos or terbufos, was significantly associated with an increased risk of developing breast cancer; risk associated with exposure to some pesticides may vary by menopausal status (Engel et al. 2017). Latinas are at lower risk of breast cancer than non-Latina white women (Cronin et al. 2018). This may be due to a number of factors, including earlier first birth and greater parity among Latinas (Sweeney et al. 2008). Despite the reduced risk of developing breast cancer among Latinas relative to non-Latinas, it is the top cause of cancer deaths among Latinas (Cronin et al. 2018). Hispanic women also have lower 5-year survival rates from breast cancer compared to non-Hispanic whites (Palmer et al. 2005).

Lower breast cancer survival rates for Latina farmworkers have been attributed to underuse of mammograms to screen for breast cancer. The US Preventive Services Task Force currently recommends that women with average risk of breast cancer aged 50–74 get a mammogram every 2 years (CDC 2019b). In a study of 200 Hispanic women over 50 years old and living in a farmworker community in the Lower Rio Grande Valley of Texas, Palmer et al. (2005) found that fewer than half (38%) of participants adhered to screening guidelines.

Research on knowledge about breast cancer and breast cancer screening guidelines among Latina farmworkers is mixed. Compared to permanent Latina residents, Latinas working as migrant farmworkers in Maryland had less knowledge about factors that contribute to breast cancer (Schlehofer and Brown-Reid 2015). Latinas have a low level of knowledge of breast cancer (Ramirez et al. 2000). Coughlin and Wilson (2002) report low levels of knowledge about breast cancer screening among Latina farmworkers. However, Sunil et al. (2014) reported low to moderate knowledge among Hispanic women living in South Texas, while Furgurson et al. (2019) and Meade et al. (2002) reported moderate levels among Latina farmworkers in North Carolina and Florida, respectively. These mixed reports suggest local variability in breast cancer knowledge among Latina farmworkers.

Latina farmworkers who are knowledgeable about mammogram screening recommendations still face access barriers to screening. Many Latina farmworkers do not have health insurance, and some do not regularly see a healthcare provider. The National Breast and Cervical Cancer Early Detection Program (NBCCEDP) offers free or low-cost screenings to women without insurance or coverage for screenings who make less than 250% of the federal poverty level a year (CDC 2019c; Palmer et al. 2005). However, some women are unaware of this program. Long work hours and childcare responsibilities also limit the time Latina farmworkers have to visit a healthcare provider for screening. Because of the technology required for mammography, women usually must travel to a center or health clinic for breast screening. Additionally, language barriers, fear of immigration authorities, and lack of transportation hinder these women from adhering to screening guidelines. Sociocultural beliefs such as a fatalistic attitude toward cancer, fear of cancer, emphasis on acute vs. preventive care, and embarrassment associated with exposing the body to healthcare providers may also prevent Latina farmworkers from getting cancer screening (Coughlin and Wilson 2002).

Reducing barriers to screening may reduce mortality rates due to breast cancer in this population. Cancer education has been employed to address sociocultural barriers and increase screening rates. The National Center for Farmworker Health implemented the Cultivando la Salud program to train health workers in breast and cervical cancer education at sites serving Latinx populations (NCFH 2014a, b). Furgurson et al. (2019) reported high awareness of cancer screening and treatment options among Latina farmworkers in North Carolina. This contrasts with literature reporting fatalistic outlooks on cancer among Latinx farmworkers (Coughlin and Wilson 2002). High BMI is associated with increased risk of developing some types of breast cancer (Picon-Ruiz et al. 2017). It is also associated with high mortality among breast cancer patients. This suggests that interventions focused on diet may reduce breast cancer incidence and mortality among Latina farmworkers and members of farmworker households.

Cervical Cancer

Overall, cervical cancer incidence and mortality rates in the US have been declining. However, Latinas continue to experience the highest cervical cancer incidence rate among any racial or ethnic groups and a higher mortality rate than non-Latina white women (Cronin et al. 2018). The US Preventive Services Task Force recommends Pap testing every 3 years for average-risk women between the ages of 21 and 65 (CDC 2019d). While a study from Michigan suggests recent increased use of Pap tests among Latina farmworker women, knowledge about risk factors, the purpose of Pap tests, and screening recommendations still appears to be low (Coughlin and Wilson 2002; Castañeda et al. 2012; Knoff et al. 2013). Surveyed Latina migrant farmworkers from central Florida and southern Georgia also reported low levels of knowledge about HPV and cancer (25%) and HPV vaccines (30%) (Luque et al. 2010).

Similar to breast cancer rates, higher cervical cancer incidence and mortality rates among Latinas have been tied to low screening rates, limited English language, lack of knowledge, sociocultural beliefs, schedule conflicts, lack of transportation, fear of immigration authorities, and structural barriers, such as low insurance coverage (Luque et al. 2010; Jacobs et al. 2005; Shah et al. 2006; Coronado et al. 2004). The fact that cervical cancer rates are high among Latina farmworkers, even though the NBCCEDP covers cervical cancer screening for low-income women and the federal Vaccines for Children (VFC) Program covers the cost of HPV vaccination for girls under the age of 18, points to the influence that nonfinancial barriers pose to cervical cancer prevention (CDC 2019c; Luque et al. 2012). In addition, beliefs about the HPV vaccine may discourage Latina farmworkers from getting the HPV vaccine to protect against cervical cancer. Participants in a study by Luque et al. (2012) were concerned that getting vaccinated would damage their reputations because of the vaccine's association with sexual activity and promiscuity. Furthermore, some were opposed to vaccinating their children because they viewed it as giving permission to engage in sexual activity.

6.3.2.3   HIV

There are few recent studies on the prevalence of human immunodeficiency virus (HIV) in farmworkers. Estimates from the late 1980s and early 1990s range from 2.6% to 13% among Latinx farmworkers in the eastern US (CDC 1988; Jones et al. 1991). A report from the National Center for Farmworker Health (2014a, b) indicates a prevalence of 133.1 HIV/AIDS cases per 100,000 migrant and seasonal agricultural workers in the eastern US. HIV disproportionately affects Latinx immigrants, and Latinas in particular, compared to the non-Latino white population

(CDC 2019a). While Latinx individuals account for 18% of the US population, they account for 24% of new HIV cases (NCFH 2018). Transmission of HIV infections among Latinas is primarily attributable to heterosexual contact (88%) (CDC 2019a).

Risk Factors and Barriers to Preventive Behaviors

Engaging in unprotected sex and having multiple sexual partners are known risk factors for acquiring HIV. These risks may be elevated in circumstances that Latina farmworkers face. In a study from Florida, Latina farmworkers who had lower sexual relationship power or experienced interpersonal violence were significantly more likely to engage in risky sexual behavior (Kim et al. 2019). Latinas in farmworker communities whose male partner migrates without them may be at higher risk of contracting HIV due to a greater chance that their partner will engage in sexual encounters with other individuals (Rao et al. 2008). Loneliness among migrant male farmworkers is common, and it drives some to pursue extramarital relations while away from their families (Apostolopoulos et al. 2006; NCFH 2018). The low proportion of women to men in rural work communities also leads some men to pay sex workers. It has been reported that as much as 44% of single and unaccompanied married migrant and seasonal farmworkers use sex workers (Rao et al. 2008). Some commercial sex workers move frequently between rural communities, increasing the risk of transmission among rural communities. Condoms are not often used in these encounters (Apostolopoulos et al. 2006; Rao et al. 2008). The *machismo* gender norm, wherein men are expected to emphasize their sexuality, has been implicated in encouraging men to have multiple partners and increasing the risk of heterosexual transmission (Kim et al. 2019; Rao et al. 2008). Heavy alcohol use in migrant communities may exacerbate risky sexual behavior. A study of North Carolina Latino migrant farmworkers found that 40% of participants who had sex within the past 3 months reported being under the influence of alcohol at least once during a sexual encounter (Rhodes et al. 2010). Binge drinking is a pattern reported in this population, with heavier drinking during celebrations (Rhodes et al. 2010). Injection drug use has also been reported as a risk factor for HIV transmission; however, it appears to be less prevalent in this population (Rao et al. 2008).

Self-efficacy for HIV prevention, HIV-related knowledge, and intention to negotiate safe sex are three HIV preventive factors (Ramirez-Ortiz et al. 2019). Cultural norms and attitudes among the Latinx community can act as barriers to engaging in preventive behaviors. The *marianismo* gender norm, wherein women are expected to model virtues of sexual purity and passivity, has been implicated as a deterrent to engaging in HIV-preventive behaviors (Kim et al. 2019; Levison et al. 2018). Under this social construct, women are blamed if they become impure. Therefore, a woman who engages in HIV-preventive behaviors and discusses safe sex practices, such as condom use, is seen as admitting to promiscuity or distrusting her male partner. Serious social repercussions for a woman transgressing cultural norms can include shaming, abuse from her partner, and her partner withdrawing financial support (Levison et al. 2018). Fear of such social repercussions can lead Latinas to engage in self-silencing behaviors, such as suppressing their complaints, in order to maintain a relationship. Latinas may feel embarrassed about discussing their sexual health and engage in self-silencing behaviors with health service providers, especially those they do not trust. Self-silencing behaviors and discriminating attitudes were negatively associated with HIV-preventive behaviors among Latina farmworkers in Florida (Ramirez-Ortiz et al. 2019). Low levels of HIV knowledge, low perceived personal risk of HIV infection, misconceptions on how to use condoms, and misidentification of HIV risk factors have been reported among the Latinx farmworker population (Rhodes et al. 2010; Apostolopoulos et al. 2006; AIDS Institute 2007).

Barriers to Prevention and Treatment Services

Immigration status, lack of knowledge about healthcare rights, limited transportation, lack of trust, and stigma are barriers to accessing HIV prevention and treatment services (Kim et al. 2019). Lack of health insurance is a major obstacle to HIV treatment access. The AIDS Drug Assistance Program (ADAP) is a federal program that provides antiretroviral drugs for low-income individuals regardless of immigration status (Levison et al. 2018). However, eligibility varies by state, and enrollment caps have been implemented in recent years. The HIV testing rate in the Latinx farmworker population appears to be low. A study of migrant and seasonal farmworkers in New York found that fewer than a third (31%) of participants had been tested for HIV (AIDS Institute 2007). The study cited structural and financial barriers along with stigma as underlying the low testing rate.

Viral suppression of HIV requires long-term access to antiretroviral therapy (ART), which may be difficult for Latinx farmworkers to obtain and maintain. HIV-positive Latinx have lower rates of viral suppression than non-Latinx whites (Levison et al. 2018). Lack of knowledge, sociocultural deterrents, and structural barriers contribute to the higher disease burden among Latinx farmworkers by affecting ART treatment adherence in addition to initial HIV screening and treatment (Levison et al. 2018). In their study of Latinx immigrants in Boston, Levison et al. (2017) identified avoidance of HIV service attendance as a common coping mechanism to HIV-related stigma. Limited patient-provider trust may also decrease ART adherence. For Latina farmworkers in particular, job instability, seasonality of work, and distance from healthcare services can make ART adherence difficult.

Interventions

Community-based HIV prevention interventions have demonstrated the value of home-based HIV testing, lay health advisors, and internet outreach in addressing HIV among the Latinx community (Levison et al. 2018). Strengthening patient-provider trust may help address gaps in HIV knowledge and health-seeking behaviors among this community. Engaging in personal interactions, patient-centered interviews, graphical handouts tailored to the average English literacy level in this population, and assurance of patient privacy are recommended for retaining Latina patients (Caal et al. 2012). Studies in North Carolina and south Florida indicate that HIV home testing kits may also appeal to migrant and seasonal farmworkers, although women were less likely than men to intend to accept a free testing kit (Fernandez et al. 2005; Kinney et al. 2015). Reduction of community-level stigma, especially for Latinas, is an important aim of some current HIV interventions (Levison et al. 2018).

6.3.2.4 Other Sexually Transmitted Infections

The prevalence of sexually transmitted diseases, other than HIV/AIDS, among farmworkers in the eastern US was estimated to be 217.0 cases per 100,000 migrant and seasonal agricultural workers in 2014 (NCFH 2014a, b). Prevalence of sexually transmitted infections (STIs) is generally more than twice as high among Latinx than non-Latinx whites (Rhodes et al. 2010; CDC 2017). STIs of relevance to this population include chlamydia, gonorrhea, syphilis, and hepatitis B. The same risk factors that make female farmworkers vulnerable to HIV, including risky sexual behavior, structural and financial barriers to prevention and treatment health services, sociocultural norms, and stigma, make them vulnerable to other STIs.

Chlamydia and Gonorrhea

Among 20- to 24-year-old Latinx females in 2017, the prevalence of chlamydia infections was 2605.7 cases per 100,000 people, and the prevalence of gonorrhea was 339.6 cases per 100,000 people (CDC 2017). Data on the burden of these diseases in the Latina farmworker population is scarce. In a study of predominantly Latinx farmworker communities in California, Brammeier et al. (2008) reported 1.6% of males tested positive for chlamydia, while no respondents tested positive for gonorrhea.

Syphilis

Syphilis has been reported in migrant and seasonal farmworker populations at a higher prevalence than national averages. In 2017, the average prevalence of syphilis per 100,000 people was 5.4 cases for whites and 11.8 cases for Hispanics (CDC 2017). Rhodes et al. (2010) found 2% of migrant and seasonal farmworkers surveyed in North Carolina tested positive by rapid plasma reagin (RPR) for syphilis, while Brammeier et al. (2008) found 0.86% of participants recruited from farmworker communities in California tested positive by RPR for syphilis.

Hepatitis B

The prevalence of hepatitis B among farmworkers in the eastern US was estimated to be 30.8 cases per 100,000 migrant and seasonal agricultural workers in 2016 (NCFH 2014a, b). This was higher than the prevalence estimated in the West and Midwest. A study among North Carolina Latinx farmworkers found that over 55% of participants had not heard of hepatitis B (Rhodes et al. 2010). The results indicate lower levels of knowledge about non-HIV STIs may pose a challenge to reproductive health in the Latinx farmworker population.

6.3.3   Mental Health

The mental health challenges that Latina farmworkers face put them at high risk of depression. Studies in North Carolina indicate poor mental health in Latinx farmworker populations (Grzywacz et al. 2010; Hiott et al. 2008; Fox and Kim-Godwin 2011). Latina women have a higher risk of depression than white and African American women and Latino men (Fox and Kim-Godwin 2011). Although not extensive, mental health research conducted among farmworker women in the eastern US has similar outcomes to research conducted among other farmworker women in other parts of the country (see Chap. 4). Farmworker women in the eastern US reported greater stress and anxiety than non-farmworker women (Arcury et al. 2018). In their study on Latina farmworkers in North Carolina, Fox and Kim-Godwin (2011) found nearly half (47.6%) of respondents had scores of at least 16 on the Center for Epidemiological Studies Depression Scale. Stressors for this population include family hardship, social isolation, sexual harassment and assault, exposure to intimate partner violence, economic hardship, job insecurity, immigration status, and acculturation (Roblyer et al. 2016; Fox and Kim-Godwin 2011). Financial and logistical barriers to accessing mental health services pose a challenge to improving mental health among Latina farmworkers.

For Latina farmworkers in particular, family functioning may relate strongly to depression (Sarmiento and Cardemil 2009). In a study by Roblyer et al. (2016), depressive symptoms among farmworker women were associated with family conflict. Cultural expectations on women to nurture and dutifully care for the family may underlie this finding. Lack of social support is associated with increased risk of depression for immigrant Latinas. Being away from family members is a reliable predictor of stress among Latinas in the eastern US (Fox and Kim-Godwin 2011). Discrimination and harassment are also associated with depressive symptoms among Latina farmworker women (Roblyer et al. 2016). Kim-Godwin et al. (2014) reported that among Latinx migrant and seasonal farmworkers in rural southeastern North Carolina, those with high stress levels also had high levels of intimate partner violence and depression. Cultural norms and stigma often act as deterrents to discussing abusive relationships or assault for Latina farmworkers. This can increase feelings of isolation and hinder mental health-seeking behaviors.

Work safety climate and work organization dimensions are correlates of exposure to stressors and resultant symptoms in manual laborers. A study on Latina manual workers in North Carolina found that workers who had nonstandard shifts reported increased stress and depressive symptoms (Arcury et al. 2014b). Perceived supervisor control was also linked with mental health. Greater job demand and less decision latitude were associated with more depressive symptoms among the cohort. Those with greater psychological demands had greater depressive symptoms. Skill variety was also associated with greater family conflict and depressive symptoms. Farm work is labor intensive, and female farmworkers often are assigned to repetitive tasks under supervisor control. In a study in North Carolina, Arcury et al. (2018) found that Latina farmworkers had a significantly greater mean anxiety score compared to non-farmworker or unemployed Latinas. However, economic hardship appears to be a greater stressor than general farm work among female farmworkers (Pulgar et al. 2016; Roblyer et al. 2016). Latina farmworkers face economic and lifestyle stressors due to the seasonal nature of their job and often inadequate compensation. Fox and Kim-Godwin (2011) found that job and medical insecurities, along with migrant lifestyle, were reliable predictors of stress among Latinas in the eastern US. Among farmworker women, Arcury et al. (2015b) found that those in migrant families "had more depressive symptoms, more physical activity and less economic security," than those in seasonal farmworker families.

Immigration status and acculturation are also strong stressors that impact Latina farmworker mental health. Fox and Kim-Godwin (2011) found that immigration status and difficulty understanding spoken English were predictors of depression among Latina farmworkers in North Carolina. Among participants in the study, worry about being deported and worry about not having a permit to work were the greatest stressors reported.

According to the NAWS data, approximately two-thirds of Eastern Region Latina farmworkers lack health insurance (USDOL 2016) and the physical and mental health benefits associated with it. Migrating farmworkers have a harder time accessing Medicaid, if eligible, or maintaining consistent and appropriate care due to their mobility as they move from state to state (Hetrick 2015). Latinas are also less likely to get mental health services than non-Latina white or African American women (Fox and Kim-Godwin 2011). Access to mental health services can also be difficult due to language barriers and lack of such services in rural communities (Pulgar et al. 2016). Linguistic and cultural barriers may be particularly pronounced in mental health services. Women who seek out mental health services may find that they are inaccessible, too expensive, or unavailable in their language.

6.3.4   Oral Health

Oral health is one of the greatest unmet health needs for farmworkers. Oral health is important for maintaining nutritious diets and interacting socially by smiling or talking (Quandt et al. 2007). Farmworker children are more likely to receive dental care than adults. A study interviewing Latinx farmworker mothers in western North Carolina found that over half (56.9%) of children received dental care every 6 months or annually (Quandt et al. 2007). Fewer than a quarter (20.95%) of adults received dental care every 6 months or annually. Fewer than half (47%) of mothers had received dental care in the past year (Quandt et al. 2007). In a study of migrant farmworkers in Florida, Carrion et al. (2011) found that about a quarter (26%) of adults reported their teeth to be in poor or very poor condition.

Oral health is particularly important for females in the farmworker community. A mother's attitude toward oral health influences her family members' oral health practices (Hoeft et al. 2009). Furthermore, several periodontal diseases have been associated with pregnancy, including gingivitis and periodontitis (Hartnett et al. 2016). Poor oral health and lack of oral care are also linked with premature birth and cardiovascular disease (Carrion et al. 2011). Latinx women are less likely than non-Latinx white women to receive oral care during pregnancy (Hartnett et al. 2016).

Many Latina farmworkers only utilize dental services for acute oral health issues. Women in farmworker families in a North Carolina study were most likely to receive oral health care in emergencies or when experiencing pain (Quandt et al. 2007). Similar results were found among migrant farmworkers in Florida, the substantial majority of whom were women (Carrion et al. 2011; Castañeda et al. 2010). They generally visited the dentist when in pain or when receiving prenatal health services while in the US.

Recent studies indicate high levels of oral health knowledge among these Latinx farmworkers (Castañeda et al. 2010; Carrion et al. 2011). A study of Latina farmworkers by Quandt et al. (2007) found that although 60.2% of respondents never flossed, all of the respondents brushed their teeth at least once a day. Research indicates economic and logistical barriers are the primary barriers to seeking oral healthcare among Latinx farmworkers (Carrion et al. 2011; Quandt et al. 2007; Castañeda et al. 2010). Cost, lack of dental insurance, lost wages during dental visits, lack of transportation, and migrant lifestyle impede Latina farmworkers from accessing oral health services. For many, lack of dental insurance and high costs are the main deterrents to accessing oral health services.

Dental coverage for Latina farmworkers often differs from that of their family members. While Medicaid provides dental insurance for many Latinx farmworker children, most Latinx farmworker parents do not have dental insurance. Latina farmworkers often have access to oral healthcare during pregnancy due to efforts from community-based dental health programs and Medicaid coverage for pregnant women (Carrion et al. 2011; Castañeda et al. 2010). Castañeda et al. (2010) found that in their sample of migrant Latina farmworker mothers in Florida, roughly a third had seen a dentist during prenatal care. After pregnancy, women lose dental service coverage under Medicaid, and many do not continue receiving care (Castañeda et al. 2010; Carrion et al. 2011).

Even for female farmworkers who have dental insurance, some dental providers are unwilling or unavailable to provide oral health services. Reimbursement rates for dentists providing services to Medicaid patients are low. The nationwide average reimbursement rate was 60.5% in 2010, while in some states, like Florida, the rate was even lower (30.5%) (Castañeda et al. 2010). This creates a disincentive for dentists to treat Medicaid patients. Other deterrents from accepting Medicaid patients include administrative difficulties and complaints about missed appointments. A scarcity of dentists due to professional licensing restrictions along with few dentists practicing in rural areas limits farmworker access to dental care (Castañeda et al. 2010). Mobile clinics serving low-income patients are resources that many migrant farmworker families utilize (Carrion et al. 2011). However, mobile units are often unpredictable and have a limited range of dental services that they offer. This can result in one-time dental screenings without ability to do follow-up treatment of more serious dental problems (Castañeda et al. 2010).

6.4   Conclusions and Recommendations

The research literature on the health of women in the US farmworker community is spotty, at best. Few studies have focused exclusively on women, so much of what is known either is extrapolated from risks documented for male farmworkers or is concluded from small numbers of women found in general surveys of the mostly male farmworker population. A larger proportion of farmworkers in the eastern US are women than in other parts of the country, and it appears that this is reflected in an increasing number of recent studies in the eastern US. For example, North Carolina research has included a large number of women in farmworker families (some, but not all, working in the fields) (e.g., Arcury et al. 2015b; Pulgar et al. 2016). Research in Florida has begun to include worker samples that are majority women (e.g., Campbell et al. 2017; Mutic et al. 2018).

The studies that exist nationally and in the eastern US document the way unfair labor practices and other aspects of the work environment place women farmworkers at risk of occupational injuries and illnesses that include heat illness and musculoskeletal injuries and exposure to pesticides whose effects may not be evident for years. For women in farmworker families, health risks stemming from poor living conditions and take-home pesticide exposure are also known.

Compared to men in the farmworker community, women have additional risks of sexual harassment, pregnancy concerns, and a range of female cancers and sexually transmitted infections for which they likely receive inadequate screening and treatment. Mental health concerns for women in farmworker families are prevalent, many of them linked to the stress encountered due to discrimination and immigration issues, as well as the impoverished and isolated circumstances women endure.

Based on these findings, recommendations for research, practice, and policy are warranted.

Research:

- Research is needed to understand the experience of women in farmworker families in the eastern US. This includes experiences with gender and ethnic discrimination and its impact on their ability to maintain their health and that of their families. In particular, the extent of sexual harassment needs to be understood in order to gauge its impact on physical and mental health.

- Health research on work-related injuries and illnesses among women, including heat-related illness and musculoskeletal disorders, is needed to understand risks specific to women. Research focused largely on men may not be adequate to quantify the risks to women, who, on average, differ in body composition and size.
- Research on reengineered workplaces and tools for women is needed because their body sizes and shapes differ, on average, from those of men. Studies should focus on whether such engineering changes reduce the risk of injury for Latinas in farm work.

Practice:

- Ensure that women in farmworker families understand and have access to safe and culturally and linguistically appropriate reporting of sexual harassment and gender discrimination, both in the workplace and in the community.
- Provide culturally and linguistically appropriate mental health services appropriate for women in the farmworker community. These could use approaches such as telehealth and mobile screening clinics to serve these women who are often isolated with limited transportation.
- Review worker safety regulations to ensure their appropriateness for women in the agricultural workplace, including methods of delivery of worker education and reporting options.
- Train healthcare providers to conduct occupational histories with Latinas to be able to provide care that takes account of job exposures.

Policy:

- Current policies that directly or indirectly prevent women in farmworker families from accessing health-related services need to be changed. These include policies based on immigration status that prevent women from accessing affordable healthcare and nutrition services for themselves and their families. These also include policies based on length of in-state residence or transferability of benefits (e.g., Medicaid) that can prevent women in migrant farmworker families from obtaining continuity of care.
- Policies that prevent women farmworkers from receiving equitable pay and benefits with men should be amended. As in many industries, it is possible that jobs typically filled by women are underpaid and eligible for fewer benefits. Such discrimination can have far-reaching effects on women's health and that of their families.
- Programs such as the Fair Food Program should be expanded, and its Code of Conduct should be made state or federal policy so that all farmworkers, including women, receive training concerning sexual harassment protection and reporting.

References

AIDS Institute, New York State Department of Health (2007) Migrant and seasonal farmworkers health care access and HIV/AIDS in this population. New York, NY: AIDS Institute, New York State Department of Health. https://www.health.ny.gov/diseases/aids/providers/reports/migrant_farmworkers/docs/heatlhcareaccess.pdf. Accessed 13 Aug 2019

Apostolopoulos Y, Sonmez S, Kronenfeld J et al (2006) STI/HIV risks for Mexican migrant laborers: exploratory ethnographies. J Immigr Minor Health 8:291–302

Arcury TA, O'Hara H, Grzywacz JG et al (2012) Work safety climate, musculoskeletal discomfort, working while injured, and depression among migrant farmworkers in North Carolina. Am J Public Health 102:S272–S278

Arcury TA, Cartwright MS, Chen H et al (2014a) Musculoskeletal and neurological injuries associated with work organization among immigrant Latino women manual workers in North Carolina. Am J Ind Med 57:468–475

Arcury TA, Grzywacz JG, Chen H et al (2014b) Work organization and health among immigrant women: Latina manual workers in North Carolina. Am J Public Health 104:2445–2452

Arcury TA, Lu C, Chen H et al (2014c) Pesticides present in migrant farmworker housing in North Carolina. Am J Ind Med 57:312–322

Arcury TA, Summers P, Talton JW et al (2015a) Heat illness among North Carolina Latino farmworkers. J Occup Environ Med 57:1299–1304

Arcury TA, Trejo G, Suerken CK et al (2015b) Work and health among Latina mothers in farmworker families. J Occup Environ Med 57:292–299

Arcury TA, Sandberg JC, Talton JW et al (2018) Mental health among Latina farmworkers and other employed Latinas in North Carolina. Rural Ment Health 42:89–101

Auger N, Naimi AI, Smargiassi A et al (2014) Extreme heat and risk of early delivery among preterm and term pregnancies. Epidemiology 25:344–350

Bauer M, Ramírez M (2010) Injustice on our plates: immigrant women in the U.S. food industry. Available via Southern Poverty Law Center. https://www.splcenter.org/sites/default/files/d6_legacy_files/downloads/publication/Injustice_on_Our_Plates.pdf. Accessed 7 Aug 2019

Brammeier M, Chow JM, Samuel MC et al (2008) Sexually transmitted diseases and risk behaviors among California farmworkers: results from a population-based survey. J Rural Health 24:279–284

Brock M, Northcraft-Baxter L, Escoffery C et al (2012) Musculoskeletal health in south Georgia farmworkers: a mixed methods study. Work 43:223–236

Brumitt J, Reisch R, Krasnoselsky K et al (2011) Self-reported musculoskeletal pain in Latino vineyard workers. J Agromedicine 16:72–80

Caal S, Guzman L, Renteria RA et al (2012) Reproductive health care through the eyes of Latina women: insights for providers. Child Trends. Available via Migrant Clinicians Network. https://www.migrantclinician.org/files/Child_Trends-2012_08_31_FR_LatinaReproductive.pdf. Accessed 15 Aug 2019

Campbell K, Baker B, Tovar A et al (2017) The association between skin rashes and work environment, personal protective equipment, and hygiene practices among female farmworkers. Workplace Health Saf 65:313–321

Carrion IV, Castañeda H, Martinez-Tyson D et al (2011) Barriers impeding access to primary oral health care among farmworker families in central Florida. Soc Work Health Care 50:828–844

Castañeda X, Zavella P (2003) Changing constructions of sexuality and risk: Migrant Mexican women farmworkers in California. J Lat Am Caribb Anthropol 8:126–150

Castañeda H, Carrion IV, Kline N et al (2010) False hope: effects of social class and health policy on oral health inequalities for migrant farmworker families. Soc Sci Med 71:2028–2037

Castañeda SF, Rosenbaum RP, Gonzalez P et al (2012) Breast and cervical cancer screening among rural midwestern Latina migrant and seasonal farmworkers. J Prim Care Community Health 3:104–110

Centers for Disease Control and Prevention (CDC) (1988) HIV seroprevalence in migrant and seasonal farmworkers-North Carolina, 1987. MMWR Morb Mortal Wkly Rep 37(34):517–519

Centers for Disease Control and Prevention (CDC) (2017) STDs in racial and ethnic minorities. https://www.cdc.gov/std/stats17/minorities.htm. Accessed 15 Aug 2019

Centers for Disease Control and Prevention (CDC) (2019a) HIV and Hispanics/Latinos. https://www.cdc.gov/hiv/group/racialethnic/hispaniclatinos/index.html/. Accessed 18 Mar 2019

Centers for Disease Control and Prevention (CDC) (2019b) What is breast cancer screening? https://www.cdc.gov/cancer/breast/basic_info/screening.htm. Accessed 30 Jul 2019

Centers for Disease Control and Prevention (CDC) (2019c) National Breast and Cervical Cancer Early Detection Program (NBCCEDP). https://www.cdc.gov/cancer/nbccedp/index.htm. Accessed 30 Jul 2019

Centers for Disease Control and Prevention (CDC) (2019d) Screening recommendations and considerations. https://www.cdc.gov/cancer/knowledge/provider-education/cervical/recommendations.htm. Accessed 31 Jul 2019

Coalition of Immokalee Workers (CIW) (2012) Fair food program changes the norm: confronting sexual violence and harassment in the fields. https://ciw-online.org/blog/2012/03/ffp_sexual_harassment_brief/. Accessed 1 Aug 2019

Coronado GD, Thompson B, Koepsell TD et al (2004) Use of pap test among Hispanics and non-Hispanic whites in a rural setting. Prev Med 38:713–722

Coughlin SS, Wilson KM (2002) Breast and cervical cancer screening among migrant and seasonal farmworkers: a review. Cancer Detect Prev 26:203–209

Cronin KA, Lake AJ, Scott S et al (2018) Annual report to the nation on the status of cancer, part I: National cancer statistics. Cancer 124:2785–2800

Dominguez MM (1997) Sex discrimination and sexual harassment in agricultural labor. Am Univ J Gen Soc Policy Law 6:231–259

Engel LS, Werder E, Satagopan J et al (2017) Insecticide use and breast cancer risk among farmers' wives in the Agricultural Health Study. Environ Health Perspect 125:097002

Eskenazi B, Marks AR, Bradman A et al (2007) Organophosphate pesticide exposure and neurodevelopment in young Mexican-American children. Environ Health Perspect 115:792–798

Fenga C (2016) Occupational exposure and risk of breast cancer. Biomed Rep 4:282–292

Fernandez MI, Collazo JB, Bowen GS et al (2005) Predictors of HIV testing and intention to test among Hispanic farmworkers in South Florida. J Rural Health 21:56–64

Fox JA, Kim-Godwin Y (2011) Stress and depression among Latina women in rural southeastern North Carolina. J Community Health Nurs 28:223–232

Furgurson KF, Sandberg JC, Hsu FC et al (2019) Cancer knowledge among Mexican immigrant farmworkers in North Carolina. J Immigr Minor Health 21:515–521

Galarneau C (2013) Farm labor, reproductive justice: migrant women farmworkers in the US. Health Hum Rights 15:E144–E160

Ganjoo S, Kaul D, Shah PA (2018) Carpal tunnel syndrome in females: pregnancy and lactation the major risk factors. Int J Reprod Contracept Obstet Gynecol 7:3512–3515

Grzywacz JG, Quandt SA, Chen H et al (2010) Depressive symptoms among Latino farmworkers across the agricultural season: structural and situational influences. Cultur Divers Ethnic Minor Psychol 16:335–343

Gunier RB, Bradman A, Harley KG et al (2017) Prenatal residential proximity to agricultural pesticide use and IQ in 7-year-old children. Environ Health Perspect 125:057002

Habib RR, Hojeij S, Elzein K (2014) Gender in occupational health research of farmworkers: a systematic review. Am J Ind Med 57:1344–1367

Hamilton ER, Hale JM, Savinar R (2019) Immigrant legal status and health: legal status disparities in chronic conditions and musculoskeletal pain among Mexican-born farm workers in the United States. Demography 56:1–24

Hartnett E, Haber J, Krainovich-Miller B, Bella A et al (2016) Oral health in pregnancy. J Obstet Gynecol Neonatal Nurs 45:565–573

Hetrick M (2015) Medicaid and migrant farmworkers: why the state residency requirement presents a significant access barrier and what states should do about it. Health Matrix Clevel 25:437–485

Hiott AE, Grzywacz JG, Davis SW et al (2008) Migrant farmworker stress: mental health implications. J Rural Health 24:32–39

Hoeft KS, Barker JC, Masterson EE (2009) Mexican-American mothers' initiation and understanding of home oral hygiene for young children. Pediatr Dent 31:395–404

Human Rights Watch (2012) Cultivating fear: the vulnerability of immigrant farmworkers in the US to sexual violence and sexual harassment. http://www.hrw.org/sites/default/files/reports/us0512ForUpload_1.pdf. Accessed 23 Jul 2019

Jacobs EA, Karavolos K, Rathouz PJ et al (2005) Limited English proficiency and breast and cervical cancer screening in a multiethnic population. Am J Public Health 95:1410–1416

Jones JL, Rion P, Hollis S et al (1991) HIV-related characteristics of migrant workers in rural South Carolina. South Med J 84:1088–1090

Kasner EJ, Keralis JM, Mehler L et al (2012) Gender differences in acute pesticide-related illnesses and injuries among farmworkers in the United States, 1998–2007. Am J Ind Med 55:571–583

Kim NJ, Vasquez VB, Torres E et al (2016) Breaking the silence: sexual harassment of Mexican women farmworkers. J Agromedicine 21:154–162

Kim H, He Y, Pham R et al (2019) Analyzing the association between depression and high-risk sexual behavior among adult Latina immigrant farm workers in Miami-Dade county. Int J Environ Res Public Health 16(7):1120

Kim-Godwin YS, Maume MO, Fox JA (2014) Depression, stress, and intimate partner violence among Latino migrant and seasonal farmworkers in rural southeastern North Carolina. J Immigr Minor Health 16:1217–1224

Kinney S, Lea CS, Kearney G et al (2015) Predictors for using a HIV self-test among migrant and seasonal farmworkers in North Carolina. Int J Environ Res Public Health 12:8348–8358

Knoff JS, Harlow SD, Yassine M et al (2013) Cervical cancer screening practice and knowledge among Hispanic migrant and seasonal farmworkers of Michigan. J Prim Care Community Health 4:209–215

Kuehn L, McCormick S (2017) Heat exposure and maternal health in the face of climate change. Int J Environ Res Public Health 14:853

Lerro CC, Stein KD, Smith T et al (2012) A systematic review of large-scale surveys of cancer survivors conducted in North America, 2000–2011. J Cancer Surviv 6:115–145

Levison JH, Bogart LM, Khan IF et al (2017) "Where it falls apart": barriers to retention in HIV care in Latino immigrants and migrants. AIDS Patient Care STDs 31:394–405

Levison JH, Levinson JK, Alegría M (2018) A critical review and commentary on the challenges in engaging HIV-infected Latinos in the continuum of HIV care. AIDS Behav 22:2500–2512

Liebman AK, Mainster B, Lee BC (2014) Family services for migrant and seasonal farm workers: the Redlands Christian Migrant Association (RCMA) Model. J Agromedicine 19:123–129

Liebman AK, Simmons J, Salzwedel M et al (2017) Caring for children while working in agriculture—the perspective of farmworker parents. J Agromedicine 22:406–415

Lin S, Lin Z, Ou Y, National Birth Defects Prevention Study et al (2018) Maternal ambient heat exposure during early pregnancy in summer and spring and congenital heart defects—a large US population-based, case-control study. Environ Int 118:211–221

Luque JS, Castañeda H, Tyson DM et al (2010) HPV awareness among Latina immigrants and Anglo-American women in the southern United States: cultural models of cervical cancer risk factors and beliefs. NAPA Bull 34:84–104

Luque JS, Castañeda H, Tyson DM et al (2012) Formative research on HPV vaccine acceptability among Latina farmworkers. Health Promot Pract 13:617–625

Marks AR, Harley K, Bradman A et al (2010) Organophosphate pesticide exposure and attention in young Mexican-American children: the CHAMACOS study. Environ Health Perspect 118:1768–1774

Meade CD, Calvo A, Cuthbertson D (2002) Impact of culturally, linguistically, and literacy relevant cancer information among Hispanic farmworker women. J Cancer Educ 17:50–54

Mix J, Elon L, Vi Thien Mac V et al (2018) Hydration status, kidney function, and kidney injury in Florida agricultural workers. J Occup Environ Med 60:E253–E260

Mora DC, Miles CM, Chen H et al (2016) Prevalence of musculoskeletal disorders among immigrant Latino farmworkers and non-farmworkers in North Carolina. Arch Environ Occup Health 71:136–143

Mostafalou S, Abdollahi M (2017) Pesticides: an update of human exposure and toxicity. Arch Toxicol 91:549–599

Moyce S, Mitchell D, Armitage T et al (2017) Heat strain, volume depletion and kidney function in California agricultural workers. Occup Environ Med 74:402–409

Murphy J, Samples J, Morales M et al (2015) "They talk like that, but we keep working": sexual harassment and sexual assault experiences among Mexican indigenous farmworker women in Oregon. J Immigr Minor Health 17:1834–1839

Mutic AD, Mix JM, Elon L et al (2018) Classification of heat-related illness symptoms among Florida farmworkers. J Nurs Scholarsh 50:74–82

National Center for Farmworker Health (NCFH) (2014a) Regional migrant health profile. http://www.ncfh.org/uploads/3/8/6/8/38685499/ncfh_regional_mh_analysis_final_5.16.pdf. Accessed 15 Aug 2019

National Center for Farmworker Health (NCFH) (2014b) Breast cancer, health centers and U.S. agricultural workers. http://www.ncfh.org/ncfh-blog/breast-cancer-health-centers-and-us-agricultural-workers. Accessed 1 Aug 2019

National Center for Farmworker Health (NCFH) (2018) HIV/AIDS agricultural worker factsheet. http://www.ncfh.org/uploads/3/8/6/8/38685499/fshiv_aids_2018.pdf. Accessed 13 Aug 2019

Nerbass FB, Pecoits-Filho R, Clark WF et al (2017) Occupational heat stress and kidney health: from farms to factories. Kidney Int Rep 2:998–1008

O'Brien RW, Barrueco S, López ML et al (2011) Design for Migrant and Seasonal Head Start survey final design report. Administration for Children and Families, Office of Planning, Research, and Evaluation, Washington, DC. https://www.acf.hhs.gov/sites/default/files/opre/migrant_design.pdf

Padilla YC, Scott JL, Lopez O (2014) Economic insecurity and access to the social safety net among Latino farmworker families. Soc Work 59:157–165

Palmer RC, Fernandez ME, Tortolero-Luna G et al (2005) Correlates of mammography screening among Hispanic women living in lower Rio Grande Valley farmworker communities. Health Educ Behav 32:488–503

Picon-Ruiz M, Morata-Tarifa C, Valle-Goffin JJ et al (2017) Obesity and adverse breast cancer risk and outcome: mechanistic insights and strategies for intervention. CA Cancer J Clin 67:378–397

Pulgar CA, Trejo G, Suerken C et al (2016) Economic hardship and depression among women in Latino farmworker families. J Immigr Minor Health 18:497–504

Quandt SA, Clark HM, Rao P et al (2007) Oral health of children and adults in Latino migrant and seasonal farmworker families. J Immigr Minor Health 9:229–235

Quandt SA, Grzywacz JG, Trejo G et al (2014) Nutritional strategies of Latino farmworker families with preschool children: identifying leverage points for obesity prevention. Soc Sci Med 123:72–81

Quinlan M, Mayhew C, Bohle P (2001) The global expansion of precarious employment, work disorganization, and consequences for occupational health: a review of recent research. Int J Health Serv 31:335–414

Ramirez AG, Suarez L, Laufman L et al (2000) Hispanic women's breast and cervical cancer knowledge, attitudes, and screening behaviors. Am J Health Promot 14:292–300

Ramirez-Ortiz D, Rojas P, Sanchez M et al (2019) Associations of self-silencing and egalitarian attitudes with HIV prevention behaviors among Latina immigrant farmworkers. J Immigr Minor Health 21:430–433

Rao P, Hancy K, Vélez M, et al (2008) HIV/AIDS and farmworkers in the US. Farmworker justice and migrant clinicians network. https://www.migrantclinician.org/files/HIVWhitePaper08.pdf. Accessed 13 Aug 2019

Rappazzo KM, Warren JL, Meyer RE et al (2016) Maternal residential exposure to agricultural pesticides and birth defects in a 2003 to 2005 North Carolina birth cohort. Birth Defects Res A Clin Mol Teratol 6:240–249

Reid A, Schenker MB (2016) Hired farmworkers in the US: demographics, work organisation, and services. Am J Ind Med 59:644–655

Reschke KL (2012) Child care needs of farm families. J Agromedicine 17:208–213

Rhodes SD, Bischoff WE, Burnell JM et al (2010) HIV and sexually transmitted disease risk among male Hispanic/Latino migrant farmworkers in the Southeast: findings from a pilot CBPR study. Am J Ind Med 53:976–983

Robinson E, Nguyen HT, Isom S et al (2011) Wages, wage violations, and pesticide safety experienced by migrant farmworkers in North Carolina. New Solut 21:251–268

Roblyer MI, Grzywacz JG, Suerken CK et al (2016) Interpersonal and social correlates of depressive symptoms among Latinas in farmworker families living in North Carolina. Women Health 56:177–193

Runge SB, Pedersen JK, Svendsen SW et al (2013) Occupational lifting of heavy loads and preterm birth: a study within the Danish national birth cohort. Occup Environ Med 70:782–788

Sagiv SK, Harris MH, Gunier RB et al (2018) Prenatal organophosphate pesticide exposure and traits related to autism spectrum disorders in a population living in proximity to agriculture. Environ Health Perspect 126:047012

Sarmiento IA, Cardemil EV (2009) Family functioning and depression in low-income Latino couples. J Marital Fam Ther 35:432–445

Schlehofer MM, Brown-Reid TP (2015) Breast health beliefs, behaviors, and barriers among Latina permanent resident and migratory farm workers. J Community Health Nurs 32:71–88

Shah M, Zhu K, Wu H et al (2006) Hispanic acculturation and utilization of cervical cancer screening in the US. Prev Med 42:146–149

Snijder CA, te Velde E, Roeleveld N et al (2012) Occupational exposure to chemical substances and time to pregnancy: a systematic review. Hum Reprod Update 18:284–300

Summers K, Jinnett K, Bevan S (2015) Musculoskeletal disorders, workforce health and productivity in the United States. Available via The Centers for Workforce Health and Performance, The Work Foundation. http://www.theworkfoundation.com/wp-content/uploads/2016/11/385_White-paper-Musculoskeletal-disordersworkforce-health-and-productivity-in-the-USA-final.pdf. Accessed 7 Aug 2019

Sunil TS, Hurd T, Deem C et al (2014) Breast cancer knowledge, attitude and screening behaviors among Hispanics in south Texas colonias. J Community Health 39:60–71

Sweeney C, Baumgartner KB, Byers T et al (2008) Reproductive history in relation to breast cancer risk among Hispanic and non-Hispanic white women. Cancer Causes Control 19:391–401

TePoel M, Rohlman D, Shaw M (2017) The impact of work demand and gender on occupational and psychosocial stress in Hispanic farmworkers. J Agric Saf Health 23:109–123

Treaster DE, Burr D (2004) Gender differences in prevalence of upper extremity musculoskeletal disorders. Ergonomics 47:495–526

U.S. Bureau of Labor Statistics (2017) Survey of occupational injuries and illnesses: charts package. https://www.bls.gov/iif/osch0062.pdf. Accessed 15 Jul 2019

U.S. Department of Agriculture (USDA) (2019) Number of women farmworkers increasing. USDA Economic Research Service. https://www.wlj.net/top_headlines/number-of-women-farmworkers-increasing/article_40743c4e-c9b1-11e9-812f-270ffe35e704.html. Accessed 9 Sept 2019

U.S. Department of Labor (USDOL) (2005) Findings from the National Agricultural Workers Survey (NAWS) 2001–2002. A demographic and employment profile of United States farm workers. Research report no. 9. Washington, DC: Office of the Assistant Secretary for Policy and the Office of Programmatic Policy, U.S. Department of Labor. https://www.doleta.gov/agworker/report9/naws_rpt9.pdf. Accessed 12 Sept 2019

U.S. Department of Labor (USDOL) (2016) National Agricultural Workers Survey (NAWS) public data content and file formats. Washington, DC: Employment and Training Administration, U.S. Department of Labor. https://www.doleta.gov/naws/public-data/. Accessed 15 Jul 2019

Waugh IM (2010) Examining the sexual harassment experiences of Mexican immigrant farmworking women. Violence Against Women 16:237–261

Xiao H, McCurdy SA, Stoecklin-Marois MT et al (2013) Agricultural work and chronic musculoskeletal pain among Latino farm workers: the MICASA study. Am J Ind Med 56:216–225

Chapter 7
The Health of Children in the Latinx Farmworker Community in the Eastern United States

Sara A. Quandt and Taylor J. Arnold

7.1 Introduction

Children in the Latinx farmworker community include two overlapping groups: children in the families of coresident adult farmworkers and children who work as hired farmworkers. While these children share some health influences and outcomes with other Latinx children in the United States (US) (e.g., they are members of a minority ethnic group and may face discrimination), they also face a distinct constellation of factors that distinguishes them from other Latinx children.

The health of both these groups of children can be set in the context of behaviors and exposures shaped by the social and physical environments in which they live (Fig. 7.1). Farmworker families have characteristics that set them apart from other families. In the southeastern US, they work seasonally in agriculture and may migrate to work, largely up and down the East Coast, following the crop seasons. Some farm work in Florida is becoming year-round as cyclical citrus production converts to year-round organic vegetable production, but elsewhere on the East Coast, work continues to be seasonal. Many families are of mixed documentation status, with members who are foreign-born (e.g., adults and older children) being more likely to lack documents to be in the US legally. Young children in farmworker families are now usually US citizens, which may give them better access to medical and social services than their parents or older siblings. As farmworkers, these families live in rural environments, which bring with them isolation and lower density of some resources and services. Housing for farmworkers is of notoriously poor qual-

S. A. Quandt (✉)
Department of Epidemiology and Prevention, Division of Public Health Sciences, Wake Forest School of Medicine, Winston-Salem, NC, USA

T. J. Arnold
Department of Family and Community Medicine, Wake Forest School of Medicine, Winston-Salem, NC, USA

© Springer Nature Switzerland AG 2020
T. A. Arcury, S. A. Quandt (eds.), *Latinx Farmworkers in the Eastern United States*, https://doi.org/10.1007/978-3-030-36643-8_7

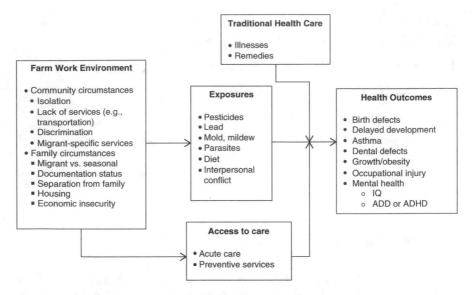

Fig. 7.1 Social ecology model of health for children in farmworker families

ity. Together, these environmental factors predict a number of exposures (e.g., pesticides, lead, low-quality diet) and limitations on access to healthcare that may lead to a pattern of health effects distinctive for children in the farmworker community.

The existing literature on the health of this child population is fragmentary, and it has not been drawn together previously. The literature pertaining to Latinx children in the western US and in states on the US-Mexico border (and, to some extent, in the Midwest) has greater time depth, reflecting the long-standing presence of Latinx farmworkers in those regions. For the eastern US, there are fewer studies, but a growing body of work shows the vulnerability of these children. This chapter will describe some work from other parts of the US, where appropriate, to highlight possible health issues for children in the eastern US.

The number of children in the Latinx farmworker community is hard to pinpoint. The National Agricultural Workers Survey (NAWS) data for 2015–2016 showed that more than half of workers interviewed were parents (Hernandez and Gabbard 2018). Of these parents, three-quarters were married or living as married; 14% were single; and 10% were separated, divorced, or widowed. Eighty percent of parents lived with all of their minor children, and 3% lived with only some of them. Two-thirds of workers with minor children in the household had one or two children, and the remainder had three or more. Of the households with minor children, 53% had children less than 6 years of age, 65% had children between 6 and 13 years of age, and 38% had children 14–17 years of age. Analyses of multiple years of NAWS data (2000–2009) showed that older children were more likely to have been foreign-born and younger ones to have been born in the US (Gabbard et al. 2014).

7.2 Children in Farmworker Families

7.2.1 Access to Healthcare

Children in the farmworker community have special needs for health services that set them apart from the general population (Council on Community Pediatrics 2013). In addition to high rates of poverty, inadequate availability of basics like housing and food exacerbates risk of health problems. The migratory lifestyle of some families and even the frequent moves typical of low-income families with unstable housing can prevent establishing a medical home for children's healthcare. Campbell-Montalvo and Castañeda (2019) characterize the situation of farmworkers as one of structural violence, as economic, political, and material factors conflate to create an environment hostile to farmworker families having access to the care they need. Farmworker parents often lack information on the workings of the US health system; even within a single family, children can have different eligibilities for accessing healthcare services. The state-by-state differences in the implementation of the Affordable Care Act provisions and its state of flux with legal challenges have made it even harder for families to understand available benefits.

It is impossible to know how many children access healthcare, but the number accessing migrant health centers nationally is known from the program grantee data at migrant health centers funded by the Health Resources and Services Administration (HRSA) (HRSA 2015). In 2015, 292,345 patients, about 35% of total patients in these clinics nationally, were children less than 18 years of age. Approximately 18,000 infants under the age of 1 and about 62,000 children ages 1–4 received care. A patient survey at migrant health centers showed that, for 2009 data, those patients received care comparable in quality and access to those at other community health centers (Hu et al. 2016). However, both migrant and community health center patients had limitations in aspects of primary care such as dental care and access to prescription medicines.

Historically, many farmworker parents have sought care for their children during return visits to Mexico. This has been the case, in particular, for families living near the border (e.g., Texas and California), where more than half of child healthcare has been obtained by returning to Mexico (Seid et al. 2003). Even recently, this desire to return to Mexico where care does not come with issues of documentation status attached has been expressed by farmworker families in Florida (Campbell-Montalvo and Castañeda 2019). Data collected in the early 2000s in eastern North Carolina found that health services used by farmworker families of children less than 13 years of age were need driven (Weathers et al. 2003). A more recent analysis of anticipatory guidance for children in farmworker families indicates the pattern still holds (Arcury et al. 2016). That is, children used health services when sick, rather than for well-child care. Younger children and girls were more likely to access care than older children and boys. Those visiting doctors were more likely to have insurance. Parents' documentation status did not predict whether or not children had insurance. Rather, parents who had been in the US for 5 or more years, had a family member with WIC benefits, had a child of female gender, had a child with age less than 2 years, and were able to leave work for child's medical care all predicted having insurance, likely because the child was born in the US (Weathers et al. 2008a, b). Children of migrant workers have greater access to some federally funded migrant health services than children of seasonal (nonmigrant) workers. However, those who migrate are less likely than other children to have continuity of care. Because parents work long hours with limited benefits, they cannot take children to receive medical care without losing work time. Parents may not have transportation to take children to clinics and may not know where the clinics are, and the clinics themselves may have limited hours and services. This type of care is likely to lead to inconsistencies in immunizations (Lee et al. 1990) and in evaluating developmental problems. Even apparently low-cost medications or treatments may be beyond a family's resources (Weathers and Garrison 2004).

It is likely that the same factors found in earlier studies for unmet needs among children in farmworker families remain constant. Unmet needs for care were explored in the North Carolina sample (Weathers et al. 2004). Over half of the children had an unmet need, defined as whether or not the child's caretaker reported a time in the past year when the caretaker felt the child needed medical care, but the child did not receive it. Reasons for the last episode of unmet needs were lack of transportation (80% of episodes), not knowing where to obtain care (32%), inconvenient clinic schedule (10%), no permission to leave work (9%), and difficulty in making appointments (9%). In multivariate analyses of factors enabling healthcare, unmet need was associated with "good," "fair," or "poor" health status (compared to "excellent" or "very good") and with depending on others for transportation. After adjustment for sociodemographic variables, unmet need was associated with ages 3–6 years and with high pressure for parents to work. Children aged 3–6 were more than twice as likely to have unmet needs than children over 6–12 years. Those whose parents reported very high pressure to work were almost six times more likely to have unmet needs.

Solutions to these healthcare access issues for children in farmworker families arc difficult to design, as the healthcare for low-income families in the US as a whole is in flux. While system-wide solutions may be scarce, there is evidence that government-sponsored programs for children in farmworker families, such as Migrant Education or Migrant Head Start, can serve as advocates and facilitators for greater access to care (Campbell-Montalvo and Castañeda 2019; Quandt et al. 2014).

7.2.2   Growth and Obesity

The prevalence of overweight and obesity, defined as ≥85th percentile and < 95th percentile of body mass index (BMI) for age and ≥95th percentile of BMI, respectively, is high among children in farmworker families. A recent systematic review found that the prevalence of overweight ranged from 10% to 33% and obesity from 15% to 37% (Lim et al. 2017). These are in line with a recently published study from California (Sadeghi et al. 2017), in which children 3–8 years of age had a prevalence of 19% for overweight and 26% for obesity. In the eastern US, almost identical prevalence figures were found for children ages 3–16 years of migrant farmworkers in Florida (overweight prevalence of 20% and obesity prevalence of 27%) (Rosado et al. 2013). Prevalence was about the same for overweight (20%) and slightly lower for obesity (22%) in slightly younger children (2.5–3.5 years) of migrant and seasonal farmworkers in North Carolina (Grzywacz et al. 2014). These investigators found that not only did these children show a propensity to overweight and obesity but they also experienced a very early adiposity rebound (Ip et al. 2017). That is, the increase children typically see in BMI in early childhood occurs for these children extremely early, predicting greater accumulation of body weight as children move toward adulthood.

The foundations of this excess overweight and obesity have been explored in a multiyear, prospective study in North Carolina. Diet quality of these young children was below optimum; in particular, their diets had excess added sugar and too few fruits, vegetables, and foods with whole grains (Quandt et al. 2016). Physical activity, as measured by accelerometers, was highly sedentary, with just a few minutes per day of moderate to vigorous activity, far below recommended levels (Grzywacz et al. 2014). This pattern of physical activity did not change during the 2 years these children were followed (Ip et al. 2016). Quandt et al. (2014) proposed the examination of the nutrition strategies of farmworker families with children to identify leverage points around child nutritional status (Fig. 7.2). Nutritional strategies include how families procure food, use food (preparation techniques, scheduling, and content of meals and snacks), and maintain food security (Quandt et al. 1998). The content of the nutritional strategies reflects *resources* such as the uncertain and uneven income schedules of farmworkers, government services, and assistance pro vided by members of social networks. Also reflected are *contextual factors* (e.g., food beliefs, parenting styles, personal experiences) and *environmental factors* (e.g., a migrant lifestyle, rural residence, housing, and cooking facilities).

Subsequent analyses examining these factors found a variety of child feeding styles practiced by parents. Those feeding styles that were somewhat disengaged (low in parent- or child-centered behaviors) were associated with poorer diet quality and higher child BMI (Ip et al. 2018). Part of parental lack of engagement with children appears due to mothers' experience of depressive symptoms. Almost a third of mothers had significant depressive symptomatology (Pulgar et al. 2016), and those with severe episodic or chronic symptoms were less likely to use a feeding style that was responsive to their children and more likely to feed children a low-quality diet (Marshall et al. 2018).

Beliefs parents hold that overexertion can be harmful to children's health and that sedentary behavior can help with learning complicate children getting sufficient physical activity (Grzywacz et al. 2016). In addition, environmental factors such as the lack of safe play spaces and play equipment in the neighborhoods in which farmworker families live likely promote sedentary activity for children (Arcury et al. 2015a, 2017).

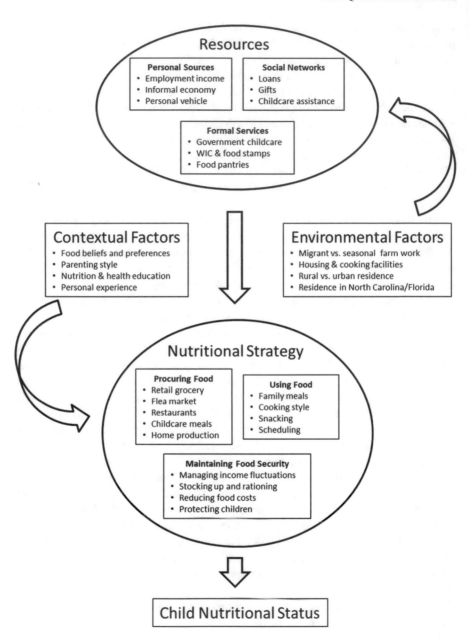

Fig. 7.2 Model of nutritional strategies of child feeding in farmworker families (Quandt et al. 2014)

Food insecurity has been documented among farmworker families with children in the eastern US, with half to two-thirds reporting lacking food security when asked retrospectively about the past year (Borre et al. 2010; Quandt et al. 2006). A more detailed analysis of food insecurity over a 2-year period showed that food insecurity for these families is largely a transient phenomenon, reflecting seasonality of work and income and documentation status, which may regulate families' access to such food safety net features as the Supplemental Nutrition Assistance Program (SNAP) (Ip et al. 2015). Food insecurity (and expectations of seasonal food insecurity) likely causes families to choose inexpensive low-quality foods and perhaps indulge children in food treats when money is available (Quandt et al. 2014).

Inappropriate levels of overweight and obesity and the dietary and physical activity patterns underlying them are likely tied to access to healthcare for children in farmworker families. An examination of the anticipatory guidance mothers reported receiving in North Carolina found that children with well-child visits annually were less likely to be obese than those who did not have such visits (14.8% obese vs. 35.5% obese) (Arcury et al. 2016). Almost all mothers reported receiving guidance on the child's weight, though much less often on dietary issues such as consuming sugar-sweetened beverages and the importance of family meals and physical activity issues such as limiting television watching and video game usage and increasing physical activity or exercise. It would appear that the lack of access to regular well-child visits may prevent parents from receiving such messages.

Further study of the role of programs such as Migrant Head Start in overweight and obesity of children in farmworker families is needed. Analyses from children in Michigan suggest that longer enrollment is associated with lower rates of obesity (Lee and Song 2015), which may reflect parental education provided by Head Start or the role of the on-site meal and physical activity programs.

7.2.3 Oral Health

Children in farmworker families are at risk of poor oral health due to a combination of factors, including ineffective oral hygiene and lack of access to dental services. Problems often start with caries in the primary dentition. Dental caries are caused by demineralization of teeth from bacteria-produced acid; dietary carbohydrates can encourage bacteria, and toothbrushing and dental sealants can protect the teeth.

Limited data are available on children in farmworker families in the eastern US. In a study of mothers of 79 children in North Carolina with an average age of 4.5 (±2.9) years, less than 20% reported their child's oral health was very good or excellent (Quandt et al. 2007). Pain, bleeding gums, and loss of permanent teeth were reported. Almost a quarter reported that they brushed their child's teeth never or only once per day. Three-quarters never flossed the child's teeth.

Carrion et al. (2011) reported a qualitative study of 40 farmworker parents in Florida drawn from a Migrant Head Start Center and a nonprofit migrant clinic sponsored by a religious organization. Quantitative data abstracted from the interviews showed that almost a third rated their children's teeth and two-thirds rated their own teeth as in fair to poor condition. About half said their children had never visited a dentist or had not visited in the past 2 years. Those who did see a dentist did so through the arrangements of the Head Start Center, which made appointments with local dentists, arranged payments, and provided transportation. Parents reported that seeing a dentist outside of the Head Start Center's program was expensive and required time off from work, during which they were not paid. They also had little knowledge of pediatric dentists who might accept Medicaid payments. These parents reported that the Head Start Center provided toothbrushes and toothpaste to the children, which they would not have had otherwise.

Programs to teach oral hygiene to parents have been developed and tested among farmworkers in the western US (Hoeft et al. 2015, 2016; Chang et al. 2018). In the eastern US, the East Coast Migrant Head Start Program (ECMHSP) has developed teaching materials for use with farmworker parents of infants and preschoolers. Cultural practices such as putting children to bed with bottles and belief that the primary dentition is unimportant obstruct the adoption of preventive practices (Hoeft et al. 2016). Dental care requirements for children in ECMHSP led to many of these children receiving preventive and restorative services, as reflected in Carrion et al.'s findings (2011).

The oral health of children can have both short- and long-term effects. In the short term, the experience of pain from caries and oral infections can reduce children's quality of life; oral health problems are one of the primary reasons for school absenteeism (Jackson et al. 2011). In the long term, functional aspects of the adult dentition can be compromised due to misaligned and lost teeth. There is also evidence that chronic oral health conditions like periodontitis lead to higher rates of heart disease (Dietrich et al. 2017).

One of the most important effects of childhood oral health problems is stigma and discrimination associated with appearance, which occur both in childhood and adulthood. Working with children in farmworker families in California, Horton and Barker (2010) show that farmworkers' poverty comes to be embodied in their visibly poor oral health. As children get older, their chances for employment and advancement are curtailed by the appearance of their teeth, and they often spend large sums trying to correct the problems of crooked or decayed teeth that result from inadequate early childhood dental care.

Being a noncitizen or naturalized citizen and lacking dental insurance are known to reduce the use of dental services by adults in the US (Wilson et al. 2016). Farmworker families are likely to lack employment-based dental insurance, but children may have some limited advantage because of their access to Migrant Head Start and, if born in the US, Medicaid insurance. Castañeda et al.'s (2010) ethnographic research with migrant farmworkers in Florida notes that, despite low dental health literacy, the real barriers to children receiving adequate dental services are structural. Although families are promised dental Medicaid assistance, this program promotes "false hope," as it is vastly underfunded. Because of the very low reimbursement rates, most dentists have begun to devote more time to providing charity care through free clinics and refuse to accept Medicaid patients in their private practices. As these free clinics serve almost exclusively adults and are only one day, they cannot help children, who often need multiple visits to address their dental problems.

7.2.4 Vision

Limited data exist about visual impairment and its treatment among children in farmworker families. One of the only studies of this was conducted in Georgia (Soares et al. 2019). Researchers screened 94 Latinx and 54 Haitian children, ages 4–17 years, at a migrant summer school during 2014 and 2015. Of these, 26% were found to have poor visual acuity (defined as less than 20/40 for ages less than 60 months, 20/30 for ages 60 months and older, or between-eye difference of at least two lines on the vision chart). Almost all (83%) of this poor visual acuity was resolved by correcting the refractive error. Most of the remaining problems were judged to be secondary to untreated amblyopia ("lazy eye") in one or both eyes. All cases of amblyopia were found among the children.

The proportion of children with poor visual acuity in this study was significantly higher than that of African American and Latinx children in larger US studies of pediatric eye disease (Varma et al. 2006; Friedman et al. 2008). The proportion with reduced acuity due to amblyopia among the Latinx children appears to be high. Because amblyopia needs to be detected early in life so that treatment can be started, this study points to needs for early life screening, as well as continuing attention to detect problems that can arise during the school years.

7.2.5 Environmental Health

Environmental exposures of children in farmworker families in the US contribute to their health disparities. Often the double jeopardy of living in impoverished environments (including living in dilapidated housing and near industrial chemicals) and inadequate public health information about detecting and preventing such exposures places these children at substantial risk. This risk is magnified in children, as their small body size, greater surface to volume ratio, higher energy need and respiratory rate, and lower ability to metabolize and eliminate environmental chemicals lead to higher exposures and doses of environmental toxins than adults would experience in the same environment (Roberts et al. 2012; Eskenazi et al. 2010; Marks et al. 2010). Children also differ from adults in that they have less mature metabolic processes, reproductive systems, and nervous systems, which may place them at greater risk of hazardous exposures. Children's longer life expectancy means that they have longer latency periods to manifest effects of exposure. Finally, children are more vulnerable in that their emotional and behavioral immaturity may make them more susceptible to poor decision-making and, if hired farmworkers, less likely to challenge supervisor demands.

Current research on environmental health among farmworker children in the eastern US focuses on pesticides; older studies focused on lead exposure and parasites (Osband and Tobin 1972; Ungar et al. 1986). Research on the health effects of pesticides that link exposures to cognitive decline and neurological disease in adults has led recently to a focus on the role of pesticides in cognitive development of children. Despite a national focus on environmental factors as asthma triggers in housing of low-income populations, little research has been conducted on asthma among farmworkers' children in the eastern US.

7.2.5.1 Housing and Neighborhoods

For young children who spend considerable time indoors, housing is their greatest source of environmental exposures. Historically, housing for the general population in the eastern US has been considered crowded (i.e., more than one person per room, excluding kitchens and bathrooms) (Housing Assistance Council 2000). Children live in more than 40% of the crowded units in states such as Florida, Kentucky, Maryland, New Jersey, New York, South Carolina, and Virginia, all states with large farmworker populations. It is important to consider all housing stock for children in farmworker families and not just camps on farms, as many families, particularly seasonal farmworker families, find housing in the local housing market and not on farms.

Beyond the housing units themselves, characteristics of the neighborhoods in which farmworker families live can present physical and mental health challenges. Arcury et al. (2014) assessed neighborhood characteristics of families with young children in North Carolina. About a third stated that the level of traffic on the street or road where they lived made it difficult to get out and walk, and this was strongly associated with stress experienced by the family and with lack of an outward orientation (e.g., to go out for social and recreational events). Other factors related to the location of farmworker family housing, such as time it took to drive to grocery stores, were also associated with family stress.

7.2.5.2 Pesticides

Crowded and low-quality housing of farmworker families frequently leads to pesticide exposure. This exposure comes from two pathways. One is the take-home pathway, which includes pesticides adult farmworkers track into dwellings and automobiles on clothes, shoes, skin, tools, and farm products. If children go into pesticide-treated fields to play, they come in contact with pesticide residues. Those residues that get into housing are slow to break down, so they circulate in the air, contaminating toys, food, and other items young children may put into their mouths. A recent literature review noted there was convincing evidence of children of farmworkers receiving more take-home exposure than children of non-farmworkers (Hyland and Laribi 2017). Of the studies included, only two were conducted in the eastern US, both in North Carolina, one using environmental samples (Quandt et al. 2004) and the other urinary metabolite biomarkers (Arcury et al. 2007). The second pathway is through the application of pesticides in housing and yards by landlords or family members to control pests. The poor condition of farmworker housing, like that of many economically disadvantaged families, often includes leaky pipes and inadequate food storage and trash disposal facilities, which attract pests. Holes in floors, walls, windows, and screens allow pests into homes (Quandt et al. 2015).

Pesticide exposure of children in farmworker communities is of concern because of the potential for developing a number of life-threatening conditions after cumulative exposure. While earlier established concerns have been for cancers, including childhood leukemia, brain cancer, and non-Hodgkin's lymphoma (Infante-Rivard and Weichenthal 2007), more recent longitudinal research among both farmworker and non-farmworker families has demonstrated the effect of pesticide exposure on child cognitive development. Bouchard et al. (2011) report that prenatal and postnatal exposure of children in a California farmworker community to organophosphate pesticides resulted in an average deficit of seven IQ points for children in the highest quintile of exposure, compared to the lowest quintile. Among non-farmworker families, similar effects of pesticides have been shown for children exposed prenatally and at early ages (Engel et al. 2011; Rauh et al. 2011).

Studies on pesticide exposure of farmworker children in the eastern US demonstrate that they are exposed to a wide variety of pesticides. A study of urinary metabolites collected in summer 2004 from 60 Latinx farmworker children aged 1–6 years in eastern North Carolina found metabolites of 13 of the 14 pesticides investigated (Arcury et al. 2007). These included metabolites of seven organophosphorus pesticides, of which those from parathion, chlorpyrifos, diazinon, and malathion were the most frequently found (Fig. 7.3). Other commonly found pesticide metabolites

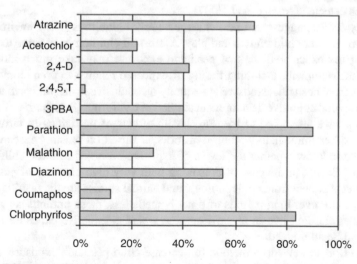

Fig. 7.3 Proportion of Latinx farmworker children aged 1–6 years with metabolites for specific pesticides in urine; North Carolina, summer 2004 (Arcury et al. 2007)

included evidence of pyrethroid insecticide 3PBA and the herbicides 2,4-D and acetochlor. The types of pesticides found demonstrate the role of drift or track-in as pathways in children's exposure. Chlorpyrifos was banned for indoor use in 2001. Parathion has no indoor use and is used in cotton, not in crops where farmworkers would work.

Urinary metabolites from organophosphate pesticides were analyzed from 16 children from ten Latinx farmworker families in western North Carolina (Arcury et al. 2005). In all cases, measurable dialkyl or dimethyl metabolites of organophosphorus pesticides were found. All but one child had at least one metabolite at or above the 50th percentile for total sample, age group, gender, and of Mexican Americans of the 1999–2000 cycle of the National Health and Nutrition Examination Survey (NHANES) (Centers for Disease Control and Prevention 2003; Barr et al. 2004). Ten of 16 children had at least one metabolite above the 90th percentile in comparison with the NHANES reference data.

Environmental wipe samples were collected from the floors, toys, and children's hands in 41 farmworker houses in western North Carolina with a child less than 7 years of age (Quandt et al. 2004). Samples were analyzed for eight pesticides known to be used in agriculture in the study area and 13 others commonly found in house dust throughout the US (Camann et al. 2000). The patterns of occurrence supported the idea of a pathway from floors to toys to children's hands. Pesticides were found in 95% of houses, with residential pesticides more common than agricultural.

All three studies tried to find predictors of exposure. In the western North Carolina studies (Quandt et al. 2004; Arcury et al. 2005), living adjacent to farm fields predicted the presence of agricultural pesticides and organophosphate metabolites; residing in a house judged hard to clean was a predictor of residential pesticides and organophosphate metabolites. In eastern North Carolina, boys, children in rental housing, and those with mothers working part-time had a greater number of pesticides detected (Arcury et al. 2007).

These studies suggest that pesticides are fairly ubiquitous in the environments where farmworker children live and play. Almost all children have some exposure. Detecting the exact predictors of pesticide exposure may take much more fine-detailed measurement, including timing of exposure relative to predictors. Health outcomes from pesticide exposure are equally inconclusive from studies in the eastern US. Beyond cognitive development studied in California (Bouchard et al. 2011), no studies have attempted to measure health effects of pesticides in farmworker children, either immediate or long-term effects. Based on existing research, it is impossible to know whether the levels of exposure observed in these children arc dangerous. Except in the case of poisoning with very high amounts of pesticides, health effects known from epidemiologic and animal studies are the result of cumulative exposure over long periods of time. Nonetheless, these findings suggest that farmworker children live in an environment where cumulative exposure is likely and should be minimized.

In an effort to develop a method to decrease child pesticide exposure, a North Carolina team implemented a six-lesson, *promotora*-led behavior change intervention with 610 farmworker families of young children. *Promotoras* are lay health advisors, who are members of the Latinx community. The home-delivered intervention was designed to increase parental knowledge of pesticide dangers for children, increase the use of integrated pest management strategies to reduce child exposures, and increase parental self-efficacy in preventing child pesticide exposure. Significant improvements in knowledge were observed, as well as significant improvements in practices related to take-home pesticide exposure and residential pest control (Quandt et al. 2013). Further data analyses showed that most of the improvement in behaviors was due to changes in pesticide knowledge rather than changes in self-efficacy or qualities of the *promotora* or the mother herself (Grzywacz et al. 2013). Although children in participating families were not tested for pesticide exposure, the study demonstrates that parents are interested in child health and willing to adopt measures that could protect their children from pesticide exposure.

7.3   Health of Hired Child Farmworkers

Much of the public has no knowledge that the fruits and vegetables piled in grocery store bins may have been harvested by hired children as young as 10 years old. That this is permissible under US labor laws is an even greater surprise for many (Fig. 7.4). Little is known about the characteristics of the Latinx child farmworkers in the US, even in the scientific community. The only nationally available data come from the National Agricultural Workers Survey (NAWS) and the Childhood

US farm job restrictions for children	
Ages	**Rules under the Fair Labor Standards Act (1938)**
16+	Any farm job, hazardous[1] or not, unlimited hours
14-15	Any nonhazardous farm job outside school hours
12-13	Any nonhazardous farm job outside school hours with parental permission or on same farm as parent(s)
Under 12	Any nonhazardous farm job outside school hours with parental permission but only where FLSA minimum wage requirements do not apply (i.e., small farms)
All ages	No rules or restrictions for children working on a farm owned or operated by their parents

[1] Hazardous tasks, as outlined in the Hazardous Occupation Orders in Agriculture, include working with and driving machinery, working with large animals, working from heights, working in confined spaces, driving passengers, working with toxic chemicals, and working with explosives

Fig. 7.4 Job restrictions for children working in agriculture, by age (USDOL 2016)

Agricultural Injury Survey (CAIS). The only regional studies that have looked at various occupational health topics for hired adolescent farmworkers come from California, Washington, Oregon, Texas, and North Carolina. Comparison across studies is difficult; however, regional comparisons can help piece together a picture of child farmworkers in the US. This section focuses on hired child crop workers. Livestock workers are excluded, as evidence points to a majority of Latinx children working in crop agriculture. Each subsection compares national and regional research and includes information about the personal and work characteristics of hired child farmworkers and their exposures.

7.3.1   What We Know About Child Farmworkers from National Data

National estimates of hired child farmworkers are difficult to calculate. The NAWS collects data from farmworkers in crop agriculture. The sample includes interviews with youths aged 14–18 and asks farmworker parents about their younger dependent children who work on farms, though the information collected on child workers under 14 years old is very limited. Two recent reports drew from NAWS data to produce profiles and estimates of hired child workers. The estimates of child workers are disparate between these reports because one included 18-year-olds (Gabbard et al. 2014) in the estimate and the other was based on child workers 17 years old and under (United States Government Accountability Office (GAO) 2018). Gabbard et al. (2014) estimated that there were 84,000 youth 14–18 years old working on crop farms each year from 2004 to 2009 (6% of all crop workers) and 4000 children under 14 years old (Gabbard et al. 2014). The 2018 Government Accountability Office (GAO) report estimated that an average of 43,000 children 17 years old and under worked on crop farms between 2005 and 2008 (GAO 2018). The GAO report also calculated estimates from years 2009–2012 and 2013–2016, estimating 30,000 and 34,000 child workers 17 years old and under each year during those periods, respectively.

The CAIS also produces national estimates of hired youth from select years between 2001 and 2014 (CDC 2018a). The most recent estimate is from 2014 and suggests that 79,325 youth 17 years old and under were working as hired crop workers. The variation in these estimates from national datasets demonstrates the need for better methods for calculating numbers of child farmworkers in the US.

7.3.1.1   National Demographics of Hired Child Farmworkers

Both the 2014 and 2018 reports drawing from NAWS indicated that hired child workers were more often male than female and more often Latinx than white and were overwhelming likely to live below the national poverty level (Gabbard et al. 2014; GAO 2018). The 2014 report that included 18-year-olds indicated that 61%

were foreign-born and 74% had been in the US less than 2 years (Gabbard et al. 2014). This stands in contrast with the 2018 GAO report, which found that most Latinx workers 17 years old and under were US citizens. The 2018 report estimated the percentage of hired crop workers 17 years old and under by region from 2005 to 2016. Estimates show that there was a relatively even distribution of child workers in California, the Midwest, and Northwest regions, with fewer in the Southeast and Southwest.

7.3.2   Regional Information About Hired Child Farmworkers

Table 7.1 shows the limited scope of research examining the occupational safety and health among young hired Latinx workers from 2002 to 2018. Few of these studies were solely focused on hired Latinx child farmworkers, but some do distinguish between white youth working on family farms and hired Latinx children. Almost all existing research has obtained data through surveys, including face-to-face, telephone, and online surveys; many have recruited samples through high schools, largely from students in agricultural curricula or clubs like the Future Farmers of America. Additionally, the generalizability of results is restricted because multiple papers have been written on different aspects of the same parent study samples (Arcury et al. 2014, 2015b). Further, the age ranges of participants vary between studies, with many excluding workers under 13 years old and some including workers as old as 20.

7.3.2.1   Non-eastern States

Regional studies in California, Texas, and Washington have different sampling frames and should be compared with caution. However, for the studies that report demographic compositions of their samples, several trends can be observed. These trends are consistent with analyses of national data from the NAWS and CAIS (GAO 2018; Gabbard et al. 2014). First, it appears that the majority of Latinx and non-Latinx children hired for farm work are male, with figures across studies ranging between 60% and 70% male. Second, most of the young Latinx hired farmworkers 17 years old and under were born in the US, with sample percentages ranging between 56% and 85% US-born and the majority of foreign-born coming from Mexico. However, in studies that focused on migrant child farmworkers, participants were more likely to be foreign-born. Finally, although several studies do not report ages of samples in detail, children 16 years and older are slightly more likely to be represented in samples. This could indicate that older children are more likely than younger children to be hired for farm work.

Table 7.1 Studies of hired child and youth farmworkers in the US, 2002–2018

Authors	Site	Topic	Methods
National studies			
GAO report (2018)	National	Summaries of injury and fatality data and compliance strategies for working children	Review of NAWS, CAIS, CPS, and NASS data pertaining to children working in agriculture from 2003 to 2016
Gabbard et al. (2014)	National	Profiles of youth, parents, and children of farmworkers in the US	Review of NAWS and CAIS data from 2004 to 2009
Westaby and Lee (2003)	Ten selected states	Longitudinal examination of antecedents to youth injury in agricultural settings	Survey, FFA students, $n = 3081$
Regional studies			
Arcury et al. (2019b)	North Carolina	Baseline characteristics of Latinx child farmworkers	Survey, ages 10–17, $n = 202$
Quandt et al. (2019)	North Carolina	Organization of work among Latinx child farmworkers	In-depth interviews, ages 10–17, $n = 30$
Arcury et al. (2015c)	North Carolina	Work safety culture among Latino youth farmworkers	Survey, ages 10–17, $n = 87$
Arcury et al. (2014)	North Carolina	Safety and injury characteristics of Latinx youth farmworkers	Survey, ages 10–17, $n = 87$
Kearney et al. (2015)	North Carolina	Work safety climate among Latino youth farmworkers	Survey, ages 10–17, $n = 87$
Perla et al. (2015)	Washington	Agricultural health and safety perspectives among Latinx youth	Survey, ages 14–18, $n = 196$
Bonauto et al. (2003)	Washington	Community-based telephone survey of work and injuries in teen agricultural workers	Survey, ages 13–19, $n = 200$ (122 Latinx teens)
Hennessy-Burt et al. (2013)	California	Factors associated with agricultural work performed by adolescents from an immigrant worker population	Survey, ages 11–18, $n = 101$
McCurdy et al. (2012)	California	Agricultural injury among public high school students in agricultural sciences curriculum	Survey, mean age of 15, $n = 1783$
McCurdy and Kwan (2012a)	California	Prospective agricultural injury experience among high school students enrolled in agricultural sciences curriculum	Survey, mean age of 15, $n = 946$
McCurdy and Kwan (2012b)	California	Ethnic and gender differences in farm tasks and safety practices among high school students	Survey, mean age of 15, $n = 946$ (212 Latinx students)
Peoples et al. (2010)	California	Health, occupational, and environmental risks of emancipated migrant farmworker youth	Focus groups, ages 13–22, $n = 29$

(continued)

Table 7.1 (continued)

Authors	Site	Topic	Methods
Salazar et al. (2004)	Oregon	Latinx adolescent farmworkers' perceptions associated with pesticide exposure	Focus groups, ages 11–18, $n = 33$
McCauley et al. (2002)	Oregon	Pesticide knowledge and risk perception among adolescent Latinx farmworkers	Survey, ages 13–18, $n = 102$
Shipp et al. (2013)	Texas	Occupational injury among adolescent farmworkers	Survey, ages 13–19, $n = 410$
Whitworth et al. (2010)	Texas	Relationship between neurotoxicity symptoms and injury among adolescent farmworkers	Survey, mean age of 15, $n = 88$
Shipp et al. (2007a)	Texas	Pesticide training among adolescent farmworkers	Survey, ages <14 to >18, high school students, grades 9–12, $n = 324$
Shipp et al. (2007b)	Texas	Lower back pain among farmworker high school students	Survey, 14–18, $n = 410$
Vela Acosta et al. (2007)	Texas	Health risk behaviors and work injury among Latinx adolescents and farmworkers	Survey, ninth graders, $n = 4914$ ($n = 1347$ with farm work experience)
Cooper et al. (2005)	Texas	Comparison of substance use, work, and injuries among migrant farmworkers vs. other rural Texas students	Survey, middle and high school students, $n = 10,867$ ($n = 545$ from farmworker families)

7.3.2.2 Eastern States

Those few eastern US studies that have collected information on nationality find trends observed in other regions that most Latinx child farmworkers 17 and under were born in the US. A 2014 study of 87 Latinx child farmworkers ages 10–17 in North Carolina found that 78% were born in the US (Arcury et al. 2014). These results are consistent with a larger North Carolina study with 202 Latinx child farmworkers ages 10–17, where 81% were US-born (Arcury et al. 2019b). Both studies found that the majority of foreign-born children were from Mexico, with a small percentage from Guatemala or another Central American country (Arcury et al. 2019b). Most Latinx child farmworkers in North Carolina are bilingual, with nearly all (99.5%) speaking Spanish and 84% speaking English (Arcury et al. 2019b). Boys make up the majority of child farmworkers, with both 2014 and 2019 studies having nearly identical gender ratios (62% boys vs. 38% girls).

North Carolina studies have found that the majority of child farmworkers are enrolled in school. Seventy-five percent (Arcury et al. 2014) and 95% of child farmworkers (Arcury et al. 2019b) reported current school enrollment. In the latter study, nearly one-quarter of those enrolled in school worked in farm work during the fall semester and nearly one-third worked during the spring semester. Of those who worked during the school year, very few children (4%) reported that they had missed school days in order to do farm work. The majority of children in both studies reported working during summer vacation (Arcury et al. 2014, 2019b). A Texas study found that migrant farmworker students were more likely to work before school than nonmigrant students (Cooper et al. 2005).

7.3.3 Model of Risks Stemming from Organization of Work

Collectively, existing studies paint a picture of the elevated risk of performing agricultural work at a young age. Farm work in the US is organized in a way that places farmworkers at risk of injury and poor health outcomes, with children being especially vulnerable to such risks. The conceptual model of hired child farmworkers (Fig. 7.5) is helpful for delineating factors that influence health outcomes. Additionally, this framework helps extend analyses to compare the experiences of Latinx child farmworkers in the US, as many of the macro-level forces affecting risk are not specific to one region. In this model, child farmworker health is directly influenced by occupational, social, and environmental hazards. However, characteristics of the child and the work itself can buffer or exacerbate health outcomes from work hazards. Child characteristics that can protect against work hazards include both personal (e.g., gender, age, status, accompanied by adult family member) and developmental (e.g., physical, emotional, cognitive). Characteristics of the work environment include multilevel factors including the external context (economic, legal, political, technological, and legal forces), organizational context (manage-

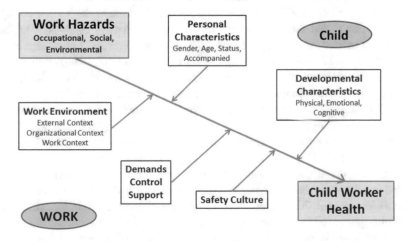

Fig. 7.5 Conceptual model of the organization of work for child farmworkers (Quandt et al. 2019)

ment structure, supervisory practices, production methods, and policies), and work context (job characteristics) (Sauter et al. 2002; Landsbergis et al. 2014). The work's demands, control, support (Karasek and Theorell 1990; Snyder et al. 2008), and safety culture can influence child workers' health outcomes, with high-demand jobs and low levels of control or support resulting in poor health.

7.3.4 What Do We Know About the Work Child Farmworkers Perform

Child farmworkers labor in a variety of farm operations, crops, and tasks. While existing research does not always distinguish between ethnicities, it reveals several ways in which Latinx children differ from their white counterparts. Latinx children are more likely to live below the poverty level, less likely to work on an operation owned or operated by their family members, and more likely to work in tasks related to planting, cultivating, and hand harvesting rather than tasks such as operating machinery.

7.3.4.1 Nationally

The reports drawing from NAWS data (Gabbard et al. 2014; GAO 2018) estimate that, of all hired crop workers surveyed (children and adults) between 2003 and 2016, more than one-third (39%) began working in US agriculture when they were 18 or younger. Seven percent reported beginning farm work before the age of 14 years, and 32% reported beginning between ages 14 and 18 years. Between 2004 and 2009, 85% of youths were employed directly by a grower, and the other 15% reported employment by a farm labor contractor (Gabbard et al. 2014). However, this has likely changed in the last 10 years, as farm consolidation continues to shift farm labor employment to contractor arrangements, particularly in crop agriculture. In a study of 410 high school farmworkers in Texas, a little over one-third reported working for a small owner or grower, and a little under one-quarter reported working for a contractor only; over one-quarter reported working for a combination of employers or other arrangements (Shipp et al. 2013). Such results should be interpreted with caution, as a qualitative study in North Carolina highlighted that child workers may not fully understand the arrangements of their employment (Quandt et al. 2019).

From 2004 to 2009, the largest group of 14- to 18-year olds were working in vegetable crops (30%), with a little over a quarter (27%) working in horticulture and less than a quarter (24%) working in fruits and nuts. Field crops and miscellaneous made up the remainder (Gabbard et al. 2014). Over one-half of youth crop workers (55%) performed preharvest and harvest tasks, while 45% performed postharvest, technical, or other tasks (Gabbard et al. 2014). Almost 90% of 14- to 18-year olds from 2004 to 2009 were paid by the hour, with the rest being paid piece rate. Average wages were very low, around $7.25 per hour; and the majority of youth who had worked in the previous year made less than $10,000 from farm work.

7.3.4.2 Regionally

A California sample of 946 rural students working in agriculture included 212 Latinx students (McCurdy and Kwan 2012a). Latinx students were more likely to work in hand harvesting of crops and were less likely to perform hazardous tasks involving chemicals and machinery, respectively, than white males (McCurdy and Kwan 2012b). Another California study consisting of 101 Latinx farmworkers between 11 and 18 found that participants worked in melons, tomatoes, cotton, and nuts and completed tasks including hoeing, packing, and picking (Hennessy-Burt et al. 2013). Fifteen percent of the sample started farmwork at age 14 or younger, and youth with lower acculturation levels were four times more likely to begin working at a younger age (Hennessy-Burt et al. 2013).

In Washington, a 2003 study of 200 Latinx and white teenage agricultural workers found that Latinx teens were less likely to work or live on a farm owned by a family member (Bonauto et al. 2003). Forty-four percent of the Latinx teens reported that they had started working in agriculture when they were 12 years of age or younger (Bonauto et al. 2003). Consistent with what was observed in California and national findings, other studies in Washington and Oregon found that most Latinx teen farmworkers performed the tasks for harvesting crops (Perla et al. 2015; Salazar et al. 2004; McCauley et al. 2002).

Texas research with 410 high school student farmworkers aged 14–18 reported that students worked in a wide variety of crops, but those most commonly reported were cotton, corn, melons, and peanuts. In contrast to other regional studies where harvesting was the main task, Texas participants reported cutting, clearing, cleaning, and hoeing more frequently (Shipp et al. 2013).

In a sample of 202 Latinx child farmworkers aged 10–17 in North Carolina, over half reported 2 or less years working in agriculture, and a little over one-third reported 3 or more years of experience (Arcury et al. 2019b). These children worked in a variety of crops and farm labor tasks. Across two separate studies with samples of 87 and 202 Latinx child workers, topping tobacco was the most common job that child workers occupied (Arcury et al. 2014, 2019b). Picking blueberries, harvesting sweet potatoes, and working in tomatoes were also common jobs for children. Most of the tasks across crops involved activities required for the growth, maintenance, and eventual harvest of crops including planting, weeding, and picking; fewer involved driving vehicles or operating machinery (Arcury et al. 2014, 2019b).

Over three-fourths (77%) of child farmworkers in the 2019 North Carolina study were paid directly, and nearly a quarter of child farmworkers' pay was given to their parents (23%), with younger children's pay more likely to go to parents. Workers were usually paid cash rather than by check. A third of child workers reported being paid at piece rate, while two-thirds were paid by the hour. The majority who were paid at an hourly rate received between $8 and $9; however, some workers reported unpaid work time waiting for crops to dry or equipment repair or time spent traveling from field to field (Arcury et al. 2019b).

7.3.4.3 Critical Aspects of Organization of Work for Child Farmworkers

As is evident from national and regional studies cited above, the organization of work poses several threats to the health and safety of child farmworkers; Quandt et al. (2019) document many of these in qualitative data from child farmworkers in North Carolina. First, work is largely based on the crew leader system, with children being supervised by a crew leader who is tasked by a grower with completing fieldwork, often on a deadline and for a set amount of money. Such a situation may make children pressured to work more quickly than safely. Indeed, in a 2014 study, 38% of Latinx child farmworkers reported that their supervisors were only interested in doing the job fast and cheaply (Arcury et al. 2015c). With pressure to get the work finished, heat stress or reentering fields treated with pesticides too soon may occur. Some of these demands may be countered by support from coworkers and family; Quandt et al. (2019) found this support to be more common for younger children than for teen workers.

North Carolina studies have demonstrated low levels of work safety culture and poor levels of safety climate (Arcury et al. 2015c; Kearney et al. 2015). Using qualitative data, Arcury et al. (2019a) present a conflicted view of work safety culture for child farmworkers. These children are told by their families to work safely; indeed, family members often teach the children in the fields how to perform their tasks in a safe manner and ensure that children are wearing the proper personal protective equipment for the job. Yet children see their coworkers and their supervisors placing a much lower value on working safely, not wearing appropriate personal protective equipment, and taking risks. While some of the children attribute any suggestion of working safely to altruism of the supervisors, others see this behavior as more pragmatic: supervisors do not want to get into trouble, and they want to keep production levels high. Supervisors provide little safety training; most provided is simply in the context of training a child to do a task. In a few cases, children were told to watch a safety video and then sign a paper indicating they had watched it.

7.3.5 Exposures and Health Outcomes for Child Farmworkers

While there is a substantial body of literature examining the health and exposures of adult farmworkers, little to no research has documented the health of child farmworkers. Translating research on adults to child populations requires some consideration of the differences between children and adults and how these may influence outcomes from workplace exposures (see Sect. 7.2.5). These differences between adults and children raise concern about the appropriateness of children working where they are exposed to environmental hazards, including pesticides, nicotine, and heat, and social hazards such as discrimination and interpersonal violence.

7.3.5.1   Injuries and Fatalities

Nationally

The Childhood Agricultural Injury Survey (CAIS) collects injury and demographic data for youth less than 20 years old who live on, work on, or visit farms. Data are available from years 2001, 2004, 2006, 2009, 2012, and 2014 (CDC 2018b). While recent reports show a downward trend for nonfatal injuries from 2001 to 2014 for all youth, rates are still extremely high, with about 33 children injured in agriculture-related incidents every day (CDC 2018c). The CAIS does not include injuries to contract laborers, so actual numbers, especially for Latinx child workers, are likely higher.

Fatality rates for children living and working on farms are also high. From 2003 to 2016, 237 children died in agriculture-related child incidents, which accounted for 52% of work-related child fatalities across all industries (GAO 2018). In 2015, young agricultural workers were 44.8 times more likely to be fatally injured, when compared to all other industries combined (CDC 2018c). Within the broad North American industry classification of agriculture, forestry, and fishing and hunting, 60% of child fatalities from 2003 to 2016 were in crop production, 28% in animal production and aquaculture, and the rest in forestry and fishing (GAO 2018).

Regionally

Calculated injury rates are difficult to compare across studies due to different definitions of injuries and uses of self-report. A California study calculated a cumulative 1-year injury incidence of 2.4% for the 212 Latinx teen farmworkers in the sample (McCurdy et al. 2012). In Texas, severe back pain was reported by 15.7% of a sample of 410 largely migrant Latinx youth farmworkers (Shipp et al. 2007b). In this sample, the estimated rate of nonfatal injuries was 27.0/100 full time equivalents (FTE) for the most severe injury types, and this rate increased to 73.6/100 FTE when broadening the injury definition (Shipp et al. 2013). The estimated rate for severe injury in Texas is similar to that found in Washington (20.8/100 FTE) in a sample of 122 Latinx teen farmworkers (Bonauto et al. 2003). Whitworth and colleagues found a positive association between reported neurotoxicity symptoms and injury among adolescent farmworkers in Texas (Whitworth et al. 2010). Another Texas study found that migrant farmworker students were more likely to report work-related injuries than nonmigrant students (Cooper et al. 2005). A 2014 survey of 87 Latino youth farmworkers in North Carolina found that 54% reported a musculoskeletal injury, 60.9% reported a traumatic injury, and 72.4% reported a dermatological injury in the previous year (Arcury et al. 2014).

7.3.5.2 Pesticides

Agricultural workers are exposed to a wide variety of toxic chemicals including herbicides, insecticides, and other pesticides which can have both immediate and long-term health effects. Acute poisoning, characterized by vomiting, diarrhea, and excessive salivation, can result from encountering concentrated chemicals in the fields or during mixing and loading. Chronic exposure to pesticides occurs through contact with pesticide residues on plants, soil, or tools that are transferred to the skin. The long-term effects of chronic exposure are increasingly understood to include cancer, neurodegenerative disease, and reproductive problems (see Sect. 7.2.5.2). Child farmworkers may be exposed to pesticides through direct contact from mixing or applying, drift from nearby spraying, and chemical residues in the fields on plants or brought home on clothes by themselves or family members.

In NAWS data from 2003 to 2016, 14% of 16-year-olds and 8% of 17-year-olds reported that they had mixed, loaded, or applied pesticides in the previous year (GAO 2018). California research found that nearly a quarter of Latinx boys reported mixing or applying chemicals, with a median age at initiation of 14 (McCurdy and Kwan 2012b). A 2002 Oregon study had similar results; 22% of 102 Latinx adolescents reported mixing or applying chemicals in their current job (McCauley et al. 2002). Twenty-two percent of Latinx child farmworkers in North Carolina reported working within view of fertilizer or pesticide applications in the previous week, and 12% worked in an area where pesticides had been applied in the previous week (Arcury et al. 2014). They may also be at risk of exposure to chemical residues brought into the home from parents; 18% of farmworker parents in the NAWS with dependent children reported working with pesticides in the previous 12 months (Gabbard et al. 2014). Children 16 and 17 years of age are legally permitted to apply pesticides.

Pesticide safety knowledge can help workers protect themselves from pesticide exposure. Federal law mandates Worker Protection Standard (WPS) training, which includes pesticide safety, for all agricultural workers (Environmental Protection Agency 2018). Unfortunately, pesticide safety training, knowledge, and behaviors appear to be low among Latinx children working in agriculture. In Oregon, only 32% of adolescent farmworkers reported that they had received safety training; only half wore protective clothing or equipment when working; and low pesticide knowledge was associated with low use of protective measures (McCauley et al. 2002). In Texas, only 21% of adolescent farmworkers reported ever receiving pesticide safety training (Shipp et al. 2007a). In focus group interviews with 33 migrant farmworker youth in Washington, researchers noted that youth were only vaguely aware of the dangers of pesticide exposure, but were also aware that workplace constraints sometimes limited their ability to enact safe practices (Salazar et al. 2004). Training levels in North Carolina studies were significantly lower. Arcury and colleagues found that only 6% of 87 youth farmworkers reported receiving pesticide training in the previous year and 8% reported ever receiving pesticide training. Further, youth reported a negative work safety climate and culture, which were associated with increased pesticide exposure risk (Arcury et al. 2015c; Kearney et al. 2015).

7.3.5.3   Tobacco and Nicotine

Child farmworkers in the eastern US are distinct from workers in most other regions because they are likely to work in tobacco production. North Carolina is the leading tobacco-producing state, followed by Kentucky, Virginia, and Tennessee (Statista 2019). Tobacco production is particularly dangerous, compared to other crops, yet limited research is available documenting the health effects of child involvement in the US.

In North Carolina, 46% of a 2013 sample of 87 child farmworkers and 57% of a 2017 sample of 202 child farmworkers stated that they had worked in tobacco in the last week that they worked in agriculture (Arcury et al. 2014, 2019b). The most common job reported for child tobacco workers was topping tobacco (50% of entire sample), while only 4% reported working in the task of barning harvested tobacco. Topping tobacco involves inspecting individual plants to break off the flower that grows on top, removing "suckers" (*retoños*) that grow at the joint between the main stem and secondary leaf stems and applying a growth regulatory chemical. This task results in contact with the leaves and can lead to green tobacco sickness (GTS). GTS is acute nicotine poisoning that occurs when nicotine is absorbed through the skin (Arcury et al. 2003; Quandt et al. 2001). The differential diagnosis for GTS is nausea or vomiting and headache or dizziness within 24 h of working in tobacco (Arcury et al. 2001a). Contact with plants wet from dew, rain, and perspiration, as well as working in wet clothes, increases risk of GTS, as water on the plants contains high amounts of nicotine (Arcury et al. 2001b; Gehlbach et al. 1975). Two Human Rights Watch reports interviewed child tobacco workers in four states and found that most reported experiencing symptoms consistent with GTS (Human Rights Watch 2014, 2015). In a study of adult tobacco workers in North Carolina, workers with four or less years of experience were more likely to experience GTS than those with 5 or more years (Arcury et al. 2001a). This is a cause for concern among child tobacco workers, as they are unexperienced, have a lower tolerance to nicotine, and may not know how to work safely with tobacco plants.

Workers generally recover from GTS within a few hours to a few days. Long-term effects of work-related nicotine poisoning are unknown; however, evidence from adolescent smoking studies shows that childhood nicotine exposure has detrimental effects on long-term brain development (Goriounova and Mansvelder 2012; Dwyer et al. 2009). Adolescent nicotine exposure affects gene expression and neuron structure, which can lead to functional and structural cognition changes including attention deficit and lower impulse control (Goriounova and Mansvelder 2012). Studies from rodent models have demonstrated that brain changes during sensitive maturational periods are due to nicotine rather than other chemicals found in cigarettes (Dwyer et al. 2009).

An examination of global tobacco production that compared child labor in the US, Kazakhstan, and Malawi highlights the fact that, although the US has ratified the International Labor Organization's (ILO) Convention Number 182 (one of the eight fundamental conventions of the ILO, which seeks to eliminate some of the worst forms of child labor such as slavery and work that, by its nature, is likely to harm the health, safety, and morals of children), it has not passed any laws (e.g., age restrictions) that would protect child tobacco workers (Ramos 2018). Human Rights Watch (Human Rights Watch 2014, 2015) and others have called for federal regulations to prohibit children under 18 from engaging in hazardous work on tobacco farms in the US, but there has been no action.

7.3.5.4   Heat

Much of the work that hired child farmworkers do in the US occurs during the hottest months, regardless of region. Crop workers are at increased risk of heat-related illnesses including heat rash, heat cramps, heat exhaustion, and heat stroke, which can be life threatening. Symptoms vary, but commonly include nausea, dizziness, headache, and fainting. A national review of heat-related fatalities from 1992 to 2006 found that the fatality rate for crop workers was 20 times greater than US civilian workers (CDC 2008). Nineteen percent of crop worker fatalities during that timeframe occurred in North Carolina (CDC 2008).

A substantial amount of research has documented heat-related illness fatalities among adult farmworkers in the US and specifically in North Carolina; however, child workers are absent from these analyses. In a survey of 300 North Carolina farmworkers, 94% reported working in extreme heat; of those, 40% reported heat-related symptoms (Mirabelli et al. 2010). These results are consistent with a later study in which 35.6% of farmworkers surveyed reported heat-related symptoms; associated factors were working in wet clothes and shoes, harvesting and topping tobacco, and spending after-work time in an extremely hot house (Arcury et al. 2015b). Another North Carolina study reported heat-related illness prevalence of 72% among workers reporting one heat-related illness symptom and 27% among those reporting three or more symptoms (Kearney et al. 2016). Child workers may be at greater risk than adults of heat-related illness due to their inexperience in maintaining hydration during physical activity and their susceptibility to pressure from supervisors and coworkers to continue working in dangerous conditions (Quandt et al. 2019).

7.3.5.5   Social Exposures

In addition to environmental hazards, child farmworkers are also at risk of detrimental social exposures such as interpersonal violence and discrimination. Several aspects of the organization of farm work increase risk of interpersonal violence and discrimination. Farm work fields are generally isolated in rural environments away from regulatory or law enforcement entities. Workers may be susceptible to violence and discrimination perpetrated by employers or local residents because they fear retaliation, loss of job, or, in some cases, deportation, if they complain. Ten percent of a sample of 87 youth farmworkers in North Carolina experienced some level of sexual harassment, and this was likely underreported (Arcury et al. 2014).

Another qualitative study with 30 child farmworkers in North Carolina described a work environment with little oversight and few protections from potential violence, harassment, and discrimination (Quandt et al. 2019). Several other qualitative studies of adult farmworkers in California and Oregon have reported high levels of sexual harassment in the fields (Castañeda and Zavella 2003; Murphy et al. 2015; Waugh 2010). A Human Rights Watch report describes the myriad ways in which immigrant farmworkers are vulnerable to sexual violence and sexual harassment (Human Rights Watch 2012) (see also Chap. 6). With limited studies and the sensitive nature of the topic, it is difficult to quantify this problem. Any amount of sexual violence and discrimination in workplaces is unacceptable; it is particularly egregious for vulnerable children to be subjected to these environments.

7.4   Conclusions

Children in farmworker families, whether employed as hired farmworkers themselves or not, face significant health threats. Like many children in low-income families, they lack adequate access to healthcare. The situation may be worse for these children because of issues with documentation status, restriction placed on access to government safety net programs for immigrants, and fear of deportation in an uncertain political climate. Limited parental resources, whether housing or access to healthy food, link to health threats.

Hired child farmworkers constitute a hidden population within the larger farmworker population. They are at risk due to their immaturity: their bodies, particularly the brain and nervous system, are still developing; and they may not have sufficient experience to make good decisions about health and safety. Policies to protect child workers are weaker in agriculture than in other industries.

The research base for Latinx children in farmworker families in the eastern US is thinner than in other parts of the US that have a longer history of Latinx farmworkers. There have been two significant advances in the last 10 years. These have been the research focused on overweight and obesity among children in farmworker families and the research on health risks of Latinx hired child farmworkers. The last 10 years has also seen considerable attention by journalists and advocacy groups (e.g., Human Rights Watch, Association of Farmworker Opportunity Programs) to the situation of hired child farmworkers (Human Rights Watch 2014, 2015; Association of Farmworker Opportunity Programs 2019). Additional research studies are needed to identify and design prevention programs for health and safety risks.

7.5   Recommendations

Research should be conducted to better document conditions of children in the farmworker community. Future research should prioritize the perspectives of farmworker communities and ensure that they have a voice in how the research proceeds from beginning to end (see Chap. 8). These children are often unseen, because of their rural residence and the hidden nature of farmworker residences, and fail to access services for multiple reasons, including parents' fear generated by immigration tensions. In the eastern US, a larger proportion of farmworkers, and, consequently, children in farmworker communities, live in the southern states. These states, on the whole, have a history of denying services to minority residents, passing anti-union legislation, and providing more limited social and health programs. These factors make the research and policy needs of these children all the more imperative.

For children in farmworker families, these research recommendations include the following:

- Documenting the numbers of such children and their personal and health characteristics.
- Evaluating evidence-based interventions, including those to (1) reduce overweight and obesity and (2) increase access to healthcare, particularly at early ages.

For child farmworkers, research recommendations include the following:

- Implementing surveillance systems to document the personal and work characteristics of hired child labor. While such data are currently collected in the NAWS, data are inconsistent across ages, with very little collected on the youngest workers.
- Implementing surveillance systems to record occupational illness, injury, and death data from hired child labor. Such data could be collected in the NAWS, though more focused studies on children are necessary, and would likely require a greater emphasis on finding minors.
- Conducting focused research on the impact of hired farm work on children, including examination of the educational and health impact of such work. Prospective data collection is essential to be able to establish causality of farm work on such outcomes.

Beyond research, policy regarding children in the farmworker community must be changed. For children in farmworker families, greater access to the full range of state and federal health services is crucial. These include medical, nutritional, dental, and educational services. While many of these children are US citizens and therefore should have full access to services, greater implementation of outreach to ensure the use of services is needed to achieve equity with other citizen children. In particular, children should have full access to well-child medical and dental care and to the anticipatory guidance provided at such healthcare visits. Policy changes to increase the portability of Medicaid and other state-based insurance systems from one state to another are important for children in the eastern US whose families migrate. Likewise, policy changes are needed to extend programs for migrant farmworkers (e.g., Migrant Education and Migrant Head Start) to seasonal farmworkers as they settle out of the migrant stream.

For child farmworkers, the need for policy change is clear. The rationale is outdated for exempting agriculture from the child labor provisions of the Fair Labor Standards Act that are applied to all other industries. These hired child farmworkers are not working on their parents' farms. They are working in much the same conditions and often alongside adult farmworkers. Policies should be implemented at the federal level to protect these children by (1) eliminating all work in agriculture until age 16 and (2) prohibiting hazardous work until age 18. This will bring child labor in agriculture to the standard enforced for all other industries in the US. Many children go to the fields to work out of the necessity to supplement the low wages of their farmworker parents. Raising the federal minimum wage and eliminating the exemption of overtime pay for agricultural workers would increase the incomes of farmworker parents and reduce the need of children to work alongside their parents.

References

Arcury TA, Quandt SA, Preisser JS et al (2001a) The incidence of green tobacco sickness among Latino farmworkers. J Occup Environ Med 43:601–609

Arcury TA, Quandt SA, Preisser JS (2001b) Predictors of incidence and prevalence of green tobacco sickness among Latino farmworkers in North Carolina, USA. J Epidemiol Commun Health 55:818–824

Arcury TA, Quandt SA, Preisser JS et al (2003) High levels of transdermal nicotine exposure produce green tobacco sickness in Latino farmworkers. Nicotine Tob Res 5:315–321

Arcury TA, Quandt SA, Rao P et al (2005) Organophosphate pesticide exposure in farmworker family members in western North Carolina and Virginia: case comparisons. Hum Organ 64:40–51

Arcury TA, Grzywacz JG, Barr DB et al (2007) Pesticide urinary metabolite levels of children in eastern North Carolina farmworker households. Environ Health Perspect 115:1254–1260

Arcury TA, Rodriguez G, Kearney GD et al (2014) Safety and injury characteristics of youth farmworkers in North Carolina: a pilot study. J Agromedicine 19:354–363

Arcury TA, Trejo G, Suerken CK et al (2015a) Housing and neighborhood characteristics and Latino farmworker family well-being. J Immigr Minor Health 17:1458–1467

Arcury TA, Summers P, Talton JW et al (2015b) Heat illness among North Carolina Latino farmworkers. J Occup Environ Med 57:1299–1304

Arcury TA, Kearney GD, Rodriguez G et al (2015c) Work safety culture of youth farmworkers in North Carolina: a pilot study. Am J Public Health 105:344–350

Arcury TA, Skelton JA, Ip EH et al (2016) Anticipatory guidance about child diet and physical activity for Latino farmworker mothers. J Health Care Poor Underserved 27:1064–1079

Arcury TA, Suerken CK, Ip EH et al (2017) Residential environment for outdoor play among children in Latino farmworker families. J Immigr Minor Health 19:267–274

Arcury TA, Arnold TJ, Mora DC et al (2019a) "Be careful!" Perceptions of work safety culture among hired Latinx child farmworkers in North Carolina. Am J Ind Med 62:1091–1102

Arcury TA, Arnold TJ, Sandberg JC et al (2019b) Latinx child farmworkers in North Carolina: study design and participant baseline characteristics. Am J Ind Med 62:156–167

Association of Farmworker Opportunity Programs (2019) Children in the fields: the stories you should know. Available via AFOP. https://afop.org/wp-content/uploads/2019/04/AFOP-CIFC-Publication-The-Stories-You-Should-Know-2019.pdf. Accessed 23 May 2019

Barr DB, Bravo R, Weerasekera G et al (2004) Concentrations of dialkyl phosphate metabolites of organophosphorus pesticides in the US population. Environ Health Perspect 112:186–200

Bonauto DK, Keifer M, Rivara FP et al (2003) A community-based telephone survey of work and injuries in teenage agricultural workers. J Agric Saf Health 9:303–317

Borre K, Ertle L, Graff M (2010) Working to eat: vulnerability, food insecurity, and obesity among migrant and seasonal farmworker families. Am J Ind Med 53:443–462

Bouchard MF, Chevrier J, Harley KG et al (2011) Prenatal exposure to organophosphate pesticides and IQ in 7-year-old children. Environ Health Perspect 119:1189–1195

Camann DE, Colt JS, Teitelbaum SL et al (2000) Pesticide and PAH distributions in house dust from seven areas of USA. Paper presented at the 21st Annual Meeting of the Society of Environmental Toxicology, Nashville, TN, 12–16 November 2000

Campbell-Montalvo R, Castañeda H (2019) School employees as health care brokers for multiply-marginalized migrant families. Med Anthropol (8):1–14

Carrion IV, Castañeda H, Martinez-Tyson D et al (2011) Barriers impeding access to primary oral health care among farmworker families in Central Florida. Soc Work Health Care 50:828–844

Castañeda X, Zavella P (2003) Changing constructions of sexuality and risk: migrant Mexican women farmworkers in California. J Lat Am Anthropol 8:126–151

Castañeda H, Carrion IV, Kline N et al (2010) False hope: effects of social class and health policy on oral health inequalities for migrant farmworker families. Soc Sci Med 71:2028–2037

Centers for Disease Control and Prevention (CDC) (2003) Second national report on human exposure to environmental chemicals. Centers for Disease Control and Prevention, National Center Environmental Health, Atlanta, GA

Centers for Disease Control and Prevention (CDC) (2008) Heat-related deaths among crop workers—United States, 1992–2006. MMWR Morb Mortal Wkly Rep 57:649–653

Centers for Disease Control and Prevention (CDC) (2018a) Childhood agricultural injury survey (CAIS) results technical information. https://www.cdc.gov/niosh/topics/childag/cais/techinfo.html#Datasource. Accessed 22 May 2019

Centers for Disease Control and Prevention (CDC) (2018b) Childhood agriculture injury survey (CAIS) results. https://www.cdc.gov/niosh/topics/childag/cais/default.html. Accessed 22 May 2019

Centers for Disease Control and Prevention (CDC) (2018c) The national institute for occupational safety and health (NIOSH): National children's center for rural and agricultural health and safety. https://www.cdc.gov/niosh/docs/2018-111/default.html. Accessed 22 May 2019

Chang CP, Barker JC, Hoeft KS et al (2018) Importance of content and format of oral health instruction to low-income Mexican immigrant parents: a qualitative study. Pediatr Dent 40:30–36

Cooper SP, Weller NF, Fox EE et al (2005) Comparative description of migrant farmworkers versus other students attending rural South Texas schools: substance use, work, and injuries. J Rural Health 21:361–366

Council on Community Pediatrics (2013) Providing care for immigrant, migrant, and border children. Pediatrics 131:e2028–e2034

Dietrich T, Webb I, Stenhouse L et al (2017) Evidence summary: the relationship between oral and cardiovascular disease. Br Dent J 222:381–385

Dwyer JB, McQuown SC, Leslie FM (2009) The dynamic effects of nicotine on the developing brain. Pharmacol Ther 122:125–139

Engel SM, Wetmur J, Chen J et al (2011) Prenatal exposure to organophosphates, paraoxonase 1, and cognitive development in childhood. Environ Health Perspect 119:1182–1188

Environmental Protection Agency (2018) Agricultural Worker Protection Standard (WPS). https://www.epa.gov/pesticide-worker-safety/agricultural-worker-protection-standard-wps. Accessed 22 May 2019

Eskenazi B, Huen K, Marks A et al (2010) PON1 and neurodevelopment in children from the CHAMACOS study exposed to organophosphate pesticides in utero. Environ Health Perspect 118:1775–1781

Friedman DS, Repka MX, Katz J et al (2008) Prevalence of decreased visual acuity among preschool-aged children in an American urban population: the Baltimore pediatric eye disease study, methods, and results. Ophthalmology 115:1786–1795.e1–4

Gabbard S, Georges A, Hernandez T et al (2014) Findings from the National Agricultural Workers Survey (NAWS) 2000–2009: profiles of youth, parents, and children of farm workers in the United States. Rockville, MD: JBS International. https://www.doleta.gov/naws/research/docs/NAWS_Research_Report_10.pdf. Accessed 25 Apr 2019

Gehlbach SH, Williams WA, Perry LD et al (1975) Nicotine absorption by workers harvesting green tobacco. Lancet 305(7905):478–480

Goriounova NA, Mansvelder HD (2012) Short- and long-term consequences of nicotine exposure during adolescence for prefrontal cortex neuronal network function. Cold Spring Harb Perspect Med 2:a012120

Grzywacz JG, Arcury TA, Talton JW et al (2013) "Causes" of pesticide safety behavior change in Latino farmworker families. Am J Health Behav 37:449–457

Grzywacz JG, Suerken CK, Zapata Roblyer MI et al (2014) Physical activity of preschool-aged Latino children in farmworker families. Am J Health Behav 38:717–725

Grzywacz JG, Arcury TA, Trejo G et al (2016) Latino mothers in farmworker families' beliefs about preschool children's physical activity and play. J Immigr Minor Health 18:234–242

Health Resources and Services Administration (HRSA) (2015) National migrant health centers program grantee data. Bureau of Primary Health Care. https://bphc.hrsa.gov/uds2015/datacenter.aspx?q=t3a&year=2015&state=&fd=mh. Accessed 19 Dec 2019

Hennessy-Burt TE, Stoecklin-Marois MT, McCurdy SA et al (2013) Factors associated with agricultural work performed by adolescents from an immigrant farm worker population (MICASA study). J Agric Saf Health 19:163–173

Hernandez T, Gabbard S (2018) Findings from the National Agricultural Workers Survey (NAWS) 2015–2016: a demographic and employment profile of United States farmworkers. Report prepared for the U.S. Department of Labor, Employment and Training Administration, Office of Policy Development and Research. Rockville, MD: JBS International. https://www.doleta.gov/naws/research/docs/NAWS_Research_Report_13.pdf. Accessed 25 Apr 2019

Hoeft KS, Rios SM, Pantoja Guzman E et al (2015) Using community participation to assess acceptability of "contra caries", a theory-based, promotora-led oral health education program for rural Latino parents: a mixed methods study. BMC Oral Health 15:103

Hoeft KS, Barker JC, Shiboski S et al (2016) Effectiveness evaluation of contra caries oral health education program for improving Spanish-speaking parents' preventive oral health knowledge and behaviors for their young children. Community Dent Oral Epidemiol 44:564–576

Horton S, Barker JC (2010) Stigmatized biologies: examining the cumulative effects of oral health disparities for Mexican American farmworker children. Med Anthropol Q 24:199–219

Housing Assistance Council (2000) Abundant fields, meager shelter: findings from a survey of farmworker housing in the eastern migrant stream. Housing Assistance Council, Washington, DC

Hu R, Shi L, Lee DC et al (2016) Access to and disparities in care among migrant and seasonal farm workers (MSFWs) at U.S. health centers. J Health Care Poor Underserved 27:1484–1502

Human Rights Watch (2012) Cultivating fear: the vulnerability of immigrant farmworkers in the US to sexual violence and sexual harassment. Available via HRW. https://www.hrw.org/report/2012/05/15/cultivating-fear/vulnerability-immigrant-farmworkers-us-sexual-violence-and-sexual. Accessed 23 May 2019

Human Rights Watch (2014) Tobacco's hidden children: hazardous child labor in United States farming. Available via HRW. https://www.hrw.org/report/2014/05/13/tobaccos-hidden-children/hazardous-child-labor-united-states-tobaccofarming. Accessed 23 May 2019

Human Rights Watch (2015) Teens of the tobacco fields: child labor in United States farming. Available via HRW. https://www.hrw.org/report/2015/12/09/teens-tobacco-fields/child-labor-united-states-tobacco-farming. Accessed 23 May 2019

Hyland C, Laribi O (2017) Review of take-home pesticide exposure pathway in children living in agricultural areas. Environ Res 156:559–570

Infante-Rivard C, Weichenthal S (2007) Pesticides and childhood cancer: an update of Zahm and Ward's 1998 review. J Toxicol Environ Health B Crit Rev 10:81–99

Ip EH, Saldana S, Arcury TA et al (2015) Profiles of food security for US farmworker households and factors related to dynamic of change. Am J Public Health 105:e42–e47

Ip EH, Saldana S, Trejo G et al (2016) Physical activity states of preschool-aged Latino children in farmworker families: predictive factors and relationship with BMI percentile. J Phys Act Health 13:726–732

Ip EH, Marshall SA, Saldana S et al (2017) Determinants of adiposity rebound timing in children. J Pediatr 184:151–156.e2

Ip EH, Marshall SA, Arcury TA et al (2018) Child feeding style and dietary outcomes in a cohort of Latino farmworker families. J Acad Nutr Diet 118:1208–1219

Jackson SL, Vann WF Jr, Kotch JB et al (2011) Impact of poor oral health on children's school attendance and performance. Am J Public Health 101:1900–1906

Karasek R, Theorell T (1990) Healthy work: stress, productivity, and the reconstruction of working life. Basic Books, New York

Kearney GD, Rodriguez G, Quandt SA et al (2015) Work safety climate, safety behaviors, and occupational injuries of youth farmworkers in North Carolina. Am J Public Health 105:1336–1343

Kearney GD, Hu H, Xu X et al (2016) Estimating the prevalence of heat-related symptoms and sun safety-related behavior among Latino farmworkers in eastern North Carolina. J Agromedicine 21:15–23

Landsbergis PA, Grzywacz JG, LaMontagne AD (2014) Work organization, job insecurity, and occupational health disparities. Am J Ind Med 57:495–515

Lee K, Song W (2015) Effect of enrollment length in migrant head start on children's weight outcomes. Health Soc Work 40:142–150

Lee CV, McDermott SW, Elliott C (1990) The delayed immunization of children of migrant farm workers in South Carolina. Public Health Rep 105:317–320

Lim YM, Song S, Song WO (2017) Prevalence and determinants of overweight and obesity in children and adolescents from migrant and seasonal farmworker families in the United States—a systematic review and qualitative assessment. Nutrients 9:E188

Marks AR, Harley K, Bradman A et al (2010) Organophosphate pesticide exposure and attention in young Mexican-American children: the CHAMACOS study. Environ Health Perspect 118:1768–1774

Marshall SA, Ip EH, Suerken CK et al (2018) Relationship between maternal depression symptoms and child weight outcomes in Latino farmworker families. Matern Child Nutr 14:e12614

McCauley LA, Sticker D, Bryan C et al (2002) Pesticide knowledge and risk perception among adolescent Latino farmworkers. J Agric Saf Health 8:397–409

McCurdy SA, Kwan JA (2012a) Agricultural injury risk among rural California public high school students: prospective results. Am J Ind Med 55:631–642

McCurdy SA, Kwan JA (2012b) Ethnic and gender differences in farm tasks and safety practices among rural California farm youth. J Occup Environ Hyg 9:362–370

McCurdy SA, Xiao H, Kwan JA (2012) Agricultural injury among rural California public high school students. Am J Ind Med 55:63–75

Mirabelli MC, Quandt SA, Crain R et al (2010) Symptoms of heat illness among Latino farm workers in North Carolina. Am J Prev Med 39:468–471

Murphy J, Samples J, Morales M et al (2015) "They talk like that, but we keep working": sexual harassment and sexual assault experiences among Mexican indigenous farmworker women in Oregon. J Immigr Minor Health 17:1834–1839

Osband ME, Tobin JR (1972) Lead paint exposure in migrant labor camps. Pediatrics 49:604–606

Peoples JD, Bishop J, Barrera B et al (2010) Health, occupational and environmental risks of emancipated migrant farmworker youth. J Health Care Poor Underserved 21(4):1215–1226

Perla ME, Iman E, Campos L et al (2015) Agricultural occupational health and safety perspectives among Latino-American youth. J Agromedicine 20:167–177

Pulgar CA, Trejo G, Suerken C et al (2016) Economic hardship and depression among women in Latino farmworker families. J Immigr Minor Health 18:497–504

Quandt SA, Arcury TA, Bell RA (1998) Self-management of nutritional risk among older adults: a conceptual model and case studies from rural communities. J Aging Stud 12:351–368

Quandt SA, Arcury TA, Preisser JS et al (2001) Environmental and behavioral predictors of salivary cotinine in Latino tobacco workers. J Occup Environ Med 43:844–852

Quandt SA, Arcury TA, Rao P et al (2004) Agricultural and residential pesticides in wipe samples from farmworker family residences in North Carolina and Virginia. Environ Health Perspect 112:382–387

Quandt SA, Shoaf JI, Tapia J et al (2006) Experiences of Latino immigrant families in North Carolina help explain elevated levels of food insecurity and hunger. J Nutr 136:2638–2644

Quandt SA, Clark HM, Rao P et al (2007) Oral health of children and adults in Latino migrant and seasonal farmworker families. J Immigr Minor Health 9:229–235

Quandt SA, Grzywacz JG, Talton JW et al (2013) Evaluating the effectiveness of a lay health promoter-led, community-based participatory pesticide safety intervention with farmworker families. Health Promot Pract 14:425–432

Quandt SA, Grzywacz JG, Trejo G et al (2014) Nutritional strategies of Latino farmworker families with preschool children: identifying leverage points for obesity prevention. Soc Sci Med 123:72–81

Quandt SA, Brooke C, Fagan K et al (2015) Farmworker housing in the United States and its impact on health. New Solut 25:263–286

Quandt SA, Trejo G, Suerken CK et al (2016) Diet quality among preschool-age children of Latino migrant and seasonal farmworkers in the United States. J Immigr Minor Health 18:505–512

Quandt SA, Arnold TJ, Mora DC et al (2019) Hired Latinx child farm labor in North Carolina: the demand-support-control model applied to a vulnerable worker population. Am J Ind Med 62:1079-1090

Ramos AK (2018) Child labor in global tobacco production: a human rights approach to an enduring dilemma. Health Hum Rights 20:235–248

Rauh V, Arunajadai S, Horton M et al (2011) Seven-year neurodevelopmental scores and prenatal exposure to chlorpyrifos, a common agricultural pesticide. Environ Health Perspect 119:1196–1201

Roberts JR, Karr CJ, Council on Environmental Health (2012) Pesticide exposure in children. Pediatrics 130:e1765–e1788

Rosado JI, Johnson SB, McGinnity KA et al (2013) Obesity among Latino children within a migrant farmworker community. Am J Prev Med 44:S274–S281

Sadeghi B, Schaefer S, Tseregounis IE et al (2017) Prevalence and perception of childhood obesity in California's farmworker communities. J Community Health 42:377–384

Salazar MK, Napolitano M, Scherer JA et al (2004) Hispanic adolescent farmworkers' perceptions associated with pesticide exposure. West J Nurs Res 26:146–166. discussion 167–175

Sauter SL, Brightwell WS, Colligan MJ et al (2002) The changing organization of work and the safety and health of working people. OH DHHS (NIOSH) No 2002–116. Dept of Health and Human Services, Cincinnati, OH

Seid M, Castañeda D, Mize R et al (2003) Crossing the border for health care: access and primary care characteristics for young children of Latino farm workers along the US-Mexico border. Ambul Pediatr 3:121–130

Shipp EM, Cooper SP, del Junco DJ et al (2007a) Pesticide safety training among farmworker adolescents from Starr County, Texas. J Agric Saf Health 13:311–321

Shipp EM, Cooper SP, Del Junco DJ et al (2007b) Severe back pain among farmworker high school students from Starr County, Texas: baseline results. Ann Epidemiol 17:132–141

Shipp EM, Cooper SP, del Junco DJ et al (2013) Acute occupational injury among adolescent farmworkers from South Texas. Inj Prev 19:264–270

Snyder LA, Krauss AD, Chen PY et al (2008) Occupational safety: application of the job demand-control-support model. Accid Anal Prev 40:1713–1723

Soares RR, Rothschild M, Haddad D et al (2019) Visual impairment and eye disease among children of migrant farmworkers. J Pediatr Ophthalmol Strabismus 56:28–34

Statista (2019) Major U.S. states in tobacco production 2015–2018. https://www.statista.com/statistics/192022/top-10-tobacco-producing-us-states/. Accessed 22 May 2019

Ungar BL, Iscoe E, Cutler J et al (1986) Intestinal parasites in a migrant farmworker population. Arch Intern Med 146:513–515

United States Department of Labor (USDOL), Wage and Hour Division (2016) Child Labor Bulletin 102. Child labor requirements in agricultural occupations under the Fair Labor

Standards Act. WH1295. Washington, DC: US Department of Labor. https://www.dol.gov/whd/regs/compliance/childlabor102.pdf. Accessed 30 May 2019

United States Government Accountability Office (GAO) (2018) Working children: federal injury data and compliance strategies could be strengthened. https://www.gao.gov/assets/700/695209.pdf. Accessed 15 Apr 2019

Varma R, Deneen J, Cotter S, Multi-Ethnic Pediatric Eye Disease Study Group et al (2006) The multi-ethnic pediatric eye disease study: design and methods. Ophthalmic Epidemiol 13:253–262

Vela Acosta MS, Sanderson M, Cooper SP et al (2007) Health risk behaviors and work injury among hispanic adolescents and farmworkers. J Agric Saf Health 13(2):117–136

Waugh IM (2010) Examining the sexual harassment experiences of Mexican immigrant farmworking women. Violence Against Women 16(3):237–261

Weathers AC, Garrison HG (2004) Children of migratory agricultural workers: the ecological context of acute care for a mobile population of immigrant children. Clin Pediatr Emerg Med 5:120–129

Weathers A, Minkovitz C, O'Campo P et al (2003) Health services use by children of migratory agricultural workers: exploring the role of need for care. Pediatrics 111:956–963

Weathers A, Minkovitz C, O'Campo P et al (2004) Access to care for children of migratory agricultural workers: factors associated with unmet need for medical care. Pediatrics 113:e276–e282

Weathers AC, Minkovitz CS, Diener-West M et al (2008a) The effect of parental immigration authorization on health insurance coverage for migrant Latino children. J Immigr Minor Health 10:247–254

Weathers AC, Novak SP, Sastry N et al (2008b) Parental nativity affects children's health and access to care. J Immigr Minor Health 10:155–165

Westaby JD, Lee BC (2003) Antecedents of injury among youth in agricultural settings: a longitudinal examination of safety consciousness, dangerous risk taking, and safety knowledge. J Saf Res 34(3):227–240

Whitworth KW, Shipp EM, Cooper SP et al (2010) A pilot study of symptoms of neurotoxicity and injury among adolescent farmworkers in Starr County, Texas. Int J Occup Environ Health 16:138–144

Wilson FA, Wang Y, Stimpson JP et al (2016) Use of dental services by immigration status in the United States. J Am Dent Assoc 147:162–169.e4

Chapter 8
Community-Based Participatory Research (CBPR) and Other Community-Engaged Research with Latinx Farmworker Communities in the Eastern United States

Thomas A. Arcury and Sara A. Quandt

8.1 Introduction

Latinx farmworkers constitute a vulnerable and hidden population. They are vulnerable because they are often poor, generally have little formal education, have limited English language skills, experience discrimination, and often lack documentation. Farmworkers also have limited access to health care (Arcury and Quandt 2007). They are a hidden population because no list of farmworkers exists. Most farmworkers in the eastern United States (US) live in the general community rather than in employer-provided housing or farmworker camps. Among those who live in the general community, no particular characteristics indicate that they are farmworkers. No state in the eastern US has a comprehensive list or database of the farmworker camps in which some migrant farmworkers live. Whether an individual is considered a farmworker can change from month to month and is affected by the policies of different agencies and organizations. Agricultural work is seasonal for farmworkers, and individuals who work on farms in a particular month may be employed in other occupations in other months. Organizations providing health, education, and other human services vary in their definitions of who is a farmworker and therefore eligible for the services they provide. Whether the spouse, children, or others living with a farmworker are considered members of the farmworker population can also vary for different organizations.

T. A. Arcury (✉)
Department of Family and Community Medicine, Wake Forest School of Medicine, Winston-Salem, NC, USA

S. A. Quandt
Department of Epidemiology and Prevention, Division of Public Health Sciences, Wake Forest School of Medicine, Winston-Salem, NC, USA

© Springer Nature Switzerland AG 2020
T. A. Arcury, S. A. Quandt (eds.), *Latinx Farmworkers in the Eastern United States*, https://doi.org/10.1007/978-3-030-36643-8_8

Farmworkers' vulnerabilities make them want to remain hidden from human services programs and from research (Heckathorn 1997). Farmworkers are members of a population that has characteristics that put them at risk of legal jeopardy (lacking documentation) and of discrimination (being immigrants, speaking Spanish). They may be unwilling to participate in research studies for fear of losing their jobs or disclosure to local or federal authorities. Compounding this circumstance, employers often warn Latinx farmworkers not to speak to strangers in general, and to advocates and researchers in particular.

Community-based participatory research (CBPR) and other forms of community-engaged research provide a framework that can enhance the participation of farmworkers and the members of other vulnerable and hidden communities in research studies. Community-engaged research involves individuals and organizations whom farmworkers trust. These individuals and organizations ensure that the research addresses health concerns that farmworkers share. This approach provides a pathway for involving individual community members in project leadership. It enables the identification of community members who can be recruited to the research. Community engagement allows investigators to work with community members and to use research results to improve health and well-being of both the individuals who participate in the research and the larger farmworker community.

8.2 Community-Based Participatory Research

8.2.1 CBPR: A Form of Community Engagement

CBPR is a joint process by which health scientists and community members collaborate to critically investigate and change the environment, both physical and social, in an effort to improve people's health (Arcury et al. 2001a). Israel et al. (2005) define "community" as a unit of identity reinforced through social interaction and characterized by shared values.

CBPR is a form of community engagement. In their report, *Principles of Community Engagement*, the Clinical and Translational Science Awards Consortium (CTSAC 2011) defines community engagement as the process of working collaboratively with and through communities in an effort to "mobilize resources and influence systems, change relationships among partners, and serve as catalysts for changing policies, programs, and practices." They present a typology of community engagement that begins with "outreach" (the least engaged form of community engagement) through "consultation," "involvement," and "collaboration" to "shared leadership," the most engaged form of community engagement (Fig. 8.1). CBPR, at its best, reflects shared leadership, a strong bidirectional relationship based on a strong partnership in which final decision-making is at the community level, and must minimally reflect collaboration, community involvement with bidirectional communication and community partnerships for each project component.

	Increasing Level of Community Involvement, Impact, Trust, and Communication Flow →				
	Outreach	**Consult**	**Involve**	**Collaborate**	**Shared Leadership**
	Some community involvement Communication flows from one to the other, to inform Provides community with information. Entities coexist. Outcomes: Optimally, establishes communication channels and channels for outreach.	More community involvement Communication flows to the community and then back, answer seeking Gets information or feed-back from the community. Entities share information. Outcomes: Develops connections.	Better community involvement Communication flows both ways, participatory form of communication Involves more participation with community on issues. Entities cooperate with each other. Outcomes: Visibility of partnership established with increased cooperation	Community involvement Communication flow is bidirectional Forms partnerships with community on each aspect of project from development to solution. Entities form bidirectional communication channels. Outcomes: Partnership building, trust building	Strong bidirectional relationship Final decision making is at community level. Entities have formed strong partnership structures. Outcomes: Broader health outcomes affecting broader community. Strong bidirectional trust built

Fig. 8.1 Community engagement continuum (adapted from the Clinical and Translational Science Awards Consortium, Community Engagement Key Function Committee Task Force on the Principles of Community Engagement 2011:8)

8.2.2 Reasons for Using CBPR

The CTSAC (2011) lists nine reasons to use a community-engaged approach. We submit that ethical considerations are the primary justification for using CBPR and other community-engaged research approaches with vulnerable communities, such as Latinx farmworkers. It is ethical to include members of vulnerable communities as partners in research for which they are the "subjects," particularly when the results of this research may benefit other communities and populations.

CBPR provides the members of these vulnerable communities with a voice in deciding whether the research should be done, how it is done, and how the results are used. It helps to ensure that the results of this research benefit the vulnerable community members as well as the members of other, less vulnerable communities (Quandt et al. 2001a). For example, research on pesticide exposure is important to farmworkers because this exposure can affect their health, their ability to have children, and the health of their children. CBPR can help ensure that the results of pesticide research actually benefit the safety and health of farmworkers and that they are not used only to help reduce pesticide exposure or the health effects of pesticides among less vulnerable populations (e.g., farm owners, suburban gardeners).

CBPR helps build the capacity of professional researchers to communicate study results to community members and increases the capacity of community members to extract study results from professional researchers. It ensures that professional researchers work with community members so that study results inform policy that improves the health and justice of vulnerable communities.

CBPR provides members of these vulnerable communities some financial reward by paying them to be members of the research team (e.g., co-investigators, project managers, data collectors), just as the professional scientists receive financial reward from the conduct of the research (e.g., their salaries, career advancement). It also provides members of these communities with skills that they can use to further address concerns in their communities and to improve their individual circumstances by providing them with financial capital, knowledge and skill capital, social capital, and political capital.

Improving research quality is a secondary justification for using a CBPR approach in conducting research with vulnerable communities. Involvement by the community helps in delineating the important research questions. For example, our research on farmworker pesticide exposure was of interest to those providing health care to and advocating for farmworkers. It was also of interest to farmworkers. However, a question that was more important in the everyday lives of farmworkers revolved around food security and access to food. Therefore, we added these issues to our research and tested an intervention to improve food access (Arcury et al. 2004a; Ip et al. 2015; Quandt et al. 2004a, 2006a, 2014b, 2018). We shared our results with those providing health and education services to farmworkers (Quandt 2007; Quandt and Arcury 2003; Quandt et al. 2003). Similarly, although our initial pesticide research addressed workplace exposure of workers, we learned from farmworkers that they were concerned about their children's pesticide exposure. Therefore, we developed studies that documented child pesticide exposure (Arcury et al. 2005, 2006; Quandt et al. 2004b; Rao et al. 2007; Rohlman et al. 2005) and developed interventions that can be used by lay health advisors (LHAs) to reduce this exposure (Arcury et al. 2004b, 2009a; Quandt et al. 2013a).

Involvement by the community directs the policy issues that the research should consider. For example, by selecting the topics addressed in our research (e.g., pesticides, housing, green tobacco sickness), our community partners indicate the policy issues that are important for the health and justice of the farmworker community. Similarly, our community partners are involved in producing policy briefs that summarize our research results for presentation to policy makers as well as to the public (Arcury et al. 2017b).

Community partners help to determine what data to collect and how best to collect them. They provide insight into the individual characteristics and work organization for farmworkers and the potential associations of these individual and organizational characteristics with farmworkers' health and justice. For example, our community partners raised questions about the occurrence of wage theft and its justice implications (Robinson et al. 2011). Community partners can vet the appropriate vocabulary and wording (e.g., the appropriate terms used for applying pesticides, labor contractor, and respiratory wheeze) to use in questionnaire items and community education materials; this is particularly important when materials must be prepared for vernacular usage in a second language. Community partners can inform sample design by identifying important community characteristics, and they can support participant recruitment and retention.

The ethics of returning study results to individual research participants and to their communities is gaining increased recognition. The National Academies of Sciences, Engineering, and Medicine issued a report in 2018 on returning individual research results (Botkin et al. 2018), and "Reporting Back Research Results" was the theme for the 2018 Partnerships for Environmental Public Health Annual Meeting sponsored by the National Institute of Environmental Health Sciences in December 2018. The importance and ethics of reporting individual results to study participants in CBPR have been discussed in the general literature (Brody et al. 2007; Chen et al. 2010; Morello-Frosch et al. 2009) and specifically for Latinx farmworkers (Quandt et al. 2004c). The CBPR process supports the return of research results to individuals and to the community by indicating the information that is important to individuals and the appropriate language to use when presenting this information (Quandt et al. 2004c). Community partners are essential to determining how best to inform general community members about research results. We have noted the importance of disseminating results to address public policy issues (Arcury et al. 2017b). The CBPR process also informs general community dissemination and community education programs. For example, our community partners indicated that we should present information about pesticide safety to the community using radio spots (Lane et al. 2009). Community members specified the information to be included and the radio stations for broadcasting. Similarly, in developing a lay health intervention to reduce occupational pesticide exposure, community members indicated that it was important to receive information from "experts" as well as from community health educators (Quandt et al. 2001b).

8.2.3 A Model of CBPR

We present a model for CBPR with vulnerable communities, developed and expanded through our work with farmworker communities in North Carolina (Arcury et al. 1999; Arcury and Quandt 2017). This model argues that CBPR must engage in high-quality research, both because all research should be high quality and because CBPR is a political endeavor. CBPR is political because it supports vulnerable communities in demanding social and environmental change to improve their health and justice; they want an equitable share of benefits from those with power, who have an inequitable share of these benefits (Arcury et al. 2001a). This model acknowledges that the members of low-income and vulnerable communities, such as Latinx farmworkers, often have limited resources (e.g., education, time, finances) to participate in research. It is the responsibility of the professional researchers, who generally have substantial educational, temporal, and financial resources, to ensure multiple *modes* of participation are available for community members to engage in the different *domains* of community participation.

This model suggests four domains in which community members can participate (Fig. 8.2). Community members can engage in *consultation*, helping to delineate needed research. They can engage in *strategic planning*, helping to decide how to

Community Participation Modes and Domains					
Examples of Modes	**Domains**				
	Consultation	Strategic Planning	Execution	**Translation**	
				Dissemination	Implementation
Academic – Community-based organization partnership	X	X	X	X	X
Community advisory committee	X	X			
Health care provider advisory committee	X	X			X
Partnership with service organizations	X	X	X	X	X
Community meetings	X				
Training community members			X		
Engaging Students			X		

Fig. 8.2 Multimode, multi-domain community-based participatory research model indicating examples of the domains in which different modes might be used (adapted from Arcury and Quandt 2017:93)

conduct the research. They can work toward the *execution* of research and intervention studies by helping to recruit participants, executing intervention programs, collecting data, analyzing data, and reporting results. Finally, they can engage in *translation*, sharing results with other community residents and policy makers. The importance of translation has become more apparent in recent years and includes *dissemination* (to research participants, to the community, and to policy) and *implementation* (ensuring that results are integrated into laws, policy, regulation, and practice).

8.3 CBPR to Address Latinx Farmworker Health, Safety, and Justice

This chapter's focus is CBPR and other community-engaged research projects conducted with Latinx farmworker communities in the eastern US. However, projects conducted with Latinx non-farmworker communities in the eastern US and with Latinx farmworker communities in other regions inform this discussion.

8.3.1 CBPR with Latinx Communities in the Eastern US

A number of projects have used CBPR or other community-engaged approaches to address health among Latinx communities in the eastern US. For example, Rhodes et al. (2016, 2018) have developed and implemented programs to address HIV. The results of their research have been used to develop intervention programs, including health navigators and social media, to reduce health disparities among Latinx men who have sex with men (MSM) and trans women (Rhodes et al. 2017; Sun et al. 2015; Tanner et al. 2018). Luque et al. (2017) developed and implemented a program to improve cervical cancer screening among Latinas in southeastern Georgia with lay health advisors.

Quandt and colleagues have addressed the occupational health of Latinx poultry processing workers with two projects. One project used CBPR to document occupational health hazards and other community concerns of poultry processing workers (Quandt et al. 2006b, 2013b) and used this information to develop a LHA intervention to help workers address these hazards (Grzywacz et al. 2009; Marín et al. 2009). The second used a community-engaged approach focused on documenting the risk factors and prevalence of occupational injuries among these workers (Arcury et al. 2012a, 2013, 2014a, 2015a; Cartwright et al. 2012, 2013; Quandt et al. 2014a; Walker et al. 2013).

These projects indicate the importance of long-term commitment to working with the communities, involving local residents in the data collection process, and disseminating the results. They highlight the common feature of using LHAs in providing health education and interventions for vulnerable communities. They note the importance of expanding communication and dissemination from traditional forms of communication to the use of contemporary approaches, such as social media. They also document the difficulty of working with poorly funded community organizations. The 4-year *JUSTA: Justice and Health for Poultry Workers* project (Quandt et al. 2006b) worked with a succession of four community organization partners. The first three community organizations disbanded due to lack of adequate long-term funding.

Inadequate funding also contributes to frequent staff turnover in some community-based organizations; for example, over a 25-year period, one organization collaborating with the Wake Forest School of Medicine team had nine different directors (several of whom were part-time), and during a 2-year period, the organization had no director.

8.3.2 CBPR with Farmworker Communities Across the United States

Several community-engaged projects with farmworkers have been conducted in regions outside the eastern US, with most being located on the West Coast, in California, Oregon, and Washington. For example, the Center for Environmental

Research and Children's Health (CERCH) at the University of California, Berkeley, School of Public Health, manages several projects with Latinx residents living in agricultural communities: *Center for the Health Assessment of Mothers and Children of Salinas (CHAMACOS), Chamacos of Salinas Evaluating Chemicals in Homes and Agriculture (COSECHA), and Health and Environmental Research in Make-Up of Salinas Adolescents (HERMOSA)*. Publications from these projects (e.g., Bradman et al. 2009; Salvatore et al. 2009; Madrigal et al. 2016) note the use of a CBPR framework and CBPR principles.

Projects conducted in Oregon with the general Latinx farmworker population (McCauley et al. 2001; Napolitano et al. 2002) and indigenous farmworker communities (Farquhar et al. 2013; Gregg et al. 2010), as well as in Washington (Ortega et al. 2018; Thompson et al. 2008, 2017), describe and evaluate their community engagement processes. For example, McCauley et al. (2001) present their model of community engagement and evaluate the effectiveness of their approach. Thompson et al. (2017) evaluate their approach to disseminating research results to farmworker community members and analyze the perceptions of community advisory committee members (Ortega et al. 2018).

A theme repeated for these community-engaged projects with Latinx farmworkers is the engagement of LHAs. Projects with limited community engagement also commonly use LHAs (Forst et al. 2006).

8.3.3 CBPR with Farmworker Communities in the Eastern United States

CBPR and other community-engaged projects have been conducted with Latinx farmworker communities across the eastern US, with multiple projects conducted in Florida and North Carolina (Table 8.1). They reflect collaborations dedicated to involving farmworker communities. It is possible that other community-engaged projects exist; if so, they have not produced materials documenting their approach, goals, or results. The research methods used in these community-engaged projects are highly varied. They have used qualitative and survey interview methods to learn what farmworkers know and believe about their work and safety and to document their characteristics and experiences. Several of the studies have used biomonitoring and environmental assessment techniques to measure exposure and risk.

The community-engaged projects with Latinx farmworkers have a limited geographic distribution. Most of these projects have been conducted in North Carolina and Florida, states with large numbers of Latinx farmworkers, with one project each in Georgia, Tennessee, Kentucky and Maryland, and New York and Maine. No community-engaged projects have been reported in the other New England (Vermont, New Hampshire, Massachusetts, Rhode Island, Connecticut), Mid-Atlantic (New Jersey, Delaware, Pennsylvania, Ohio), or southern (South Carolina, Alabama, Mississippi, Louisiana) states. Among the seven North Carolina

Table 8.1 Location, academic partners, community partners, and project titles of Latinx farmworker community-engaged research projects in the eastern US

State	Academic partners	Community partners	Project
• Florida	• University of Florida • University of South Florida	• Farmworker Association of Florida	• Together for Agricultural Safety • Partnership for Citrus Worker Health • *Girasoles*
• Florida	• Florida International University • University of Miami	• Latina immigrant farmworkers	• HIV behavior change intervention
• Georgia	• Georgia Southern University	• Southeast Georgia communities project	• *Salud es Vida*
• North Carolina	• Wake Forest School of Medicine • East Carolina University • University of North Carolina, Chapel Hill	• North Carolina Farmworkers' Project • Student Action with Farmworkers • NC Justice Center • NC FIELD • NC Farmworker Health Program • El Buen Pastor Latino Community Services	• Preventing Agricultural Chemical Exposure (PACE) 1–5 • *Casa y campo* • *La Familia Sana*: Promotora Program • Green Tobacco Sickness • Farmworker Housing, Exposures and Health • Youth Health Educator Program • Hired Child Farmworker Study
• Kentucky and Maryland	• University of Kentucky • University of Maryland	• Community advisory council • Industry advisory council	• Thoroughbred Worker Health and Safety Study
• Tennessee	• East Tennessee State University	• Rural Medical Services	• Tomato Workers
• New York and Maine	• Northeast Center for Occupational Safety and Health for Agriculture, Forestry and Fishing	• Maine Migrant Health Program • Farmworker community coalitions	• Community Collaborations for Farmworker Safety and Health Project

projects listed, the Preventing Agricultural Chemical Exposure (PACE) project has been functioning continuously since 1996 and will continue at least through 2020, having received five rounds of funding from the National Institute of Environmental Health Sciences.

The academic and research organizations that have participated in community-engaged research are quite limited. Eleven universities plus a research center affiliated with a regional health system have collaborated in community-engaged research with Latinx farmworkers in the eastern US, with seven of the 11 universities located in North Carolina and Florida. The community partners in these projects are varied, but also limited. Other than North Carolina, the projects in each state each include a single formal organization or agency partner; six organizations or agencies have collaborated on the community-engaged projects in North Carolina. In two instances, the community partners are not well defined. The Thoroughbred Worker Health and Safety Study conducted in Kentucky and Maryland lists a "community advisory council" and an "industry advisory council" with little information about their composition; the Community Collaborations for Farmworker Safety and Health Project conducted in New York and Maine lists "farmworker community coalitions" as well as the Maine Migrant Health Program.

Pesticides have been the major specific occupational health and safety risk addressed by community-engaged projects with Latinx farmworkers in the eastern US (Table 8.2). These include several Florida, North Carolina, and Tennessee projects designed to measure pesticide exposure (Arcury et al. 2009b, 2014b), delineate the health effects of pesticide exposure (Kim et al. 2018; Quandt et al. 2015a, 2017), and reduce pesticide exposure (Arcury et al. 2009a; Flocks et al. 2001, 2007, 2012; Silver et al. 2014; Trejo et al. 2013). Several Florida and North Carolina projects have also addressed the prevalence (Arcury et al. 2015b; Flocks et al. 2013; Mac et al. 2017; Mirabelli et al. 2010; Mutic et al. 2018) and prevention (Quandt et al. 2013c; Spears et al. 2013) of heat stress. One North Carolina project investigated the prevalence, causes, and prevention of green tobacco sickness (Arcury et al. 2001b; Quandt et al. 2001c; Rao et al. 2002), acute nicotine poisoning, which is unpleasant on its own and can exacerbate the effects of heat.

Ergonomic and musculoskeletal disorders (MSDs) have been the focus of community-engaged projects in North Carolina, Tennessee, Kentucky and Maryland, and New York and Maine. This is a diverse set of research in its methods and goals. The North Carolina studies used self-report and physical examination to measure the prevalence of MSDs (Arcury et al. 2012d; Mora et al. 2016), and the Kentucky and Maryland research also used self-report (Swanberg et al. 2017). The Tennessee project developed vehicle designs that would reduce MSD injuries (Silver et al. 2014). The New York and Maine research conducted detailed ergonomic assessments to refine the tools used by farmworkers who harvest wild blueberries (blueberry rake) and apples (apple bucket) to reduce MSDs (see Chap. 3) (Earle-Richardson et al. 2009; May et al. 2008).

Community-engaged projects in North Carolina have investigated eye symptoms (Quandt et al. 2001d, 2008) and vision problems among Latinx farmworkers (Quandt et al. 2016), as well as eye injuries (Quandt et al. 2012). Projects in New York (Earle-Richardson et al. 2014) and Florida (Luque et al. 2007; Monaghan et al. 2011; Tovar-Aguilar et al. 2014) have developed interventions to reduce eye injuries.

Projects in North Carolina (Mirabelli et al. 2011; Kearney et al. 2014) as well as in Kentucky (Flunker et al. 2017) have examined problems with pulmonary function among Latinx farmworkers using questionnaires and spirometry data. These analyses indicated relatively high abnormal pulmonary function. Finally, Swanberg et al. (2013, 2016) report on the general occupational injuries of Latinx farmworkers in Kentucky and Maryland employed on thoroughbred horse farms.

Table 8.2 Major health and justice issues addressed by Latinx farmworker community-engaged research projects in the eastern US

Project	Health and justice issues addressed										
	Occupational health and safety								General health		
	Pesticides	Heat stress	Green tobacco sickness	Ergonomics/ musculoskeletal disorders	Vision/ eye injuries	Pulmonary function	General occupational injuries	Child labor	Mental health	Cancer	Housing, family, women's health
Florida											
Together for Agricultural Safety	X										
Partnership for Citrus Worker Health					X						X
Girasoles		X									
HIV behavior change intervention											X
Georgia											
Salud es Vida										X	X
North Carolina											
Preventing Agricultural Chemical Exposure (PACE) 1–5	X	X			X	X			X	X	X
Casa y Campo	X										X
La Familia Sana: Promotora program	X										X
Green Tobacco Sickness			X								

(continued)

Table 8.2 (continued)

	Health and justice issues addressed										
	Occupational health and safety								General health		
Project	Pesticides	Heat stress	Green tobacco sickness	Ergonomics/ musculoskeletal disorders	Vision/ eye injuries	Pulmonary function	General occupational injuries	Child labor	Mental health	Cancer	Housing, family, women's health
Farmworker Housing, Exposures and Health	X	X				X					X
Youth Health Educator (YHE) Program		X						X			
Hired Child Farmworker Study	X	X		X				X			
Tennessee											
Tomato Workers	X			X							
Kentucky/Maryland											
Thoroughbred Worker Health and Saftey Study				X		X	X				
New York/Maine											
Community Collaborations for Farmworker Safety and Health Project				X	X						

Several community-engaged projects in North Carolina have focused on Latinx child farmworkers. It is legal to hire children as young as 10 years old for agricultural labor. One of these projects developed an intervention based on youth health educators to reduce heat-related illnesses (Spears et al. 2013). A pilot study examined how work safety culture and organization of work are associated with child farmworker injuries (Arcury et al. 2015c; Kearney et al. 2015). A current longitudinal study (Arcury et al. 2019; Arnold et al. 2019) focuses on the effects of agricultural labor on the physical and cognitive development of child farmworkers.

The mental health of male (Arcury et al. 2012d; Crain et al. 2012; Grzywacz et al. 2010) and female (Arcury et al. 2018) Latinx farmworkers is one area of general health considered by community-engaged projects. In addition, one project has developed an intervention to increase cancer screening among Latinx farmworker women (Luque et al. 2011; Wells et al. 2012), while another has described Latinx farmworker knowledge of cancer and cancer prevention (Furgurson et al. 2019a, b).

Housing is a major thrust of the community-engaged research in North Carolina. Adequate housing is a basic human right (United Nations General Assembly 1948), and inadequate housing causes poor physical and mental health (Quandt et al. 2015b). One component of this housing research investigated housing quality in migrant farmworker camps and documented whether employers met regulatory requirements (Arcury et al. 2012b, c; Bischoff et al. 2012). Other housing research examined the general housing conditions of seasonal farmworker families (Arcury et al. 2017a; Early et al. 2006; Gentry et al. 2007), with a focus on pesticide exposure for Latinx farmworker spouses and children (Arcury et al. 2006, 2007; Quandt et al. 2004b; Rao et al. 2007). Greater attention is being directed toward health and justice among Latinx women farmworkers in the eastern US, with analysis of health during pregnancy (Kelley et al. 2013), mental health (Arcury et al. 2018), HIV prevention (Sanchez et al. 2016), and cancer prevention (Luque et al. 2011) (see Chap 6).

8.4 Latinx Farmworker CBPR in the Eastern United States: Commonalities and Lessons Learned

Although all of the CBPR and community-engaged projects with Latinx farmworkers in the eastern US have published their scientific results, fewer have written about their community-engaged organization, processes, or evaluations. This shortcoming is also common among farmworker community-engaged research conducted in other regions of the US. This lack of documentation makes it difficult to use lessons learned from this research to inform new partnerships and projects. Exceptions exist; for example, Arcury et al. (2001a) organized a conference on community-engaged approaches in addressing farmworker pesticide exposure with two of the resulting papers (Quandt et al. 2001a; Flocks et al. 2001) describing CBPR projects with Latinx farmworkers in the eastern US. Arcury and Quandt (2017) provide a comprehensive review of the community engagement process in a single project with Latinx farmworkers (PACE3), and Quandt and Arcury (2017) describe CBPR procedures for development of occupational health educational programs.

This discussion uses the CBPR model developed by Arcury and colleagues (Arcury et al. 1999; Arcury and Quandt 2017) to explore organizational and processual commonalities across the projects listed in Tables 8.1 and 8.2. This discussion is limited to published materials from these projects describing their organizations, processes, and evaluation of their community-engaged approaches (Table 8.3). Some of the projects listed in Tables 8.1 and 8.2 have not reported on their organizations and processes (e.g., the Green Tobacco Sickness project in North Carolina and the Thoroughbred Worker Health and Safety Study conducted in Kentucky and Maryland) and are not included in this discussion.

8.4.1 Commonalities

8.4.1.1 Community-Based Organizations

Flocks et al. (2001) and Quandt et al. (2001b) present thorough discussions of the roles of community-based organizations in providing consultation, strategic planning, and execution of their community-engaged projects. Both papers include detailed models describing the role of community-based organizations in these domains and evaluate the importance of this participation in project success. Arcury and Quandt (2017) also discuss how their several community partners were involved in the domains of consultation, strategic planning, and execution.

8.4.1.2 Advisory Committees

Although most Latinx farmworker community-engaged research projects note that they have advisory committees, only one project (Arnold et al. 2019) has discussed how the advisory committee has actually contributed to consultation, delineating what research is needed, and strategic planning, deciding how the research should be conducted. Arnold et al. (2019) discuss how their project's youth advisory committee discussed what topics should be included in their project, interview content, and wording for interview items.

8.4.1.3 Student Involvement

Arnold et al. (2019) and Rao et al. (2004) provide discussions of how students were consulted in the development of community-engaged projects. These include high school and college students from the farmworker community (Arnold et al. 2019), as well as college student interns (Rao et al. 2004). Spears et al. (2013) discuss how

Table 8.3 How community-engaged projects with Latinx farmworkers in the eastern US reflect the components of the CBPR model

| | | Execution | | Translation | | | |
| | | | | Dissemination | | | |
Consultation	Strategic planning	Research	Intervention	Research participants	Community	Policy	Implementation
Community-based organizations Flocks et al. (2001) Quandt et al. (2001b) Arcury and Quandt (2017)	*Community-based organizations* Flocks et al. (2001) Quandt et al. (2001b) Arcury and Quandt (2017)	*Community-based organizations* Flocks et al. (2001) Quandt et al. (2001b) Arcury and Quandt (2017)	*Lay health advisors/ Promotoras/ navigators* Quandt et al. (2001b) Luque et al. (2007) Arcury et al. (2009a) Luque et al. (2011) Monaghan et al. (2011) Wells et al. (2012) Quandt et al. (2013a) Spears et al. (2013) Trejo et al. (2013) Tovar-Aguilar et al. (2014)	*Returning individual results* Quandt et al. (2004c) Arcury and Quandt (2017) Flocks et al. (2018)	*Community education* Quandt et al. (2001a) Quandt et al. (2013a) Arcury and Quandt (2017) Quandt and Arcury (2017)	*Policy briefs* Arcury et al. (2017b) Arcury and Quandt (2017)	
Advisory committees Arnold et al. (2019)	*Advisory committees* Arnold et al. (2019)		*Social marketing* Flocks et al. (2001) Tovar-Aguilar et al. (2014)				

(continued)

Table 8.3 (continued)

| Consultation | Strategic planning | Execution | | Translation | | | |
| | | | | Dissemination | | | Implementation |
		Research	Intervention	Research participants	Community	Policy	
Student involvement Rao et al. (2004) Arnold et al. (2019)	*Student involvement* Rao et al. (2004) Arnold et al. (2019)	*Student involvement* Rao et al. (2004) Spears et al. (2013) Silver et al. (2014) Arnold et al. (2019)	*Equipment redesign* May et al. (2008) Earle-Richardson et al. (2005) Earle-Richardson et al. (2009)				
Literature review Quandt et al. (1999) Hiott et al. (2006)	*Literature review* Quandt et al. (2001a) Hiott et al. (2006)	*Community members* Arcury and Quandt (2017)	*Safety training* Earle-Richardson et al. (2014)				
			Risk mapping Cravey et al. (2000)				

they trained high school students to implement a lay health education program to reduce heat-related illness among child farmworkers. Silver et al. (2014) show how health sciences students can collect data during health screening interviews. Arnold et al. (2019) describe how student co-investigators from Student Action with Farmworkers, a partner community organization, supported participant recruitment and data collection.

8.4.1.4 Literature Review

Two projects (Hiott et al. 2006; Quandt et al. 1999, 2001a) discuss how they used literature reviews of pesticide education materials available for health-care providers and for farmworkers to delineate needed research and inform the development of interventions. Community-based organization staff members participated in these literature reviews to evaluate the acceptability of the available materials.

8.4.1.5 Community Members

Although most community-engaged projects mention that community members are hired as data collectors, few provide further information describing or evaluating how community members are involved in the execution of other research tasks, such as the design of data collection instruments and protocols, project management, data analysis and interpretation of results, or publishing results. Arcury and Quandt (2017) discuss the importance of community-members as project staff for improving participant recruitment and retention.

8.4.1.6 Lay Health Advisors

Discussions of the execution of community-engaged intervention projects have focused on the role of LHAs (*promotoras de salud*, lay health workers, navigators) in these interventions. The importance of LHAs has been noted for community-engaged projects with Latinx farmworkers in other regions (e.g., McCauley et al. 2013) and for community-engaged projects with other Latinx communities in the eastern US (Grzywacz et al. 2009; Marín et al. 2009; Rhodes et al. 2016; Sun et al. 2015). These LHA interventions use individuals from Latinx communities to deliver information, training, and support for individuals and families. Community members accept others from their communities, as these individuals share the language and culture of the community.

Among Latinx farmworkers, LHA occupational interventions have focused on occupational pesticide exposures (Quandt et al. 2001b), eye injuries (Luque et al. 2007; Monaghan et al. 2011; Tovar-Aguilar et al. 2014) and heat-related illness among child farmworkers (Spears et al. 2013). Non-occupational LHA interventions have addressed cervical cancer screening (Luque et al. 2011; Wells et al. 2012) and residential pesticide exposure (Arcury et al. 2009a; Quandt et al. 2013a; Trejo et al. 2013). The evaluations of these LHA interventions indicate that they are effective in improving safety and health. However, the projects provide no information that the interventions continue after specific projects end or that other organizations adopted them.

8.4.1.7 Social Marketing

Social marketing is "the use of marketing to design and implement programs to promote socially beneficial behavior change" (Grier and Bryant 2005:319). CBPR projects have developed successful social marketing interventions to improve pesticide safety behaviors (Flocks et al. 2001) and the use of eye safety personal protective equipment (Tovar-Aguilar et al. 2014) in Florida. As with the LHA interventions, the investigators offer no evidence that these social marketing interventions continued beyond the end of these specific projects.

8.4.1.8 Equipment Redesign

Community-engaged projects in New York and Maine used community-engaged approaches to redesign tools used by Latinx farmworkers, such as the apple bucket and blueberry rake, to reduce musculoskeletal pain and injuries (May et al. 2008; Earle-Richardson et al. 2005, 2009). These new tools have not been widely adopted by the industry due to their cost.

8.4.1.9 Safety Training

Earle-Richardson et al. (2014) describe the success of a short safety presentation by a project coordinator, along with the provision of eye drops and protective eyewear for improving Latinx farmworker eye health. As with the other interventions, no information is available indicating that the intervention continued after the end of the project.

8.4.1.10 Risk Mapping

Cravey et al. (2000) describe the use of risk mapping to educate Latinx farmworkers about the risks of pesticide exposure in locations where they work and live. This technique involves farmworkers drawing actual maps of the farms on which they work, on which they highlight the locations in which pesticides are applied and stored. Such an approach intends to raise awareness of exposure risk.

8.4.1.11   Returning Individual Results

The importance and ethics of educating study participants about their individual results from environmental monitoring, biomonitoring, and clinical tests is receiving wide attention (Botkin et al. 2018). Only three Latinx farmworker community-engaged projects report on their processes for returning individual results. Quandt et al. (2004c) describe their process for developing and then executing a process to inform Latinx farmworker families about the pesticides found in their home. Arcury and Quandt (2017) discuss the manner in which they returned pesticide urinary metabolite results to individual Latinx farmworkers. Flocks et al. (2018) indicate that they referred about one-third of the Latinx farmworkers screened for heat-related illness for follow-up and treatment. One of these individuals had chronic renal failure.

8.4.1.12   Community Education

Many projects develop community and occupational safety education materials, but do not provide a discussion of this process in the literature. Quandt and Arcury (2017) present an entire chapter on their process for developing culturally, linguistically, and educationally appropriate educational materials for Latinx farmworkers. Overwhelmingly, these materials have addressed issues surrounding occupational and residential pesticide safety (Quandt et al. 2001a, 2013a; Arcury and Quandt 2017).

8.4.1.13   Policy Briefs

Working with the North Carolina Farmworker Advocacy Network, Arcury and Quandt (2017) and Arcury et al. (2017b) have developed policy briefs to summarize community-engaged research results and put them in a short, digestible format (two-page documents using graphics) with policy recommendations. Others have not engaged in developing statements; this may reflect a perception that this may violate a prohibition on lobbying by federal research funders and organizational rules against policy advocacy among academic partners at state institutions.

8.4.1.14   Implementation

None of the Latinx farmworker community-engaged projects conducted in the eastern US have reported on efforts at implementation, where implementation is the "systematic uptake of research findings and other evidence-based practices into routine practice, and, hence, to improve the quality and effectiveness of health services and care" (Eccles and Mittman 2006). Although these projects have documented the causes of illness and injuries among Latinx farmworkers and developed interventions that improve the health and safety of these farmworkers, they have provided little evidence of their uptake into routine practice.

8.4.2 Lessons Learned

The literature on CBPR and other community-engaged research with Latinx farmworkers in the eastern US has largely focused on intervention execution, particularly the role of LHAs and other farmworker training and education programs. Several papers provide discussions of the community engagement process and methods for consultation and strategic planning and research execution. Only a few papers discuss translation, sharing results with community residents and policy makers.

Most of the Latinx farmworker community-engaged projects in the eastern US have involved community-based organizations, have had community advisory committees, and have included community members in consultation, strategic planning, and research execution activities, but they have not published descriptions or evaluations of these activities. Due to this lack of documentation, the "quality" of the relationships and involvement of the community in these projects is difficult to judge. No one has written about problems in attempting to use a CBPR or other community-engaged approaches with Latinx farmworker communities. For example, the lack of published accounts of community engagement in strategic planning may reflect the dominance of professional researchers vs. community members or community organizations in research design and applications for funding.

These projects indicate the importance of long-term commitment to working with communities, involving local residents in the data collection process, and disseminating the results. Arcury and Quandt (2017) discuss how their PACE3 project built on relationships established over 10 years in PACE1 and PACE2 and how these relationships with the North Carolina Farmworkers' Project, Student Action with Farmworkers, and other organizations continued into PACE4 (and now into PACE5). Other CBPR projects conducted by these investigators have had the benefit of these 20-year relationships. Similarly, the CBPR projects conducted in Florida (Flocks et al. 2001, 2018) have included a 20-year relationship with the Farmworker Association of Florida. However, most community-engaged projects have not documented the difficulties experienced in collaborations between academic investigators and community organizations, particularly poorly funded community organizations (see Quandt et al. 2001a).

The literature includes descriptions of successful interventions for improving the occupational health and safety of Latinx farmworkers and the members of their families. These interventions have increased knowledge, improved safety behaviors, increased health screening, and reduced musculoskeletal injuries. Although successful, these interventions ended with the conclusion of specific projects. A limited exception is a residential pesticide safety intervention developed by Arcury et al. (2009a). This intervention was adapted for a project in Colorado (Liebman et al. 2007) and then used in a North Carolina demonstration project (Quandt et al. 2013a; Trejo et al. 2013). This residential pesticide safety intervention did not survive the end of specific projects, even with its repeated successes.

Most of the interventions (LHAs, social marketing, safety training, and risk mapping) have concentrated on educating or training farmworkers to improve health and safety. These training interventions put the onus for safety on farmworkers but do not ensure that the work is organized in such a fashion that allows farmworkers to be safe. These Latinx farmworker community-engaged projects have not substantially addressed the policy and regulatory issues that are required to affect the organization of farm work. The organization of farm work must change before farmworkers can use their safety education and before safety and justice are achieved.

8.5 Recommendations: Research, Advocate, Educate

Much of the research on farmworkers in the eastern US has claimed use of CBPR or other community-engaged approaches. This may reflect the priorities of those agencies that have funded much of the farmworker research (e.g., National Institute of Environmental Health Sciences, National Institute for Occupational Safety and Health), as well as the proclivities of the small group of investigators conducting this research. Academic and community partners using CBPR and other community-engaged approaches with Latinx farmworkers can take several steps to improve the value of their efforts for improving the health and justice of farmworkers and other vulnerable communities.

1. Develop community-engaged methods: Those using CBPR or other community-engaged research approaches with farmworkers or other vulnerable communities should document how they implemented these approaches, how the community actually benefitted, and how the science benefitted. If they do not write papers describing their community engagement models, processes, and evaluation, they should at least discuss the substance of their collaboration in their scientific papers.

    Several journals provide mechanisms for publishing analyses of community-engaged approaches:

    • *Health Education & Behavior* (https://journals.sagepub.com/home/heb).
    • *Health Education Research* (https://academic.oup.com/her/).
    • *Health Promotion Practice* (https://journals.sagepub.com/home/hpp).
    • *Journal of Community Health* (https://link.springer.com/journal/10900).
    • *New Solutions: A Journal of Environmental and Occupational Health Policy (https://journals.sagepub.com/home/new)*.
    • *Preventing Chronic Disease: Public Health Research, Practice, and Policy (https://www.cdc.gov/pcd/index.htm)*.

- *Progress in Community Health Partnerships: Research, Education, and Action* (https://www.press.jhu.edu/journals/progress-community-health-partnerships-research-education-and-action).

2. Discuss problems and failures: Those engaged in community-engaged approaches should be honest about the problems they have faced, how they solved these problems, and their failures. Based on most of the published literature, it appears that all community-engaged projects function smoothly and are great successes. However, informal discussions among academic and community participants from most community-engaged projects reflect challenges they encounter and actual failures they experience (Quandt et al. 2001a). Although no one wants to air dirty laundry in public, analyses of challenges increase the face validity of these approaches and can instruct others on how to solve common problems.

3. Critical assessment: Assessment of what is CBPR and other community-engaged approaches should be more critical. The CTSAC (2011) presents a continuum of community engagement (Fig. 8.1). Academic and community investigators should be more reflective of the place of their projects on this continuum. They should have a realistic appraisal of the level of "community" involvement in a project's design, strategic planning, execution, and translation. They should assess who is in the community and who can represent it. For example, working with an industry advisory group may reflect one community and may help get access to workers at worksites, but such a partnership may not reflect the needs, perspectives, and justice for vulnerable communities.

4. Organization of work: Several Latinx farmworker CBPR projects in the eastern US have begun documenting the organization of work and work safety culture and how they affect health, safety, and justice (Arcury et al. 2012d, 2015c, d; Kearney et al. 2015; Swanberg et al. 2012, 2013, 2017). This research should be expanded and used to change policy.

5. Policy relevance: Those conducting community-engaged research should not consider their efforts completed when they publish their results in a scientific journal. Such publication alone will not improve the health and justice of the vulnerable communities that participated in the study. Community-engaged investigators should invest their efforts beyond the research to present results to policy makers, educating these policy makers and arguing for the implementation of needed policy changes.

6. Improve the lives of vulnerable community members: The members of vulnerable communities often lack the resources and power to address the forces that degrade their environments, affect their health, and limit their attaining justice. Academic investigators argue that the involvement of vulnerable community members improves research reliability, validity, and overall quality. Research quality is important to academic investigators; it is the basis of their professional appraisal, promotion, and income. However, research quality may mean little to community members if the results of the research do not improve their lives.

Community-engaged investigators also need to address the dissemination and implementation of their research results. Community-engaged investigators should return research results to community members who participated in the research by providing and explaining their individual results and by providing education to community members on how to use these results to improve their health (e.g., providing Latinx farmworkers communities with ways to reduce their family members' exposure to pesticides). Some results are ambiguous (e.g., no one knows who will eventually develop cancer or a neurological disorder from pesticide exposure), making these efforts all the more important.

Community-engaged investigators must also educate the public about how vulnerable communities experience health injustice. In terms of Latinx farmworkers, community-engaged investigators should educate consumers about the human cost of their food and other agricultural products (Christmas trees, tobacco, ornamental scrubs, flowers, and ferns).

7. Invest in community capital: CBPR and other community-engaged projects should use project resources to improve the intellectual and skill capital of community members. They should ensure that members of the community are hired, educated, and mentored to complete project tasks—such as project management, data collection, public speaking, and community education—that improve their ability to continue their efforts to promote the well-being of their community. These skills can also improve their financial well-being through future employment.

8. Social media: Community-engaged investigators should explore the potential of social media to inform vulnerable community members, the public, and policy makers. Access to and use of social media by the general public and policy makers to communicate and persuade is widely understood. Research has documented that the mobile technology needed for social media has become widely available and is used by Latinx farmworkers in the eastern US (Price et al. 2013; Sandberg et al. 2016).

9. Implementation science: Community-engaged research has resulted in important new knowledge, successful intervention programs for HIV and pesticide exposure, and new tools that reduce the ergonomic effects of work on Latinx farmworkers. These successes have not been widely adopted for use. Those conducting community-engaged research should now integrate implementation science into their translation scheme.

References

Arcury TA, Quandt SA (2007) Delivery of health services to migrant and seasonal farmworkers. Annu Rev Public Health 28:345–363

Arcury TA, Quandt SA (2017) Community-based participatory research and occupational health disparities: pesticide exposure among immigrant farmworkers. In: Leong FTL, Eggerth DE, Chang DH, Flynn MA, Ford JK, Martinez RO (eds) Occupational health disparities: improving the well-being of ethnic and racial minority workers. APA Press, Washington, DC, pp 89–112

Arcury TA, Austin CK, Quandt SA et al (1999) Enhancing community participation in intervention research: farmworkers and agricultural chemicals in North Carolina. Health Educ Behav 26:563–578

Arcury TA, Quandt SA, Dearry A (2001a) Farmworker pesticide exposure and community-based participatory research: rationale and practical applications. Environ Health Perspect 109(Suppl 3):429–434

Arcury TA, Quandt SA, Preisser JS et al (2001b) The incidence of green tobacco sickness among Latino farmworkers. J Occup Environ Med 43(7):601–609

Arcury TA, Quandt SA, Rao P et al (2004a) Programa la promotora: nutrition education materials. Department of Family and Community Medicine, Wake Forest University School of Medicine, Winston-Salem, NC

Arcury TA, Quandt SA, Rao P et al (2004b) Programa la promotora: pesticide safety education materials. Department of Family and Community Medicine, Wake Forest University School of Medicine, Winston-Salem, NC

Arcury TA, Quandt SA, Rao P et al (2005) Organophosphate pesticide exposure in farmworker family members in western North Carolina and Virginia: case comparisons. Hum Organ 64:40–51

Arcury TA, Grzywacz JG, Davis SW et al (2006) Organophosphorus pesticide urinary metabolite levels of children in farmworker households in eastern North Carolina. Am J Ind Med 49:751–760

Arcury TA, Grzywacz JG, Barr DB et al (2007) Pesticide urinary metabolite levels of children in eastern North Carolina farmworker households. Environ Health Perspect 115(8):1254–1260

Arcury TA, Marín A, Snively BM et al (2009a) Reducing farmworker residential pesticide exposure: evaluation of a lay health advisor intervention. Health Promot Pract 10:447–455

Arcury TA, Grzywacz JG, Chen H et al (2009b) Variation across the agricultural season in organophosphorus pesticide urinary metabolite levels for Latino farmworkers in eastern North Carolina: project design and descriptive results. Am J Ind Med 52(7):539–550

Arcury TA, Grzywacz JG, Anderson AM et al (2012a) Personal protective equipment and work safety climate among Latino poultry processing workers in western North Carolina, USA. Int J Occup Environ Health 18:320–328

Arcury TA, Weir M, Chen H et al (2012b) Migrant farmworker housing regulation violations in North Carolina. Am J Ind Med 55:191–204

Arcury TA, Weir MM, Summers P et al (2012c) Safety, security, hygiene and privacy in migrant farmworker housing. New Solut 22:153–173

Arcury TA, O'Hara H, Grzywacz JG et al (2012d) Work safety climate, musculoskeletal discomfort, working while injured, and depression among migrant farmworkers in North Carolina. Am J Public Health 102(Suppl 2):S272–S278

Arcury TA, Grzywacz JG, Anderson AM et al (2013) Employer, use of personal protective equipment, and work safety climate: Latino poultry processing workers. Am J Ind Med 56:180–188

Arcury TA, Cartwright MS, Chen H et al (2014a) Musculoskeletal and neurological injuries associated with work organization among immigrant Latino women manual workers in North Carolina. Am J Ind Med 57:468–475

Arcury TA, Lu C, Chen H et al (2014b) Pesticides present in migrant farmworker housing in North Carolina. Am J Ind Med 57(3):312–322

Arcury TA, Mora DC, Quandt SA (2015a) "…you earn money by suffering pain": beliefs about carpal tunnel syndrome among Latino poultry processing workers. J Immigr Minor Health 17(3):791–801

Arcury TA, Summers P, Talton JW et al (2015b) Heat illness among North Carolina Latino farmworkers. J Occup Environ Med 57(12):1299–1304

Arcury TA, Kearney GD, Rodriguez G et al (2015c) Work safety culture of youth farmworkers in North Carolina: a pilot study. Am J Public Health 105(2):344–350

Arcury TA, Summers P, Talton JW et al (2015d) Job characteristics and work safety climate among North Carolina farmworkers with H-2A visas. J Agromedicine 20(1):64–76

Arcury TA, Suerken CK, Ip EH et al (2017a) Residential environment for outdoor play among children in Latino farmworker families. J Immigr Minor Health 19(2):267–274

Arcury TA, Wiggins MF, Brooke C et al (2017b) Using "policy briefs" to present scientific results of CBPR: farmworkers in North Carolina. Prog Community Health Partnersh 11(2):137–147

Arcury TA, Sandberg JC, Talton JW et al (2018) Mental health among Latina farmworkers and other employed Latinas in North Carolina. Rural Mental Health 42(2):89–101

Arcury TA, Arnold TJ, Sandberg JC et al (2019) Latinx child farmworkers in North Carolina: study design and participant baseline characteristics. Am J Ind Med 62(2):156–167

Arnold TJ, Malki A, Leyva J et al (2019) Engaging youth advocates in community-based participatory research on child farmworker health in North Carolina. Prog Community Health Partnersh 13(2):191–199

Bischoff WE, Weir M, Summers P et al (2012) The quality of drinking water in North Carolina farmworker camps. Am J Public Health 102(10):e49–e54

Botkin JR, Mancher M, Busta ER et al (eds) (2018) Returning individual research results to participants: guidance for a new research paradigm. The National Academies Press, Washington, DC

Bradman A, Salvatore AL, Boeniger M et al (2009) Community-based intervention to reduce pesticide exposure to farmworkers and potential take-home exposure to their families. J Expo Sci Environ Epidemiol 19(1):79–89

Brody JG, Morello-Frosch R, Brown P et al (2007) Improving disclosure and consent: "is it safe?": new ethics for reporting personal exposures to environmental chemicals. Am J Public Health 97(9):1547–1554

Cartwright MS, Walker FO, Blocker JN et al (2012) The prevalence of carpal tunnel syndrome in Latino poultry-processing workers and other Latino manual workers. J Occup Environ Med 54:198–201

Cartwright MS, Walker FO, Blocker JN et al (2013) Ultrasound for carpal tunnel syndrome screening in manual laborers. Muscle Nerve 48:127–131

Chen PG, Diaz N, Lucas G et al (2010) Dissemination of results in community-based participatory research. Am J Prev Med 39(4):372–378

Clinical and Translational Science Awards Consortium (2011) Principles of community engagement (2nd ed). Bethesda, MD: National Institute of Health. National Institute of Health Publication No. 11–7782. https://www.atsdr.cdc.gov/communityengagement/. Accessed 7 November 2018

Crain R, Grzywacz JG, Schwantes M et al (2012) Correlates of mental health among Latino farmworkers in North Carolina. J Rural Health 28(3):277–285

Cravey AJ, Arcury TA, Quandt SA (2000) Mapping as a means of farmworker education and empowerment. J Geogr 99:229–237

Earle-Richardson G, Jenkins P, Fulmer S et al (2005) An ergonomic intervention to reduce back strain among apple harvest workers in New York state. Appl Ergon 36:327–334

Earle-Richardson G, Sorensen J, Brower M et al (2009) Community collaborations for farmworker health in New York and Maine: process analysis of two successful interventions. Am J Public Health 99(Suppl 3):S584–S587

Earle-Richardson G, Wyckoff L, Carrasquillo M et al (2014) Evaluation of a community-based participatory farmworker eye health intervention in the "black dirt" region of New York state. Am J Ind Med 57(9):1053–1063

Early J, Davis SW, Quandt SA et al (2006) Housing characteristics of farmworker families in North Carolina. J Immigr Minor Health 8(2):173–184

Eccles MP, Mittman B (2006) Welcome to implementation science. Implement Sci 1(1):1

Farquhar S, de Jesus Gonzalez C, Hall J et al (2013) Integrating the wisdom and experience of indigenous farmworkers to improve farmworker safety and health. Prog Community Health Partnersh 7(4):413–418

Flocks J, Clarke L, Albrecht S et al (2001) Implementing a community-based social marketing project to improve agricultural worker health. Environ Health Perspect 109(Suppl 3):461–468

Flocks J, Monaghan P, Albrecht S et al (2007) Florida farmworkers' perceptions and lay knowledge of occupational pesticides. J Community Health 32(3):181–194

Flocks J, Kelley M, Economos J et al (2012) Female farmworkers' perceptions of pesticide exposure and pregnancy health. J Immigr Minor Health 14(4):626–632

Flocks J, Vi Thien Mac V, Runkle J et al (2013) Female farmworkers' perceptions of heat-related illness and pregnancy health. J Agromedicine 18(4):350–358

Flocks J, Tovar JA, Economos E et al (2018) Lessons learned from data collection as health screening in underserved farmworker communities. Prog Community Health Partnersh 12(1S):93–100

Flunker JC, Clouser JM, Mannino D et al (2017) Pulmonary function among Latino thoroughbred horse farmworkers. Am J Ind Med 60(1):35–44

Forst L, Noth IM, Lacey S et al (2006) Barriers and benefits of protective eyewear use by Latino farm workers. J Agromedicine 11(2):11–17

Furgurson KF, Sandberg JC, Hsu FC et al (2019a) HPV knowledge and vaccine initiation among Mexican-born farmworkers in North Carolina. Health Promot Pract 20(3):445–454

Furgurson KF, Sandberg JC, Hsu FC et al (2019b) Cancer knowledge among Mexican immigrant farmworkers in North Carolina. J Immigr Minor Health 21(3):515–521

Gentry AL, Grzywacz JG, Quandt SA et al (2007) Housing quality among North Carolina farmworker families. J Agric Saf Health 13(3):323–337

Gregg J, Centurion L, Maldonado et al (2010) Interpretations of interpretations: combining community-based participatory research and interpretive inquiry to improve health. Prog Community Health Partnersh 4(2):149–154

Grier S, Bryant CA (2005) Social marketing in public health. Annu Rev Public Health 26:319–339

Grzywacz JG, Arcury TA, Marín A et al (2009) Using lay health promoters in occupational health: outcome evaluation in a sample of Latino poultry-processing workers. New Solut 19:449–466

Grzywacz JG, Quandt SA, Chen H et al (2010) Depressive symptoms among Latino farmworkers across the agricultural season: structural and situational influences. Cultur Divers Ethnic Minor Psychol 16(3):335–343

Heckathorn D (1997) Respondent-driven sampling: a new approach to the study of hidden populations. Soc Probl 44:174–199

Hiott AE, Quandt SA, Early J et al (2006) Review of pesticide education materials for health care providers providing care to agricultural workers. J Rural Health 22(1):17–25

Ip EH, Saldana S, Arcury TA et al (2015) Profiles of food security for US farmworker households and factors related to dynamic of change. Am J Public Health 105(10):e42–e47

Israel BA, Parker EA, Rowe Z et al (2005) Community-based participatory research: Lessons learned from the centers for children's environmental health and disease prevention research. Environ Health Perspect 113(10):1463–1471

Kearney GD, Chatterjee AB, Talton J et al (2014) The association of respiratory symptoms and indoor housing conditions among migrant farmworkers in eastern North Carolina. J Agromedicine 19(4):395–405

Kearney GD, Rodriguez G, Quandt SA et al (2015) Work safety climate, safety behaviors, and occupational injuries of youth farmworkers in North Carolina. Am J Public Health 105(7):1336–1343

Kelley MA, Flocks JD, Economos J et al (2013) Female farmworkers' health during pregnancy: health care providers' perspectives. Workplace Health Saf 61(7):308–313

Kim S, Nussbaum MA, Laurienti PJ et al (2018) Exploring associations between postural balance and levels of urinary organophosphorus pesticide metabolites. J Occup Environ Med 60(2):174–179

Lane CM Jr, Vallejos QM, Marín AJ et al (2009) Pesticide safety radio public service announcements. Center for Worker Health, Wake Forest University School of Medicine, Winston-Salem, NC

Liebman AK, Juárez PM, Leyva C et al (2007) A pilot program using promotoras de salud to educate farmworker families about the risk from pesticide exposure. J Agromedicine 12(2):33–43

Luque JS, Monaghan P, Contreras RB et al (2007) Implementation evaluation of a culturally competent eye injury prevention program for citrus workers in a Florida migrant community. Prog Community Health Partnersh 1(4):359–369

Luque JS, Mason M, Reyes-Garcia C et al (2011) Salud es Vida: development of a cervical cancer education curriculum for promotora outreach with Latina farmworkers in rural southern Georgia. Am J Public Health 101(12):2233–2235

Luque JS, Tarasenko YN, Reyes-Garcia C et al (2017) Salud es Vida: a cervical cancer screening intervention for rural Latina immigrant women. J Cancer Educ 32(4):690–699

Mac VV, Tovar-Aguilar JA, Flocks J et al (2017) Heat exposure in central Florida fernery workers: results of a feasibility study. J Agromedicine 22(2):89–99

Madrigal DS, Minkler M, Parra KL et al (2016) Improving Latino youths' environmental health literacy and leadership skills through participatory research on chemical exposures in cosmetics: the HERMOSA study. Int Q Community Health Educ 36(4):231–240

Marín A, Carrillo L, Arcury TA et al (2009) Ethnographic evaluation of a lay health promoter program to reduce occupational injuries among Latino poultry processing workers. Public Health Rep 124(Suppl 1):36–43

May J, Hawkes L, Jones A et al (2008) Evaluation of a community-based effort to reduce blueberry harvesting injury. Am J Ind Med 51(4):307–315

McCauley LA, Beltran M, Phillips J et al (2001) The Oregon migrant farmworker community: an evolving model for participatory research. Environ Health Perspect 109(Suppl 3):449–455

McCauley L, Runkle JD, Samples J et al (2013) Oregon indigenous farmworkers: results of promotor intervention on pesticide knowledge and organophosphate metabolite levels. J Occup Environ Med 55(10):1164–1170

Mirabelli MC, Quandt SA, Crain R et al (2010) Symptoms of heat illness among Latino farm workers in North Carolina. Am J Prev Med 39(5):468–471

Mirabelli MC, Hoppin JA, Chatterjee AB et al (2011) Job activities and respiratory symptoms among farmworkers in North Carolina. Arch Environ Occup Health 66(3):178–182

Monaghan PF, Forst LS, Tovar-Aguilar JA et al (2011) Preventing eye injuries among citrus harvesters: the community health worker model. Am J Public Health 101(12):2269–2274

Mora DC, Miles CM, Chen H et al (2016) Prevalence of musculoskeletal disorders among immigrant Latino farmworkers and non-farmworkers in North Carolina. Arch Environ Occup Health 71(3):136–143

Morello-Frosch R, Brody JG, Brown P et al (2009) Toxic ignorance and right-to-know in biomonitoring results communication: a survey of scientists and study participants. Environ Health 8:6

Mutic AD, Mix JM, Elon L et al (2018) Classification of heat-related illness symptoms among Florida farmworkers. J Nurs Scholarsh 50(1):74–82

Napolitano M, Lasarev M, Beltran M et al (2002) Un lugar seguro para sus ninos: development and evaluation of a pesticide education video. J Immigr Health 4(1):35–45

Ortega S, McAlvain MS, Briant KJ et al (2018) Perspectives of community advisory board members in a community-academic partnership. J Health Care Poor Underserved 29(4):1529–1543

Price M, Williamson D, McCandless R et al (2013) Hispanic migrant farm workers' attitudes toward mobile phone-based telehealth for management of chronic health conditions. J Med Internet Res 15(4):e76

Quandt SA (2007) Nutrition curriculum for promotora programs. Migrant Health Newsline 24(4):3

Quandt SA, Arcury TA (2003) Food insecurity and household pesticide exposure: threats to health for farmworker children. 34th Migrant and Seasonal Head Start National Conference, Washington, DC, February 2003

Quandt SA, Arcury TA (2017) Developing occupational safety and health training programs for immigrant workers: translating research to practice. In: Leong FTL, Eggerth DE, Chang DH, Flynn MA, Ford JK, Martinez RO (eds) Occupational health disparities: improving the well-being of ethnic and racial minority workers. APA Press, Washington, DC, pp 161–180

Quandt SA, Austin CK, Arcury TA et al (1999) Agricultural chemical training materials for farmworkers: review and annotated bibliography. J Agromedicine 6(1):3–24

Quandt SA, Arcury TA, Pell AI (2001a) Something for everyone? A community and academic partnership to address farmworker pesticide exposure in North Carolina. Environ Health Perspect 109(Suppl 3):435–441

Quandt SA, Arcury TA, Austin CK et al (2001b) Preventing occupational exposure to pesticides: using participatory research with Latino farmworkers to develop an intervention. J Immigr Health 3(2):85–96

Quandt SA, Arcury TA, Preisser JS et al (2001c) Environmental and behavioral predictors of salivary cotinine in Latino tobacco workers. J Occup Environ Med 43(10):844–852

Quandt SA, Elmore RC, Arcury TA et al (2001d) Eye symptoms and use of eye protection among seasonal and migrant farmworkers. South Med J 94(6):603–607

Quandt SA, Arcury TA, Early J et al (2003) Hunger and food insecurity among Latino migrant and seasonal farmworkers in North Carolina. Proceedings of the 2002–2003. Migrant Farmworker Stream Forums, 2003, 81–86

Quandt SA, Arcury TA, Early J et al (2004a) Household food security among migrant and seasonal Latino farmworkers in North Carolina. Public Health Rep 119:568–576

Quandt SA, Arcury TA, Rao P et al (2004b) Agricultural and residential pesticides in wipe samples from farmworker family residences in North Carolina and Virginia. Environ Health Perspect 112(3):382–387

Quandt SA, Doran AM, Rao P et al (2004c) Reporting pesticide assessment results to farmworker families: development, implementation, and evaluation of a risk communication strategy. Environ Health Perspect 112(5):636–642

Quandt SA, Shoaf JI, Tapia J et al (2006a) Experiences of Latino immigrant families in North Carolina help explain elevated levels of food insecurity and hunger. J Nutr 136:2638–2644

Quandt SA, Grzywacz JG, Marín A et al (2006b) Illnesses and injuries reported by Latino poultry workers in western North Carolina. Am J Ind Med 49:343–351

Quandt SA, Feldman SR, Vallejos QM et al (2008) Vision problems, eye care history, and ocular protection among migrant farmworkers. Arch Environ Occup Health 63:13–16

Quandt SA, Schulz MR, Talton JW et al (2012) Occupational eye injuries experienced by migrant farmworkers. J Agromedicine 17(1):63–69

Quandt SA, Grzywacz JG, Talton JW et al (2013a) Evaluating the effectiveness of a lay health promoter-led community-based participatory pesticide safety intervention with farmworker families. Health Promot Pract 14:425–432

Quandt SA, Arcury-Quandt AE, Lawlor EJ et al (2013b) 3-D jobs and health disparities: the health implications of Latino chicken catchers' working conditions. Am J Ind Med 56:206–215

Quandt SA, Wiggins MF, Chen H et al (2013c) Heat index in migrant farmworker housing: implications for rest and recovery from work-related heat stress. Am J Public Health 103:e24–e26

Quandt SA, Newman JC, Pichardo-Geisinger R et al (2014a) Self-reported skin symptoms and skin-related quality of life among Latino immigrant poultry processing and other manual workers. Am J Ind Med 57(5):605–614

Quandt SA, Grzywacz JG, Trejo G et al (2014b) Nutritional strategies of Latino farmworker families with preschool children: identifying leverage points for obesity prevention. Soc Sci Med 123:72–81

Quandt SA, Pope CN, Chen H et al (2015a) Longitudinal assessment of blood cholinesterase activities over 2 consecutive years among Latino nonfarmworkers and pesticide-exposed farmworkers in North Carolina. J Occup Environ Med 57(8):851–857

Quandt SA, Brooke C, Fagan K et al (2015b) Farmworker housing in the United States and its impact on health. New Solut 25(3):263–286

Quandt SA, Schulz MR, Chen H et al (2016) Visual acuity and self-reported visual function among migrant farmworkers. Optom Vis Sci 93(10):1189–1195

Quandt SA, Walker FO, Talton JW et al (2017) Olfactory function in Latino farmworkers over 2 years: longitudinal exploration of subclinical neurological effects of pesticide exposure. J Occup Environ Med 59(12):1148–1152

Quandt SA, Groeschel-Johnson A, Kinzer HT et al (2018) Migrant farmworker nutritional strategies: implications for diabetes management. J Agromedicine 23(4):347–354

Rao P, Quandt SA, Arcury TA (2002) Hispanic farmworker interpretations of green tobacco sickness. J Rural Health 18(4):503–511

Rao P, Arcury TA, Quandt SA (2004) Student participation in community-based participatory research to improve migrant and seasonal farmworker health: issues for success. J Environ Educ 35:3–15

Rao P, Quandt SA, Doran AM et al (2007) Pesticides in the homes of farmworkers: Latino mothers' perceptions of risk to their children's health. Health Educ Behav 34(2):335–353

Rhodes SD, Leichliter JS, Sun CJ et al (2016) The HoMBReS and HoMBReS por un Cambio interventions to reduce HIV disparities among immigrant Hispanic/Latino men. MMWR Suppl 65(1):51–56

Rhodes SD, Mann-Jackson L, Alonzo J et al (2017) Engaged for change: a community-engaged process for developing interventions to reduce health disparities. AIDS Educ Prev 29(6):491–502

Rhodes SD, Tanner AE, Mann-Jackson L et al (2018) Community-engaged research as an approach to expedite advances in HIV prevention, care, and treatment: a call to action. AIDS Educ Prev 30(3):243–253

Robinson E, Nguyen HT, Isom S et al (2011) Wages, wage violations, and pesticide safety experienced by migrant farmworkers in North Carolina. New Solut 21(2):251–268

Rohlman DS, Arcury TA, Quandt SA et al (2005) Neurobehavioral performance in preschool children from agricultural and non-agricultural communities in Oregon and North Carolina. Neurotoxicology 26:589–598

Salvatore AL, Chevrier J, Bradman A et al (2009) A community-based participatory worksite intervention to reduce pesticide exposures to farmworkers and their families. Am J Public Health 99(Suppl 3):S578–S581

Sanchez M, Rojas P, Li T et al (2016) Evaluating a culturally tailored HIV risk reduction intervention among Latina immigrants in the farmworker community. World Med Health Policy 8(3):245–262

Sandberg JC, Spears Johnson CR, Nguyen HT et al (2016) Mobile and traditional modes of communication among male Latino farmworkers: implications for health communication and dissemination. J Immigr Minor Health 18(3):522–531

Silver K, Hoffman K, Loury S et al (2014) A campus-community partnership for farmworkers' health: interventions for tomato workers in Tennessee. Prog Community Health Partnersh 8(4):501–510

Spears CR, Kraemer Diaz AE, Bailey M et al (2013) Empowering Latino youth farmworkers as youth health educators for occupational heat-related illness safety education in eastern North Carolina. Pract Anthropol 35:38–43

Sun CJ, Mann L, Eng E et al (2015) Once a navegante, always a navegante: Latino men sustain their roles as lay health advisors to promote general and sexual health to their social network. AIDS Educ Prev 27(5):465–473

Swanberg JE, Clouser JM, Westneat S (2012) Work organization and occupational health: perspectives from Latinos employed on crop and horse breeding farms. Am J Ind Med 55(8):714–728

Swanberg JE, Clouser JM, Browning SR et al (2013) Occupational health among Latino horse and crop workers in Kentucky: the role of work organization factors. J Agromedicine 18(4):312–325

Swanberg JE, Clouser JM, Bush A et al (2016) From the horse worker's mouth: a detailed account of injuries experienced by Latino horse workers. J Immigr Minor Health 18(3):513–521

Swanberg J, Clouser JM, Gan W et al (2017) Poor safety climate, long work hours, and musculoskeletal discomfort among Latino horse farm workers. Arch Environ Occup Health 72(5):264–271

Tanner AE, Song EY, Mann-Jackson L et al (2018) Preliminary impact of the weCare social media intervention to support health for young men who have sex with men and transgender women with HIV. AIDS Patient Care STDs 32(11):450–458

Thompson B, Coronado GD, Vigoren EM et al (2008) Para niños saludables: a community intervention trial to reduce organophosphate pesticide exposure in children of farmworkers. Environ Health Perspect 116(5):687–694

Thompson B, Carosso E, Griffith W et al (2017) Disseminating pesticide exposure results to farm-worker and nonfarmworker families in an agricultural community: a community-based partici-patory research approach. J Occup Environ Med 59(10):982–987

Tovar-Aguilar JA, Monaghan PF, Bryant CA et al (2014) Improving eye safety in citrus harvest crews through the acceptance of personal protective equipment, community-based participa-tory research, social marketing, and community health workers. J Agromedicine 19(2):107–116

Trejo G, Arcury TA, Grzywacz JG et al (2013) Barriers and facilitators for promotoras' success in delivering pesticide safety education to Latino farmworker families: La Familia Sana. J Agromedicine 18:75–86

United Nations General Assembly (1948) Universal declaration of human rights. Presented Paris, France, December 10, 1948. https://www.un.org/en/universaldeclaration-human-rights/index. html. Accessed 10 Jul 2019

Walker FO, Cartwright MS, Blocker JN et al (2013) Prevalence of bifid median nerves and persis-tent median arteries and their association with carpal tunnel syndrome in a sample of Latino poultry processors and other manual workers. Muscle Nerve 48(4):539–544

Wells KJ, Rivera MI, Proctor SS et al (2012) Creating a patient navigation model to address cervical cancer disparities in a rural Hispanic farmworker community. J Health Care Poor Underserved 23(4):1712–1718

Chapter 9
Farm Labor and the Struggle for Justice in the Eastern United States

Melinda F. Wiggins

9.1 Introduction

> We Mexicans work very hard in the United States, although it's so very hot, even so we work 13 hours each day without resting a single day, planting and picking fruits and vegetables so that people here can eat. Well, the truth is that we suffer a lot by being here starting with our family, abandoning them in order to push ahead.—Adalberto (Student Action with Farmworkers 2017)

> I'll tell you a little bit about what we farmworkers experience here in the United States. Life here is very hard when we harvest fruits and vegetables… and the sun burns so much…and we get weak, and you get irritated from so much heat. And despite that we have to work all day putting up with the fatigue, dehydration and hunger. We also have to work when it's raining and we get full of dirt. And wet… I'll also tell you that it's very sad to be far from our land which is Mexico…and our loved ones like my parents, my wife and my son. But we're here working hard so that we can support our family.—Angelito (Student Action with Farmworkers 2017)

Due to the lack of protections for farmworkers under the law, a large number of undocumented farmworkers, and farmworkers' lack of organization, some advocates have gone so far as to say that farmworkers are in no better place than were industrial workers before the New Deal, which brought about widespread labor reform (Schell 2002). There has been a heightened anti-immigrant sentiment in the post-9/11 United States (US) and thus even more pressure on immigrant farmworkers, particularly those who are working without work authorization. Yet in recent years, there have been tremendous strides in terms of creative solutions and new leadership models that are emerging in the farm labor field, which hold out hope for change.

Farm work is one of the lowest-paid, least protected, and most dangerous occupations in the US (Gray and Kreyche 2007; National Farm Worker Ministry 2018).

M. F. Wiggins (✉)
Student Action with Farmworkers, Durham, NC, USA

© Springer Nature Switzerland AG 2020
T. A. Arcury, S. A. Quandt (eds.), *Latinx Farmworkers in the Eastern United States*, https://doi.org/10.1007/978-3-030-36643-8_9

227

The most recent National Agricultural Workers Survey (NAWS; Hernandez and Gabbard 2018) shows that the mean and median personal incomes for farmworkers are $17,500–$19,999 for individuals and $20,000–$24,999 for families. Twenty-nine percent of farmworkers have personal incomes of $10,000–$19,999, and 33% live below the poverty line. Farm work has always been a job filled with hardships by way of stagnant sub-poverty wages and dangerous working conditions. Farmworkers earn as little as the minimum hourly wage or 35 cents a bucket for piece-rate crops, and most do not receive overtime compensation. Agricultural workers labor for long hours in severe weather conditions; are exposed to pesticides; are at risk of musculoskeletal injuries, tuberculosis, parasitic infections, and dermatitis; and live in unsafe and overcrowded housing (33% according to the most recent NAWS [Hernandez and Gabbard 2018]). Farmworkers have limited access to benefits. Only 43% of farmworkers have unemployment insurance, 47% have health insurance (18% provided by their employer), and 62% have workers' compensation (Hernandez and Gabbard 2018). Such limited access to benefits leaves few resources to help when injured on the job. The lack of protections covering farmworkers is exacerbated by the poor enforcement of labor laws and opposition by agricultural lobbies when increased protections are proposed.

The current agricultural system in the US has a connection to the country's historical system of indentured servitude and slavery. Even after slavery was abolished, most descendants of African slaves remained in the fields as sharecroppers and tenant farmers due to a two-tiered legal system that treated black people and white people differently. Even today, agriculture relies on a primarily disenfranchised group of workers who have little power to determine the conditions of their work. Just as many landowners resisted paying workers for their labor at the end of slavery, today most agricultural employers and their lobbyists strongly resist any changes that would require higher pay for workers, more regulation in the fields, or greater rights for farm laborers.

While many advocates believe that the self-determination of workers is critical to change, a number of farmworker organizations also work to strengthen labor laws covering farmworkers and to increase workers' access to services. The farmworker support organizations that are presented in this chapter help to demonstrate the many tools that farmworkers and their allies use to bring about changes in the agricultural system.

9.2 Immigration and Farm Labor

It's something I think about every day. Is it going to be like this the rest of my life? To be separated…to be far away from my family?—Demetrio (Student Action with Farmworkers 2015)

… The danger…well, it's very far from home, around three days away. And you can be robbed, mugged… Two years ago, we were mugged—we were robbed. That's what it means to be away from home—the risks. Oh, about my baby… yes, when he was born—he was born one day before my birthday, and I was in the hospital for three days… and it's beautiful to see him grow and everything, although right now I'm far away from him. He will be 10 months old and I've been here three—three months without seeing him.— Nicasio (Student Action with Farmworkers 2016)

9.2.1 Immigration from Mexico

Historically, family separation and disenfranchisement have been cornerstones of our agricultural industry as agricultural employers recruit both undocumented and documented immigrants to work on US farms. Currently, only 40% of farmworkers have authorization to work in the US, which is up from 14% in 1989–1991 (Zong et al. 2019). Sixty-nine percent of farmworkers in the US come from Mexico, primarily from Michoacán, Guanajuato, Jalisco, Oaxaca, and Guerrero, with 40% being unaccompanied or living apart from their nuclear family (Hernandez and Gabbard 2018). The largest number of immigrants in general is from Mexico (26% of the total foreign-born group in the US). Mexico also accounts for the largest percentage of legal permanent residents, the most immigrants without authorization, and the largest group of individuals without lawful presence who were brought to the US as children and have applied for Deferred Action for Childhood Arrivals (DACA) (Zong et al. 2019).

The political and economic situation in Mexico over the last several decades has created the climate in which many poor *campesinos* have had to leave in search of a better life.

My parents had some fields, I think fifteen acres, and we dedicated our lives to planting cotton, corn, beans, watermelon, melons, different crops. But everything changed when the Mexican president gave people the opportunity to sell the fields. Everybody sold the fields, and agriculture came down. Right now my parents don't have any more money without the fields…I never before thought to come to the United States, because I was very comfortable in my town…I was very happy. I like to remember that. I dream sometimes that I am still planting cotton in Mexico with my brothers and my father. (Kleist and Resor 2008)

When faced with not being able to feed their families or migration, millions of impoverished Mexican farmers have chosen the latter.

Starting before NAFTA [North American Free Trade Agreement] was passed, Mexican president Carlos Salinas de Gortari rammed through the Congress changes in the Constitution's guarantees of land reform, to make private land ownership easier. Many of the communal *ejidos*, created in previous decades, were dissolved and their lands sold to investors. (Bacon 2019b)

The change in access to communal land in Mexico left thousands of small farmers without the means to feed their families. The push factors of land loss and subsequent inability to work and provide for their families in Mexico converged with the pull of active recruitment by US employers and led to increased migration from Mexico.

9.2.2 Recent Immigration Trends

While the largest number of immigrants is still living in traditional immigrant states like California and Texas, a number of states in the eastern US, including North Carolina, Georgia, Arkansas, South Carolina, Tennessee, and Delaware, saw the largest percentage increase of immigrants between the years 2000 and 2016 (Zong et al. 2019). North Carolina led the nation in terms of percent growth with a 274% increase in the immigrant population. North Carolina, Florida, and New York are also where some of the largest percentage of DACA recipients reside, meaning that young immigrants who were brought to the US at an early age are choosing to stay and make these states their home. Texas, Florida, and North Carolina are also the home to some of the largest numbers of farmworkers (Student Action with Farmworkers 2007).

In recent years, there has been an increase of immigrant workers from Central America who are fleeing from economic and political violence in search of political asylum in the US. The highest number of asylum applications since 1995 was filed in 2016, which follows a trend in increasing numbers over the last 7 years. Recent applications saw tremendous increases from El Salvador, Guatemala, and Honduras (from 7723 to 25,801) (Zong et al. 2019). Six percent of the most recent agricultural workers surveyed in the NAWS came from Central America, and 6% identify as indigenous (Hernandez and Gabbard 2018). Recent farmworkers from Central America are often in very precarious situations as many speak indigenous languages, have completed few years of high school, and are undocumented.

The recent focus on the US-Mexico border has brought to light the long-standing migration of Latinx individuals to the US. The lack of access to land and increase in violence in their home countries, coupled with the abiding commitment to create a better life for their families, have meant that many migrants must continue to make the hard choice of leaving their home countries to face an increasingly dangerous and hostile border.

9.2.3 Migrant and Seasonal Farmworkers

The most recent national data reveal a shift to more seasonal (81%) and less migrant workers (19%) (Hernandez and Gabbard 2018), an increase from 59% seasonal workers and 41% migrant workers in the 1989–1991 NAWS (United States Department of Labor Employment and Training Administration 2019). A third of these migrant farmworkers are international migrants, many through the H-2A guest worker program (see Chap. 2).

> I arrived here in 1999, in April of 1999, contracted by the H-2A program. I returned to Mexico on October seventh of the same year. Since that year, each year is practically the same date of coming and the same date of going… For necessity I came from Mexico to the United States to work. (Pérez 2006)

A long-time economic expert on agriculture, Philip Martin, believes that farmers are responding to the current labor market by bringing in more workers with H-2A temporary agricultural visas and using machines to replace unauthorized workers (Pullano 2017). The practice of using government subsidies to purchase farm implements to put farmworkers out of jobs dates back to the early efforts of the Southern Tenant Farmers Union after the Great Depression (Ortiz 2002). Although in many cases the introduction of machines has not replaced workers, this continues to be a common threat used by agricultural employers when they are faced with an organized workforce advancing toward a more just workplace.

Historian Cindy Hahamovitch argues that guest worker programs were originally initiated to thwart worker organization. In the 1940s, growers lobbied the federal government to quash the struggle of African American bean pickers who were organizing in Florida. This eventually led to the government approving and providing for an endless supply of foreign-born agricultural workers through temporary guest worker visa programs. "African American farmworkers' wartime struggle did not fail for lack of organization. It was the growers' ability to enlist the aid of federal authorities that crushed their promising but short-lived initiative" (Hahamovitch 2002:104).

9.2.4   Recruitment Fraud

Because information about H-2A (agricultural) and H-2B (nonagricultural) jobs is limited and in English only, those outside of the US seeking jobs do not have access to all the information they need to verify if the information is accurate or if the job is even real. Most agricultural employers seeking to fill H-2 positions rely on private recruitment agencies or independent recruiters to share information about their jobs, arrange transportation, and process applications. Like agricultural work in general, Mexico is the largest sending country for H-2 workers, with 86% of H-2 visas going to Mexican workers in 2017 (Centro de Los Derechos Del Migrante 2019).

Mexicans seeking work in the US are often charged exorbitant illegal fees to be considered for a job. Although federal laws regulate crew leaders, the system in which recruiters operate is largely unregulated. Centro de los Derechos del Migrante, Inc. released a report that documents recruitment fraud in the majority of Mexican states (Centro de Los Derechos Del Migrante 2019). They found that 10% of migrant workers paid fees averaging 3 ½ month's salary in Mexico for a job that did not exist. Although many who seek agricultural jobs in the US do so *por necesidad*, or out of economic necessity, having to pay additional recruitment fees only adds to their economic burden and debt. "Many of the largest employers of H-2A workers are associations and farm labor contractors that recruit workers in Mexico and move them from farm to farm in the United States" (Schuster 2018). Thus, many of the same groups that are involved in the unscrupulous labor recruitment system are also charging farmworkers fees for housing, food, and transportation once they are working on US farms.

9.3 Agricultural Exceptionalism

I didn't have another choice. Cause I don't have a social. I can't work anywhere.—Griselda
(Student Action with Farmworkers 2013a)

I worked there when I was pregnant and I would fall down, but you work there out of necessity.—Farmworker (Student Action with Farmworkers 2015)

9.3.1 Federal Exemptions

While the New Deal federal labor laws made significant and long-term changes to the industrial workplace, farmworkers were exempt from most of these changes and have been consistently governed by different labor standards and treated differently from other employees. Farmworkers endure the effects of "agricultural exceptionalism," a historic practice of excluding farmworkers from legal protections benefiting other workers. Most of these exceptions date back to the 1930s, when southern legislators and other power holders did not want the nearly 65% of African Americans who were farmworkers or domestic workers to receive the same treatment as white workers (Triplett 2004). While individual states can pass their own laws regulating farm labor, few have done so, especially in the eastern US.

Notably, farmworkers are excluded from the National Labor Relations Act (NLRA) passed in 1935, which governs worker organizing and collective bargaining. California led the way in the effort to rectify this exclusion, passing its own state Agricultural Labor Relations Act in 1975. But not until 2019 had any state in the eastern US provided farmworkers the same labor organizing protections as other workers who are covered by the NLRA. In May 2019, New York farmworkers won a significant victory when an appellate court ruled that excluding farmworkers from the right to organize was unconstitutional. Even so, most farmworkers who organize in the workplace are at risk of being fired, and employers have no legal obligation to negotiate a contract with them.

Another major labor law that treats farmworkers differently is the Fair Labor Standards Act (USDOL 2019), which covers minimum wage, overtime provisions, and child labor standards, among other protections. Nationally, farmworkers do not receive overtime pay, and those who labor on small farms (those using less than 500 person-days of labor in a quarter in the preceding year, as defined by USDOL) are not guaranteed the minimum wage. In addition, children as young as 10 years are allowed to work in the fields, compared to 16 years in other industries (see Chap. 7). No state in the eastern US has enforced stricter standards on child labor, even though recent data show that nearly 500,000 children currently work in agriculture (National Center for Farmworker Health 2018). Only New York has passed a law granting farmworkers overtime.

The lack of resources for farm labor advocacy and the opposition by the farm lobby has affected farmworkers' ability to lobby for better legal protections and has led to a piece-meal approach to legislative change. Instead of incorporating farmworkers fully into the two key labor laws mentioned above, a special Migrant and Seasonal Agricultural Worker Protection Act (AWPA or MSPA) was passed in 1983 to specify certain housing, employment, and transportation standards for farmworkers. And while these areas are regulated for H-2A guest workers, these workers are exempt from the AWPA (USDOL 2007).

Though not originally included in the 1970 Occupational Safety and Health Act (OSHA), farmworkers were afforded minimal health and safety protections through the Field Sanitation Standard in 1987, 17 years after all other workers were covered under OSHA. Yet again, farmworkers who work on small farms, which OSHA defines as fewer than 11 workers, are exempt from this law mandating water and handwashing in the fields. It took even longer for the federal government to pass basic pesticide protections for field workers. It was not until the mid-1990s that the Environmental Protection Agency's (EPA) Worker Protection Standard (WPS) was implemented. While these regulations do not include a system to track pesticide exposure, twelve states, including Louisiana, North Carolina, and New York, voluntarily participate in a formal tracking system, and health-care providers in 30 states must report related injuries and illnesses (Oxfam America 2004). The EPA updated the federal WPS in November 2015, with the protections going into effect in January 2017 and January 2018. Key improvements include increased pesticide training, additional personal protective equipment (Fig. 9.1) and decontamination supplies, sharing further information about

Fig. 9.1 Tobacco workers create their own personal protective equipment, 2011 (Photo by Abigail Bissette, Katie Cox Shrader, and Nandini Kumar. Published with kind permission of © Student Action with Farmworkers 2011. All Rights Reserved)

pesticide applications and the state agency where violations can be reported, and, most notably, prohibiting children under 18 from entering restricted areas early or from handling pesticides (Farmworker Justice and Migrant Clinicians Network 2016).

9.3.2 State Protections

The lack of federal protections of farmworkers has led some advocates to lobby for state laws benefiting farmworkers. Yet, most advocates agree that gains on a state and federal level are equally difficult to achieve. "On the federal level, farm interests represent only one of thousands of organized groups trying to press their agendas on Congress.... [By contrast, in] major farm states, agricultural groups have few peers in terms of influence" (Schell 2002:152). In addition to being out-resourced by agribusiness, farmworker advocacy groups often face direct opposition by growers. In North Carolina, some grower representatives resisted changes to the North Carolina Migrant Housing Act, calling the demand for mattresses in migrant labor camps an embarrassment to farmers statewide. At times, successful state wins can activate reform efforts elsewhere. For instance, the recent passage of heat stress standards and overtime requirements for farmworkers in California has led to national coalitions and conversations about what might be possible in other states and at the federal level.

Because of the resistance by agricultural interests, farmworkers remain in jobs with little state or federal protection. For instance, in half of the states, farmworkers do not receive the same workers' compensation coverage as do other employees, and in many states workers' compensation for farmworkers is optional (Schell 2002). In the eastern US, Florida and New York appear to have the most progressive laws protecting farmworkers. Florida affords workers the "right" of self-organization and access to visitors in labor camps. Florida also requires farms that employ as few as five workers to abide by the Field Sanitation Standard. In the 1990s, New York passed more stringent laws covering farmworkers' wages, sanitation, and access to drinking water (Gray and Kreyche 2007). And in the summer of 2019, New York passed comprehensive legislation, which provides workers' compensation, the right to organize, overtime, safe housing, unemployment, and disability benefits for farmworkers (Beyond Pesticides 2019). Several additional states in the eastern US, including North Carolina and Maryland, have slightly stronger migrant housing codes than the federal OSHA standard. Yet, for the most part, states in the eastern US have not passed stronger laws protecting farmworkers, but have simply adopted the few federal labor standards covering farmworkers as their ceiling.

9.3.3   Enforcement

Because of exemptions, exceptions, and under-enforcement of employment laws, agricultural labor is a largely unregulated workplace. Where legal protections do exist, the violations are rampant, many employers simply ignore the law, and workers are often unable or unwilling to make a formal complaint. Thus, the laws protecting farmworkers are rarely enforced. Reports about compliance with farm labor regulations indicate that while some areas may have improved, there is still the need for change. For instance, in 1990 the US Government Accountability Office (1992) found that a majority of growers were in violation of the Field Sanitation Standard, and in 2015–2016 the NAWS found that 11% of growers did not provide water and cups every day (Hernandez and Gabbard 2018). Enforcement at a state level often mirrors poor federal enforcement. Members of the Farmworker Advocacy Network, a coalition working on policy reform in North Carolina, have found that inadequate enforcement is due to government enforcement agencies being understaffed, having close ties with employers, rarely speaking the language of the workers, and not always providing information about how to file complaints to workers in a culturally appropriate manner.

Because the state and federal laws protecting farmworkers are weak and poorly enforced, some advocates look to international laws and labor clauses embedded in free trade agreements to hold international agribusiness companies accountable for upholding workers' rights. Even though the US is a member of the International Labor Organization (ILO), it has failed to adopt most of the standards that would improve farm labor conditions. Furthermore, the US has not ratified the ILO conventions protecting workers' right to organize or the convention on safety and health in agriculture (Oxfam America 2004). So again, advocates find themselves faced with the US government's accommodation of employer interests and refusal to protect the health, safety, and labor rights of its agricultural workforce.

9.4   The Birth of a Movement

> For the first few years, we didn't have any break besides lunch at noon. But afterwards, with the help of the union, they gave us a break in the morning, the lunch hour, and a break at 3 p.m.—Miguel (Oxfam America 2011)

The organization of farm employers, as well as agribusiness' partnership with the government, has contributed to the inability of advocates to make any real national improvements for farmworkers. Lack of documentation status, anti-union sentiment, isolation, and a number of other obstacles make it difficult for workers to organize. Many advocates agree that farmworkers' need to take care of their families often takes precedence over their own personal welfare and safety. "My description about the housing conditions is very bad. But [the farmworkers] don't care very much, because, for them, it is very important to make the money to send to their families" (Kleist and

Resor 2008). Many workers often resist complaining about work conditions, joining a union, or even talking with advocates for fear of losing their job or being deported. Heine et al. (2017) describe the limits to migrant farmworker agency stemming from a tendency to "put up with" bad conditions because the "structural barriers to agentive action are multiple and reinforcing". Poor conditions alone do not usually create the environment necessary for farmworkers to organize. A number of circumstances, including a progressive and supportive political, religious, and consumer conscious-ness, are needed in order for agricultural conditions to change. To make improvements to farmworkers' health, safety, and general well-being, many workers and advocates believe that the key is an empowered workforce.

The United Farm Workers (UFW) (https://ufw.org/), which grew out of the National Farm Workers Association of America and the Agricultural Workers Organizing Committee, developed the most significant early model of farm labor organizing in the 1960s. Combining union organizing strategies with civil rights tactics, founders Cesar Chavez and Dolores Huerta built a base of local workers in California, which was supported by allies across the country. Chavez and Huerta's focus on labor, partnerships with liberal politicians, use of religious traditions, and multiethnic organizing was often at odds with the more militaristic aims of the bur-geoning Chicano Movement. Chavez followed in the steps of Gandhi and Martin Luther King Jr. as he led the farmworker movement with a commitment to "militant nonviolence," a focus on change and empathy for the oppressor. Combining Christian practices, such as fasting and pilgrimages and use of religio-cultural sym-bols such as *La Virgen de Guadalupe* and *Don Quixote*, with references to Emiliano Zapata and the Mexican Revolution, the burgeoning union raised consciousness about "tensions" that existed in the day-to-day lives of many Mexicans living in the US. Chavez's public and political emphasis on the poor conditions experienced by farmworkers and workers' rights issues positioned him as the leader of the farm-workers (Mariscal 2004; Buss 1993; Ferriss and Sandoval 1997).

> By the time Chavez died, the UFW had shrunk to a few thousand members from a peak of about 40,000 in the late 1970s. Over 160,000 workers had voted for the union under California's Agricultural Labor Relations Act, the law the union had fought for in 1975…[But] most growers wouldn't sign contracts. Many others who did either went out of business, changed their names and dumped their workers, or simply refused to renew their agreements…In 1996, Bruce Church finally did sign a contract to settle its decades-long legal war with the union, and over the next 25 years, the UFW stabilized and began to grow. According to [Arturo] Rodriguez, 10,000 people now work under union agreements, mostly in California. (Bacon 2019a)

The UFW has also seen success on the legislative front, with requirements for grow-ers to negotiate if the workers vote for the union, passing heat stress protections, and phasing in overtime pay for field workers. Like many groups organizing farmwork-ers, they have had to adapt to the changing demographics and needs of new workers. From 2012 to 2017, the number of H-2A workers grew by 500%, and there has been an increasing number of indigenous workers in the fields. One way the UFW has responded to changes is by hiring its first immigrant woman president, Teresa Romero, in 2018.

9.5   Organizing for Change

I am a guy who has a lot of dreams. I think that one day the labor of farmworkers will be valued.—Rigoberto (Student Action with Farmworkers 2012)

My dreams were never realized. Now I have to fight so that my children can achieve what they want.—Luz (Student Action with Farmworkers 2012)

9.5.1   Alinsky Organizing

Many farm labor union leaders, including Cesar Chavez, studied and utilized strategies popularized by the late community organizer Saul Alinsky. The Alinsky model focuses on mass meetings, cumulative victories, direct confrontations with targets, and concrete wins. Its separation of professional organizers and community leaders has at times led to a lack of leadership development of rank and file workers (Castelloe et al. 2002). Even though Chavez and many other union leaders were farmworkers, they maintained their role as public spokespersons and leaders of their organizations without fully developing lay leaders as their peers in the movement. During the 1960s, the Chicano Movement critiqued the UFW's Alinsky style of organizing by calling for the union to focus less on the wins and more on building, less on campaigns and more on the movement. Their prodding begged the question that still plagues farm labor organizing today, "Does winning campaigns build a social movement" (VeneKlasen and Patel 2006)?

Other farm labor unions, Oregon-based *Pineros y Campesinos Unidos del Noroeste*/Northwest Treeplanters and Farmworkers United (PCUN) (https://pcun.org/) and the Ohio- and NC-focused Farm Labor Organizing Committee (FLOC) (http://www.floc.com/wordpress/), also rely on many Alinsky organizing strategies. They often initiate direct action campaigns targeted at growers or agricultural companies, which have the power to hand over concrete wins to agricultural workers. While these unions tend to focus on specific commodities in a state or region, they are also involved in legislative advocacy, health and safety training, housing reform, immigrants' rights coalitions, and monitoring recruitment fraud at the state and national levels.

These unions have each achieved significant victories for farmworkers. In the eastern US, FLOC negotiated a successful contract with over 8000 H-2A guest workers in North Carolina in 2004. This campaign, which lasted over a decade and culminated with the end of a 5-year boycott of Mt. Olive Pickle Company, Inc., relied heavily on mass events and marches and rallying consumers to demand that the pickle company negotiate with the workers. This was the first contract with H-2A guest workers in the country and has been used as a model for subsequent collective bargaining agreements with guest workers. In addition to providing basic health and safety protections, a day of rest, and bereavement leave, the contract also provides workers a grievance procedure to redress workplace problems. A recent

Fig. 9.2 Student Action with Farmworkers interns protesting in support of the Farm Labor Organizing Committee's VUSE boycott, 2018 (Photo by Patricia Valle. Published with kind permission of © Student Action with Farmworkers 2018. All Rights Reserved)

unpublished FLOC report showed that in 2018 alone, they used the contract to resolve over 450 issues, including recouping hundreds of thousands of dollars of pay due to workers from wage theft. FLOC's newest campaign to organize tobacco workers has been met with resistance by R.J. Reynolds Tobacco and its new parent company, British American Tobacco. An April 2018 boycott of Reynolds VUSE e-cigarette has invigorated support for this corporate campaign (Fig. 9.2).

9.5.2   Women-Centered Organizing

The Alinsky model is often juxtaposed with that of more process-oriented organizing models, which emphasize the building of relationships, consensus decision-making, and human interdependence. For instance, women-centered organizing models tend to focus on the ongoing leadership development and empowerment of community members (Castelloe et al. 2002). This multicultural model includes "work that is specifically anti-racist, anti-sexist, anti-homophobic, or has as its primary goal the development of equitable, multicultural communities" (Stall and Stoecker 1997).

Though women only make up 32% of the agricultural workforce nationwide (40% in the eastern US) (Hernandez and Gabbard 2018), they have played a critical role in many community and union organizing efforts. While women tend to work slightly fewer hours than men in the fields, they often work a "double day," meaning that in addition to farm work, they are still expected to fulfill traditional gendered roles in the home with regard to cooking, cleaning, and childcare. For those women who also become community organizers, they may in fact have a "triple day" (Blackwell 2010).

Because farmworker women are more likely to live with their families than their male counterparts (98% of farmworker women who have children are accompanied), there is an opportunity for them to engage their whole families in the work of organizing. Many farmworker women begin engaging in their community because of their concern for their children (Fig. 9.3).

> Organizing approaches that blur the boundaries between women's political and maternal roles, that include sex-segregated activities and children, and that feed family members are especially promising for women who are unaccustomed to public speaking, short of time and money, invested in the political training of the next generation, and must overcome male partners' wariness of their activism. (Seif 2008:94)

A number of scholars have discussed how women have often been relegated to the "private" sphere of organizing, while men were offered more "public" positions in terms of leadership in organizations. This has led to many women organizers challenging the notion that there is only one way in which women can support change. For instance, in the 1960s and 1970s in the Lower Rio Grande Valley of Texas, the union that was often affiliated with the UFW relegated women workers to their *campesino* center, which focused more on social services instead of the political work of the organization (Jepson 2005). It was not until the union faced some hardships with organizing and elected a new woman leader to address these issues that the division between the administrative and political work began to break down. "Rather than remain the 'social services' of the union structure, the *campesino* center became a school for women, fostering political consciousness and providing

Fig. 9.3 Worker who harvests melon, cucumbers, squash, and zucchini in South Carolina, seen here with her children, 2013 (Photo by Cindy Ramirez and Eric Britton. Published with kind permission of © Student Action with Farmworkers 2013. All Rights Reserved)

support for those who wanted to develop their organizing skills" (Jepson 2005:692). Through this new lens, women were able to participate both formally and informally in the organization, bringing along their entire family into the movement.

Though not based in the eastern US, *Líderes Campesinas* (http://www.lideres-campesinas.org/index.php) is "the only statewide organization of women farmworkers in the country" (Blackwell 2010:18). The group focuses on empowerment, intersectionality of oppressions, and "a form of community organizing that defies the categories of public and private and challenges the assumption that labor organizing happens primarily in the workplace and is limited to workplace issues, in this case, the fields" (Blackwell 2010:15). Like many women-centered models, *Líderes Campesinas* employ popular education as their organizing pedagogy. The women utilize community meetings in women's homes, facilitating discussions about how the roles of women in the fields are often mirrored at home; they have positively responded to demands by indigenous women to include issues affecting them differently; and they have pushed the national conversation on domestic violence with their advocacy for the inclusion of migrant women's experiences in the Violence Against Women Act. Women organizing on multiple issues with their entire family, workplace, and community are working in what Gloria Anzaldúa called "liminal space" and show great promise for change for farmworker communities (Blackwell 2010) (Fig. 9.3).

9.5.3   Worker-Driven Social Responsibility

Women workers with the Florida-based Coalition of Immokalee Workers (CIW) (http://ciw-online.org) have been leading the local and national fight against violence toward women in the workplace. The CIW demonstrates their emphasis on the community-based model of organizing through its development of farmworker leaders:

> We strive to build our strength as a community on a basis of reflection and analysis, constant attention to coalition building across ethnic divisions, and an ongoing investment in leadership development to help our members continually develop their skills in community education and organization. (Coalition of Immokalee Workers, http://www.ciw-online.org/about.html)

At the same time, the CIW has also successfully used mass rallies, general strikes, boycotts, and other direct action tactics to fight for fair wages and working conditions.

The CIW has gained international recognition for its innovative worker-driven social responsibility program. This model works to reform the agricultural supply chain, with an emphasis on worker leadership, legally binding industry standards, and monitoring of the agreed-upon standards. The Fair Food Program (FFP) developed from the CIW's early fast-food boycott of Taco Bell has grown to cover 35,000 workers and includes more than 16 participating buyers, including giants like

Walmart and Whole Foods Market. The program covers 90% of Florida's tomato production, as well as additional crops in Florida and tomato farms in other states in the eastern US. The key to this model is creating incentives for buyers to participate, repercussions when groups do not abide by the agreement, and worker participation.

Some of the key tenets of the program include zero tolerance of forced labor, child labor, violence, and sexual assault; company-led trainings on sexual harassment and discrimination; direct hiring by employers of qualifying workers, a progressive disciplinary process instead of arbitrary firing; working with sole recruitment channels for workers with H-2A visas instead of informal recruitment networks; paying workers a bonus on all Fair Food Program tomato purchases; creating health and safety committees; and ensuring shade, breaks, and bathrooms for workers in the fields. According to the 2017 Fair Food Annual Report, which looks at the history of the Fair Food Program since its inception, there has been overwhelming success with responses to nearly 1800 worker complaints from November 2011 to October 2017 and a workplace apparently free of sexual harassment (Fair Food Standards Council 2018). One impacted worker said,

> There is a huge difference now since we have started this season, the conditions here are really improving. For example, the supervisors used to get angry, and now they behave respectfully towards us. Now we can make a complaint without fear of retaliation, and [the supervisors] treat us well and as if we are all equals, without preference for one over the other. Now I feel happy to harvest here. (Fair Food Standards Council 2018)

Because of the increasing awareness and request for transparency and sustainability in food systems by consumers, this model has led to other worker victories both in the eastern US and abroad. Most notably is the support provided by the CIW and the Fair Food Program model for the worker-based human rights organization, Migrant Justice. The Milk with Dignity Standards Council (see Chap. 5) is now in place after Migrant Justice (https://migrantjustice.net), and Ben & Jerry's signed an agreement to adopt a worker-driven social responsibility model affecting Vermont dairy workers in the fall of 2017.

Another more recent example of this model is the Equitable Food Initiative (EFI), a nonprofit that was formed in 2015 after being a part of Oxfam America for several years (https://equitablefood.org). Like the Fair Food Program, EFI asserts that essential to successful reform of the food system is the coordination among workers, growers, retailers, and consumers. Keys to EFI's model include a trained leadership team of management and workers, compliance with the law, health and safety, freedom of association, fair compensation, fair working conditions, nondiscrimination, dispute settlement, employer-provided housing, protections for guest workers, and worker involvement. According to Equitable Food Initiative's 2017 Annual Report, 26 farming operations and 37 unique commodities have been certified in the US, Canada, Mexico, and Guatemala, which have brought in more than $4 million dollars as bonuses to workers. "The improved communication between workers and managers that emerges within the Leadership Teams has been defined as 'one of the most notable impacts of EFI'" (Equitable Food Initiative 2017 Annual

Report). This team receives training and uses a popular education model to facilitate dialogue and action. As with the Fair Food Program, EFI's model promotes leadership of women and a focus on ending sexual harassment in the fields as central to creating a respectful and democratic workplace.

9.5.4 Community Organizing and Leadership Development

Other organizations in the eastern US that emphasize the process-oriented model of organizing include *El Comité de Apoyo a Los Trabajadores Agrícolas*/The Farmworker Support Committee (CATA) in New Jersey and Pennsylvania (https://cata-farmworkers.org), Student Action with Farmworkers (SAF) in North Carolina (www.saf-unite.org), and the Farmworker Association of Florida in central and southern Florida (http://floridafarmworkers.org). These organizations pursue worker empowerment and leadership development and address the root causes of problems faced by agricultural workers. Many of these groups utilize Paulo Freire's popular education methodology, which hinges on constituent participation, equalizing of power, action, and reflection. Some of these organizations, such as CATA, focus primarily on increasing wages for farmworkers through contracts or agreements with employers, while others, such as SAF and the Farmworker Association, focus more on leadership development and health and safety issues.

One of SAF's key programs mobilizes, trains, and supports young people from across the country to advocate for improved farm labor conditions. Since its inception in 1992, SAF has supported over 1000 youth and college students with leadership development opportunities working with over 100,000 farmworkers in the Carolinas. Through this program, SAF stresses relationship-building among a diverse group of student activists, as well as leadership development of students from farmworker families. Cultural arts work is an important tool that SAF uses to build worker confidence; for instance, with SAF's popular theater group, workers practice addressing solutions to problems that they are experiencing. SAF also uses advocacy to create policy reform and employs marches, rallies, teach-ins, and boycotts to educate and organize young people to act in solidarity with farm labor organizing efforts.

CATA is another good example of how organizations use a number of strategies to make change. CATA was involved in New Jersey's recent effort to raise the minimum wage to $15/h, which included a phased-in raise for farmworkers, and has long been involved in housing reform and environmental justice efforts. For instance, CATA supports workers to create community gardens under the concept of the more internationally recognized food sovereignty framework.

> My name is Jose Luis and I am from Moroleon, Guanajuato, Mexico. I work at Kaolin Mushroom Farms. I water the tops of the mushroom beds. I have been coming to the community garden for 4–5 months. I like to grow organic because fruits and vegetables are healthier. I like tomatoes, chili peppers, summer squash and corn. I like everything we grow. (Ramirez 2018)

CATA has also worked to bring farmworkers into the national domestic fair trade movement. In collaboration with the Rural Advancement Foundation International-USA, Northeast Organic Farming Association, and Florida Certified Organic Growers and Consumers, they created the Agricultural Justice Project, which focuses on fair working conditions for workers in the organic and sustainable agricultural system. Like other alternative models being developed at the same time, this Food Justice Certification is partly a response to an increasing interest by consumers in knowing from where their food comes and includes building direct relationships between workers and buyers.

While it is important to note what distinguishes different organizing approaches, what is clear is that more often than not, farmworker organizers and advocates utilize a combination of strategies and tactics. At times and places one model or strategy may be more appropriate than another, and they usually work in tandem. What remains a key challenge for community and labor organizing groups is how to facilitate meaningful participation by farmworkers, especially when professional staff employed by the organizations have greater access to policy makers, employer groups, and other decision-makers (VeneKlasen and Patel 2006) (see Chap. 8).

9.6   Legal and Advocacy

It's hard to hear people not understand why we want better treatment. Their simple answer is to get another job. It's not that easy for me, especially because I am undocumented in this country. My answer to them is, it's not the only option I have but it is the closest to my reach, and it's my hands that harvest the food you eat.—Jesús (Student Action with Farmworkers 2012)

9.6.1   Policy Advocacy

Instead of focusing on improvements in the laws that govern agricultural labor, most organizing and advocacy groups are often forced to work diligently to block policies that would have a negative impact on farmworkers. This is partly due to the lack of resources available to organizations dedicated to farm labor advocacy, the abundance of funds available to support corporate agribusiness interests, and the seeming lack of interest by elected officials in interfering in farm labor issues. Advocacy organizations are often met with strong opposition by grower associations that decry any government regulation of farms. Many farmworkers and their advocates believe that because legislators have not prioritized and may never prioritize farmworkers, advocates need to utilize more creative means for change.

Though farmworkers often have an understanding of basic human rights, most do not know what rights the US government or state governments afford them, nor do they have knowledge of or access to resources or support in their community.

Based on research with farmworkers in New York, researcher and advocate Margaret Gray found that "lack of knowledge of labor laws is critical because it contributes to workers' perceptions that labor rights in the US are associated with citizenship or residency and not with job tenure" (Gray and Kreyche 2007:7). While workers may fully understand that they are being taken advantage of, many may not know what support they will receive if they confront their employer, are not fully aware of the procedures for making a formal complaint to the government, or may not think they have the power to impact anything beyond their individual situation. The scarcity of instances of formal resistance (i.e., filing a lawsuit under a private right to action, lodging a complaint to the North Carolina Department of Labor, or even simply threatening to do so) "suggests that migrant farmworkers felt their agency did not extend into institutionalized mechanisms of resistance and redress" (Heine et al. 2017:247).

There are few farmworker organizations primarily dedicated to policy advocacy. Washington, DC-based Farmworker Justice (https://www.farmworkerjustice.org/) is the premier farmworker organization focused on administrative and legislative advocacy at the federal level. As is the case with many farmworker organizations that must meet many needs at once, Farmworker Justice uses education, coalition building, litigation, and support of organizing to improve farm labor conditions. For over 35 years, they have focused on monitoring legislative and policy issues affecting farmworkers. They work in collaboration with farmworker groups across the country to keep them informed of current regulations, proposed policy changes, and litigation efforts affecting farmworkers on the state, regional, and national level.

In New York, advocates identified farmworkers' exclusion from state labor laws as the leading reason that farmworkers are so vulnerable. The Rural and Migrant Ministry (RMM) (http://ruralmigrantministry.org/), a multi-faith organization that has coordinated accompaniment, education, and youth empowerment programs for rural and migrant people in New York since 1981, leads the Justice for Farmworkers Campaign in New York. As with many statewide efforts, their legislative campaign had limited success, only ensuring that farmworkers in New York had minimum wage and field sanitation. But on July 17, 2019, the historic Farmworker Fair Labor Practices Act was signed into law, thus removing agricultural exceptionalism from New York law. This new law guarantees farmworkers an 8-h workday, overtime pay, a day off each week, safe and sanitary housing, unemployment, workers' compensation, disability, and protections for injured workers. The Worker Justice Center of New York (https://www.wjcny.org) and the Workers' Center of Central New York (https://workerscny.org/en/home/) have also been engaged with advocating for policy reform with farmworkers and immigrants in New York, as well as organizing dairy workers.

The Farmworker Advocacy Network is the first and only network dedicated to government accountability and policy formation in support of farmworkers in North Carolina. Through this coalition, a diverse group of organizations monitor government agencies that enforce housing, wage, and pesticide safety regulations affecting farmworkers; influence policies around these key issues; and bring farmworkers' voices into the policy arena. Since its inception in 2003, the Farmworker Advocacy

Fig. 9.4 Workers at the Farmworker Advocacy Network's *Día de los Muertos* event calling on OSHA to strengthen health and safety regulations, 2014 (Photo by Chris Johnson. Published with kind permission of © Student Action with Farmworkers 2014. All Rights Reserved)

Network has successfully reformed the migrant housing and pesticide laws in North Carolina, developed an Emmy award-winning documentary *Harvest of Dignity* (https://vimeo.com/41172333), and initiated a statewide farm labor camp database and mapping project.

The Farmworker Advocacy Network's participation in community-based participatory research (CBPR) (see Chap. 8) with Wake Forest School of Medicine has been critical to their success. Coalition members are involved in many components of the research projects, from serving as co-investigators to collecting data, to co-presenting the results, and to implementing the intervention. This partnership has led to policy briefs documenting disparities in the living and working conditions of farmworkers, which the Farmworker Advocacy Network utilizes to elevate campaigns and garner visibility and attention among policy makers and the larger public (Arcury et al. 2017) (Fig. 9.4).

9.6.2   Legal Services

There are also organizations that provide individual advocacy through legal services and litigation on behalf of farmworkers when laws that govern them are violated. Most notable are the organizations funded by the federal Legal Services Corporation, begun in the early 1970s to provide legal aid for low-income people throughout the country. The farmworker-specific programs provide agricultural workers with legal support to address workplace protections covered under the Agricultural Worker Protection Act and the few other laws covering farm laborers. Unfortunately, since 1996, legal aid money has been restricted from being used to lobby legislators, represent undocumented workers, or file class action lawsuits. Each of these restrictions severely limits the ability of organizations funded by the Legal Services Corporation to advocate for the majority of farmworkers or to efficiently represent farm labor crews experiencing workplace problems on a specific farm. While they can represent groups, each plaintiff has to be named individually instead of filing a class action, so it is not the best use of resources and it is often difficult to get each worker to agree to participate.

In response to the limitations placed on federally funded legal services, some states have independently funded nonprofit legal organizations that are able to file class action lawsuits and represent undocumented workers. Often these organizations work closely with legal aid offices to share information about common legal issues experienced by workers and share joint educational materials and strategies for reaching out to workers (Fig. 9.5). For instance, the North Carolina Justice Center is a nonprofit organization housed in the Legal Aid of North Carolina's office building that utilizes litigation, research, advocacy, and grassroots action to support improvements for low-wealth communities. The Justice Center has a strong immigrant rights program that includes education and litigation on behalf of farmworkers, as well as a statewide immigrant advocacy program.

Fig. 9.5 Legal aid outreach staff educating workers about their rights in the fields, 2010 (Photo by Joanna Welborn. Published with kind permission of © Student Action with Farmworkers 2010. All Rights Reserved)

9.7   Service to Workers

I consider myself a piece of the puzzle when it comes to community. And…even though puzzles are different shapes, they are important to make a whole.—Blanco, health counselor (Student Action with Farmworkers 2013b)

Another service I provide for OSY [out of school youth]… [is] English as a Second Language activities…. Survival English is the most basic English that migrants and out of school youth need to know to basically function and get around in everyday life in our country. The types of English the lessons that we teach looking for work, directions, basic needs….—Zach, migrant educator (Student Action with Farmworkers 2013a)

Because organizing a primarily undocumented and immigrant workforce is a long-term commitment that yields slow change, many advocates utilize a number of short- and long-term strategies to improve the lives of farmworkers. While many advocacy and organizing groups are sometimes critical of programs that only provide direct services to workers, they also often partner with service agencies to provide basic health, education, and social services to farmworkers as an immediate amelioration.

Some of the most significant services provided for mostly migrant farmworkers came about through policy changes enacted nearly 60 years ago. Consumer response to the CBS television documentary *Harvest of Shame* influenced the development of federal health, education, housing, and job training services for farmworkers nationwide. During this historic documentary shown during Thanksgiving in 1960, Edward R. Murrow interviewed black and white farmworkers, as well as Mexican *bracero* workers who worked seasonally in the US, about their poor living conditions, inadequate housing, and lack of protections under the law. As a result, federal funding programs such as the US Department of Education's migrant education program and the US Department of Health and Human Services' farmworker health program were created to address issues raised in the film.

Since the development of these early federally funded services, a number of other farmworker agencies, such as the National Center for Farmworker Health (http://www.ncfh.org/), East Coast Migrant Head Start (http://www.ecmhsp.org/), and National High School Equivalency Program/College Assistance Migrant Program (HEP-CAMP) Association (https://hepcampassociation.org/), have received federal funding or have collaborated with federally funded programs to assist farmworkers in need. Many of these agencies provide bilingual and bicultural support services that range from transportation to education to interpretation. Some also provide preventive care, English as a Second Language classes, scholarships, and childcare for farmworkers and their families. Some agencies, such as Telamon Corporation (http://telamon.org/), also provide skill development resources for farmworkers so that they can be qualified for full-time year-round non-farm jobs.

While it is hard to imagine farmworkers' lives without these critical services in the here and now, it is imperative to question why a group of wage-earning people needs government benefits in the form of housing, health care, and social services. If they work full time and contribute to the agricultural economy, they should earn a good living. If service agencies provide transportation, health care, and other basic services to workers for free, are they actually subsidizing agricultural employers who in turn pay workers less than a living wage (Morrissey 1999)? Some workers' rights and advocacy groups hold that direct service may actually sustain workers' below-poverty wages and undermine strategies addressing the systemic problems experienced by farmworkers. Social services sometimes act as a government subsidy to agribusiness by meeting basic needs not covered by low wages and the few benefits provided by employers.

9.8 Conclusion

Throughout the history of commercial agriculture in the US, there has been a reliance on an easily exploited group of workers. The eastern US and the South in particular play a distinct role in this history because of the significant numbers of slaves, sharecroppers, tenant farmers, and farmworkers who have lived and worked in this region. The failure of the US government to protect farmworkers, oppressive practices on many farms, right-to-work laws, and resistance by a highly organized agricultural industry have kept farmwork as one of the most dangerous and lowest-paid jobs in the country. Recent changes in global agriculture, including the consolidation of farms, increase of free trade agreements, and reliance on undocumented workers, have only added to an overwhelmingly challenging reality for agricultural workers. The increased militarization of the border, anti-immigrant rhetoric, and a growing number of hate groups focused on immigrants have created a climate of fear and repression for many farmworkers and their families.

Farmworkers have always relied on students, academics, people of faith, and other advocates serving as allies in their struggle for change. Consumers have played a key role in collaboration with farmworkers beginning with the United Farm Workers' first successful grape boycott in the 1960s to the Coalition of Immokalee Workers' recent victories against fast-food giants and most recently in worker-driven social responsibility models. Allies need to be active participants in the farmworker movement, yet leadership needs to come from the workers and their families.

Service agencies need to continue providing free health, legal, and education services for farmworkers, while advocacy and organizing groups need increased resources to address the underlying causes of farmworkers' poverty and unsafe workplaces. Undocumented workers need protections in the workplace, and workers' rights issues need to be at the forefront of community and labor organizing drives. Farmworkers deserve to be protected by the Universal Declaration of Human Rights (United Nations General Assembly 1948), including having the right to freedom of movement, free choice of employment, just and favorable conditions of work, protection against unemployment, equal pay for equal work, the right to form and join trade unions, and a standard of living adequate for the health and well-being of themselves and their families. The changes needed to improve farm labor conditions are both immediate and long term.

Workers are exploring new, creative ways to make change in the industry. For example, while women only account for about one-third of the workforce, they continue to emerge as leaders of the farmworker movement and issues affecting women, most notably sexual harassment in the fields, becoming one of the keys to organizing agricultural workplaces. From women leadership to local food sovereignty projects to worker-driven social responsibility efforts, farmworkers are forging new ways to challenge old industry standards.

References

Arcury TA, Wiggins MF, Brooke C et al (2017) Using "policy briefs" to present scientific results of CBPR: farmworkers in North Carolina. Prog Community Health Partnersh 11(2):137–147

Bacon D (2019a) An immigrant woman takes charge of the United Farm Workers. The American Prospect. http://prospect.org/article/immigrant-woman-takes-charge-united-farm-workers-0. Accessed 27 Aug 2019

Bacon D (2019b) A new day for Mexican workers. The American Prospect. https://prospect.org/article/new-day-mexican-workers. Accessed 27 Aug 2019

Beyond Pesticide (2019) New York bill and lawsuit push for farmworkers' right to organize. https://beyondpesticides.org/dailynewsblog/2019/02/mew-york-billand-lawsuit-push-forfarm-workers-right-to-organize. Accessed 21 Dec 2019

Blackwell M (2010) Líderes campesinas. Nepantla strategies and grassroots organizing at the intersection of gender and globalization. Aztlán: J Chicano Studies 35(1):13–47

Buss F (ed) (1993) Forged under the sun/Forjada bajo el sol. The University of Michigan Press, Ann Arbor, MI

Castelloe P, Watson T, White C (2002) Participatory change: an integrative approach to community practice. J Community Pract 10(4):7–31

Centro de los Derechos del Migrante, Inc (2019) Fake jobs for sale: analyzing fraud and advancing transparency in US labor recruitment. Baltimore, MD: Centro de los Derechos del Migrante, Inc. https://cdmigrante.org/wp-content/uploads/2019/04/Fake-Jobs-for-Sale-Report.pdf. Accessed 27 Aug 2019

Equitable Food Initiative (2017) 2017 Annual report: maximizing impact, creating assurance, driving business performance. Washington, DC. Available via EFI. https://equitablefood.org/wp-content/uploads/eVersion-EFI-2017-Annual-Report.pdf. Accessed 27 Aug 2019

Fair Food Standards Council (2018) Fair food 2017 annual report: consumer powered, worker certified. http://fairfoodstandards.org/2017-annualreport.pdf. Accessed 27 Aug 2019

Farmworker Justice, Migrant Clinicians Network (2016) Clinician's guide to EPA's worker protection standard. https://www.farmworkerjustice.org/sites/default/files/2016-WPS%20Clinician%27s%20Guide%20%28Online%29.pdf. Accessed 27 Aug 2019

Ferriss S, Sandoval R (1997) The fight in the fields: Cesar Chavez and the farmworkers movement. Harcourt Brace & Company, New York, NY

Gray M, Kreyche E (2007) The Hudson Valley farmworker report: understanding the needs and aspirations of a voiceless population. Bard College Migrant Labor Project. http://lib.ncfh.org/pdfs/7527.pdf . Accessed 27 Aug 2019

Hahamovitch C (2002) Standing idly by: "organized" farmworkers in south Florida during the depression and World War II. In: Thompson C, Wiggins M (eds) The human cost of food: farmworkers' lives, labor & advocacy. University of Texas Press, Austin, TX

Heine B, Quandt SA, Arcury TA (2017) 'Aguantamos': limits to Latino migrant farmworker agency in North Carolina labor camps. Hum Organ 76(3):240–250

Hernandez T, Gabbard S (2018) Findings from the National Agricultural Workers Survey (NAWS) 2015–2016: a demographic and employment profile of United States farmworkers research report no. 13. Washington, DC: US Department of Labor, Employment and Training Administration, Office of Policy Development and Research. https://wdr.doleta.gov/research/FullText_Documents/ETAOP_2019-01_NAWS_Research_Report_13.pdf. Accessed 27 Aug 2019

Jepson W (2005) Spaces of labor activism, Mexican-American women and the farm worker movement in south Texas since 1966. Antipode 37(4):679–702

Kleist P, Resor A (2008) Interview with Leonardo. In A. Blair (Ed.), Nuestras historias, nuestros sueños: Immigrantes Latinos en las Carolinas/Our stories, our dreams: Latino immigrants in the Carolinas (p. 47). Durham: Center for Documentary Studies at Duke University in association with Student Action with Farmworkers. http://saf-unite.org/sites/default/files/nuestras_historias_0.pdf. Accessed 27 Aug 2019

Mariscal J (2004) Negotiating César: César Chávez in the Chicano movement. Aztlán: J Chicano Studies 29(1):21–50

Morrissey M (1999) Serving farm workers, serving farmers: migrant social services in northwest Ohio. Aztlán: J Chicano Studies 24(2):95–118

National Center for Farmworker Health (2018) Child labor in agriculture factsheet. Buda, TX: National Center for Farmworker Health. http://www.ncfh.org/uploads/3/8/6/8/38685499/fs-child_labor2018.pdf. Accessed 27 Aug 2019

Ortiz P (2002) From slavery to Cesar Chavez and beyond: farmworker organizing in the United States. In: Thompson C, Wiggins M (eds) The human cost of food: farmworkers' lives, labor & advocacy. University of Texas Press, Austin, TX

Oxfam America (2004) Like machines in the fields: workers without rights in American agriculture. An Oxfam America report. https://www.oxfamamerica.org/static/media/files/like-machines-in-the-fields.pdf. Accessed 27 Aug 2019

Oxfam America (2011) A state of fear: human rights abuses in North Carolina's tobacco industry. An Oxfam America report. http://www.floc.com/wordpress/wp-content/uploads/2013/11/Oxfam-A-state-of-fear-full-report-final.pdf. Accessed 27 Aug 2019

Pérez L (2006) Unpublished interview. Deposited in Duke University Libraries, Rare Book, Manuscript and Special Collections Library

Pullano G (2017) Economist: farm operators scramce to secure labor. Fruit Growers News. https://fruitgrowersnews.com/news/economist-farm-operators-scramblesecure-labor/. Accessed 21 December 2019

Ramirez K (2018) Food sovereignty at the local level: testimonies from CATA members. Siembra: a newsletter for farmworker friends and advocates. https://cata-farmworkers.org/wp-content/uploads/2018/10/Summer-2018-color.pdf . Accessed 27 Aug 2019

Schell G (2002) Farmworker exceptionalism under the law: how the legal system contributes to farmworker poverty and powerlessness. In: Thompson C, Wiggins M (eds) The human cost of food: farmworkers' lives, labor & advocacy. University of Texas Press, Austin, TX

Schuster S (2018) Requests for farm guest worker visas surge. AgriPulse. https://www.agri-pulse.com/articles/10598-requests-for-farm-guestworker-visas-surge. Accessed 27 aug 2019

Seif H (2008) Wearing union t-shirts. Undocumented women farm workers and gendered circuits of political power. Lat Am Perspect 158(35):78–98

Stall S, Stoecker R (1997) Community organizing or organizing community? Gender and the crafts of empowerment. COMM-ORG working paper. http://comm-org.wisc.edu/papers96/gender2.html. Accessed 27 Aug 2019

Student Action with Farmworkers (2007) United States farmworker factsheet. https://www.saf-unite.org/content/united-states-farmworker-factsheet. Accessed 27 Aug 2019

Student Action with Farmworkers (2012) Más de una historia/More than one story. https://saf.atavist.com/more-than-one-story. Accessed 27 Aug 2019

Student Action with Farmworkers (2013a) Aspire to change: accounts from the migrant front. Interview of Zach by Cindy Ramirez and Eric Britton. https://saf-unite.org/content/community-comunidad-2013-documentary-work. Accessed 27 Aug 2019

Student Action with Farmworkers (2013b) Rompecabezas/Puzzles. Interview of Blanco Brito by Beatriz Cruz, Edith Valle, and Jaslina Paintal. https://safunite.org/content/community-comunidad-2013-documentary-work. Accessed 27 Aug 2019

Student Action with Farmworkers (2015) I am, I see, I think, I wonder: 2015 documentary work. https://saf-unite.org/content/i-am-i-see-i-think-i-wonder-2015-documentary-work. Accessed 27 Aug 2019

Student Action with Farmworkers (2016) Recuerdos y Sueños/Memories and Dreams: 2016 documentary work. https://saf-unite.org/content/2016-documentary-work. Accessed 27 Aug 2019

Student Action with Farmworkers (2017) Crossing thresholds, harvesting stories: 2017 documentary work. https://www.saf-unite.org/content/2017-documentary-work-0. Accessed 27 Aug 2019

Triplett W (2004) Migrant farmworkers: is government doing enough to protect them? Congress Q Inc 14(35):829–852

United Nations General Assembly (1948) Universal declaration of human rights. Presented Paris, France, 10 December 1948. http://www.un.org/en/universaldeclaration-human-rights/index.html. Accessed 27 Aug 2019

United States Department of Labor (USDOL) Employment & Training Administration (2007) Foreign labor certification: helping US employers fill jobs while protecting US and foreign workers: H-2A regional summary. Washington, DC: US Department of Labor. http://www.foreignlaborcert.doleta.gov/h-2a_region2007.cfm. Accessed 27 Aug 2019

United States Department of Labor, Wage and Hour Division (2019) Compliance assistance—Wages and the Fair Labor Standards Act (FLSA). Washington, DC: US Department of Labor. https://www.dol.gov/whd/flsa/. Accessed 27 Aug 2019

United States Government Accountability Office (1992) Hired farmworkers: health and well-being at risk. Report no. GAO/HRD-92–46. Office of Public Affairs, Washington, DC

VeneKlasen L, Patel D (2006) Citizen action, knowledge and global economic power: intersections of popular education, organizing, and advocacy. Just Associates. COMM-ORG Papers Volume 12. http://comm-org.wisc.edu/papers2006/darshana.htm. Accessed 27 Aug 2019

Zong J, Batalova J, Burrows M (2019) Frequently requested statistics on immigrants and immigration in the United States. Washington, DC: Migrant Policy Institute. https://www.migrationpolicy.org/article/frequently-requested-statistics-immigrants-and-immigration-united-states/#Numbers. Accessed 27 Aug 2019

Chapter 10
Conclusions: An Updated Agenda for Farmworker Social Justice in the Eastern United States

Thomas A. Arcury and Sara A. Quandt

10.1 Introduction

Improving the health, safety, and justice of farmworkers in the eastern United States (US) will require advocacy to effect changes in labor policy, health policy, and environmental policy. Major obstacles to policy change exist. In this chapter, we delineate common themes about health and safety for farmworker advocacy and present an agenda for farmworker social justice. Most of the policy needs that we identified in 2009 (Arcury et al. 2009) continue and need to be addressed.

10.2 Common Themes

The chapters in this volume summarize different components of health, safety, and justice for farmworkers and their families in the eastern US. Although the chapters address diverse aspects of exposure to health risks and the prevalence of injury or illness, four common themes about farmworker emerge. First, consistent trends have occurred since 2009 in changes to the context for farmworker health, safety, and justice, and in the characteristics of the farmworker population. Second, the information needed to document farmworker health and safety remains incomplete. Third, the changes of the past decade and the limited available information provoke grave concerns about farmworker health and justice. Finally, deficits in farmworker health and achieving farm labor justice result largely from agricultural labor policy.

T. A. Arcury (✉)
Department of Family and Community Medicine, Wake Forest School of Medicine, Winston-Salem, NC, USA

S. A. Quandt
Department of Epidemiology and Prevention, Division of Public Health Sciences, Wake Forest School of Medicine, Winston-Salem, NC, USA

© Springer Nature Switzerland AG 2020
T. A. Arcury, S. A. Quandt (eds.), *Latinx Farmworkers in the Eastern United States*, https://doi.org/10.1007/978-3-030-36643-8_10

10.2.1   Trends Since 2009

Since 2009, the political and social climate in the US has been infused with an increasing amount of xenophobic and anti-immigrant rhetoric. This is directed broadly at all people of color in the US, including documented and undocumented immigrants and US citizens. However, political and public sentiment has zeroed in on persons coming from Mexico and other points in Latin America. Calls to create a physical wall at the southern US border have increasingly been issued by political leaders, and citizen groups have participated in patrolling some areas of the border, increasing tension in the area. At the same time, deportations of undocumented individuals, including groups apprehended at worksites, have received considerable publicity and produced fear and anxiety among all immigrants.

The rhetoric about illegal immigration contrasts with available data. The Pew Research Center reports that the total number of unauthorized immigrants in the US fell to 10.5 million in 2017, from its peak of 12.2 million in 2007 (Krogstad et al. 2019). Unauthorized immigrants from Mexico have steadily dropped in the same decade (6.9 million down to 4.9 million); at the same time, there was a slight uptick in those from Central America (1.5–1.9 million). By and large, unauthorized immigrants living in the US are not new immigrants. About two-thirds of those in the US in 2017 had been in the country for more than 10 years.

Accompanying this rhetoric and the downturn in undocumented individuals from Mexico are reports of an increasing shortage of farmworkers. The work performed by farmworkers is wanted by few native-born Americans, and immigrant workers with documents often move from farm work to jobs in other sectors of the economy, such as construction and hospitality, that offer year-round employment and often higher pay. The fewer number of undocumented workers and the fear of many to move freely have decreased the mobility of the farmworker population and reduced the pool of workers farmers can draw upon during their cyclic need for workers.

These trends have resulted in changes in the composition of the farmworker population in the eastern US and across the country since 2009 (see Chap. 2). The numbers of migrant workers have decreased, and seasonal workers have increased. Workers choose to remain in one place year round for diverse reasons: keeping continuity in children's schooling, maintaining state-sited benefits such as health insurance, and taking advantage of the growing availability of full-year employment in farm work with the greater cultivation of organic produce in Florida and the Deep South.

At the same time, the numbers of workers in the H-2A guest worker program have increased nationally and in the eastern US. These increases are largely due to shortages of workers in specific sections of the country and employer concerns that immigration raids on undocumented workers might deplete the supply of workers at harvest and other key times in the production cycle.

Overall, the trend among farmworkers is for the worker population to be somewhat older and to include more American-born Latinx workers. The proportion of workers who are women has risen nationally, particularly in the eastern US (see Chap. 6). Children continue to be allowed to work as hired workers. While it is impossible to know if the numbers have changed over the last decade, there have been some additions to the small body of research on this population since 2009, both in the West and border states, and in North Carolina (see Chap. 7).

Trends to watch in the coming decade include the ramifications of the reduction in number of farms and the mechanization of fruit and vegetable harvesting. As discussed in Chap. 2, the aging of the farmer population and financial difficulties of maintaining small farms have led to greater consolidation and commercialization of agriculture. This suggests a continued and perhaps greater demand for hired labor. At the same time, technological advances to produce machines that can harvest fruits and vegetables in place of humans are in process (Huffman 2012). Acceptable machines are available for picking fruits and vegetables that will be processed: tomatoes, juice oranges, tart cherries, and wine grapes. Challenges remain in picking fresh market fruits and vegetables. The uncertainties of the demand for these products in the face of international imports may reduce the willingness of growers to invest in expensive machinery and therefore keep the demand for hand labor strong.

10.2.2 Lack of Information About Farmworkers

The chapters in this revised edition echo the calls in the first edition for more data to document the status of health and safety for farmworkers in the eastern US. Although federal, state, and local agencies and programs provide services to farmworkers, these governmental entities seldom collect or publish information about farmworkers. The definitions of who is a farmworker differ among agencies and programs, making it extremely difficult to compare or combine the limited information that they do publish. Therefore, the characteristics of the populations served by these programs are not known.

The level of academic-based research on the health and safety of farmworkers has increased nationally and in the eastern US. However, much of the research in the eastern US continues to be conducted in a few states, most notably Florida and North Carolina, with some in the Northeast. Few or no studies focused on farmworker health and safety have been conducted in other parts of the region. The National Institute for Occupational Safety and Health supports three Centers for Agricultural Disease and Injury Research, Education, and Prevention in the eastern US (in Florida, Kentucky, and New York). The three centers have provided some attention on farmworker health and safety issues, and it appears that farmworker health and safety remains a priority at the center in Florida.

The lack of data is important. The scope and magnitude of health problems faced by farmworkers cannot be understood without data. Without data, appropriate programs to address farmworker health cannot be developed. Without data, legislators and government officials can ignore farmworker problems and claim there are no problems to be addressed.

Of the research that has been produced in the past decade, a minority of it has addressed farmworker health and safety issues within a social justice framework.

While social justice may underlie individual researchers' intentions, the failure to make it explicit and to, in a sense, connect the dots does little to advance efforts to improve the health and safety of this vulnerable worker population.

10.2.3 Continuing Concerns for Farmworker Health and Justice

The information that is available documents grave concerns for the health and justice of farmworkers and their families. The housing available to farmworkers is largely substandard and exposes workers and their family members to environmental health risks. The ubiquitous nature of pesticide application in agriculture and in farmworker dwellings compounds the environmental health risks experienced by farmworker communities. In the eastern US, environmental and occupational regulations provide little protection to farmworkers from pesticide exposure, and the limited enforcement of these regulations further amplifies the potential for pesticide exposure among farmworkers.

Most farmworkers are young and physically fit. Yet, farmworkers experience high rates of musculoskeletal, dermatological, vision, and auditory injury and illness, infectious disease, and poor mental health. Farmworker injury and illness reflect the nature of agriculture and the limited regulations applied to this industry. Although farmworkers experience high rates of occupational and environmental injury and illness, few programs and regulations have been designed to help reduce these outcomes. Farmworkers and their families in the eastern US seldom have health insurance, and many of them have limited access to health care. Long-term consequences of occupational and environmental exposures are virtually unknown.

Farmworkers are not all men. Many women and children are also employed as farmworkers and experience some of the same occupational health risks, but also risks that are unique to their age and gender. The proportion of farmworkers who are women has increased in the past decade (see Chap. 6), and there is increasing attention being paid to the work of child farmworkers (see Chap. 7). The women and children who are not employed as farmworkers but who live with a farmworker are also exposed to the poor housing, pesticides, limited access to health care and other services, and poverty and food insecurity of farmworkers.

10.2.4 The Consequences of Agricultural Labor Policy

An important theme for farmworker health and justice in the eastern US is that agricultural labor policy supports the exploitation of farmworkers, increases the risk of injury and illness, and denies justice. The concept of agricultural exceptionalism (Guild and Figueroa 2018) has been cited in several chapters; little has changed in regard to this exceptionalism since 2009. Although some states, notably the western states of California and Washington, have changed the status of agricultural labor to go beyond the minimum standards set by federal law, current agriculture labor policy in most eastern US states and in federal statute continues to limit the ability of farmworkers to organize and be represented by a union. Current agricultural labor policy continues to make it acceptable for farmworkers to live in housing that does not meet standards that are minimal for other US residents (Arcury et al. 2012a, b) (see Chap. 2). Current agricultural labor policy continues to make it acceptable for child farmworkers to work in hazardous conditions that are not acceptable for any other industries in the US (Arcury et al. 2019) (see Chap. 7); efforts in 2012 to change this child labor policy were rebuffed by agribusiness (CropLife News 2012; Leven 2012). Current agricultural labor policy continues to make it acceptable for farmworkers to work long hours without the right to overtime pay. Current agricultural labor policy continues to make it acceptable for farmworkers to work without a health safety net (workers' compensation), should they be injured (Frank et al. 2013; Guild et al. 2016). While limited health and safety regulations are imposed in agriculture, regulatory agencies responsible for enforcing these limited regulations in the eastern US are not provided with sufficient funding to review workplace safety standards or living standards.

Agriculture has been exempted from many federal and state labor laws, partly in an effort to protect "the family farm." However, much of contemporary agriculture, particularly agriculture that employs migrant and seasonal farmworkers, is agribusiness. While the family farm has nostalgic connotations, perpetuating the notion has serious consequences for farmworkers and their families (Arcury 2017).

10.3   An Agenda for Farmworker Social Justice

10.3.1   Changing the Perspective of the US Consumer

A fundamental component in improving health and safety and achieving social justice for farmworkers is changing the perspective of the US consumer. US consumers need to understand where their food is grown, they need to know whose labor is used to grow that food, and they need to know how their demands for inexpensive food result in injury and illness for those providing the labor to grow their food.

Agriculture is an industry fueled by consumer demand. Some dimensions of consumer demand lead to farmworkers being exposed to pesticides. That is, the desire for blemish-free produce, as well as produce that can withstand long storage and shipping, helped bring about the use of pesticides at the levels seen today.

Consumer demand can be modified. Examples are the recent movement toward organic foods free from pesticides, hormones, and other chemicals, changes that are seen by consumers as promoting both health of the consumer and health of the environment. In a relatively short period, organic food has progressed from being food purchased only by well-heeled elites to being sold in Walmart, the nation's top food retailer. Similarly, consumer demand for animal welfare has produced cage-free eggs (although the conditions in which uncaged chickens live and lay eggs may not be much more humane than those of caged chickens). If consumer demand can be modified to protect the environment and to protect animals, why not create similar awareness of the human cost of food production itself with the goal of having consumers care as much about the people producing their food as they do about bugs?

To achieve this, US consumers need to have a better idea of the source of their food. They also need to understand that the demand for inexpensive food results in social injustice for the people—farmworkers—who plant, cultivate, and harvest the fresh fruits and vegetables that they eat. Stories of kindergartners visiting farms and being amazed at where milk really comes from are cute, but they are, unfortunately, the tip of the iceberg for consumer ignorance. Multinational agribusiness has done a good job convincing consumers that their food is produced by modern methods used by a farmer in the air-conditioned comfort of a million-dollar tractor looking out over his amber waves of grain. Most consumers have little idea of the living and working conditions of farmworkers or of the low wages that farmworkers are paid.

Several trends have begun to change the perspective of the US consumer. Writers such as Wendell Berry (1977, 2005, 2009) have had substantial influence on the thinking of Americans about agriculture and food. Berry argues for an obligation of community and environmental stewardship and for the interconnectedness of life: of people who consume food connected to the places and people who produce it and to the environment in which it is produced. The Slow Food International movement encourages consumers NOT to take their food for granted: to eat locally produced, unprocessed, and traditional foods. International Fair Trade Certification has worked to make consumers aware of the source of their food by providing guarantees about products such as coffee, tea, and chocolate. Among the components of Fair Trade Certification is the guarantee that the labor conditions on certified farms include freedom of association, safe working conditions, living wages, and no forced child labor.

Like Fair Trade Certification, farmworker advocates are pushing for agricultural products in the US to have a Fair Labor Practices Certification (Henderson et al. 2003; Scientific Certification Systems 2007). Agricultural products with Fair Labor Practices Certification indicate that they were produced by workers provided with equitable hiring and employment practices, provided with safe workplace conditions, and provided with access to health, education, and transportation services.

The Fair Food Program, championed by the Coalition of Immokalee Workers, has worked since 2011 to educate consumers about the labor conditions behind the food they eat. The Program has asked companies at the top of the agricultural supply chain—grocery store chains and fast-food restaurants—to pay a premium for produce, which is used to augment wages of farmworkers, and to only buy from growers who implement a human-rights-based Code of Conduct on their farms. The Code of Conduct includes provisions to prevent sexual harassment and forced labor and to pay at least a minimum wage. This program focuses on growers in the eastern US, particularly those producing tomatoes, peppers, and strawberries. As a worker-driven program, the Fair Food Program has made significant strides in improving conditions and has expanded to other products, as exemplified by the Milk with Dignity program instituted with Vermont dairies and supported by Ben & Jerry's ice-cream producers (Shreiber 2017).

Despite attempts to change consumer consciousness of the labor issues behind their food supply, it is difficult to know what progress has been made. The US food supply, whether through retail food supply or restaurants, continues to focus on cheap food. The Fair Food Program has been resisted by at least one of the major supermarket chains, Publix, which continues to expand across the eastern US. Growing public racism and xenophobia makes promoting empathy for Latinx workers a harder sell than it might have been a decade ago.

10.3.2 Research Needs: Documenting the Conditions of Farm Work and Testing Interventions

The struggle for farm labor justice will be served by the availability of data documenting the social and demographic characteristics of farmworkers and their families. This need continues since the original edition of this book. Data documenting the health and safety hazards that farmworkers experience and how these hazards are distributed among farmworkers are also needed, as are data documenting farmworker health status and the health care that farmworkers receive. These are essential for understanding the scope of health problems and health resources available to farmworkers. Several research initiatives would improve information about farmworkers and the conditions of farm work. In addition, taking a different perspective—the organization of work—would help identifying leverage points for action.

One research initiative that would improve information about farmworkers and the conditions of farm work is having governmental agencies and service provider organizations systematically compile information about the farmworker communities that they serve. While common definitions of what constitutes a farmworker are needed and each database will have shortcomings, this combination of sources will illuminate the characteristics of this vulnerable population. It will allow comparisons of farmworker communities across the eastern US and with farmworker communities in other regions.

Study of farmworkers must more often collect data that will allow measurement of health outcomes as well as the measurement of potential exposures. For example, research on farmworker housing has described the often abysmal conditions of such housing; research on agricultural pesticides has documented factors that might cause pesticide exposure. However, no farmworker housing research has collected data that measure health outcomes, such as asthma, mental health, or infectious disease, that are related to housing conditions. Little farmworker pesticide exposure research has measured the potential health effects of this exposure; an exception is recent research documenting subclinical outcomes of pesticide exposure (Quandt et al. 2017). Until health outcomes and exposure are measured, it will be difficult to argue for the need to limit exposure.

New, important research topics have arisen in the past decade. One is greater emphasis on climate change and its ramifications for workers (see Chap. 6). Climate change will bring increasing temperatures that constrain worker effort, possibly requiring a larger workforce, if workers need to work shorter days. It will also bring about changes in crops grown and changes in the ranges of some crops. Taken together, different physical demands on workers as well as new demands for labor in different parts of the country may emerge.

The past decade has seen an increase in research on occupational health using the perspective of organization of work, a framework developed earlier and promoted by the National Institute for Occupational Health and Safety for understanding the factors that affect safety and health (Sauter et al. 2002). This approach has been used with farmworkers in the eastern US (Arcury et al. 2016; Quandt et al. 2019). Continued research in this framework is needed, particularly as it applies to different cropping systems.

Many of the existing interventions for increasing worker safety and health focus on training workers and providing educational materials to facilitate this training. A review shows that most of the community-based participatory research projects (see Chap. 8) have taken a training focus. Yet, after decades of training, there appears to be little improvement in the health of farmworkers. Part of the problem may lie in failure to examine the context in which interventions are implemented and where responsibility for safety lies. Using an organization of work framework for implementing and testing interventions may prove productive. For example, interventions that require workers to take time for safety procedures have little traction in a piece-rate system of worker pay.

In addition, greater focus is needed on evaluating interventions. This includes interventions designed in a research context, as well as interventions prescribed by government regulations, such as the Worker Protection Standard and heat standards being developed and implemented in several states.

10.3.3   Advocacy for Policy Change

Social justice for farmworkers requires systemic changes in policy and regulation for labor, housing, pesticide safety, health care, wages, and immigration (Liebman et al. 2013). Each of the individual chapters in this volume has made recommendations for specific changes in policy and regulations. Here we outline major policy and regulation changes that will improve the health, safety, and justice for farmworkers in the eastern US and in the nation. Unfortunately, since 2009, little progress has been made in new policy that protects farmworkers or the members of their families. Two major initiatives, regulating hired child farm labor and banning the use of the organophosphorus insecticide chlorpyrifos, were defeated through the efforts of agribusiness (Begemann 2018; CropLife News 2012; Leven

2012). Efforts to improve the US Environmental Protection Agency's (USEPA) revised Agricultural Work Protection Standard (USEPA 2016) were limited to what the agency felt it could get through the approval process due to industry objections.

Advocacy groups continue to work for change in policy and regulation in states as well as nationally. These advocacy groups need training, designated staff, and partnerships with a number of organizations to be effective at policy advocacy work. The few labor unions and community organizing groups that support agricultural workers need additional financial resources, staff members, and public support in order to advance their agendas. Because many farmworkers are recent immigrants or hold temporary work visas, partnerships between farmworker organizations and immigrant rights groups could lead to strong and diverse coalitions to work on common campaigns and progressive farm labor policy agendas at the state and federal levels.

10.3.3.1 Labor Policy

Nationally and in individual states, policies exempting agriculture from labor regulations need to be changed. On the federal level, farmworkers should be treated the same as other workers under the Fair Labor Standards Act and National Labor Relations Act. All farmworkers need to be provided with overtime pay and covered by minimum wage laws. Hired child labor must be removed from the fields, but efforts to this end since 2009 have failed (CropLife News 2012; Leven 2012). Farmworkers must have the same right to organize into unions without fear of retaliation or lack of redress as do other workers.

Farmworkers' lives could be most improved if they were paid a living wage and provided with benefits, such as paid sick leave, holidays, and a grievance procedure. In addition, workers' compensation and environmental protection provided to workers in other industries must be provided to all agricultural workers. Advocates can look to international labor standards, as these tend to be much stronger than state or federal laws in the protections they provide to migrant workers.

10.3.3.2 Housing Policy

The need to document housing quality and revise regulations governing migrant farmworker housing, as well as the housing of most low-income families in rural communities, such as seasonal farmworkers, was documented in a 2014 conference (Arcury et al. 2015; Arcury and Summers 2015; Marsh et al. 2015; Moss Joyner et al. 2015; Quandt et al. 2015a). For migrant farmworker housing, regulations provide the bare minimum in sanitation and facilities. For the rental housing in which seasonal farmworkers live in most rural communities, often no regulations exist at all. Little enforcement is available for the housing regulations that do exist (Arcury et al. 2012a).

Regulations that provide farmworkers with safe and sanitary housing that includes facilities for food preparation, bathing, and laundry must be established. The housing provided to farmworkers must include security and privacy needed for mental as well as physical health (Arcury et al. 2012b). With the concerns of increased temperatures due to climate change, this housing must provide an environment in which workers can recover from work-related heat stress (Quandt et al. 2013). Sufficient staff must be provided to the agencies charged with enforcing these regulations.

10.3.3.3 Pesticide Policy

Pesticide exposure is a major concern for farmworkers and their families in the eastern US. The potential health effects of pesticides are insidious because they may not be apparent for years and because they do greater harm to children than to adults. Research conducted since 2009 documents continued pesticide exposure of male and female farmworkers (Arcury et al. 2016, 2018) and the subclinical health effects of this exposure (Kim et al. 2018; Quandt et al. 2015b, 2017). At a minimum, policy changes are needed to ensure the enforcement of existing pesticide safety regulations. These existing pesticide safety regulations, such as the US EPA's Worker Protection Standard, need to be expanded to address the multiple pathways of pesticide exposure experienced by farmworkers and their families.

The US EPA's Worker Protection Standard was revised in 2016. However, these revised standards reflect what agribusiness would accept rather than what was needed. These new standards do little to change how work is organized related to pesticide application. They still emphasize training farmworkers and telling them to be careful, and do little to improve enforcement. They have no requirements for evaluating whether training farmworkers is effective in increasing farmworker safety knowledge, whether this training changes behavior, or whether this training reduces pesticide exposure or dose. If the goal of the Worker Protection Standard is to reduce pesticide exposure and dose, then the pesticide exposure and dose of farmworkers should be measured.

The Worker Protection Standard requires that pesticide applicators maintain a record of the pesticides they apply to specific fields. However, this information cannot be accessed to document the geographic distribution or level of pesticide application in areas in which farmworkers live. California has enacted regulations that require pesticide applicators to report monthly the types and amounts of pesticides they apply and the location where the pesticides are applied (California Department of Pesticide Regulation 2000; Nuckols et al. 2007). The implementation of this reporting system nationally would show the level of pesticide exposure for farmworkers and other residents of agricultural communities.

Policy for active monitoring of the pesticide dose experienced by farmworkers would improve workers' health and safety. Washington State has a program in which cholinesterase levels for pesticide handlers are monitored (Weyrauch et al. 2005; Hofmann et al. 2008). Workers with a substantial decline in cholinesterase are removed from work. Policies requiring that workers be tested for cholinesterase depression or specific pesticide metabolites would identify individual workers who should be removed from specific tasks due to high exposure; policies requiring that at least a sample of workers be tested for cholinesterase depression or specific pesticide metabolites would indicate when work practices causing high exposure need to be changed.

10.3.3.4 Healthcare Policy

Few farmworkers in the eastern US are provided with health insurance. Many of the farmworkers in the eastern US cannot access some health services because they lack proper immigration documents. Farmworkers with H-2A visas are required to purchase health insurance through the Affordable Care Act (Guild et al. 2016; Arcury et al. 2017), but those without H-2A visas do not have access.

The current system of community and migrant clinics is insufficient to provide the health care needed by farmworkers and their families. For example, North Carolina provides state, in addition to federal, support for the 15–18 community and migrant clinics that operate across the state's 100 counties. However, several of these clinics operate on a limited schedule, and even if they operated on a full-time schedule, they would not be able to provide the care needed by the over 100,000 farmworkers in the state, as well as to the families of these farmworkers. This system of clinics needs to be expanded and funded to provide the needed care, and farmworkers need to be provided with health insurance. Further, policy changes are needed to assure adequate resources to federal and state agencies for development of interventions demonstrated to reduce effectively occupational injury and illness in farmworkers.

10.3.3.5 Immigration Policy

Immigration reform is one of the most significant policy changes needed to advance social justice for Latinx farmworkers. Immigration and Customs Enforcement causes fear for farmworkers, whether or not they have proper immigration documents. Although immigration reform is needed across the US, it would be a particularly important step for improving social justice for farmworkers. The Agricultural Worker Program Act of 2019 (S. 175/H.R. 641), also known as the "Blue Card Act," is an example of immigrant policy reform that would improve social justice for Latinx farmworkers. This policy would allow certain farmworkers who meet agricultural work and national security clearance requirements to work legally in agriculture for 3–5 years and allow them the opportunity to earn immigration status with a path to citizenship. This program would not make any changes to the existing H-2A agricultural guest worker program.

At the same time, countervailing proposals, such as the proposed H-2C temporary work program, are anti-immigrant and would reduce Latinx farmworker social justice. The H-2C program would allow employers to retain workers for up to 3 years without their ability to return to their home communities. Spouses and children would not be allowed to accompany workers. It would allow employment in year-round industries including aquaculture, dairy, meat and poultry processing, and forestry. Wages would be tied to the federal minimum wage, and it would require that 10% of workers' wages be placed into a trust fund that could only be accessed at a US embassy or consulate in the workers' home countries. It would require binding arbitration or mediation of grievances rather than litigation. Finally, it would make workers ineligible for any federal benefits, including Affordable Care Act subsidies, but would require them to pay for health insurance.

10.3.3.6 Enforcement of Regulations

Finally, in addition to improved policy, increased enforcement of regulations is greatly needed. No improvements to enforcement occurred during the past decade. Fines must be increased, and regulatory agencies must have real power to exact tangible consequences from noncompliant employers.

Evaluation of whether current regulations actually improve the health and safety of farmworkers is needed. Having regulations that do not work to protect Latinx farmworker health and safety does not improve social justice. Ineffective regulations only add to the cynicism of industry and of workers.

10.4 Conclusion

Health and safety for farmworkers and their families in the eastern US are inextricably tied to social justice. Farmworkers in the eastern US, as well as in other regions of the US, across North America, and around the world, have become entangled in a global economy and a global agricultural system. Farmworkers and their allies must build equitable and long-term relationships with advocacy groups, academic scientists, and other organizations focused on improving the lives of farmworkers nationally and internationally. Globalization has had a tremendous impact on farmworkers, and it is important for advocates to think about global solutions to their work. Advocates and the labor movement must promote international labor standards that protect all agricultural workers.

Social justice for farmworkers can only be achieved through systematic changes in the way society understands its connection to food. Consumers need to know the sources of their food and the working and living conditions of those who produce their food. Consumers must be willing to accept the costs of the food they consume. Documentation of the conditions of farm labor will help educate consumers and justify policy changes needed to provide safe working and living conditions for farm labor. Social justice in agriculture must be a commitment of a just society.

References

Arcury TA (2017) Anthropology in agricultural health and safety research and intervention. J Agromedicine 22(1):3–8

Arcury TA, Summers P (2015) Farmworker housing: a photo essay. New Solut 25(3):353–361

Arcury TA, Wiggins M, Quandt SA (2009) Conclusions: an agenda for farmworker social justice in the eastern United States. In: Arcury TA, Quandt SA (eds) Latino farmworkers in the eastern United States: health, safety, and justice. Springer, New York, NY, pp 221–233

Arcury TA, Weir M, Chen H et al (2012a) Migrant farmworker housing regulation violations in North Carolina. Am J Ind Med 55:191–204

Arcury TA, Weir MM, Summers P et al (2012b) Safety, security, hygiene and privacy in migrant farmworker housing. New Solut 22:153–173

Arcury TA, Jacobs IJ, Ruiz V (2015) Farmworker housing quality and health. New Solut 25(3):256–262

Arcury TA, Laurienti PJ, Chen H et al (2016) Organophosphate pesticide urinary metabolites among Latino immigrants: North Carolina farmworkers and non-farmworkers compared. J Occup Environ Med 58(11):1079–1086

Arcury TA, Jenson A, Mann M et al (2017) Providing health information to Latino farmworkers: the case of the affordable care act. J Agromedicine 22(3):275–281

Arcury TA, Laurienti PJ, Talton JW et al (2018) Pesticide urinary metabolites among Latina farmworkers and nonfarmworkers in North Carolina. J Occup Environ Med 60(1):e63–e71

Arcury TA, Arnold TJ, Sandberg JC et al (2019) Latinx child farmworkers in North Carolina: study design and participant baseline characteristics. Am J Ind Med 62(2):156–167

Begemann S (2018) Sonny Perdue disagrees with chlorpyrifos ban. AgPro Farm Journal. https://www.agprofessional.com/article/sonny-perdue-disagrees-chlorpyrifos-ban. Accessed 25 Sept 2019

Berry W (1977) The unsettling of America: culture & agriculture. Avon Books, New York, NY

Berry W (2005) The way of ignorance and other essays. Shoemaker & Hoard, Berkeley

Berry W (2009) Bringing it to the table: on farming and food. Counterpoint, Berkeley, CA

California Department of Pesticide Regulation (2000) Pesticide use reporting: an overview of California's unique full reporting system. California Department of Pesticide Regulation, Sacramento, CA

CropLife News (2012) ARA applauds Department of Labor's withdraw of the child labor proposal. https://www.croplife.com/management/legislation/ara-applauds-department-of-laborswith-draw-of-the-child-labor-proposal/. Accessed 11 Dec 2019

Frank AL, Liebman AK, Ryder G et al (2013) Health care access and health care workforce for immigrant workers in the Agriculture, Forestry, and Fisheries Sector in the southeastern US. Am J Ind Med 56:960–974

Guild A, Figueroa I (2018) The neighbors who feed us: farmworkers and government policy: challenges and solutions. Harvard Law Policy Rev 13:157–186

Guild A, Richards C, Ruiz V (2016) Out of sight, out of mind: the implementation and impact of the affordable care act in the U.S. farmworker communities. J Health Care Poor Underserved 27(4A):73–82

Henderson E, Mandelbaum R, Mendieta O et al (2003) Toward social justice and economic equity in the food system: a call for social stewardship standards in sustainable and organic agriculture. Rural Advancement Foundation International—USA. RAFI-USA, Pittsboro, NC

Hofmann JN, Carden A, Fenske RA (2008) Evaluation of a clinic-based cholinesterase test kit for the Washington State cholinesterase monitoring program. Am J Ind Med 51:532–538

Huffman WE (2012) The status of labor-saving mechanization in U.S. fruit and vegetable harvesting. Choices, Quarter 2. http://choicesmagazine.org/choices-magazine/theme-articles/immigration-and-agriculture/the-status-of-labor-saving-mechanization-in-us-fruit-and-vegetable-harvesting. Accessed 26 Sept 2019

Kim S, Nussbaum MA, Laurienti PJ et al (2018) Exploring associations between postural balance and levels of urinary organophosphorus pesticide metabolites. J Occup Environ Med 60(2):174–179

Krogstad JM, Passel JS, Cohn D (2019) 5 facts about illegal immigration in the U.S. Fact Tank News in the Numbers. Pew Research Center, Washington, DC. Published on line June 12, 2019. https://www.pewresearch.org/fact-tank/2019/06/12/5-facts-about-illegal-immigrationin-the-u-s/. Accessed 9 Oct 2019

Leven R (2012) Obama administration scraps child labor restrictions for farms. The Hill. https://thehill.com/business-a-lobbying/224169-obama-administration-scraps-child-labor-rules-for-farms. Accessed 23 Apr 2019

Liebman AK, Wiggins MF, Fraser C et al (2013) Occupational health policy and immigrant workers in the Agriculture, Forestry, and Fishing Sector. Am J Ind Med 56:975–984

Marsh B, Milofsky C, Kissam E et al (2015) Understanding the role of social factors in farmworker housing and health. New Solut 25(3):313–333

Moss Joyner A, George L, Hall ML et al (2015) Federal farmworker housing standards and regulations, their promise and limitations, and implications for farmworker health. New Solut 25:334–352

Nuckols JR, Gunier RB, Riggs P (2007) Linkage of the California pesticide use reporting database with spatial land use data for exposure assessment. Environ Health Perspect 115:684–689

Quandt SA, Wiggins MF, Chen H et al (2013) Heat index in migrant farmworker housing: implications for rest and recovery from work-related heat stress. Am J Public Health 103(8):e24–e26

Quandt SA, Brooke C, Fagan K et al (2015a) Farmworker housing in the United States and its impact on health. New Solut 25(3):263–286

Quandt SA, Pope CN, Chen H et al (2015b) Longitudinal assessment of blood cholinesterase activities over 2 consecutive years among Latino nonfarmworkers and pesticide-exposed farmworkers in North Carolina. J Occup Environ Med 57(8):851–857

Quandt SA, Walker FO, Talton JW et al (2017) Olfactory function in Latino farmworkers over 2 years: longitudinal exploration of subclinical neurological effects of pesticide exposure. J Occup Environ Med 59(12):1148–1152

Quandt SA, Arnold TJ, Mora DC et al (2019) Hired Latinx child farm labor in North Carolina: the demand-support-control model applied to a vulnerable worker population. Am J Ind Med 62:1079–1090

Sauter SL, Brightwell WS, Colligan MJ et al (2002) The changing organization of work and the safety and health of working people. OH DHHS (NIOSH) No. 2002–116. Department of Health and Human Services, Cincinnati, OH

Scientific Certification Systems (2007) Fair labor practices & community benefits. SCS Sustainable Agriculture Department, Emeryville, CA

Shreiber N (2017 Ben & Jerry's strikes deal to improve migrant dairy workers' conditions. New York Times. https://www.nytimes.com/2017/10/03/business/ben-jerrys-migrant-workers.html?smid=pl-share. Accessed 26 Sept 2019

United States Environmental Protection Agency (USEPA) (2016) Agricultural Worker Protection Standard. USEPA, Washington, DC. https://www.epa.gov/pesticide-worker-safety/agriculturalworker-protection-standard-wps. Accessed 26 Sept 2019

Weyrauch KF, Boiko PE, Keifer M (2005) Building informed consent for cholinesterase monitoring among pesticide handlers in Washington State. Am J Ind Med 48:175–181

Index

© Springer Nature Switzerland AG 2020
T. A. Arcury, S. A. Quandt (eds.), *Latinx Farmworkers in the Eastern United
States*, https://doi.org/10.1007/978-3-030-36643-8

Printed in the United States
by Baker & Taylor Publisher Services